KU-114-993

ANARKY
THE COMPLETE SERIES

ALAN GRANT
WRITER

NORM BREYFOGLE
PENCILLER

JOSEF RUBINSTEIN
INKER

NOELLE GIDDINGS FELIX SERRANO
COLORISTS

JOHN COSTANZA
LETTERER

NORM BREYFOGLE AND **JOSEF RUBINSTEIN**
COLLECTION AND SERIES COVER ARTISTS

ANARKY created by **ALAN GRANT** and **NORM BREYFOGLE**
BATMAN created by **BOB KANE** with **BILL FINGER**
SUPERMAN created by **JERRY SIEGEL** and **JOE SHUSTER**
By special arrangement with the Jerry Siegel family

DARREN VINCENZO
Editor - Original Series

JOSEPH ILLIDGE
Associate Editor - Original Series

FRANK BERRIOS
Assistant Editor - Original Series

JEB WOODARD
Group Editor - Collected Editions

ALEX GALER
Editor - Collected Edition

STEVE COOK
Design Director - Books

CURTIS KING JR.
Publication Design

BOB HARRAS
Senior VP - Editor-in-Chief, DC Comics

PAT McCALLUM
Executive Editor, DC Comics

DIANE NELSON
President

DAN DiDIO
Publisher

JIM LEE
Publisher

GEOFF JOHNS
President & Chief Creative Officer

AMIT DESAI
Executive VP - Business & Marketing Strategy,
Direct to Consumer & Global Franchise Management

SAM ADES
Senior VP & General Manager, Digital Services

BOBBIE CHASE
VP & Executive Editor, Young Reader
& Talent Development

MARK CHIARELLO
Senior VP - Art, Design & Collected Editions

JOHN CUNNINGHAM
Senior VP - Sales & Trade Marketing

ANNE DePIES
Senior VP - Business Strategy, Finance & Administration

DON FALLETTI
VP - Manufacturing Operations

LAWRENCE GANEM
VP - Editorial Administration & Talent Relations

ALISON GILL
Senior VP - Manufacturing & Operations

HANK KANALZ
Senior VP - Editorial Strategy & Administration

JAY KOGAN
VP - Legal Affairs

JACK MAHAN
VP - Business Affairs

NICK J. NAPOLITANO
VP - Manufacturing Administration

EDDIE SCANNELL
VP - Consumer Marketing

COURTNEY SIMMONS
Senior VP - Publicity & Communications

JIM (SKI) SOKOLOWSKI
VP - Comic Book Specialty Sales & Trade Marketing

NANCY SPEARS
VP - Mass, Book, Digital Sales & Trade Marketing

MICHELE R. WELLS
VP - Content Strategy

ANARKY: THE COMPLETE SERIES

Published by DC Comics. Compilation and all new material Copyright © 2018 DC Comics. All Rights Reserved. Originally published in single magazine form in ANARKY 1-8, DCU HEROES SECRET FILES 1. Copyright © 1998, 1999 DC Comics. All Rights Reserved. All characters, their distinctive likenesses and related elements featured in this publication are trademarks of DC Comics. The stories, characters and incidents featured in this publication are entirely fictional. DC Comics does not read or accept unsolicited submissions of ideas, stories or artwork.

DC Comics,
2900 West Alameda Ave., Burbank, CA 91505
Printed by Solisco Printers, Scott, QC, Canada.
12/15/17. First Printing. ISBN: 978-1-4012-7534-1

Library of Congress
Cataloging-in-Publication Data is available.

PEFC Certified
This product is from sustainably managed forests, recycled and controlled sources
PEFC/26-31-02   www.pefc.org

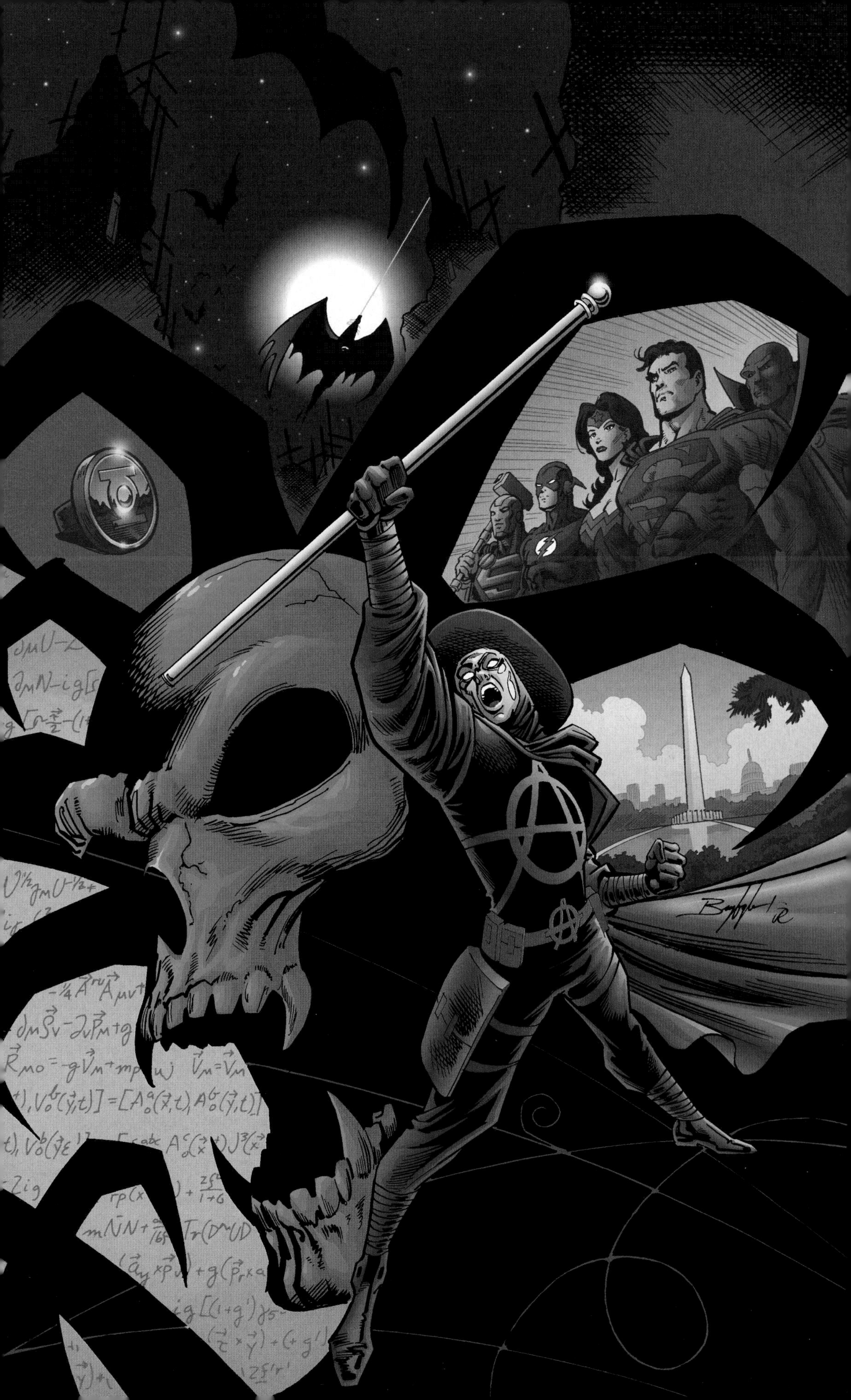

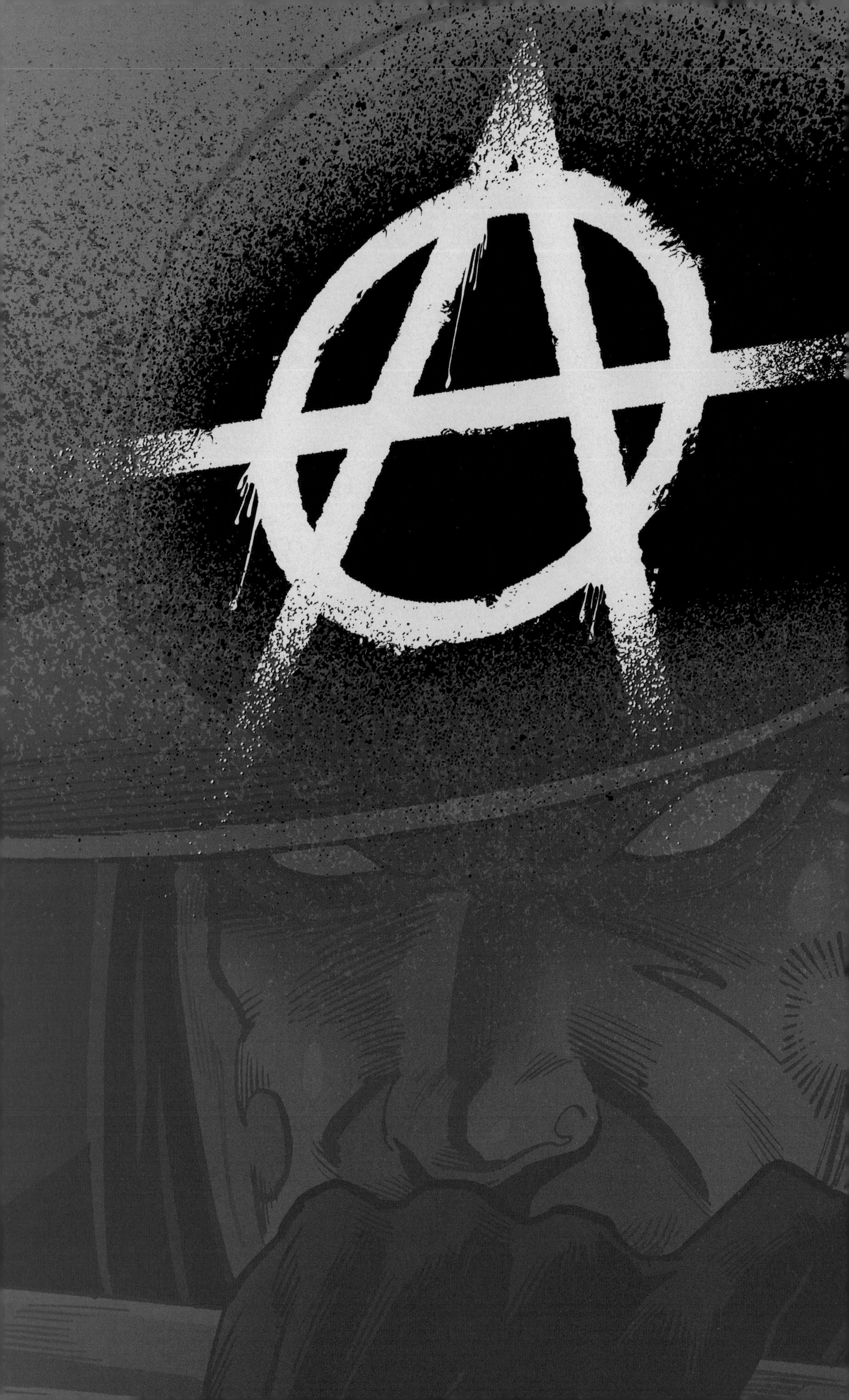

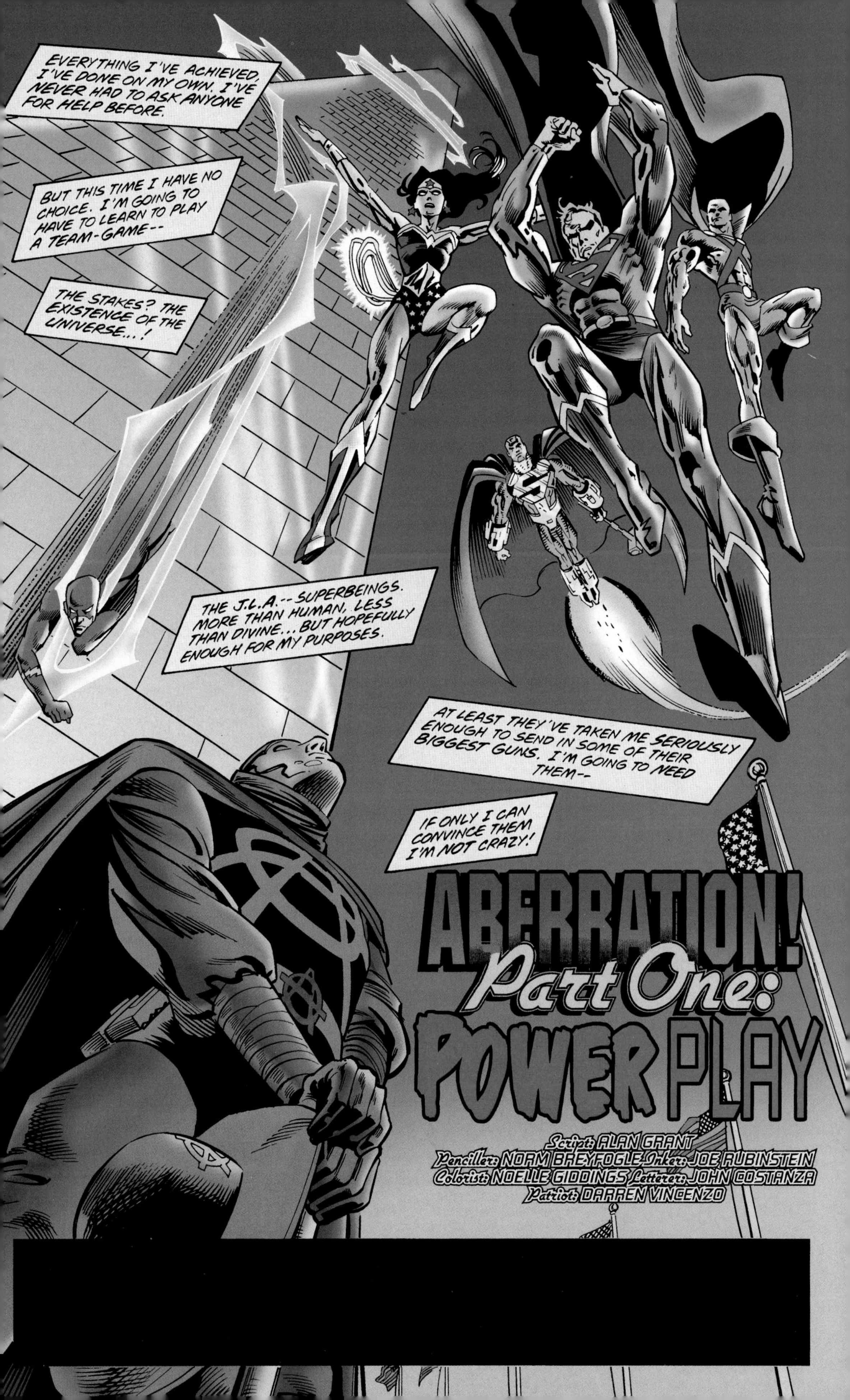
EVERYTHING I'VE ACHIEVED, I'VE DONE ON MY OWN. I'VE NEVER HAD TO ASK ANYONE FOR HELP BEFORE.
BUT THIS TIME I HAVE NO CHOICE. I'M GOING TO HAVE TO LEARN TO PLAY A TEAM-GAME--
THE STAKES? THE EXISTENCE OF THE UNIVERSE...!
THE J.L.A.--SUPERBEINGS. MORE THAN HUMAN, LESS THAN DIVINE... BUT HOPEFULLY ENOUGH FOR MY PURPOSES.
AT LEAST THEY'VE TAKEN ME SERIOUSLY ENOUGH TO SEND IN SOME OF THEIR BIGGEST GUNS. I'M GOING TO NEED THEM--
IF ONLY I CAN CONVINCE THEM I'M NOT CRAZY!
ABERRATION! Part One: POWER PLAY
Script: ALAN GRANT
Penciller: NORM BREYFOGLE Inker: JOE RUBINSTEIN
Colorist: NOELLE GIDDINGS Letterer: JOHN COSTANZA
Patriot: DARREN VINCENZO
[redacted]

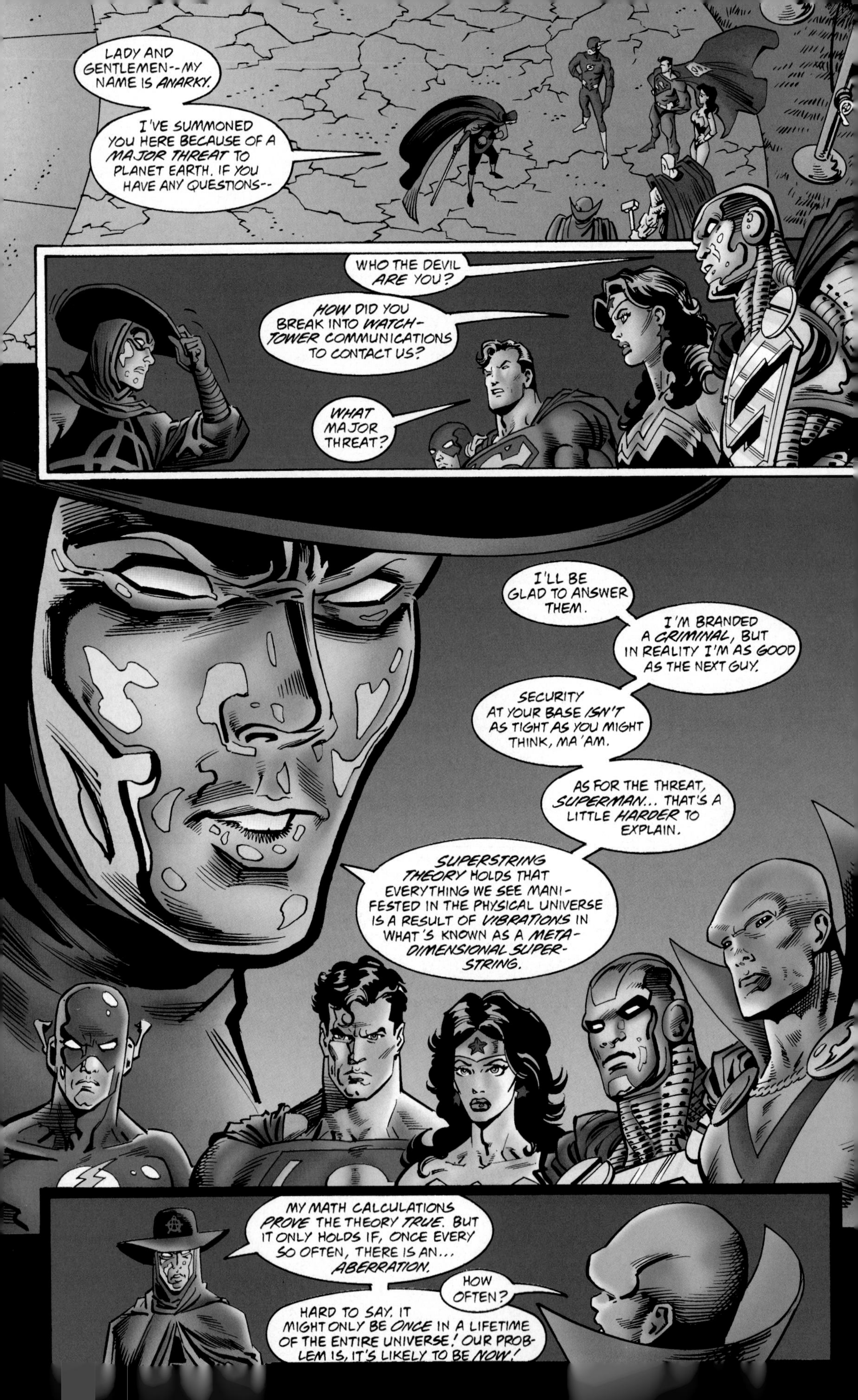
LADY AND GENTLEMEN--MY NAME IS ANARKY.
I'VE SUMMONED YOU HERE BECAUSE OF A MAJOR THREAT TO PLANET EARTH. IF YOU HAVE ANY QUESTIONS--
WHO THE DEVIL ARE YOU?
HOW DID YOU BREAK INTO WATCHTOWER COMMUNICATIONS TO CONTACT US?
WHAT MAJOR THREAT?
I'LL BE GLAD TO ANSWER THEM.
I'M BRANDED A CRIMINAL, BUT IN REALITY I'M AS GOOD AS THE NEXT GUY.
SECURITY AT YOUR BASE ISN'T AS TIGHT AS YOU MIGHT THINK, MA'AM.
AS FOR THE THREAT, SUPERMAN... THAT'S A LITTLE HARDER TO EXPLAIN.
SUPERSTRING THEORY HOLDS THAT EVERYTHING WE SEE MANIFESTED IN THE PHYSICAL UNIVERSE IS A RESULT OF VIBRATIONS IN WHAT'S KNOWN AS A META-DIMENSIONAL SUPER-STRING.
MY MATH CALCULATIONS PROVE THE THEORY TRUE. BUT IT ONLY HOLDS IF, ONCE EVERY SO OFTEN, THERE IS AN... ABERRATION.
HOW OFTEN?
HARD TO SAY. IT MIGHT ONLY BE ONCE IN A LIFETIME OF THE ENTIRE UNIVERSE! OUR PROBLEM IS, IT'S LIKELY TO BE NOW!

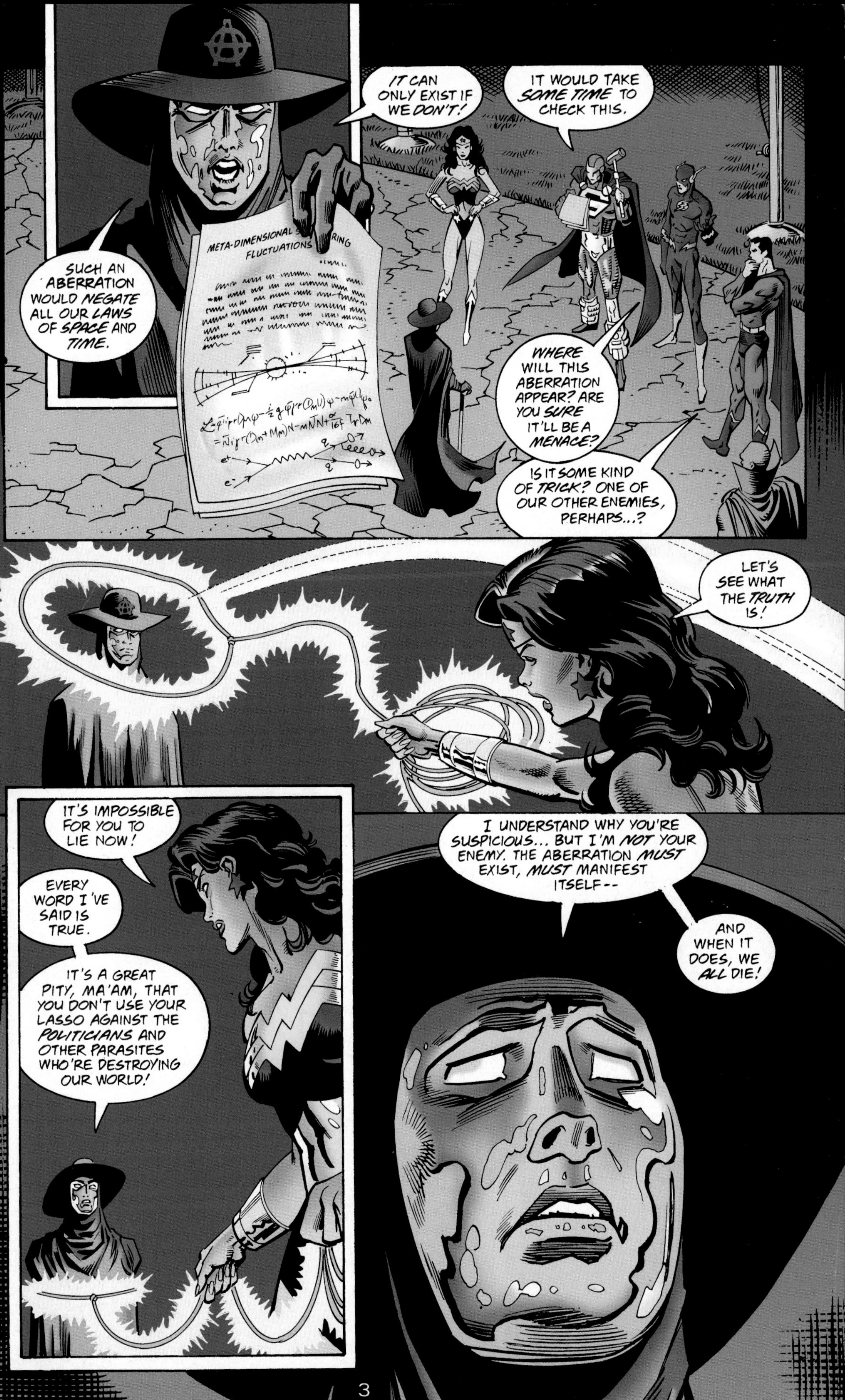
SUCH AN ABERRATION WOULD NEGATE ALL OUR LAWS OF SPACE AND TIME.
IT CAN ONLY EXIST IF WE DON'T!
IT WOULD TAKE SOME TIME TO CHECK THIS.
WHERE WILL THIS ABERRATION APPEAR? ARE YOU SURE IT'LL BE A MENACE?
IS IT SOME KIND OF TRICK? ONE OF OUR OTHER ENEMIES, PERHAPS...?
LET'S SEE WHAT THE TRUTH IS!
IT'S IMPOSSIBLE FOR YOU TO LIE NOW!
EVERY WORD I'VE SAID IS TRUE.
IT'S A GREAT PITY, MA'AM, THAT YOU DON'T USE YOUR LASSO AGAINST THE POLITICIANS AND OTHER PARASITES WHO'RE DESTROYING OUR WORLD!
I UNDERSTAND WHY YOU'RE SUSPICIOUS... BUT I'M NOT YOUR ENEMY. THE ABERRATION MUST EXIST, MUST MANIFEST ITSELF--
AND WHEN IT DOES, WE ALL DIE!

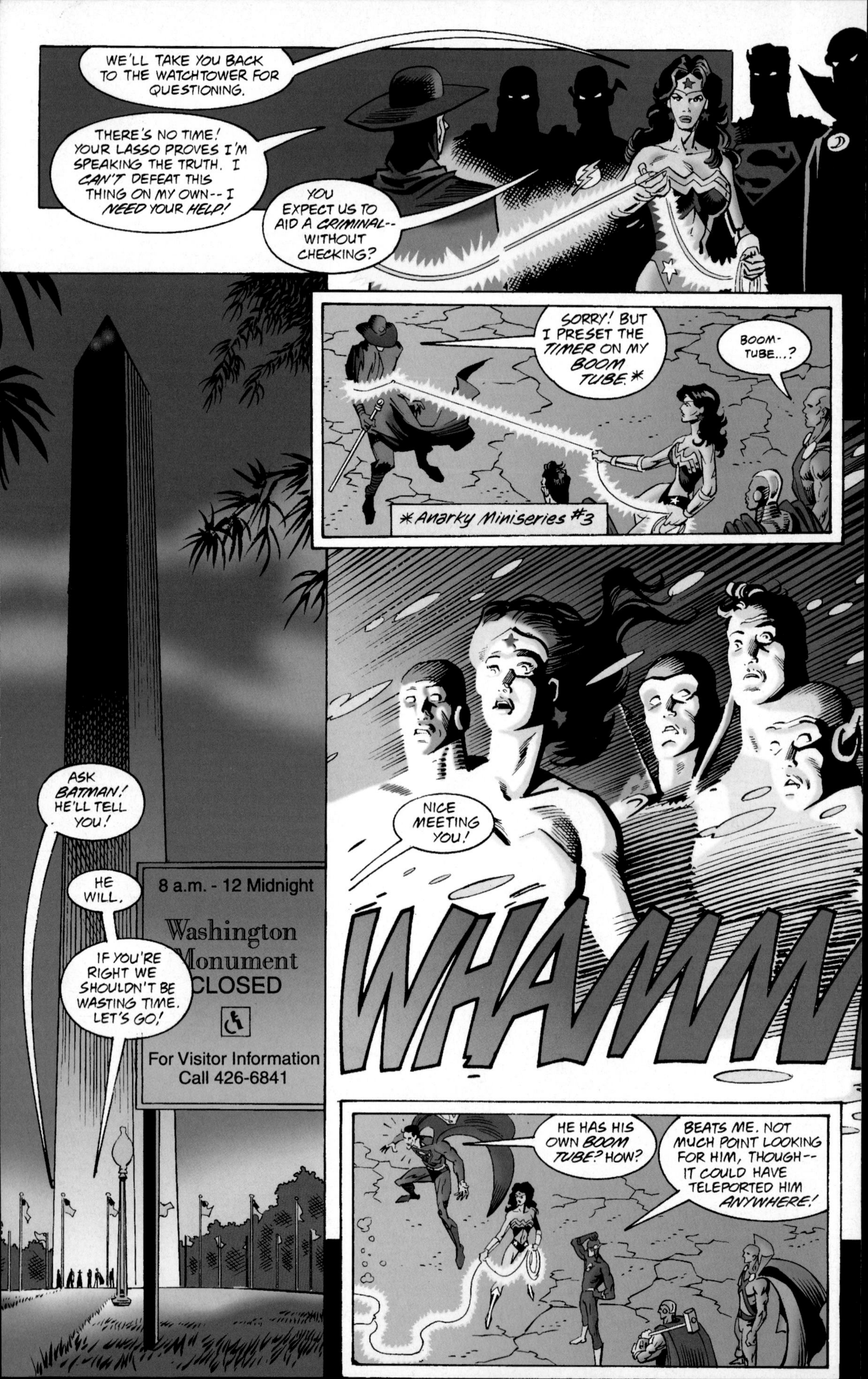
WE'LL TAKE YOU BACK TO THE WATCHTOWER FOR QUESTIONING.
THERE'S NO TIME! YOUR LASSO PROVES I'M SPEAKING THE TRUTH. I CAN'T DEFEAT THIS THING ON MY OWN-- I NEED YOUR HELP!
YOU EXPECT US TO AID A CRIMINAL-- WITHOUT CHECKING?
ASK BATMAN! HE'LL TELL YOU!
HE WILL.
IF YOU'RE RIGHT WE SHOULDN'T BE WASTING TIME. LET'S GO!
8 a.m. - 12 Midnight
Washington Monument
CLOSED
For Visitor Information Call 426-6841
SORRY! BUT I PRESET THE TIMER ON MY BOOM TUBE.*
BOOM-TUBE...?
*Anarky Miniseries #3
NICE MEETING YOU!
WHAMMM
HE HAS HIS OWN BOOM TUBE? HOW?
BEATS ME. NOT MUCH POINT LOOKING FOR HIM, THOUGH-- IT COULD HAVE TELEPORTED HIM ANYWHERE!

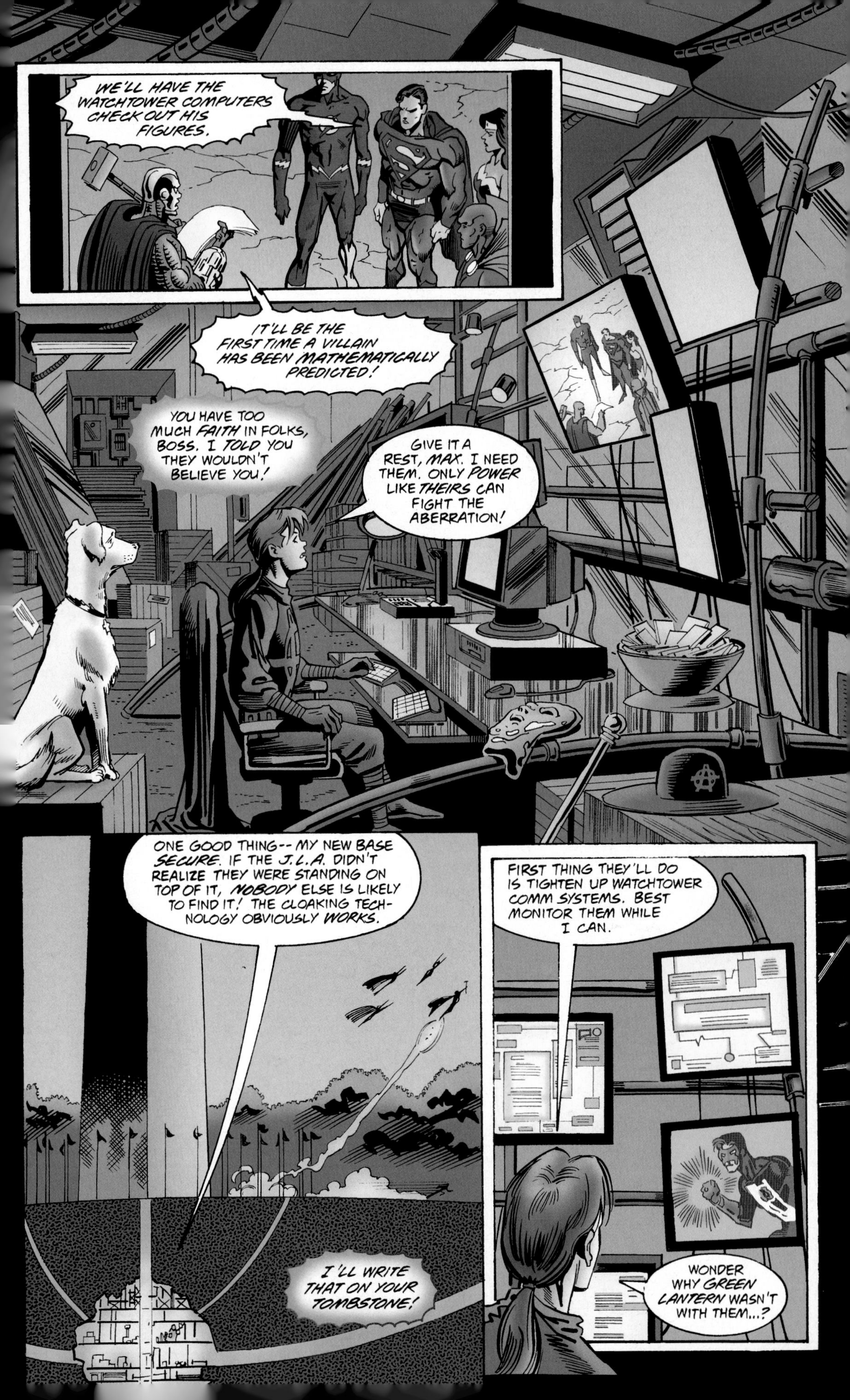
WE'LL HAVE THE WATCHTOWER COMPUTERS CHECK OUT HIS FIGURES.
IT'LL BE THE FIRST TIME A VILLAIN HAS BEEN MATHEMATICALLY PREDICTED!
YOU HAVE TOO MUCH FAITH IN FOLKS, BOSS. I TOLD YOU THEY WOULDN'T BELIEVE YOU!
GIVE IT A REST, MAX. I NEED THEM. ONLY POWER LIKE THEIRS CAN FIGHT THE ABERRATION!
ONE GOOD THING-- MY NEW BASE SECURE. IF THE J.L.A. DIDN'T REALIZE THEY WERE STANDING ON TOP OF IT, NOBODY ELSE IS LIKELY TO FIND IT! THE CLOAKING TECH-NOLOGY OBVIOUSLY WORKS.
I'LL WRITE THAT ON YOUR TOMBSTONE!
FIRST THING THEY'LL DO IS TIGHTEN UP WATCHTOWER COMM SYSTEMS. BEST MONITOR THEM WHILE I CAN.
WONDER WHY GREEN LANTERN WASN'T WITH THEM...?

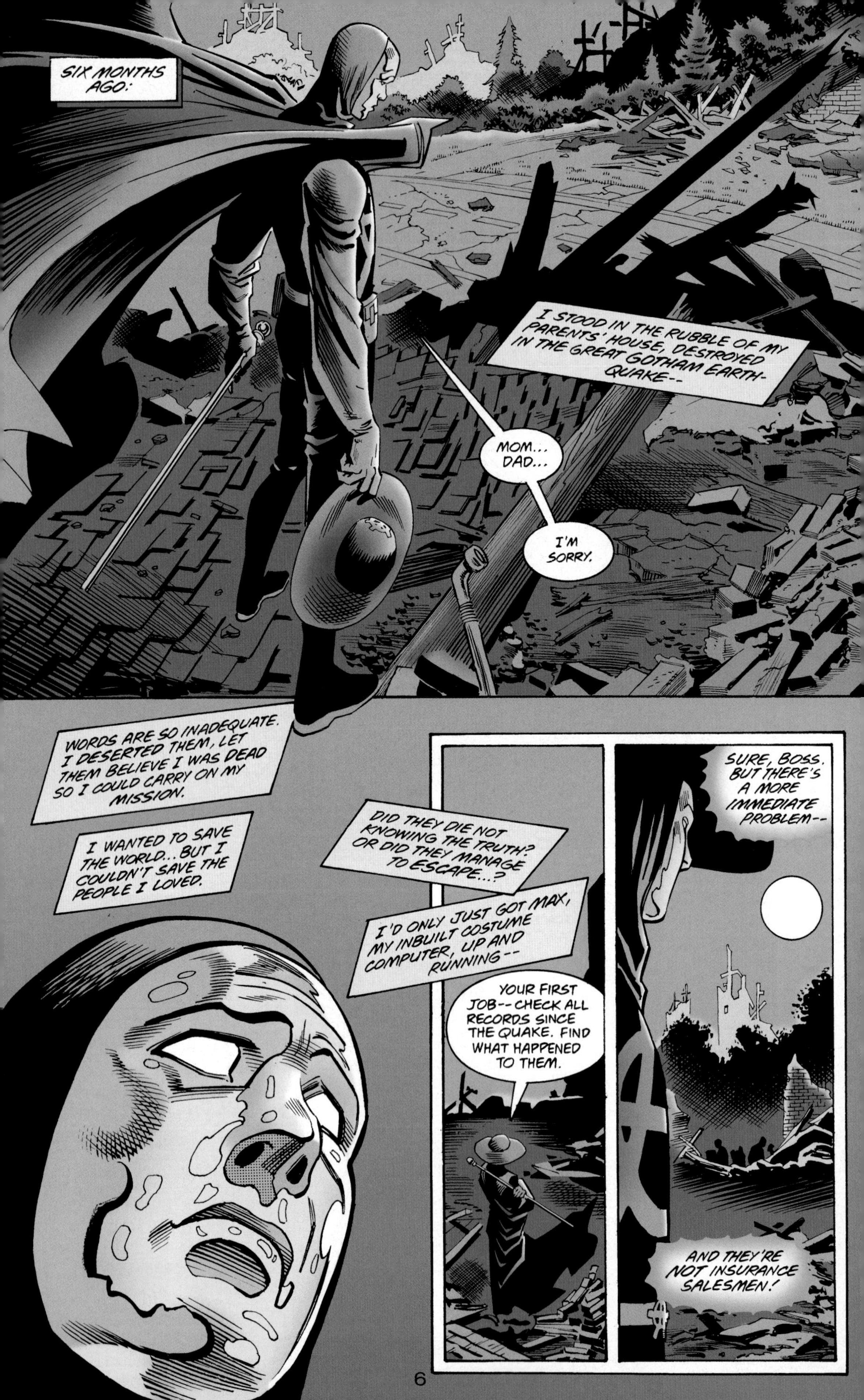
SIX MONTHS AGO:
I STOOD IN THE RUBBLE OF MY PARENTS' HOUSE, DESTROYED IN THE GREAT GOTHAM EARTH-QUAKE--
MOM... DAD...
I'M SORRY.
WORDS ARE SO INADEQUATE. I DESERTED THEM, LET THEM BELIEVE I WAS DEAD SO I COULD CARRY ON MY MISSION.
I WANTED TO SAVE THE WORLD... BUT I COULDN'T SAVE THE PEOPLE I LOVED.
DID THEY DIE NOT KNOWING THE TRUTH? OR DID THEY MANAGE TO ESCAPE...?
I'D ONLY JUST GOT MAX, MY INBUILT COSTUME COMPUTER, UP AND RUNNING--
YOUR FIRST JOB--CHECK ALL RECORDS SINCE THE QUAKE. FIND WHAT HAPPENED TO THEM.
SURE, BOSS. BUT THERE'S A MORE IMMEDIATE PROBLEM--
AND THEY'RE NOT INSURANCE SALESMEN!

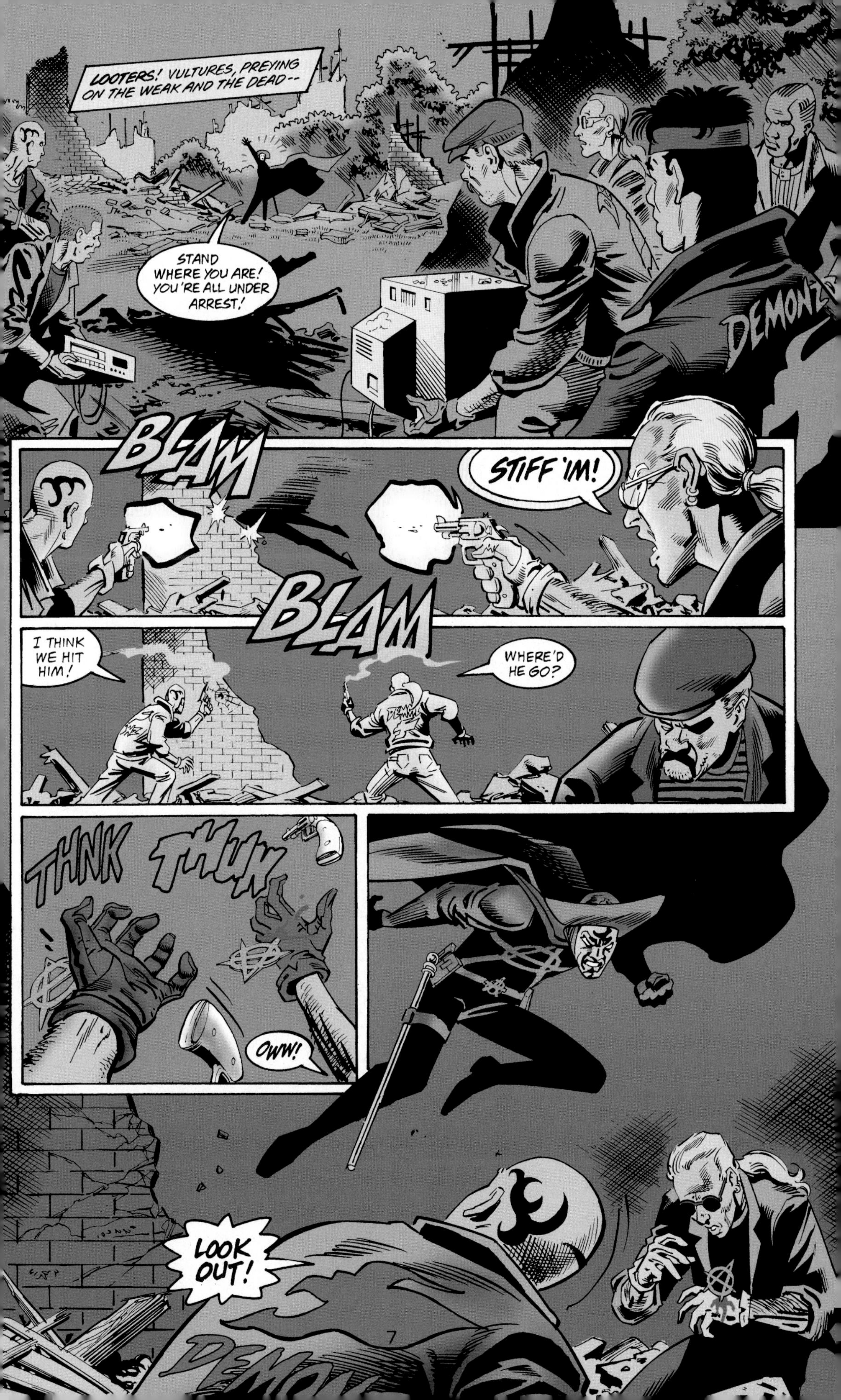
LOOTERS! VULTURES, PREYING ON THE WEAK AND THE DEAD--
STAND WHERE YOU ARE! YOU'RE ALL UNDER ARREST!
DEMONZ
BLAM
STIFF 'IM!
BLAM
I THINK WE HIT HIM!
WHERE'D HE GO?
THNK
THUN
OWW!
LOOK OUT!

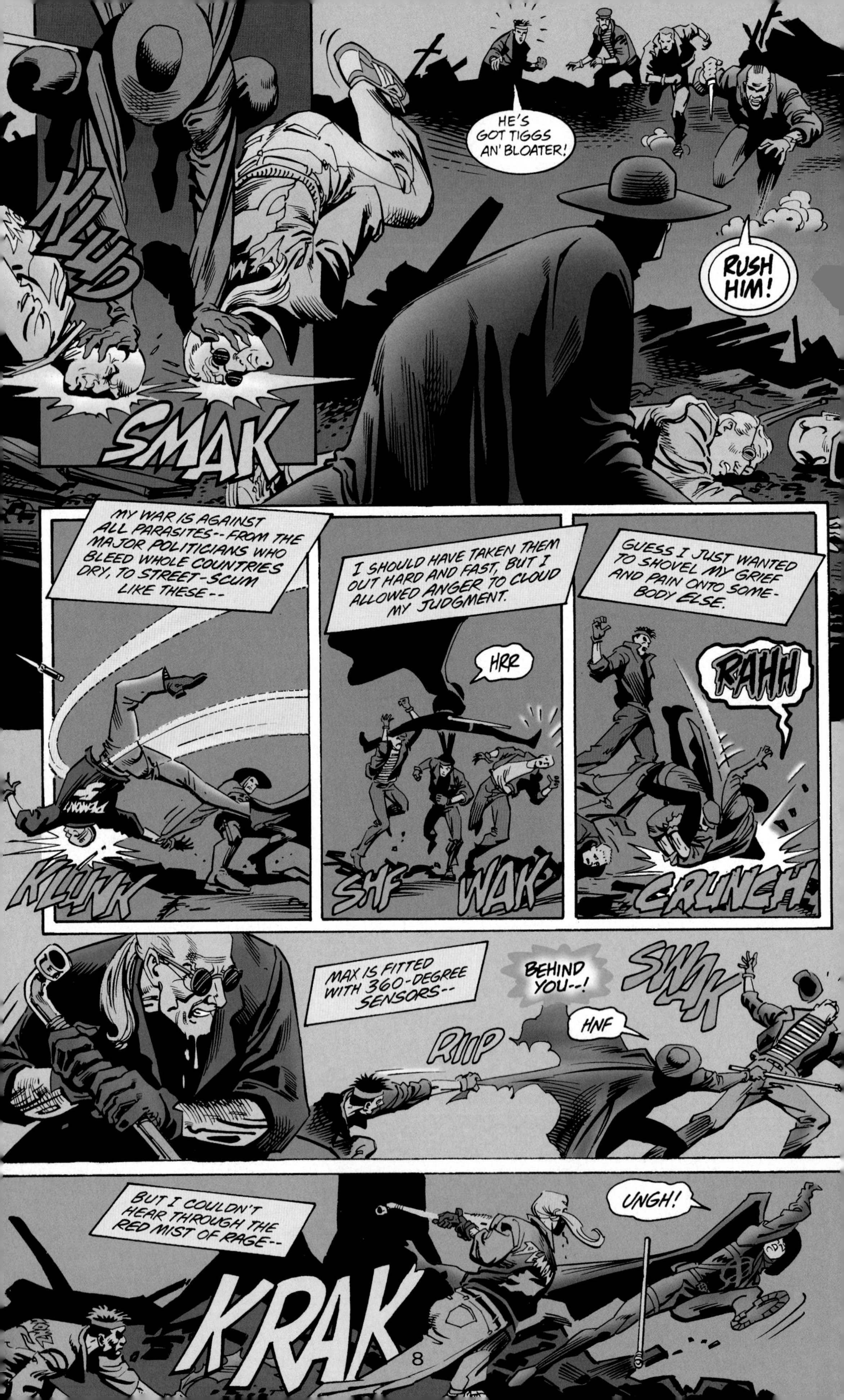
KLUD
SMAK
HE'S GOT TIGGS AN' BLOATER!
RUSH HIM!
MY WAR IS AGAINST ALL PARASITES--FROM THE MAJOR POLITICIANS WHO BLEED WHOLE COUNTRIES DRY, TO STREET-SCUM LIKE THESE--
KLUNK
I SHOULD HAVE TAKEN THEM OUT HARD AND FAST, BUT I ALLOWED ANGER TO CLOUD MY JUDGMENT.
HRR
SHF
WAK
GUESS I JUST WANTED TO SHOVEL MY GRIEF AND PAIN ONTO SOMEBODY ELSE.
RAHH
CRUNCH
MAX IS FITTED WITH 360-DEGREE SENSORS--
BEHIND YOU--!
SWAK
HNF
RIIP
BUT I COULDN'T HEAR THROUGH THE RED MIST OF RAGE--
UNGH!
KRAK

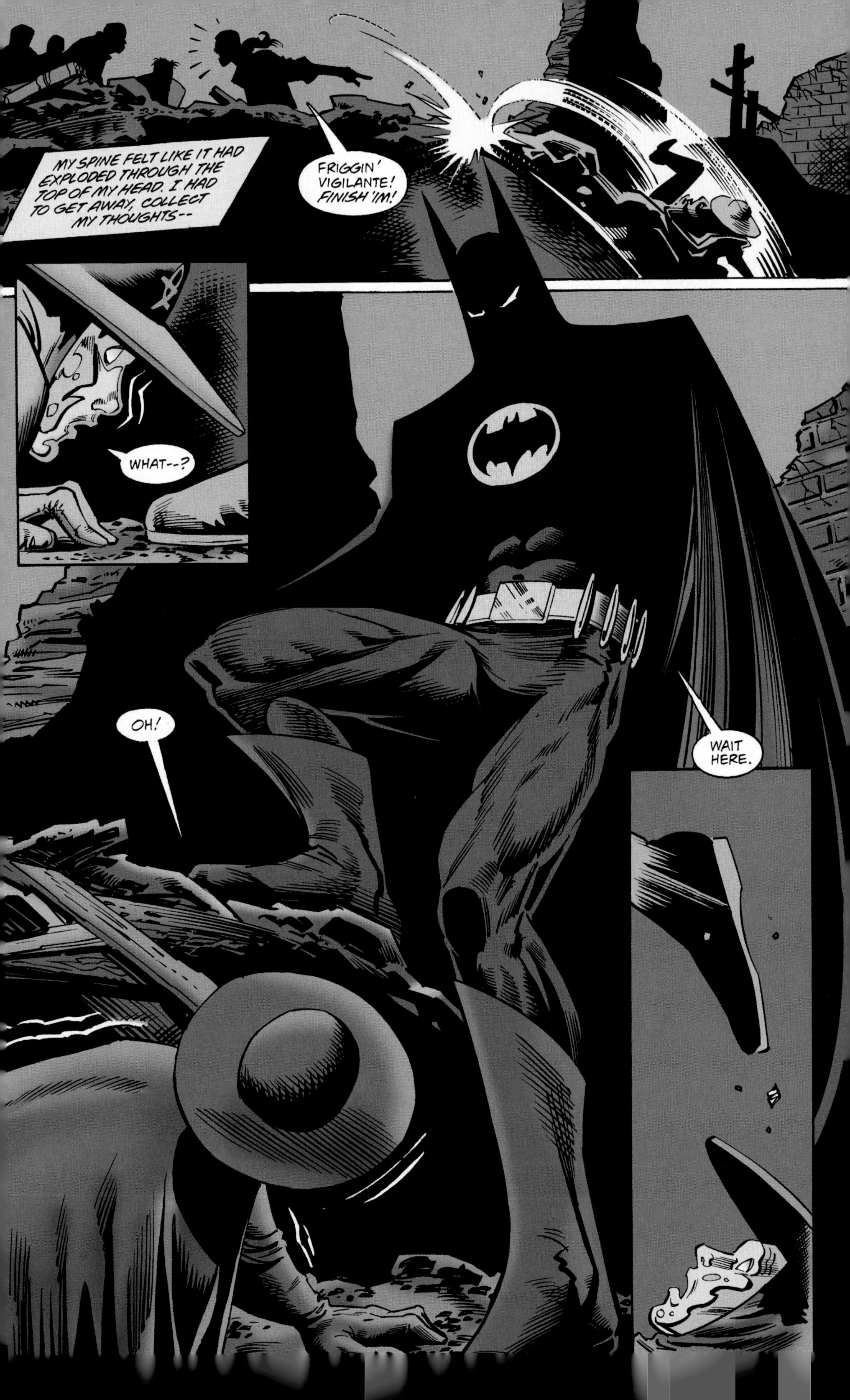
MY SPINE FELT LIKE IT HAD EXPLODED THROUGH THE TOP OF MY HEAD. I HAD TO GET AWAY, COLLECT MY THOUGHTS--
FRIGGIN' VIGILANTE! FINISH 'IM!
WHAT--?
OH!
WAIT HERE.

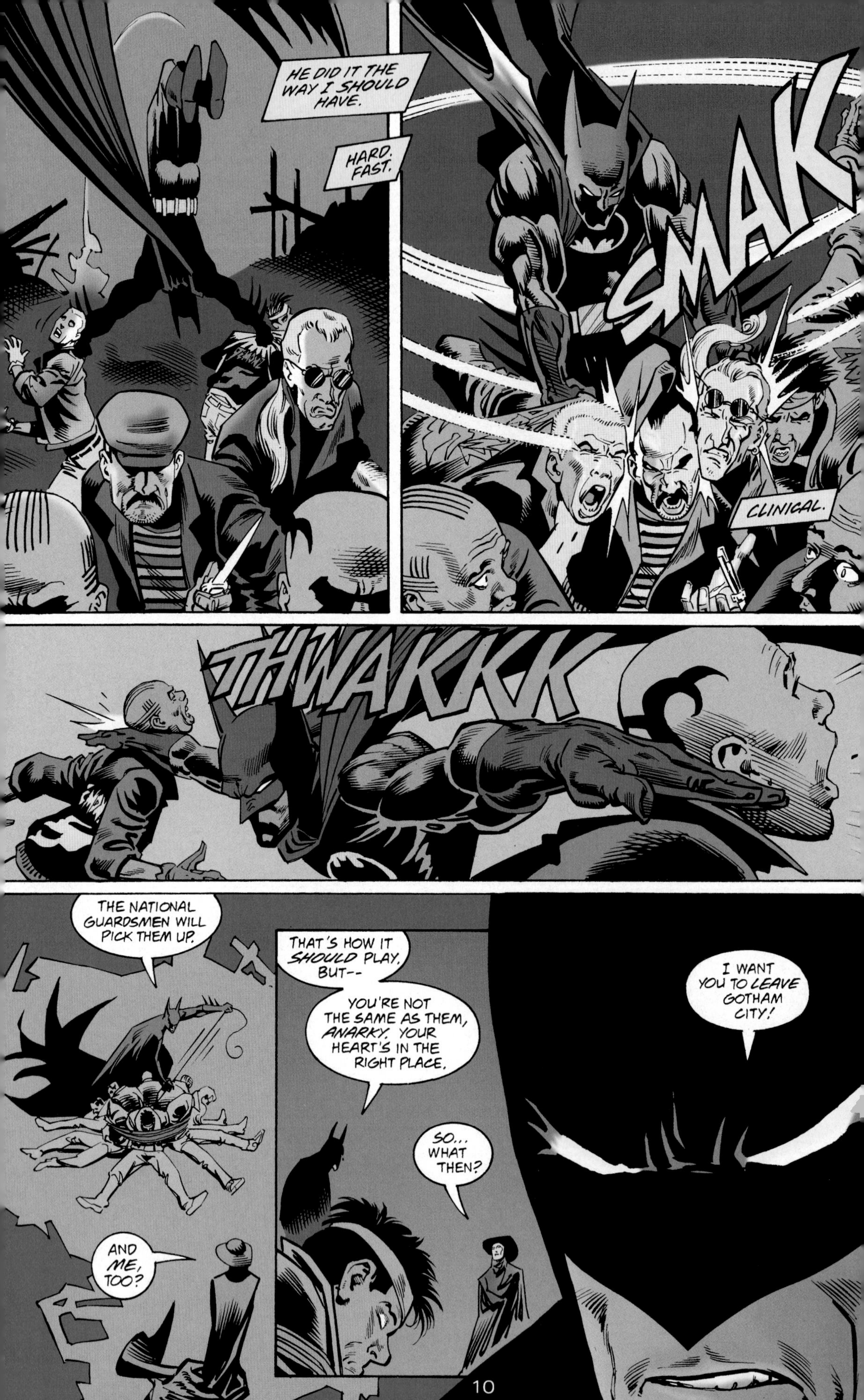
HE DID IT THE WAY I SHOULD HAVE.
HARD. FAST.
SMAK
CLINICAL.
THWAKKK
THE NATIONAL GUARDSMEN WILL PICK THEM UP.
AND ME, TOO?
THAT'S HOW IT SHOULD PLAY, BUT--
YOU'RE NOT THE SAME AS THEM, ANARKY. YOUR HEART'S IN THE RIGHT PLACE.
SO... WHAT THEN?
I WANT YOU TO LEAVE GOTHAM CITY!

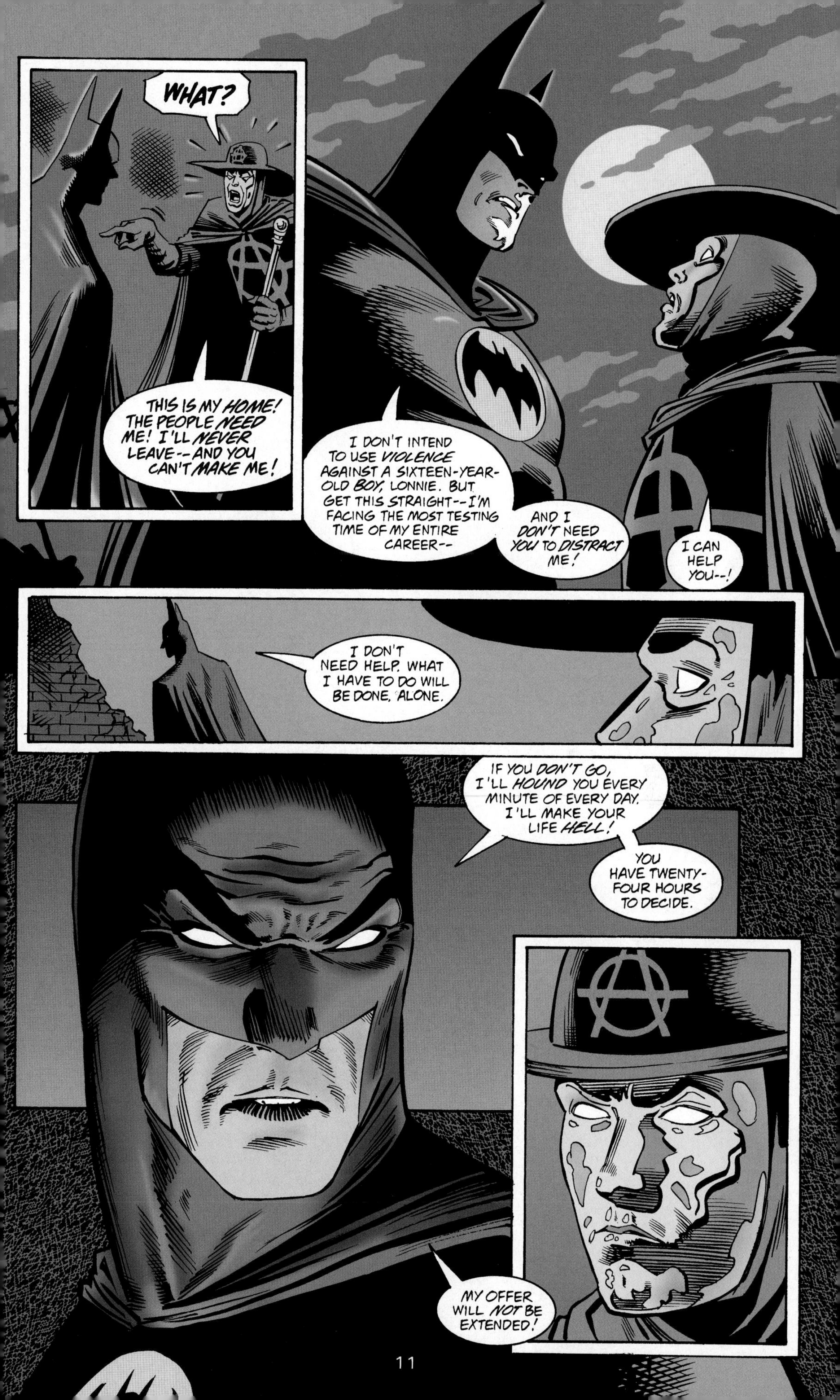
WHAT?
THIS IS MY HOME! THE PEOPLE NEED ME! I'LL NEVER LEAVE--AND YOU CAN'T MAKE ME!
I DON'T INTEND TO USE VIOLENCE AGAINST A SIXTEEN-YEAR-OLD BOY, LONNIE. BUT GET THIS STRAIGHT--I'M FACING THE MOST TESTING TIME OF MY ENTIRE CAREER--
AND I DON'T NEED YOU TO DISTRACT ME!
I CAN HELP YOU--!
I DON'T NEED HELP. WHAT I HAVE TO DO WILL BE DONE. ALONE.
IF YOU DON'T GO, I'LL HOUND YOU EVERY MINUTE OF EVERY DAY. I'LL MAKE YOUR LIFE HELL!
YOU HAVE TWENTY-FOUR HOURS TO DECIDE.
MY OFFER WILL NOT BE EXTENDED!

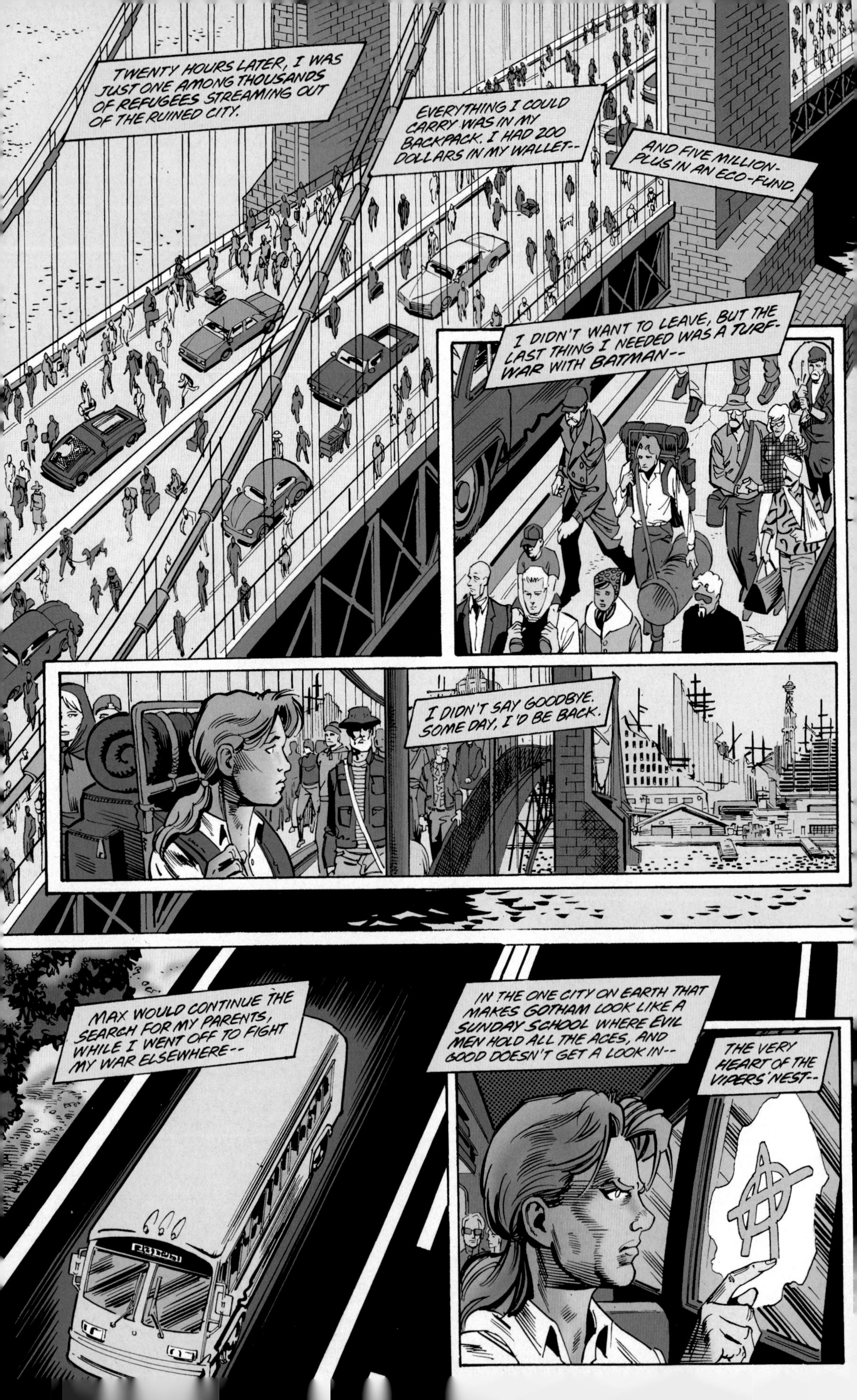
TWENTY HOURS LATER, I WAS JUST ONE AMONG THOUSANDS OF REFUGEES STREAMING OUT OF THE RUINED CITY.
EVERYTHING I COULD CARRY WAS IN MY BACKPACK. I HAD 200 DOLLARS IN MY WALLET--
AND FIVE MILLION-PLUS IN AN ECO-FUND.
I DIDN'T WANT TO LEAVE, BUT THE LAST THING I NEEDED WAS A TURF-WAR WITH BATMAN--
I DIDN'T SAY GOODBYE. SOME DAY, I'D BE BACK.
MAX WOULD CONTINUE THE SEARCH FOR MY PARENTS, WHILE I WENT OFF TO FIGHT MY WAR ELSEWHERE--
IN THE ONE CITY ON EARTH THAT MAKES GOTHAM LOOK LIKE A SUNDAY SCHOOL WHERE EVIL MEN HOLD ALL THE ACES, AND GOOD DOESN'T GET A LOOK IN--
THE VERY HEART OF THE VIPERS' NEST--

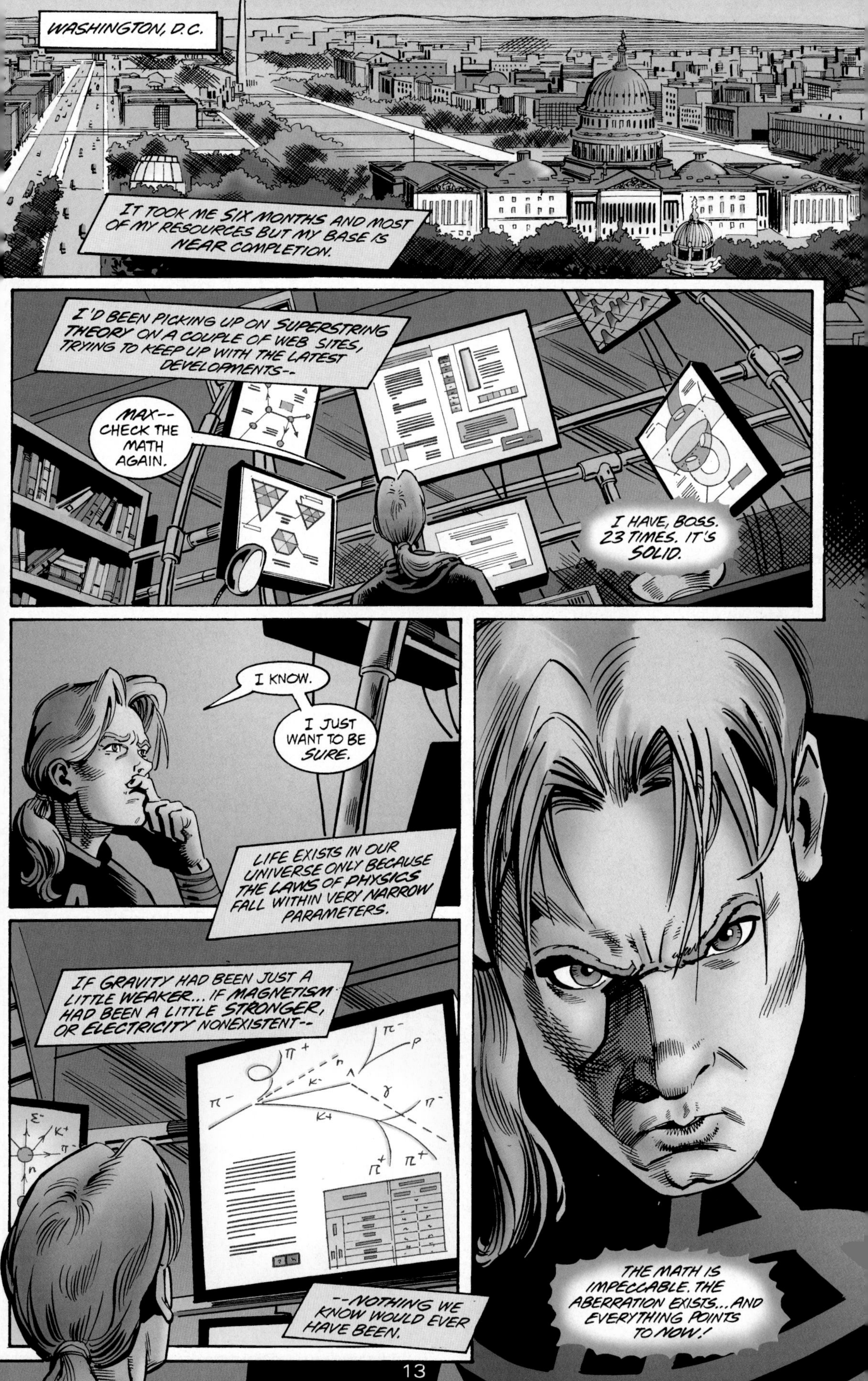
WASHINGTON, D.C.
IT TOOK ME SIX MONTHS AND MOST OF MY RESOURCES BUT MY BASE IS NEAR COMPLETION.
I'D BEEN PICKING UP ON SUPERSTRING THEORY ON A COUPLE OF WEB SITES, TRYING TO KEEP UP WITH THE LATEST DEVELOPMENTS--
MAX-- CHECK THE MATH AGAIN.
I HAVE, BOSS. 23 TIMES. IT'S SOLID.
I KNOW.
I JUST WANT TO BE SURE.
LIFE EXISTS IN OUR UNIVERSE ONLY BECAUSE THE LAWS OF PHYSICS FALL WITHIN VERY NARROW PARAMETERS.
IF GRAVITY HAD BEEN JUST A LITTLE WEAKER... IF MAGNETISM HAD BEEN A LITTLE STRONGER, OR ELECTRICITY NONEXISTENT--
--NOTHING WE KNOW WOULD EVER HAVE BEEN.
THE MATH IS IMPECCABLE. THE ABERRATION EXISTS... AND EVERYTHING POINTS TO NOW!

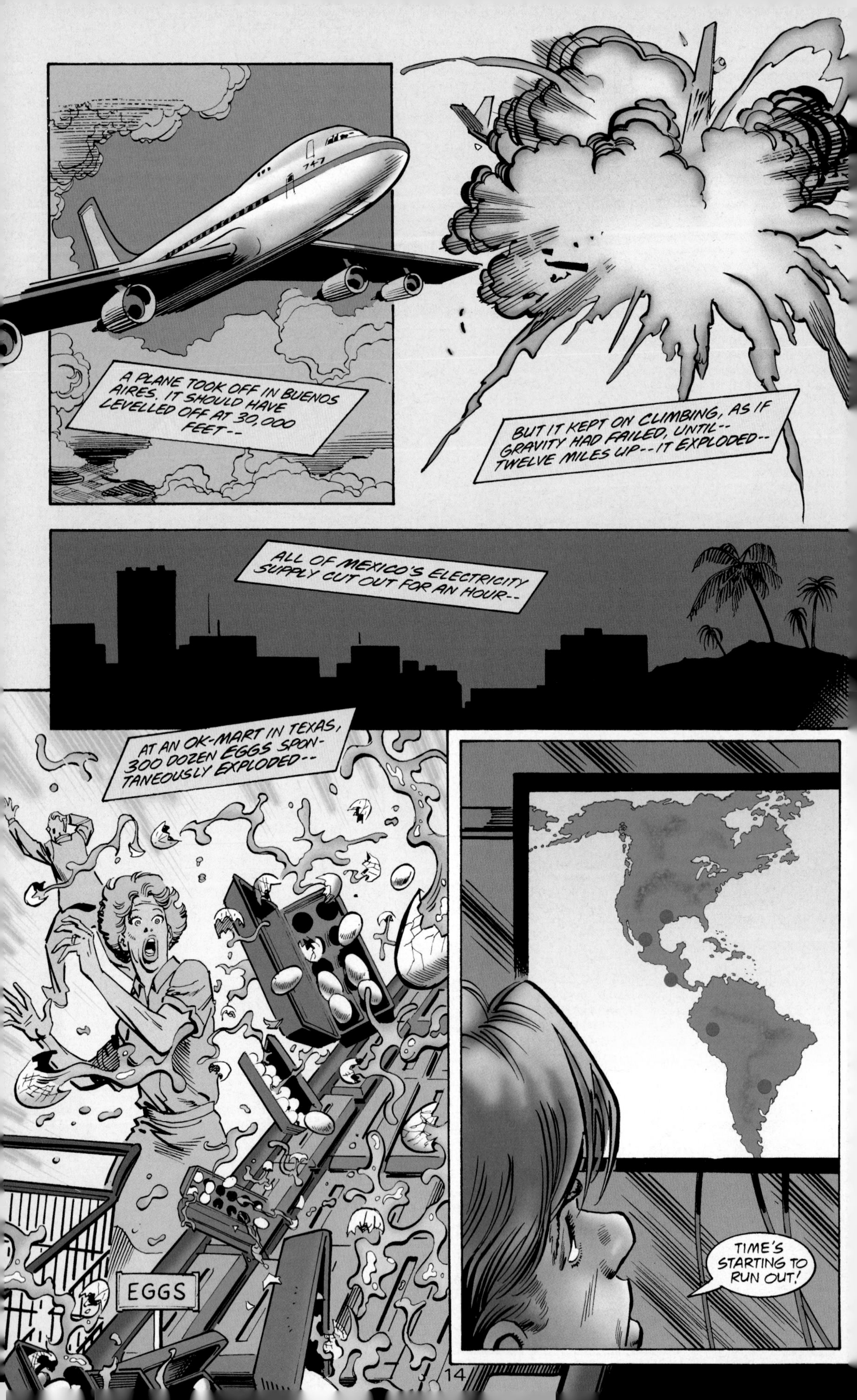
A PLANE TOOK OFF IN BUENOS AIRES. IT SHOULD HAVE LEVELLED OFF AT 30,000 FEET--
BUT IT KEPT ON CLIMBING, AS IF GRAVITY HAD FAILED, UNTIL-- TWELVE MILES UP--IT EXPLODED--
ALL OF MEXICO'S ELECTRICITY SUPPLY CUT OUT FOR AN HOUR--
AT AN OK-MART IN TEXAS, 300 DOZEN EGGS SPONTANEOUSLY EXPLODED--
EGGS
TIME'S STARTING TO RUN OUT!

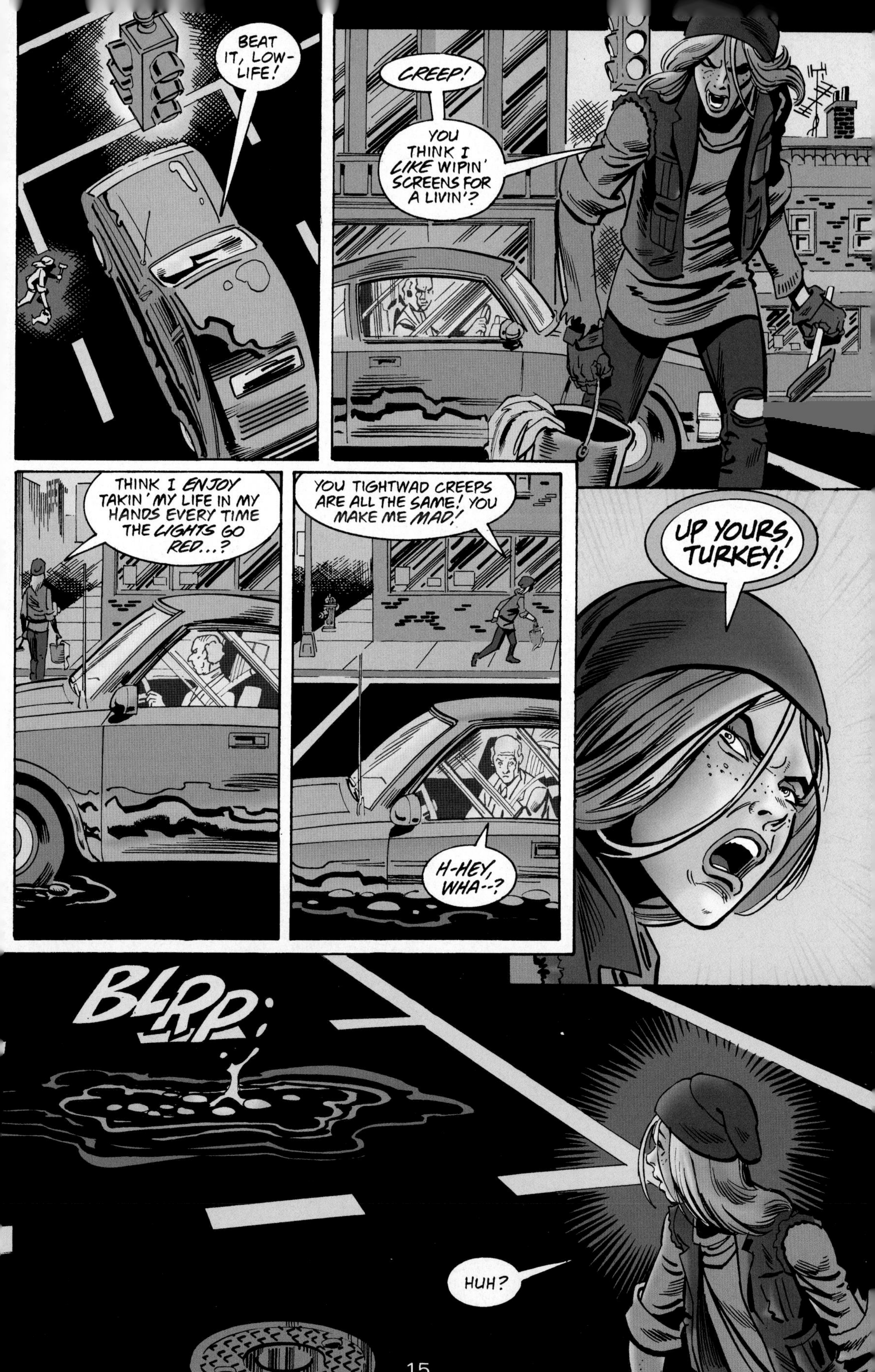
BEAT IT, LOW-LIFE!
CREEP!
YOU THINK I LIKE WIPIN' SCREENS FOR A LIVIN'?
THINK I ENJOY TAKIN' MY LIFE IN MY HANDS EVERY TIME THE LIGHTS GO RED...?
YOU TIGHTWAD CREEPS ARE ALL THE SAME! YOU MAKE ME MAD!
H-HEY, WHA--?
UP YOURS, TURKEY!
BLRP
HUH?

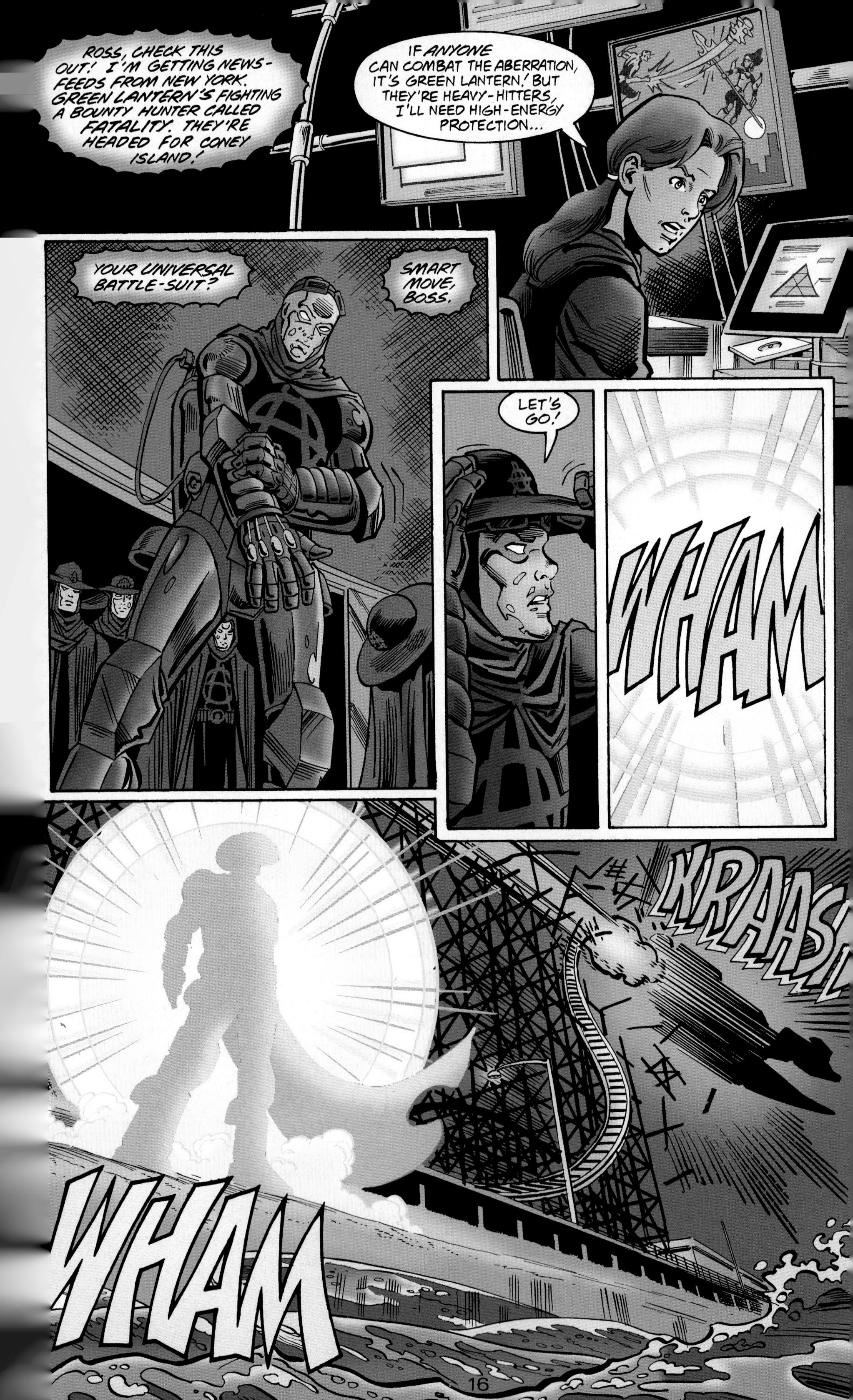
ROSS, CHECK THIS OUT! I'M GETTING NEWS-FEEDS FROM NEW YORK. GREEN LANTERN'S FIGHTING A BOUNTY HUNTER CALLED FATALITY. THEY'RE HEADED FOR CONEY ISLAND!
IF ANYONE CAN COMBAT THE ABERRATION, IT'S GREEN LANTERN! BUT THEY'RE HEAVY-HITTERS, I'LL NEED HIGH-ENERGY PROTECTION...
YOUR UNIVERSAL BATTLE-SUIT?
SMART MOVE, BOSS.
LET'S GO!
WHAM
KRAAS
WHAM

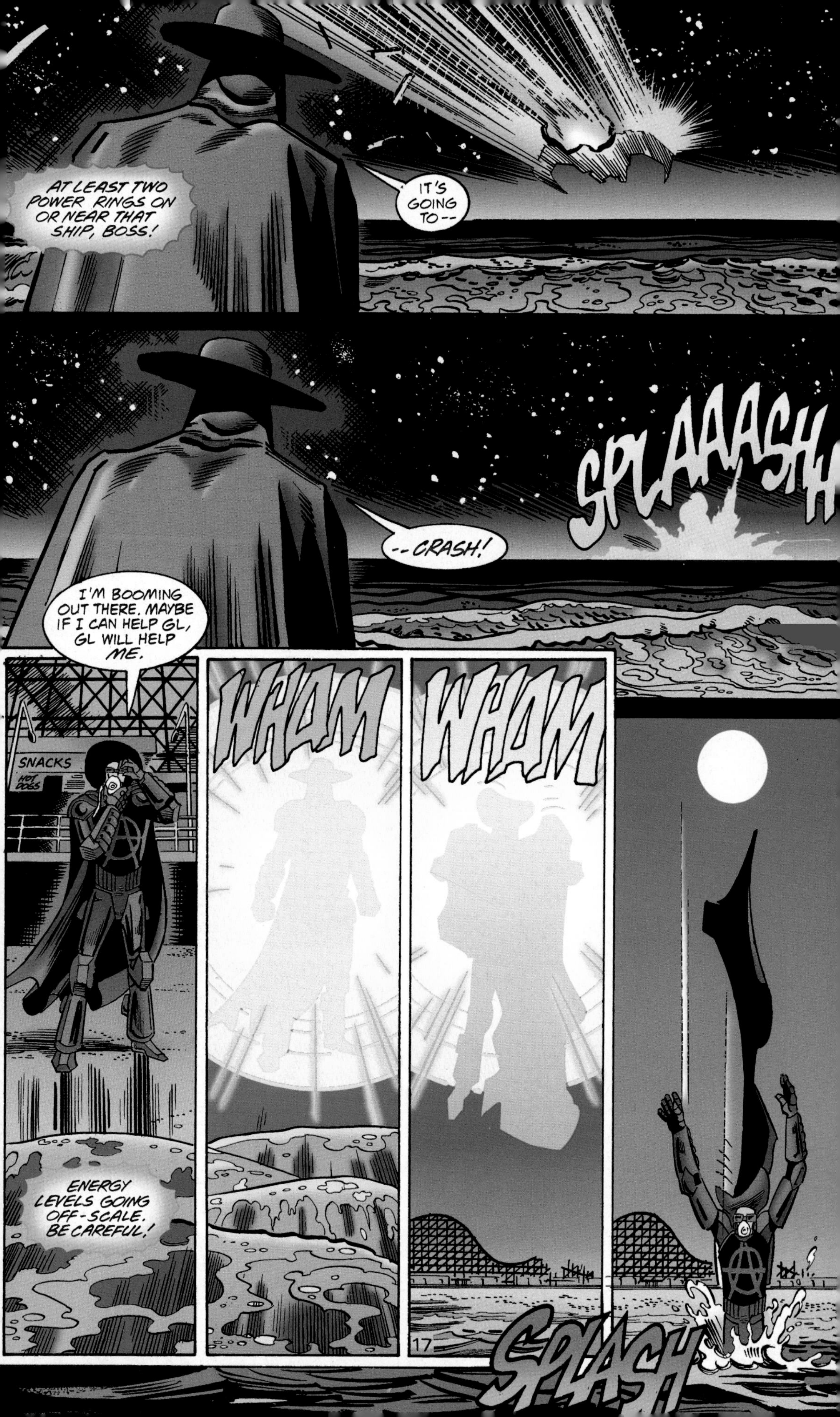
AT LEAST TWO POWER RINGS ON OR NEAR THAT SHIP, BOSS!
IT'S GOING TO--
--CRASH!
SPLAAASHH
I'M BOOMING OUT THERE. MAYBE IF I CAN HELP GL, GL WILL HELP ME.
SNACKS
HOT DOGS
WHAM
WHAM
ENERGY LEVELS GOING OFF-SCALE. BE CAREFUL!
SPLASH

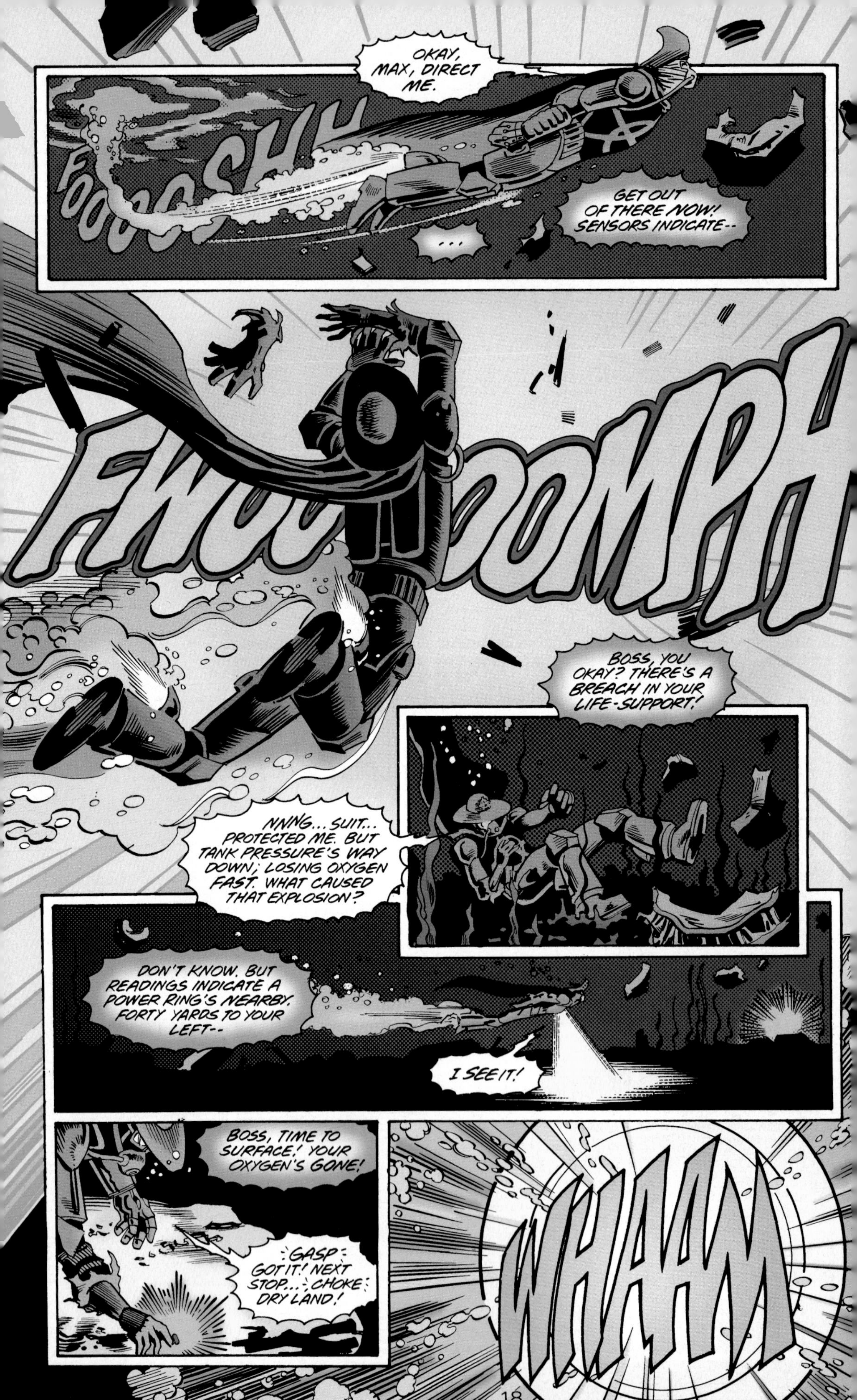

OKAY, MAX, DIRECT ME.
FOOOOSHH
GET OUT OF THERE NOW! SENSORS INDICATE--
...
FWOOOOOMPH
BOSS, YOU OKAY? THERE'S A BREACH IN YOUR LIFE-SUPPORT!
NNNG... SUIT... PROTECTED ME. BUT TANK PRESSURE'S WAY DOWN; LOSING OXYGEN FAST. WHAT CAUSED THAT EXPLOSION?
DON'T KNOW. BUT READINGS INDICATE A POWER RING'S NEARBY. FORTY YARDS TO YOUR LEFT--
I SEE IT!
BOSS, TIME TO SURFACE! YOUR OXYGEN'S GONE!
GASP GOT IT! NEXT STOP... CHOKE DRY LAND!
WHAAM

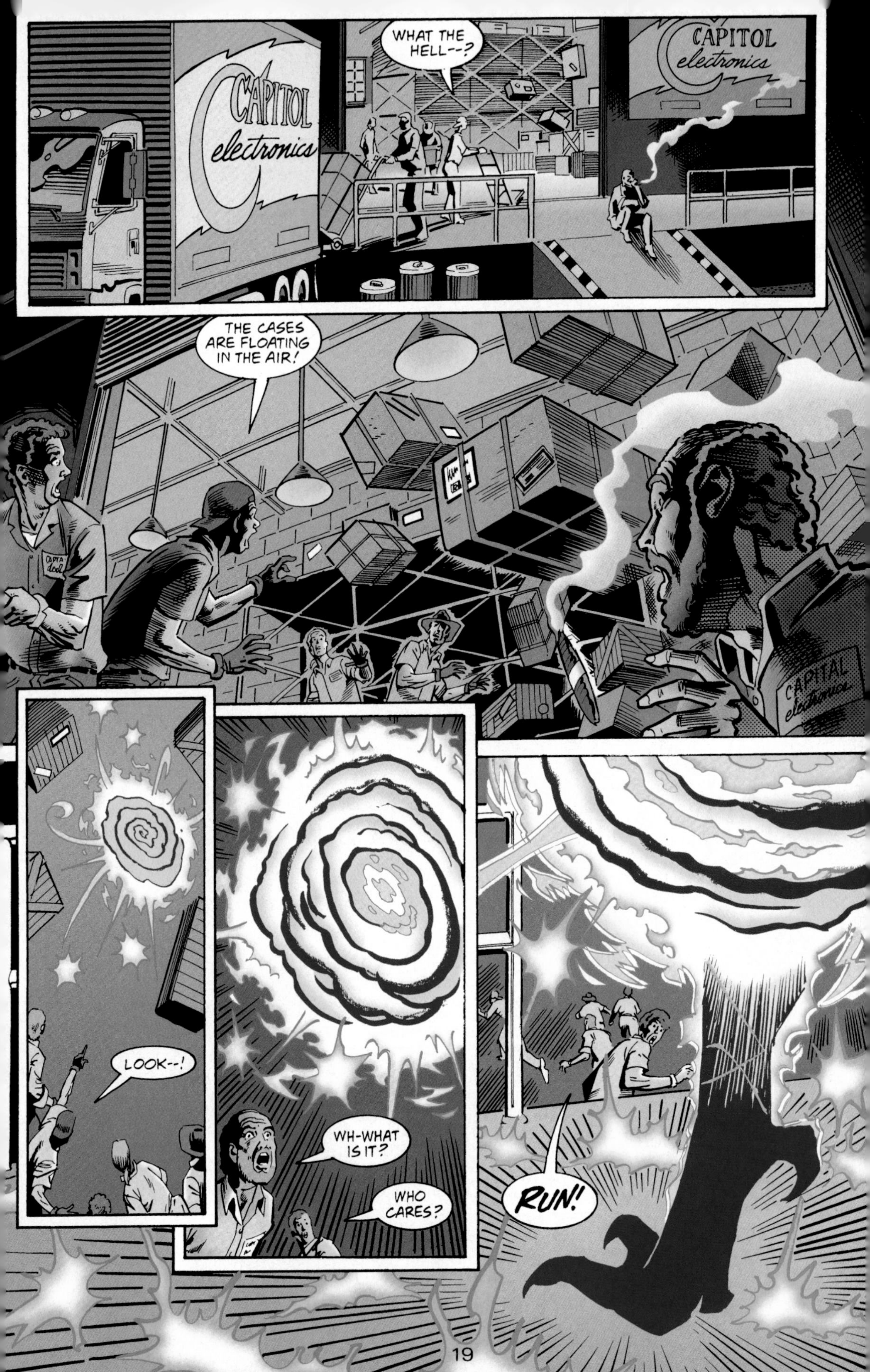
CAPITOL electronics
WHAT THE HELL--?
CAPITOL electronics
THE CASES ARE FLOATING IN THE AIR!
CAPITAL electronics
LOOK--!
WH-WHAT IS IT?
WHO CARES?
RUN!

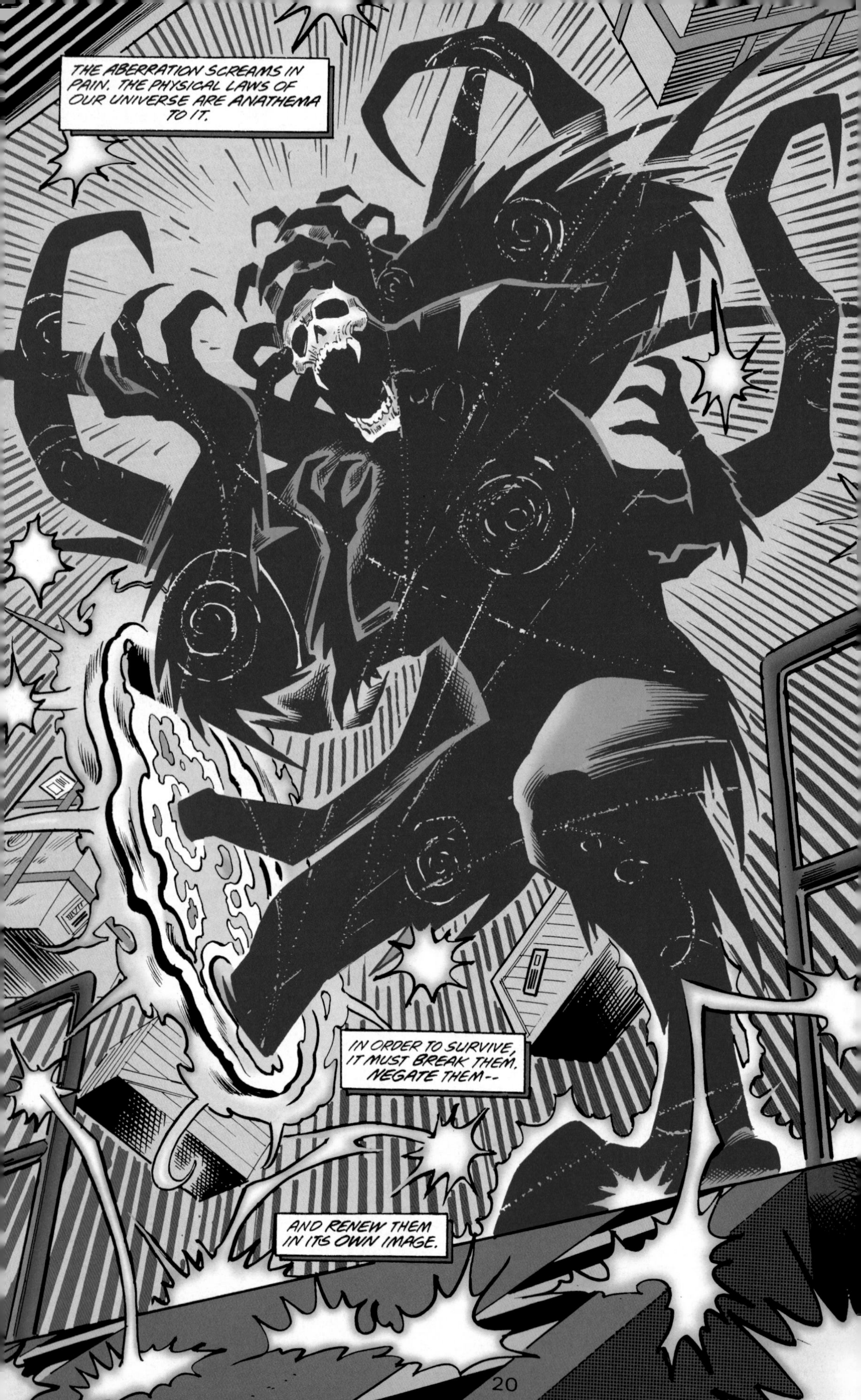
THE ABERRATION SCREAMS IN PAIN. THE PHYSICAL LAWS OF OUR UNIVERSE ARE ANATHEMA TO IT.
IN ORDER TO SURVIVE, IT MUST BREAK THEM. NEGATE THEM--
AND RENEW THEM IN ITS OWN IMAGE.

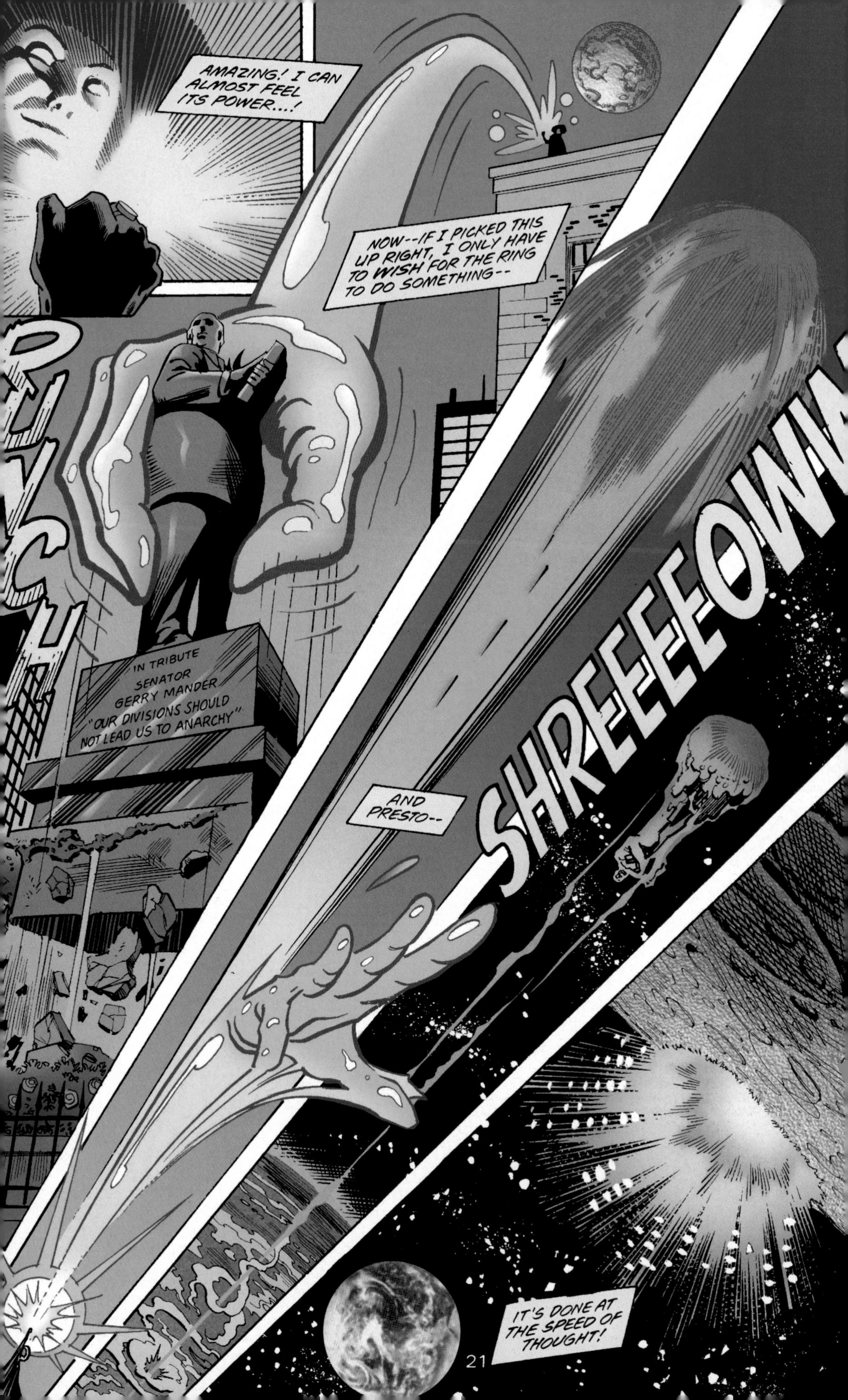
AMAZING! I CAN ALMOST FEEL ITS POWER....!
NOW--IF I PICKED THIS UP RIGHT, I ONLY HAVE TO WISH FOR THE RING TO DO SOMETHING--
IN TRIBUTE
SENATOR
GERRY MANDER
"OUR DIVISIONS SHOULD NOT LEAD US TO ANARCHY"
AND PRESTO--
SHREEEEOW
IT'S DONE AT THE SPEED OF THOUGHT!

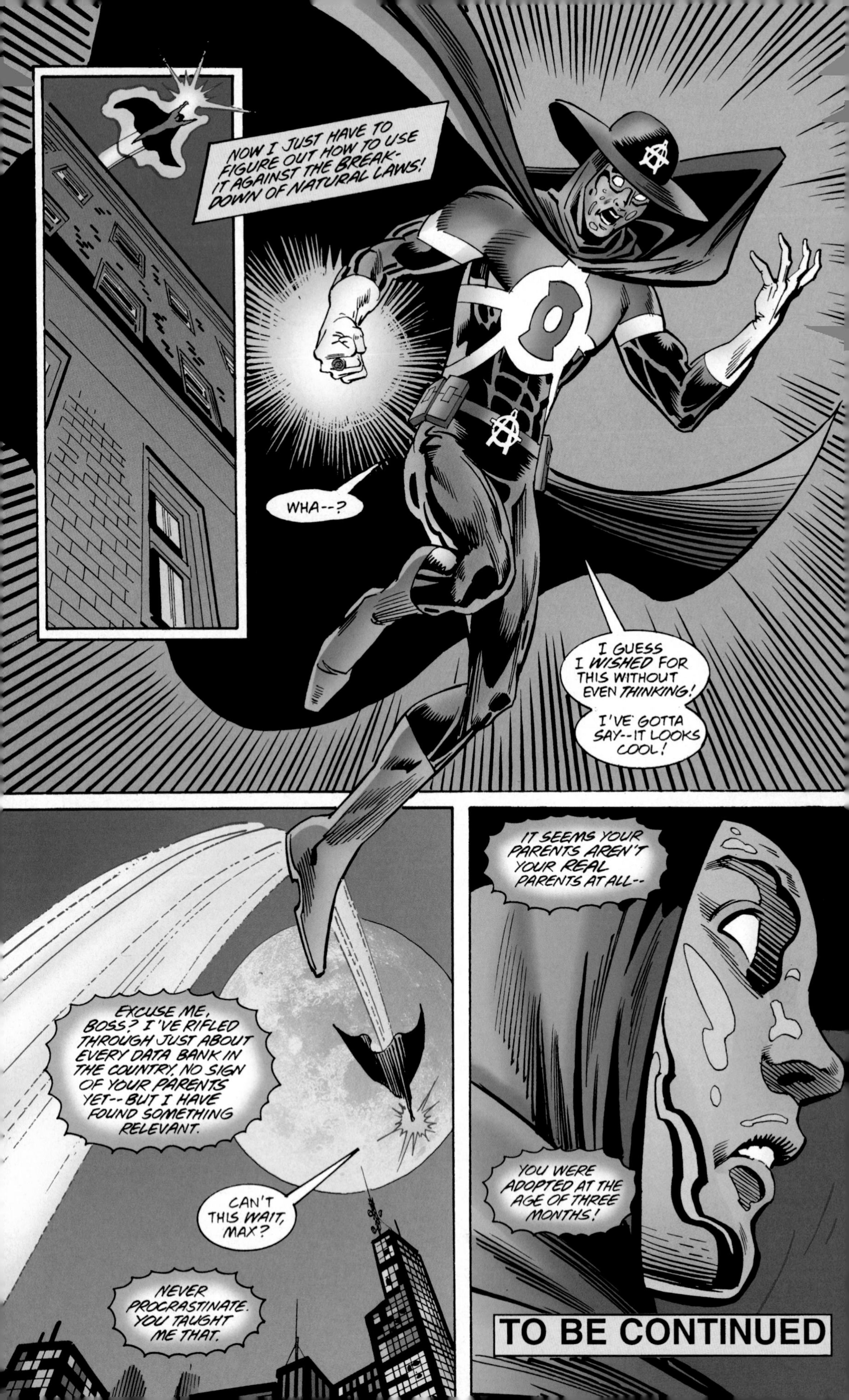
NOW I JUST HAVE TO FIGURE OUT HOW TO USE IT AGAINST THE BREAK-DOWN OF NATURAL LAWS!
WHA--?
I GUESS I WISHED FOR THIS WITHOUT EVEN THINKING!
I'VE GOTTA SAY--IT LOOKS COOL!
EXCUSE ME, BOSS? I'VE RIFLED THROUGH JUST ABOUT EVERY DATA BANK IN THE COUNTRY. NO SIGN OF YOUR PARENTS YET--BUT I HAVE FOUND SOMETHING RELEVANT.
CAN'T THIS WAIT, MAX?
NEVER PROCRASTINATE. YOU TAUGHT ME THAT.
IT SEEMS YOUR PARENTS AREN'T YOUR REAL PARENTS AT ALL--
YOU WERE ADOPTED AT THE AGE OF THREE MONTHS!
TO BE CONTINUED

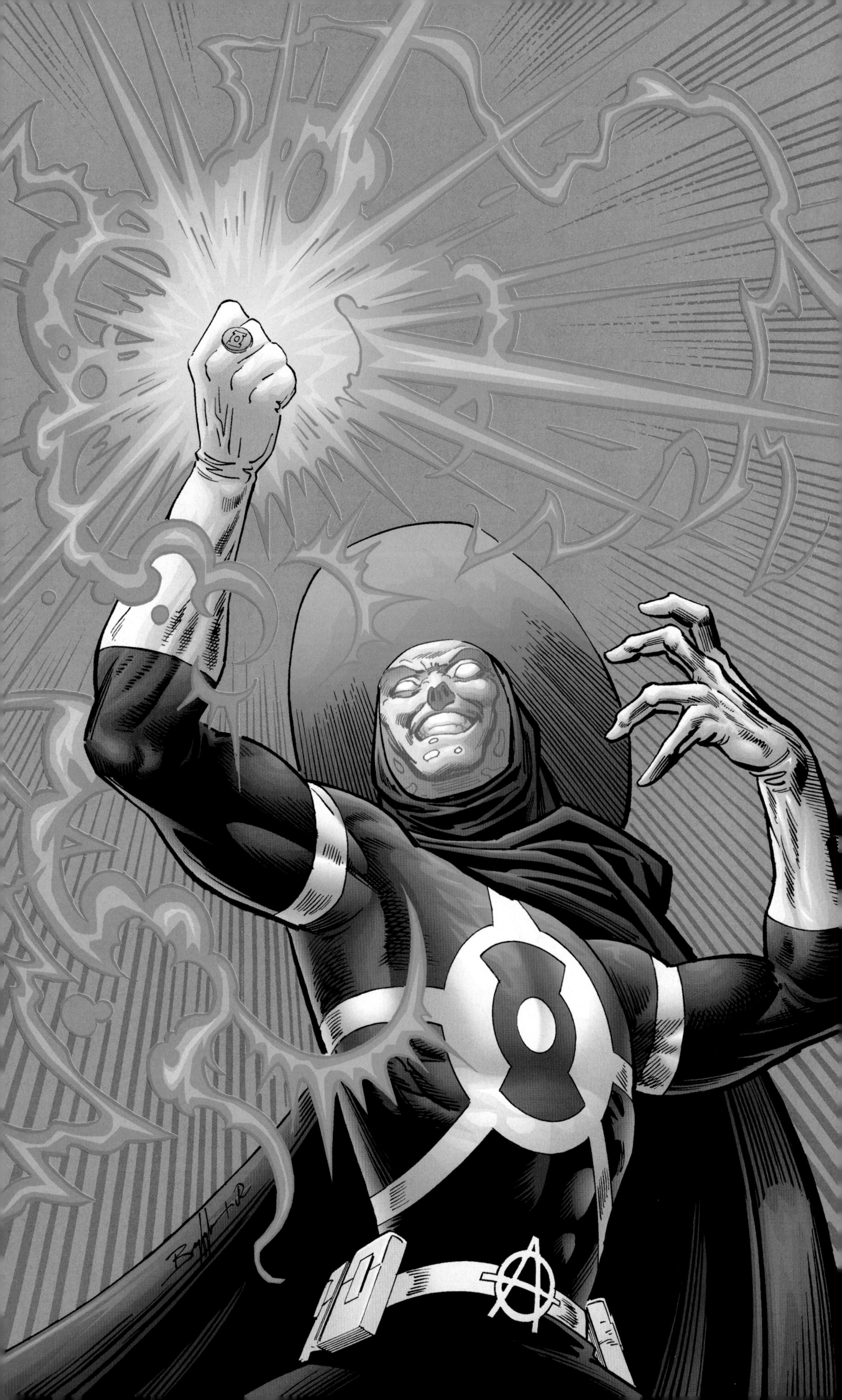

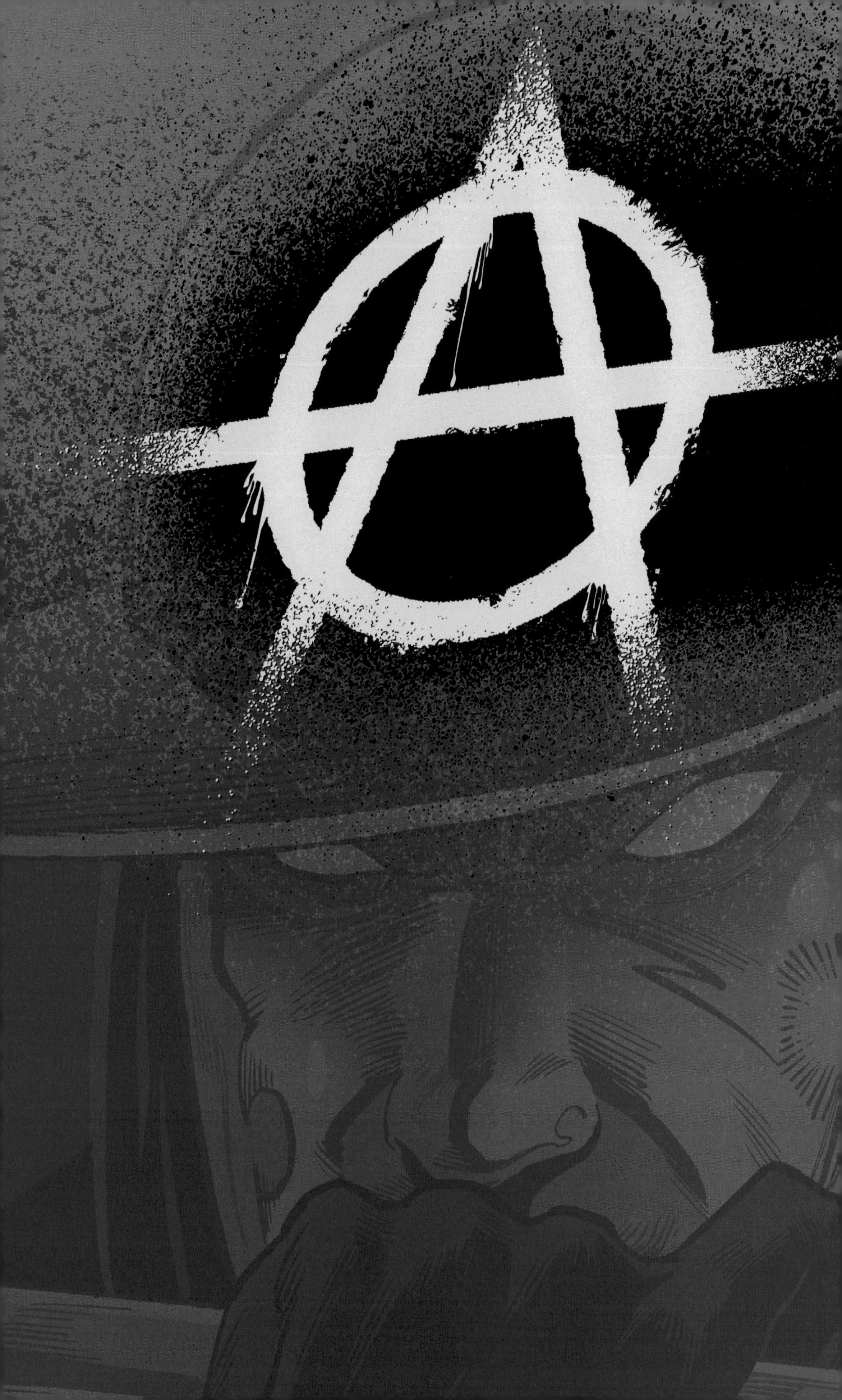

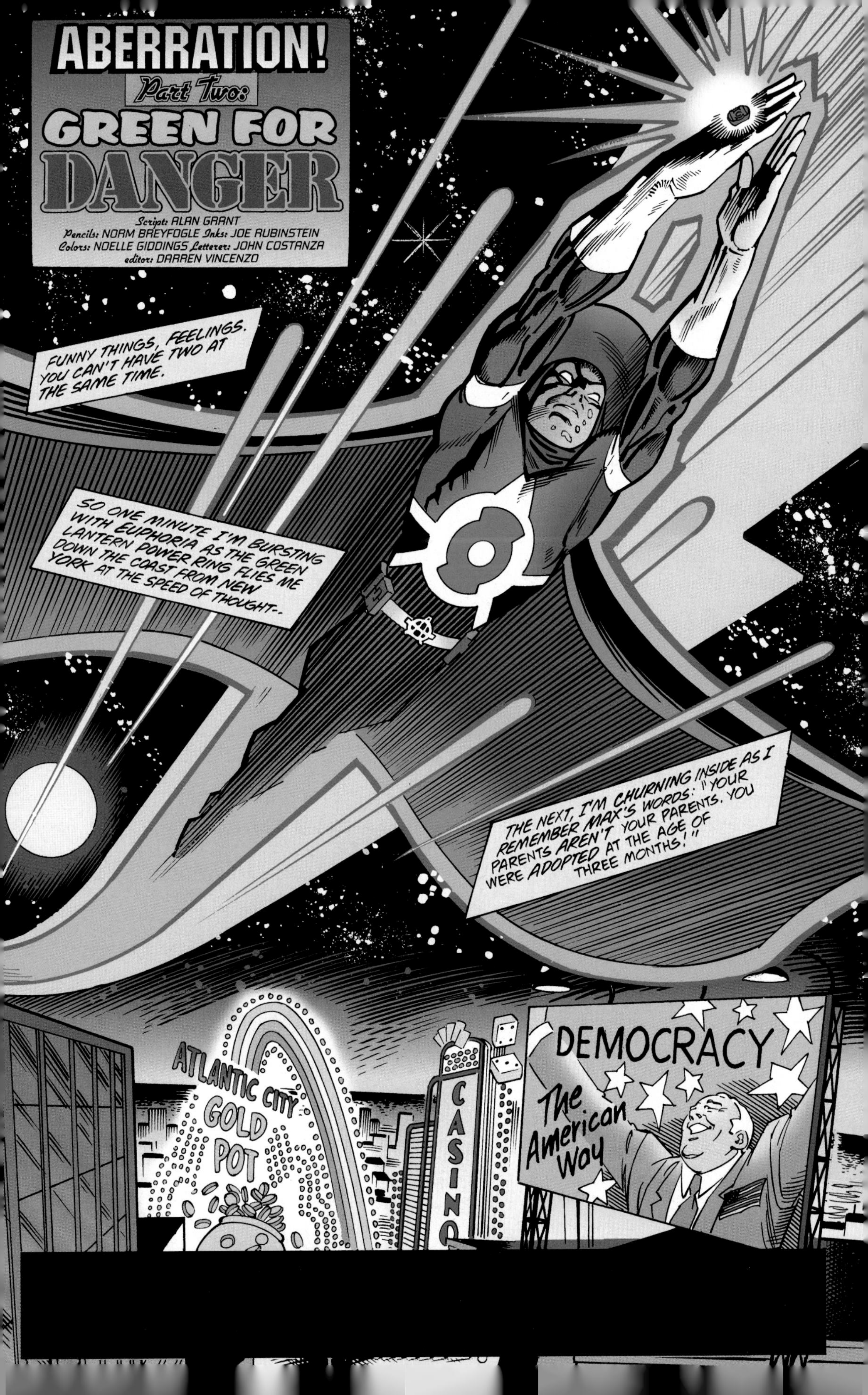
ABERRATION!
Part Two:
GREEN FOR DANGER
Script: ALAN GRANT
Pencils: NORM BREYFOGLE Inks: JOE RUBINSTEIN
Colors: NOELLE GIDDINGS Letterer: JOHN COSTANZA
editor: DARREN VINCENZO
FUNNY THINGS, FEELINGS. YOU CAN'T HAVE TWO AT THE SAME TIME.
SO ONE MINUTE I'M BURSTING WITH EUPHORIA AS THE GREEN LANTERN POWER RING FLIES ME DOWN THE COAST FROM NEW YORK AT THE SPEED OF THOUGHT--
THE NEXT, I'M CHURNING INSIDE AS I REMEMBER MAX'S WORDS: "YOUR PARENTS AREN'T YOUR PARENTS. YOU WERE ADOPTED AT THE AGE OF THREE MONTHS!"
ATLANTIC CITY GOLD POT
CASINO
DEMOCRACY
The American Way

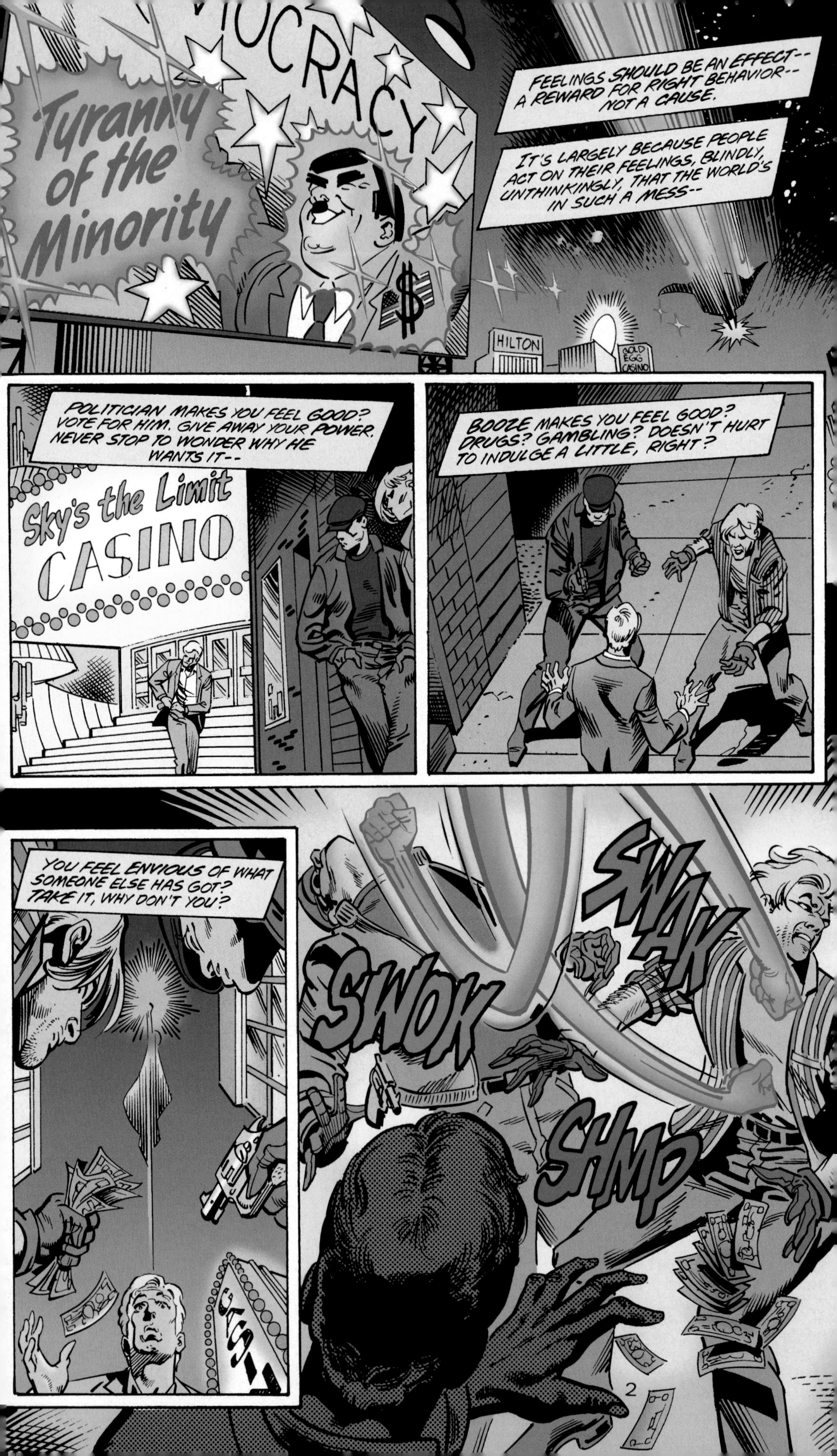
Tyranny of the Minority
FEELINGS SHOULD BE AN EFFECT-- A REWARD FOR RIGHT BEHAVIOR-- NOT A CAUSE.
IT'S LARGELY BECAUSE PEOPLE ACT ON THEIR FEELINGS, BLINDLY, UNTHINKINGLY, THAT THE WORLD'S IN SUCH A MESS--
HILTON
GOLD EGG CASINO
POLITICIAN MAKES YOU FEEL GOOD? VOTE FOR HIM. GIVE AWAY YOUR POWER. NEVER STOP TO WONDER WHY HE WANTS IT--
Sky's the Limit CASINO
BOOZE MAKES YOU FEEL GOOD? DRUGS? GAMBLING? DOESN'T HURT TO INDULGE A LITTLE, RIGHT?
YOU FEEL ENVIOUS OF WHAT SOMEONE ELSE HAS GOT? TAKE IT, WHY DON'T YOU?
SWAK
SWOK
SHMP

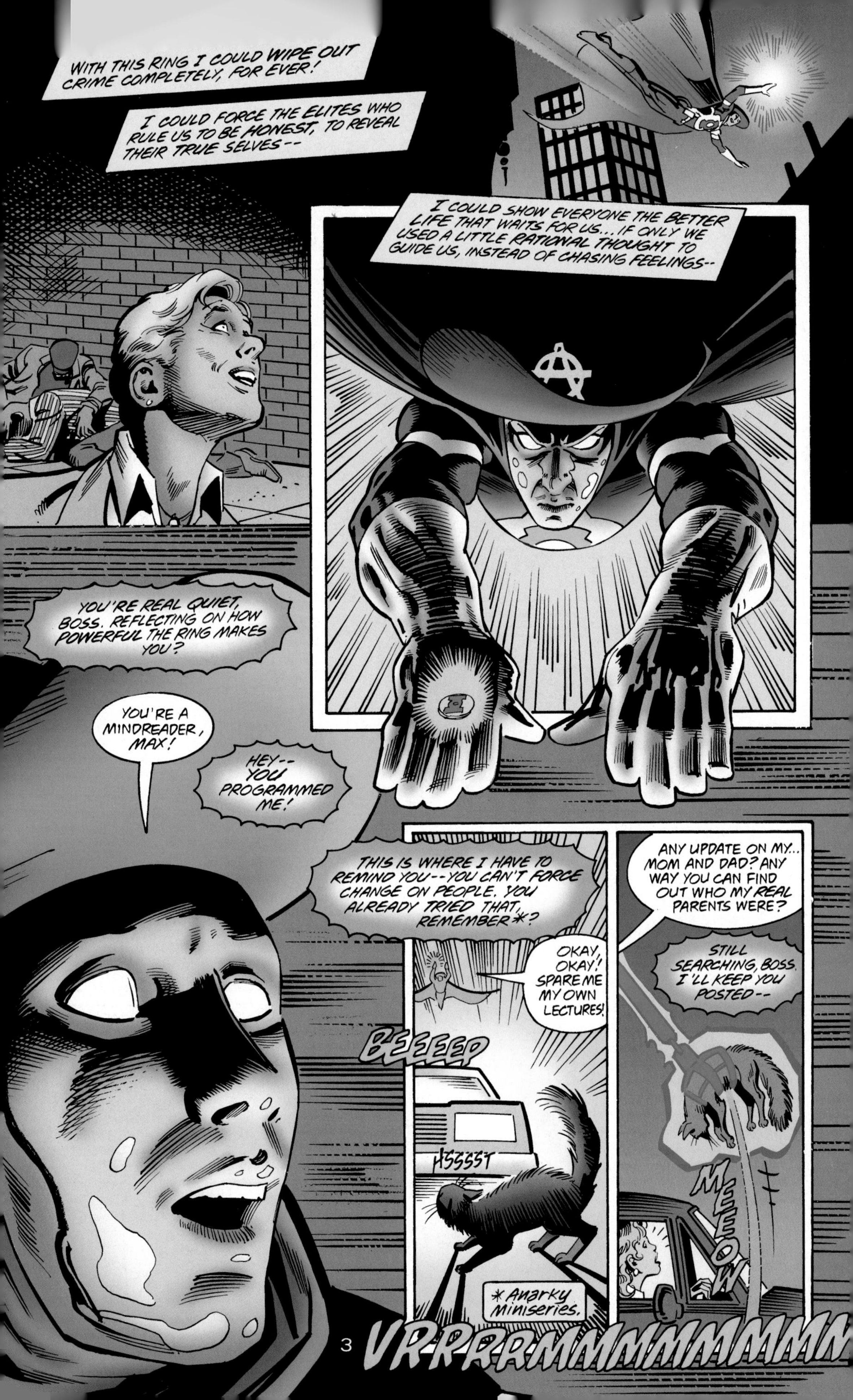

WITH THIS RING I COULD WIPE OUT CRIME COMPLETELY, FOR EVER!
I COULD FORCE THE ELITES WHO RULE US TO BE HONEST, TO REVEAL THEIR TRUE SELVES--
I COULD SHOW EVERYONE THE BETTER LIFE THAT WAITS FOR US... IF ONLY WE USED A LITTLE RATIONAL THOUGHT TO GUIDE US, INSTEAD OF CHASING FEELINGS--
YOU'RE REAL QUIET, BOSS. REFLECTING ON HOW POWERFUL THE RING MAKES YOU?
YOU'RE A MINDREADER, MAX!
HEY-- YOU PROGRAMMED ME!
THIS IS WHERE I HAVE TO REMIND YOU--YOU CAN'T FORCE CHANGE ON PEOPLE. YOU ALREADY TRIED THAT, REMEMBER*?
OKAY, OKAY! SPARE ME MY OWN LECTURES!
BEEEEP
HSSSST
*Anarky Miniseries.
ANY UPDATE ON MY... MOM AND DAD? ANY WAY YOU CAN FIND OUT WHO MY REAL PARENTS WERE?
STILL SEARCHING, BOSS. I'LL KEEP YOU POSTED--
MEEEOW
VRRRRMMMMMMMMN

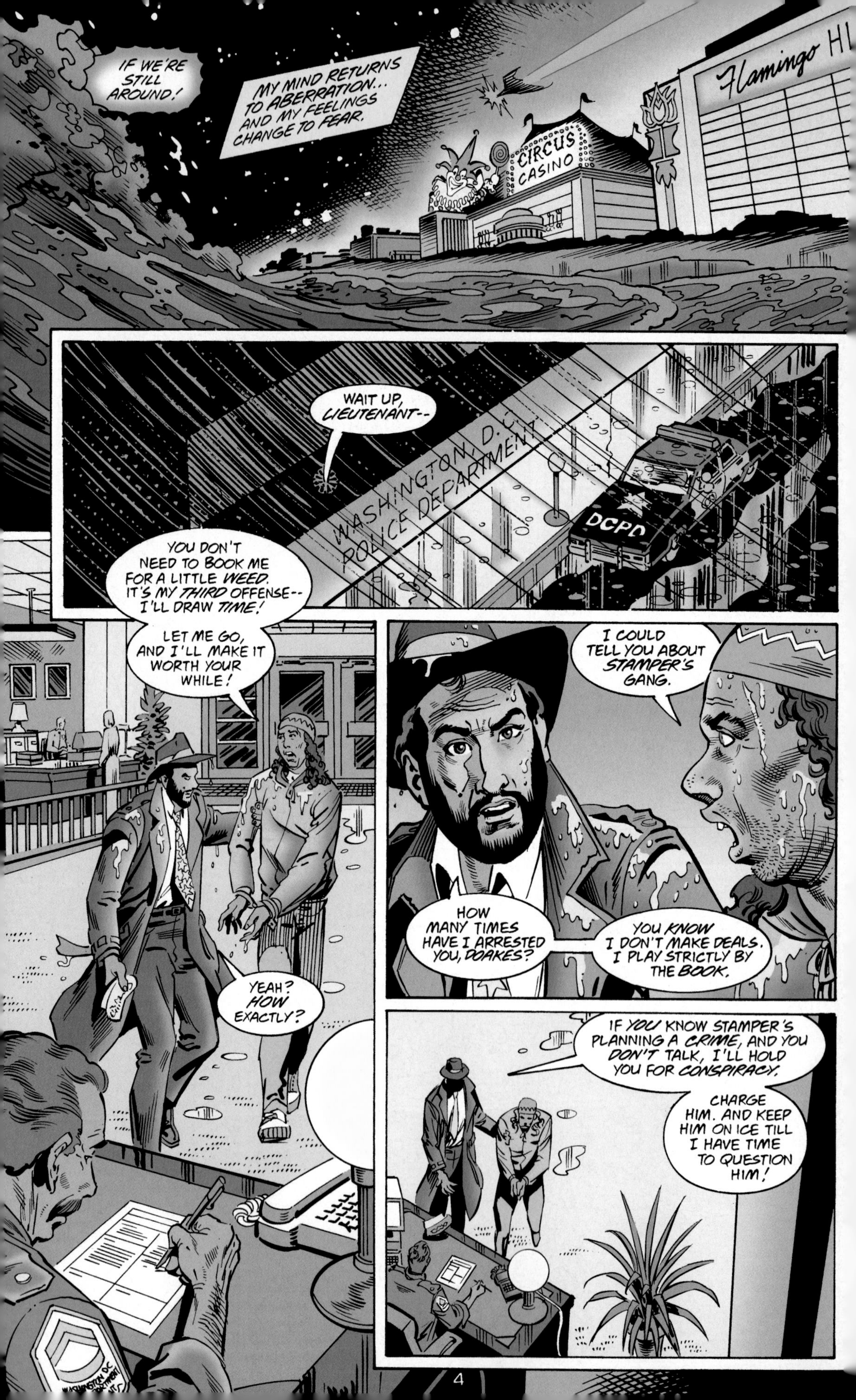
IF WE'RE STILL AROUND!
MY MIND RETURNS TO ABERRATION... AND MY FEELINGS CHANGE TO FEAR.
CIRCUS CASINO
Flamingo HI
WAIT UP, LIEUTENANT--
WASHINGTON, D.C. POLICE DEPARTMENT
DCPD
YOU DON'T NEED TO BOOK ME FOR A LITTLE WEED. IT'S MY THIRD OFFENSE-- I'LL DRAW TIME!
LET ME GO, AND I'LL MAKE IT WORTH YOUR WHILE!
YEAH? HOW EXACTLY?
I COULD TELL YOU ABOUT STAMPER'S GANG.
HOW MANY TIMES HAVE I ARRESTED YOU, DOAKES?
YOU KNOW I DON'T MAKE DEALS. I PLAY STRICTLY BY THE BOOK.
IF YOU KNOW STAMPER'S PLANNING A CRIME, AND YOU DON'T TALK, I'LL HOLD YOU FOR CONSPIRACY.
CHARGE HIM. AND KEEP HIM ON ICE TILL I HAVE TIME TO QUESTION HIM!

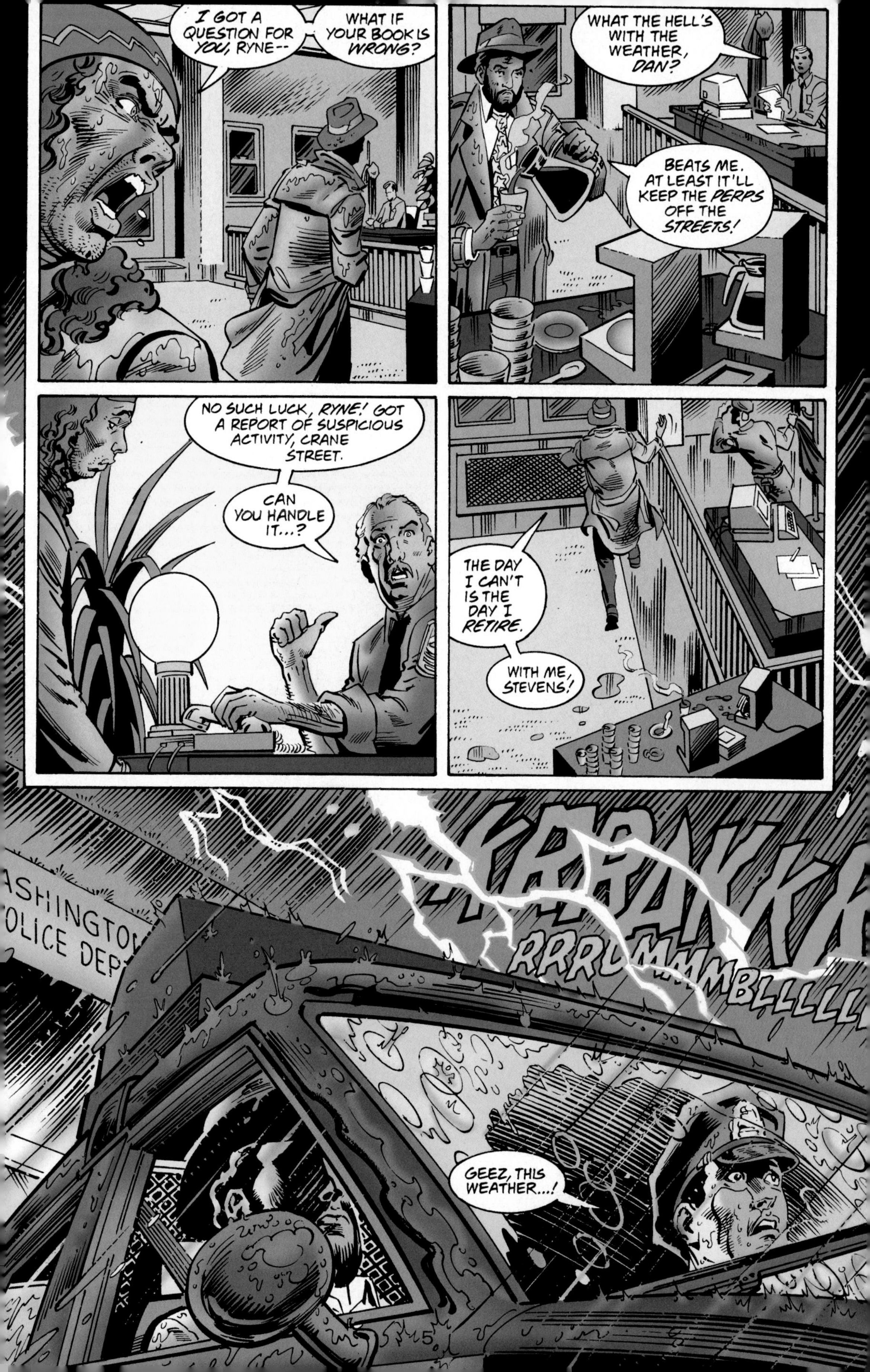
I GOT A QUESTION FOR *YOU*, RYNE--
WHAT IF YOUR BOOK IS *WRONG?*
WHAT THE HELL'S WITH THE WEATHER, *DAN?*
BEATS ME. AT LEAST IT'LL KEEP THE *PERPS* OFF THE *STREETS!*
NO SUCH LUCK, *RYNE!* GOT A REPORT OF SUSPICIOUS ACTIVITY, CRANE STREET.
CAN YOU HANDLE IT...?
THE DAY I CAN'T IS THE DAY I *RETIRE*.
WITH ME, STEVENS!
ASHINGTON
OLICE DEP
GEEZ, THIS WEATHER...!

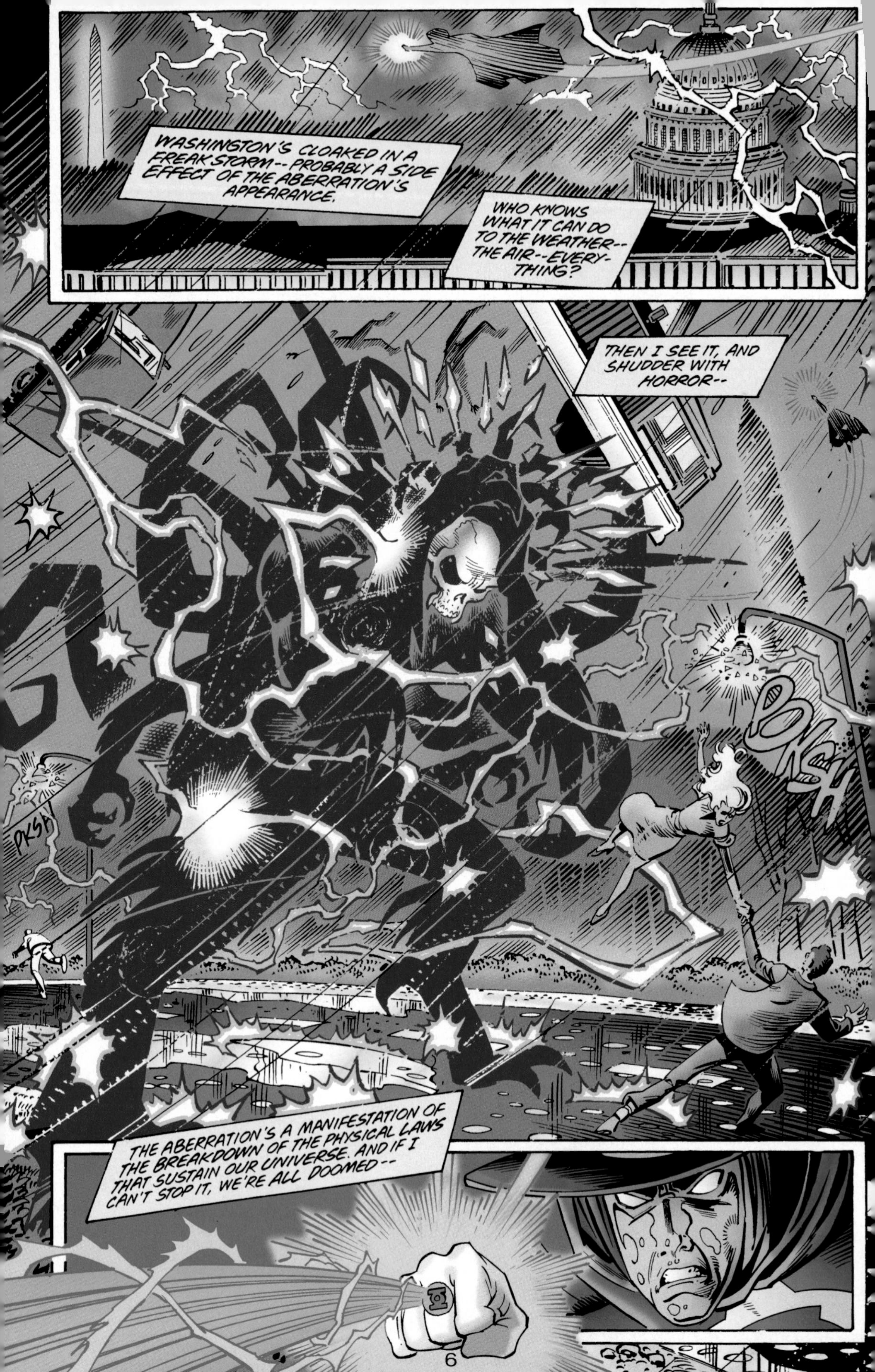
WASHINGTON'S CLOAKED IN A FREAK STORM--PROBABLY A SIDE EFFECT OF THE ABERRATION'S APPEARANCE.
WHO KNOWS WHAT IT CAN DO TO THE WEATHER--THE AIR--EVERY-THING?
THEN I SEE IT, AND SHUDDER WITH HORROR--
PKSH
PKSH
THE ABERRATION'S A MANIFESTATION OF THE BREAKDOWN OF THE PHYSICAL LAWS THAT SUSTAIN OUR UNIVERSE. AND IF I CAN'T STOP IT, WE'RE ALL DOOMED--

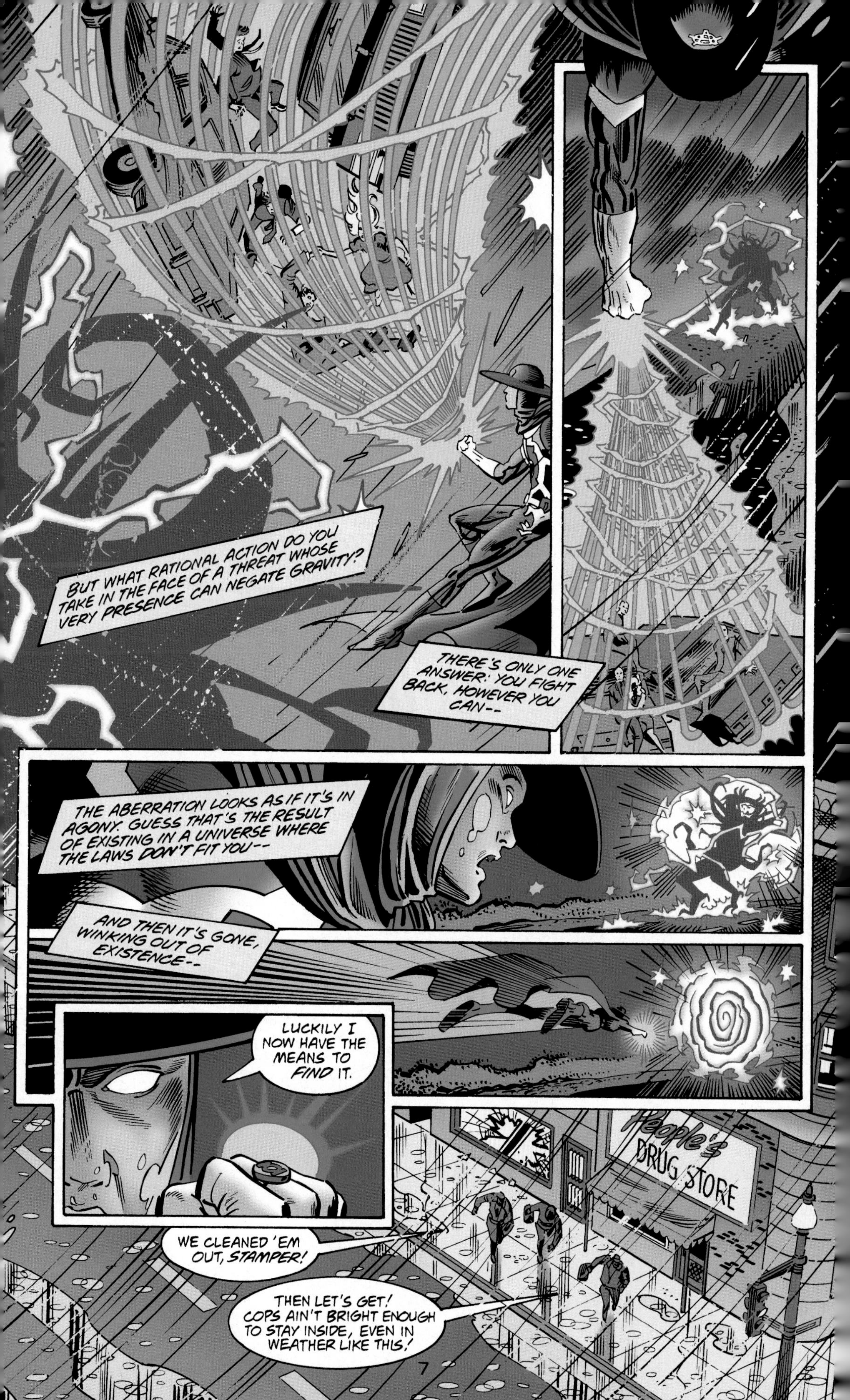

BUT WHAT RATIONAL ACTION DO YOU TAKE IN THE FACE OF A THREAT WHOSE VERY PRESENCE CAN NEGATE GRAVITY?
THERE'S ONLY ONE ANSWER: YOU FIGHT BACK, HOWEVER YOU CAN--
THE ABERRATION LOOKS AS IF IT'S IN AGONY. GUESS THAT'S THE RESULT OF EXISTING IN A UNIVERSE WHERE THE LAWS DON'T FIT YOU--
AND THEN IT'S GONE, WINKING OUT OF EXISTENCE--
LUCKILY I NOW HAVE THE MEANS TO FIND IT.
People's
DRUG STORE
WE CLEANED 'EM OUT, STAMPER!
THEN LET'S GET! COPS AIN'T BRIGHT ENOUGH TO STAY INSIDE, EVEN IN WEATHER LIKE THIS!

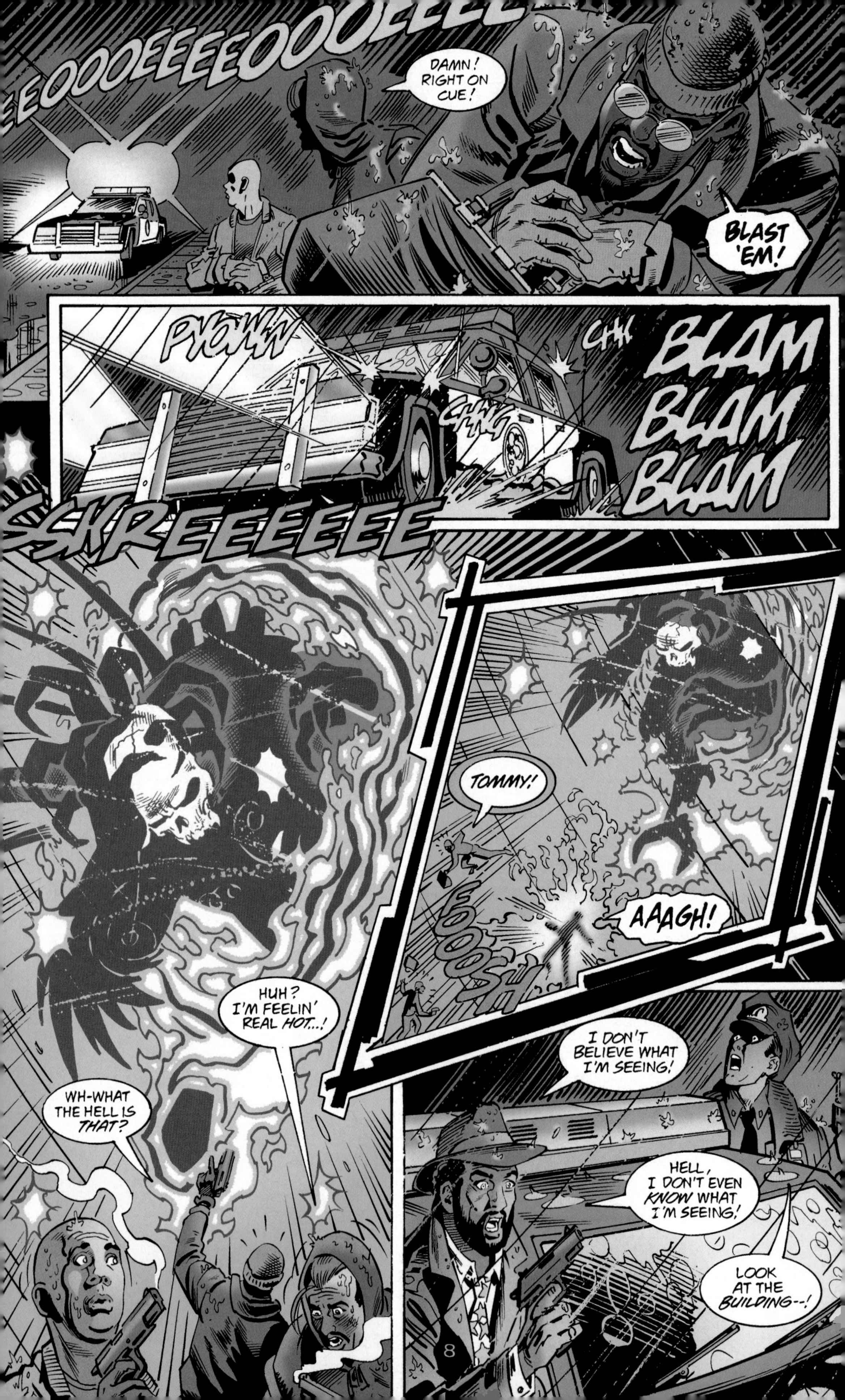
EEOOOEEEEOOOEEEE
DAMN! RIGHT ON CUE!
BLAST 'EM!
PYOWN
CHI
BLAM BLAM BLAM
CHING
SSKREEEEEEE
TOMMY!
AAAGH!
WOOOSH
HUH? I'M FEELIN' REAL HOT...!
I DON'T BELIEVE WHAT I'M SEEING!
WH-WHAT THE HELL IS THAT?
HELL, I DON'T EVEN KNOW WHAT I'M SEEING!
LOOK AT THE BUILDING--!
8

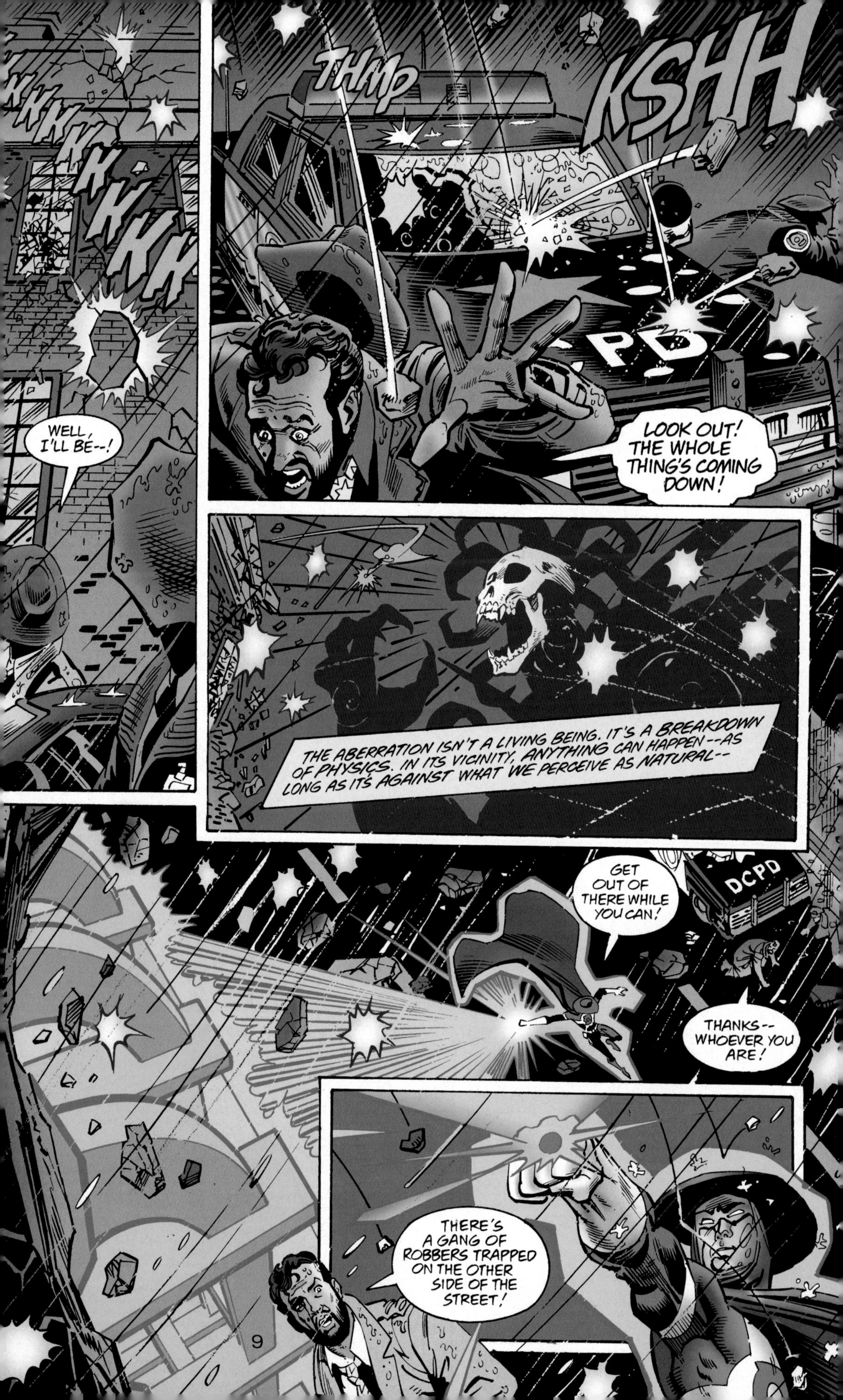

KKKKKKKKKK
THMP
KSHH
WELL, I'LL BE--!
LOOK OUT! THE WHOLE THING'S COMING DOWN!
PD
THE ABERRATION ISN'T A LIVING BEING. IT'S A BREAKDOWN OF PHYSICS. IN ITS VICINITY, ANYTHING CAN HAPPEN--AS LONG AS IT'S AGAINST WHAT WE PERCEIVE AS NATURAL--
GET OUT OF THERE WHILE YOU CAN!
DCPD
THANKS-- WHOEVER YOU ARE!
THERE'S A GANG OF ROBBERS TRAPPED ON THE OTHER SIDE OF THE STREET!

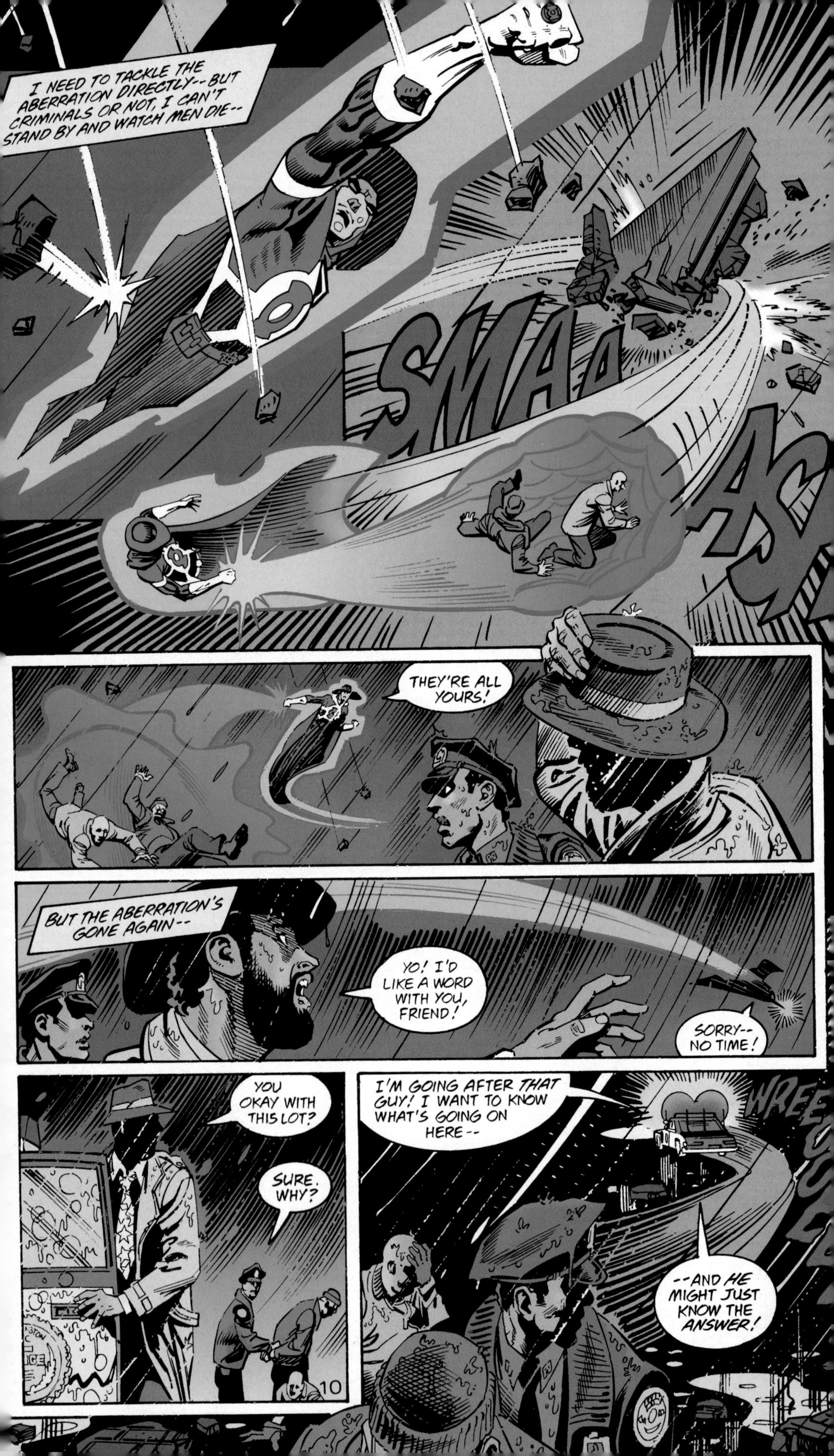
I NEED TO TACKLE THE ABERRATION DIRECTLY-- BUT CRIMINALS OR NOT, I CAN'T STAND BY AND WATCH MEN DIE--
SMAAAC
THEY'RE ALL YOURS!
BUT THE ABERRATION'S GONE AGAIN--
YO! I'D LIKE A WORD WITH YOU, FRIEND!
SORRY-- NO TIME!
YOU OKAY WITH THIS LOT?
SURE. WHY?
I'M GOING AFTER THAT GUY! I WANT TO KNOW WHAT'S GOING ON HERE--
--AND HE MIGHT JUST KNOW THE ANSWER!
10

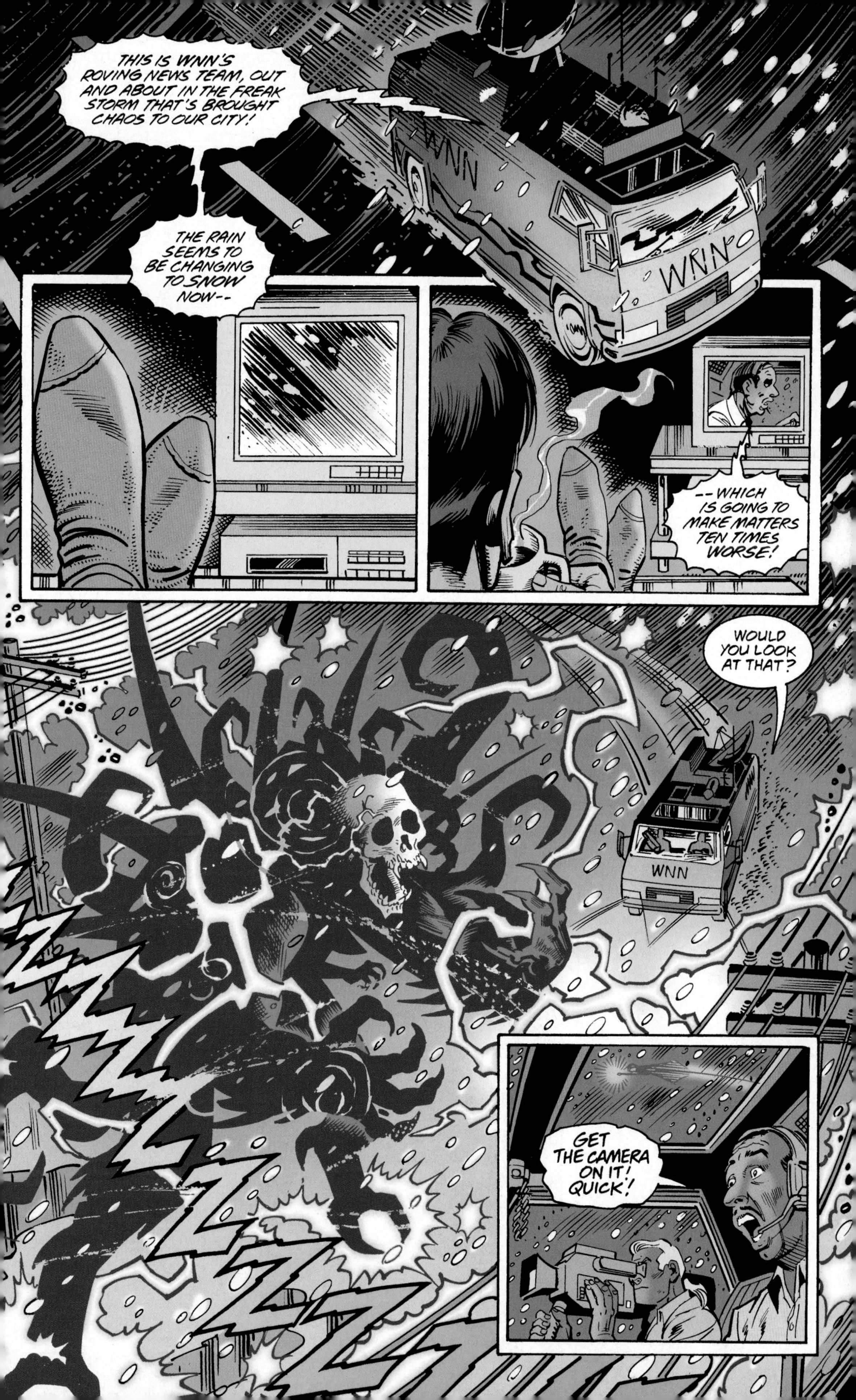
THIS IS WNN'S ROVING NEWS TEAM, OUT AND ABOUT IN THE FREAK STORM THAT'S BROUGHT CHAOS TO OUR CITY!
THE RAIN SEEMS TO BE CHANGING TO SNOW NOW--
--WHICH IS GOING TO MAKE MATTERS TEN TIMES WORSE!
WOULD YOU LOOK AT THAT?
GET THE CAMERA ON IT! QUICK!

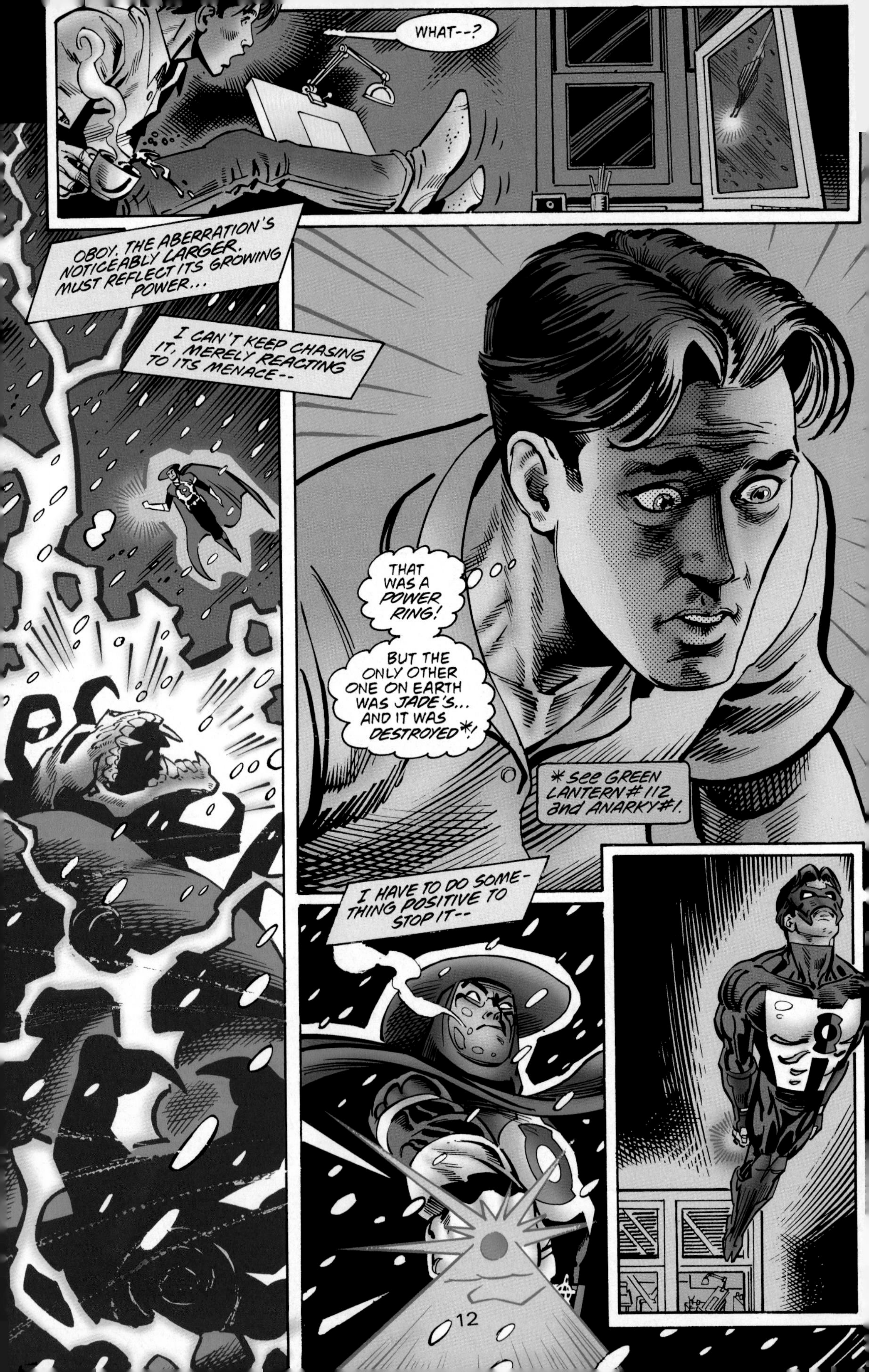
WHAT--?
OBOY, THE ABERRATION'S NOTICEABLY LARGER. MUST REFLECT ITS GROWING POWER...
I CAN'T KEEP CHASING IT, MERELY REACTING TO ITS MENACE--
THAT WAS A POWER RING!
BUT THE ONLY OTHER ONE ON EARTH WAS JADE'S... AND IT WAS DESTROYED*!
*SEE GREEN LANTERN #112 AND ANARKY #1.
I HAVE TO DO SOME-THING POSITIVE TO STOP IT--

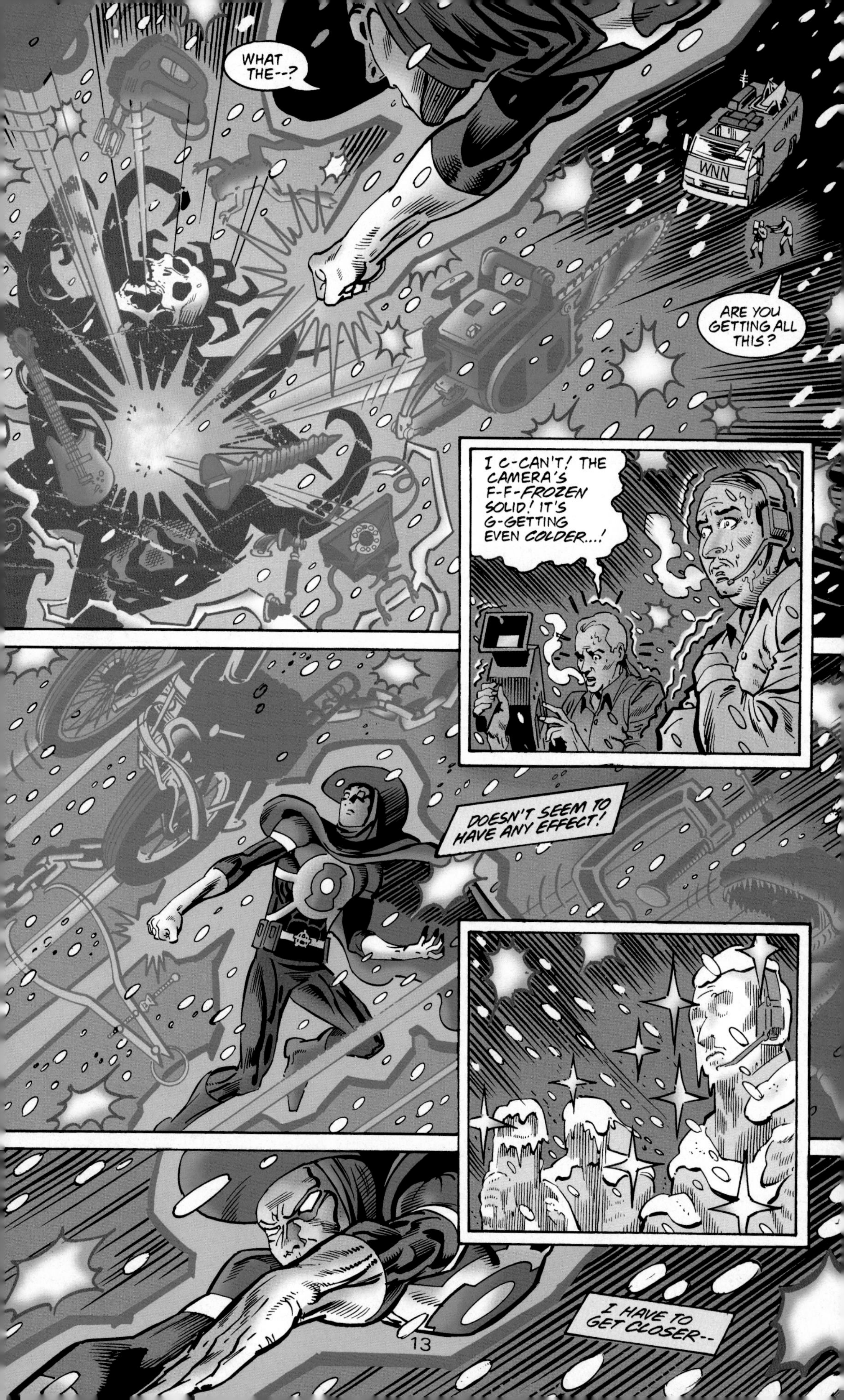
WHAT THE--?
ARE YOU GETTING ALL THIS?
I C-CAN'T! THE CAMERA'S F-F-FROZEN SOLID! IT'S G-GETTING EVEN COLDER...!
DOESN'T SEEM TO HAVE ANY EFFECT!
I HAVE TO GET CLOSER--

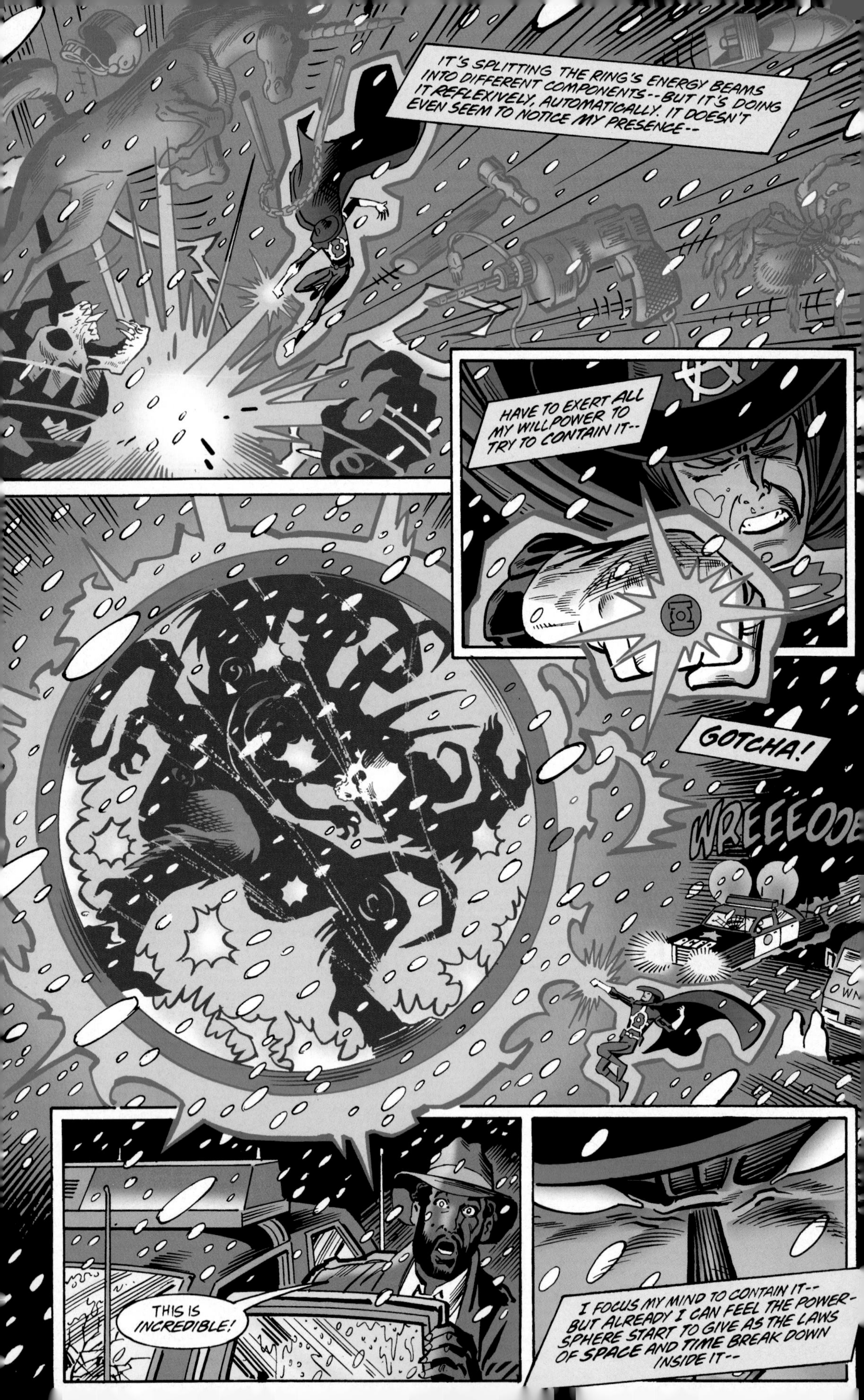
IT'S SPLITTING THE RING'S ENERGY BEAMS INTO DIFFERENT COMPONENTS--BUT IT'S DOING IT REFLEXIVELY, AUTOMATICALLY. IT DOESN'T EVEN SEEM TO NOTICE MY PRESENCE--
HAVE TO EXERT ALL MY WILLPOWER TO TRY TO CONTAIN IT--
GOTCHA!
WREEEOOE
THIS IS INCREDIBLE!
I FOCUS MY MIND TO CONTAIN IT--BUT ALREADY I CAN FEEL THE POWER-SPHERE START TO GIVE AS THE LAWS OF SPACE AND TIME BREAK DOWN INSIDE IT--

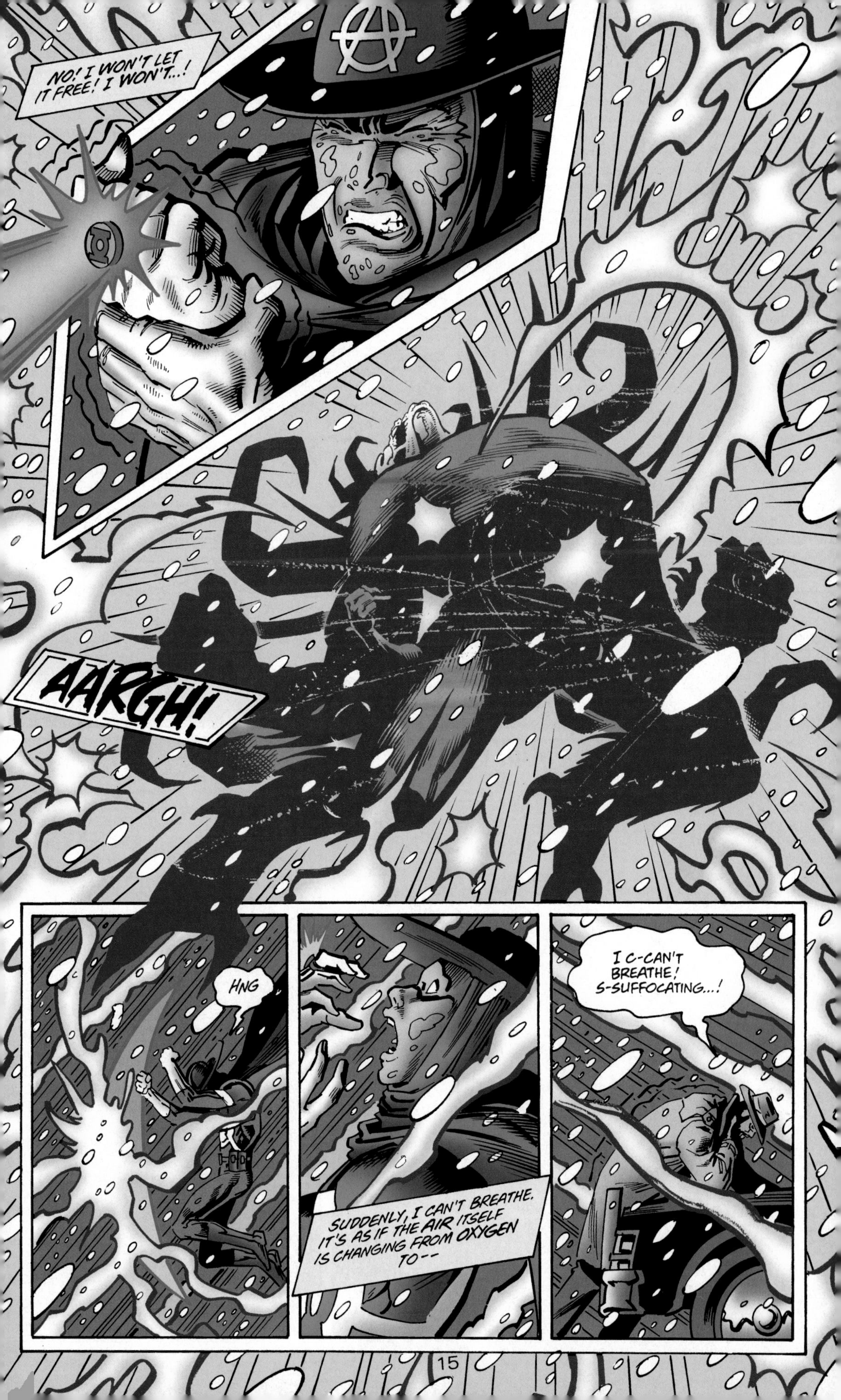
NO! I WON'T LET IT FREE! I WON'T...!
AARGH!
HNG
SUDDENLY, I CAN'T BREATHE. IT'S AS IF THE AIR ITSELF IS CHANGING FROM OXYGEN TO--
I C-CAN'T BREATHE! S-SUFFOCATING...!

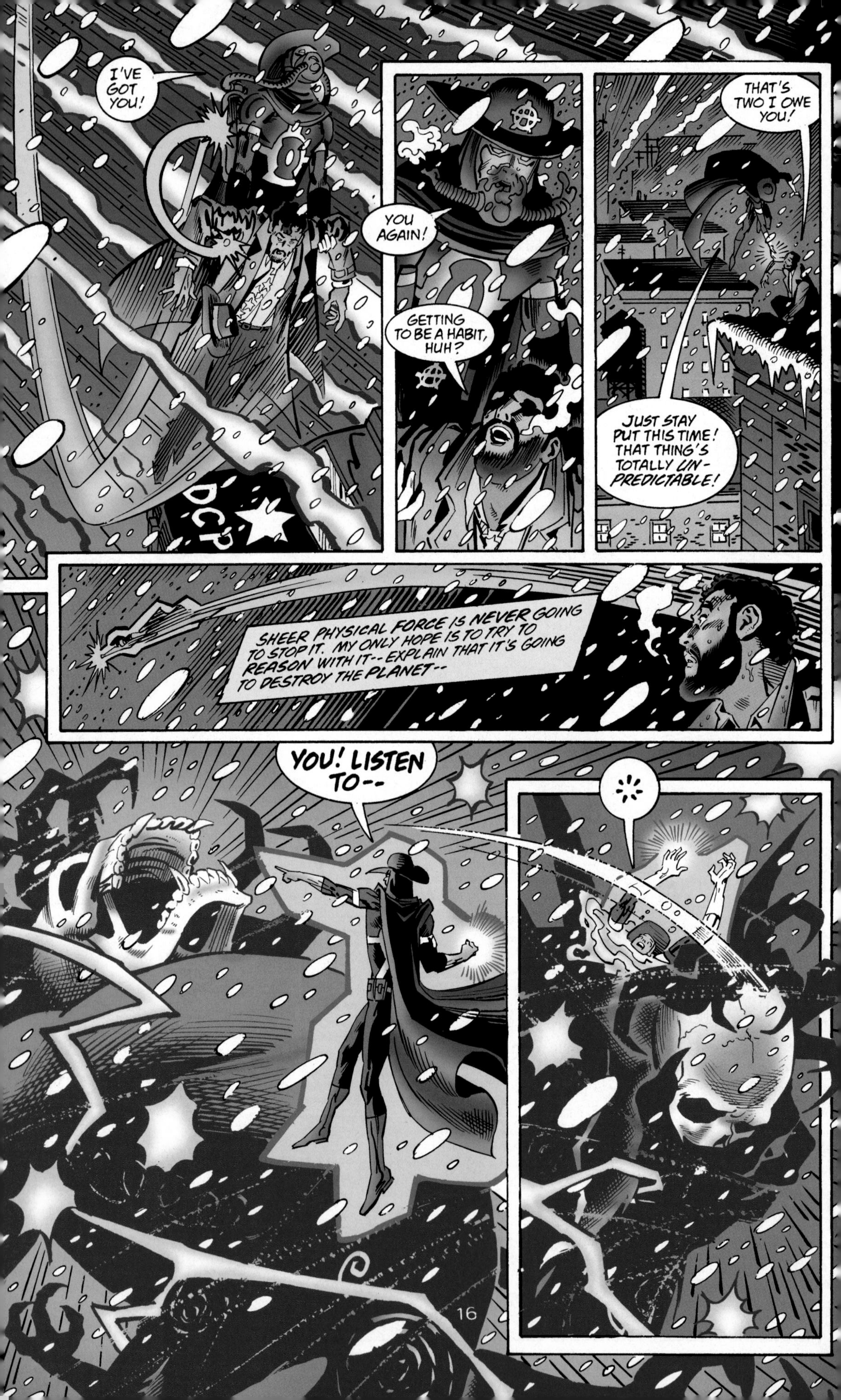

I'VE GOT YOU!
YOU AGAIN!
GETTING TO BE A HABIT, HUH?
THAT'S TWO I OWE YOU!
JUST STAY PUT THIS TIME! THAT THING'S TOTALLY UN-PREDICTABLE!
SHEER PHYSICAL FORCE IS NEVER GOING TO STOP IT. MY ONLY HOPE IS TO TRY TO REASON WITH IT-- EXPLAIN THAT IT'S GOING TO DESTROY THE PLANET--
YOU! LISTEN TO--
DCP

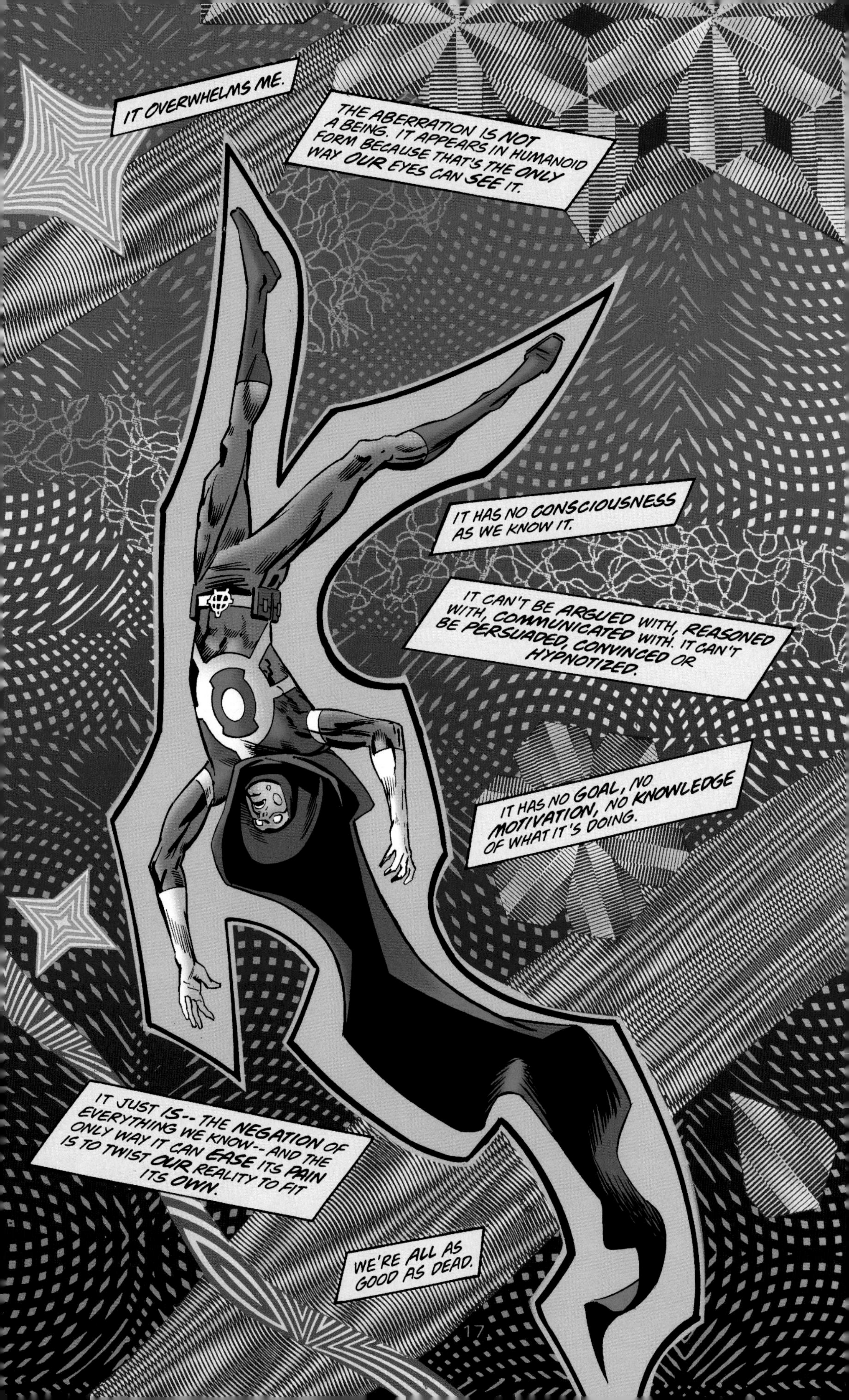
IT OVERWHELMS ME.
THE ABERRATION IS NOT A BEING. IT APPEARS IN HUMANOID FORM BECAUSE THAT'S THE ONLY WAY OUR EYES CAN SEE IT.
IT HAS NO CONSCIOUSNESS AS WE KNOW IT.
IT CAN'T BE ARGUED WITH, REASONED WITH, COMMUNICATED WITH. IT CAN'T BE PERSUADED, CONVINCED OR HYPNOTIZED.
IT HAS NO GOAL, NO MOTIVATION, NO KNOWLEDGE OF WHAT IT'S DOING.
IT JUST IS--THE NEGATION OF EVERYTHING WE KNOW--AND THE ONLY WAY IT CAN EASE ITS PAIN IS TO TWIST OUR REALITY TO FIT ITS OWN.
WE'RE ALL AS GOOD AS DEAD.

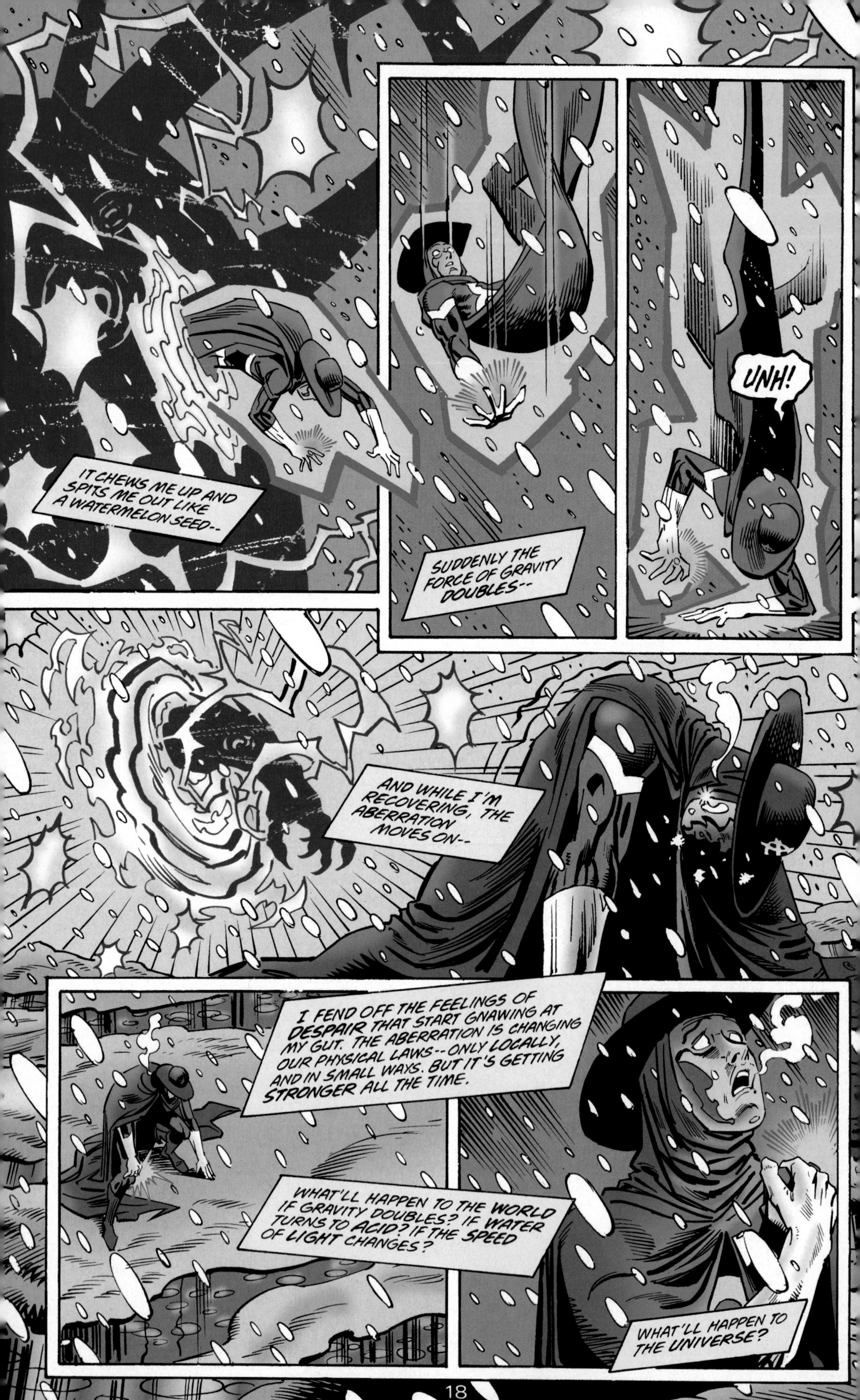

IT CHEWS ME UP AND SPITS ME OUT LIKE A WATERMELON SEED--
SUDDENLY THE FORCE OF GRAVITY DOUBLES--
UNH!
AND WHILE I'M RECOVERING, THE ABERRATION MOVES ON--
I FEND OFF THE FEELINGS OF DESPAIR THAT START GNAWING AT MY GUT. THE ABERRATION IS CHANGING OUR PHYSICAL LAWS--ONLY LOCALLY, AND IN SMALL WAYS. BUT IT'S GETTING STRONGER ALL THE TIME.
WHAT'LL HAPPEN TO THE WORLD IF GRAVITY DOUBLES? IF WATER TURNS TO ACID? IF THE SPEED OF LIGHT CHANGES?
WHAT'LL HAPPEN TO THE UNIVERSE?

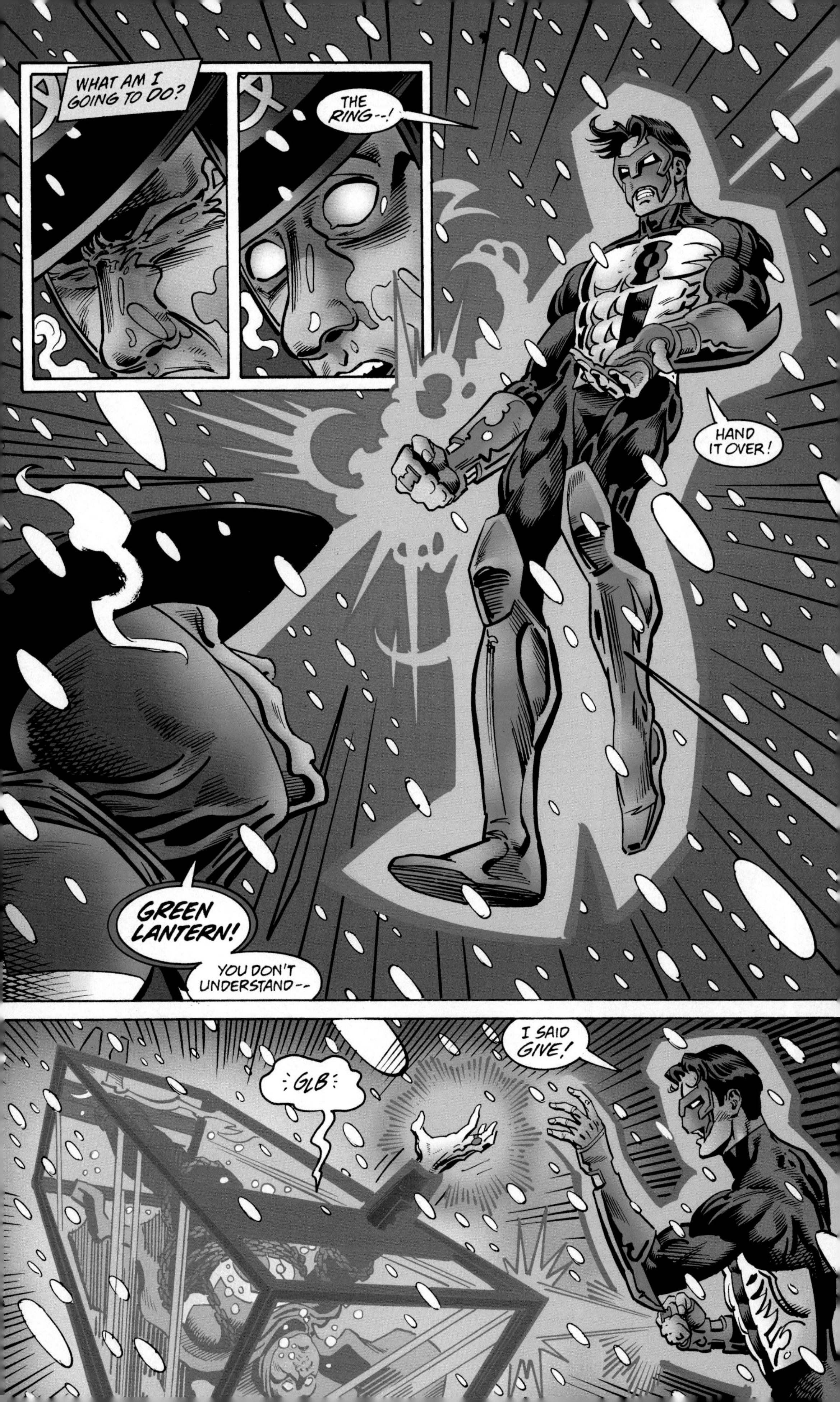
WHAT AM I GOING TO DO?
THE RING--!
HAND IT OVER!
GREEN LANTERN!
YOU DON'T UNDERSTAND--
I SAID GIVE!
GLB

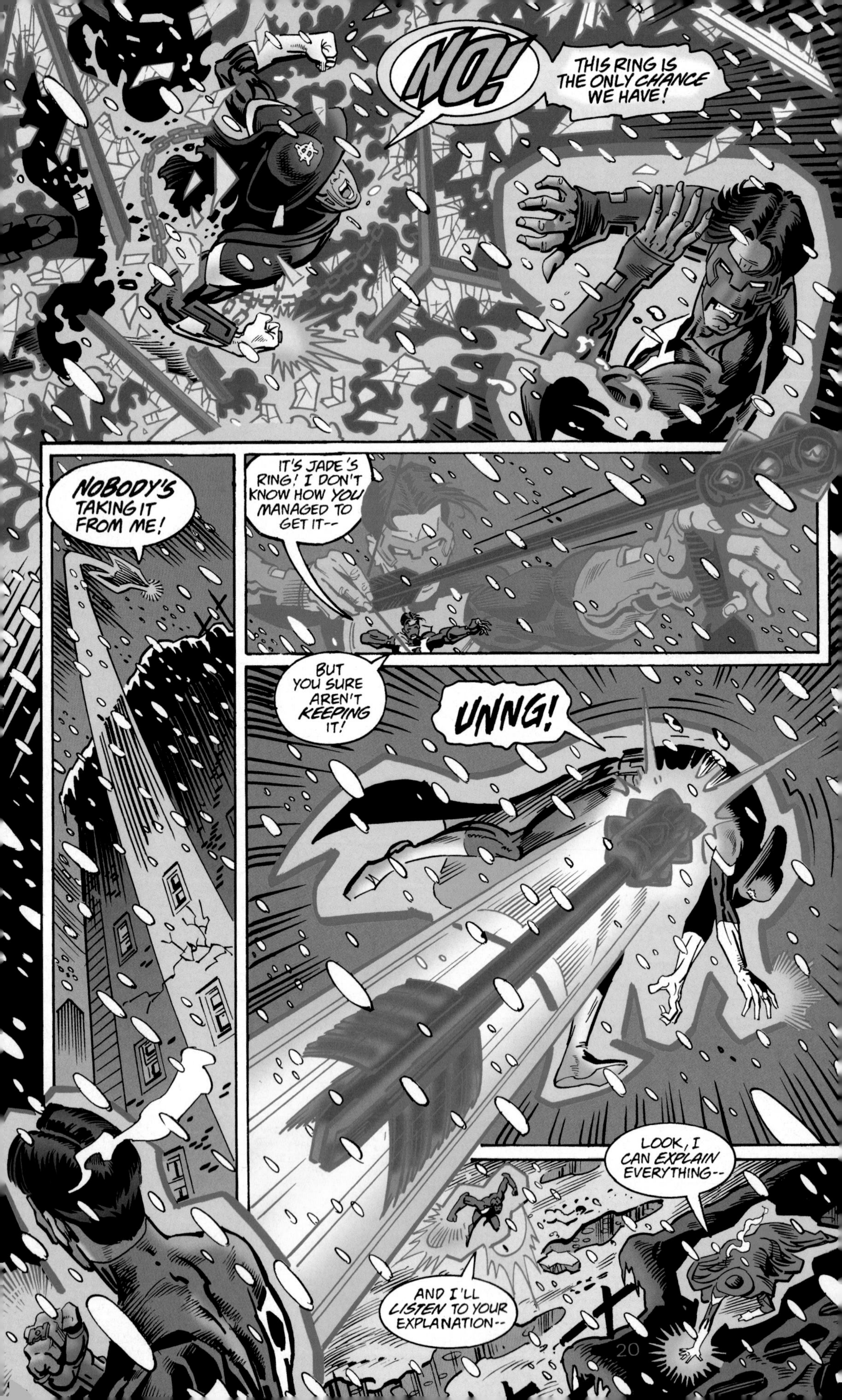
NO!
THIS RING IS THE ONLY CHANCE WE HAVE!
NOBODY'S TAKING IT FROM ME!
IT'S JADE'S RING! I DON'T KNOW HOW YOU MANAGED TO GET IT--
BUT YOU SURE AREN'T KEEPING IT!
UNNG!
LOOK, I CAN EXPLAIN EVERYTHING--
AND I'LL LISTEN TO YOUR EXPLANATION--

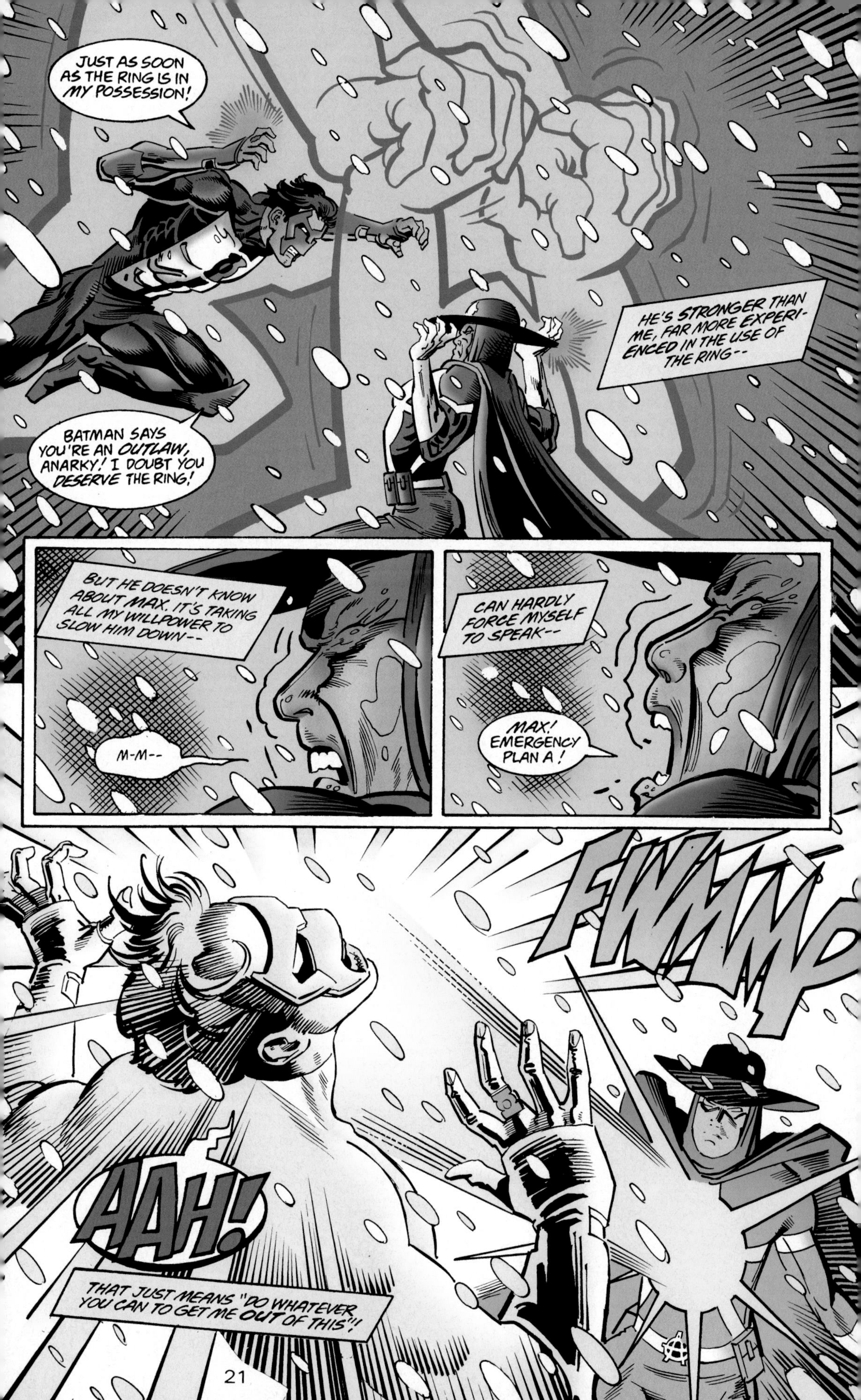
JUST AS SOON AS THE RING IS IN MY POSSESSION!
HE'S STRONGER THAN ME, FAR MORE EXPERIENCED IN THE USE OF THE RING--
BATMAN SAYS YOU'RE AN OUTLAW, ANARKY! I DOUBT YOU DESERVE THE RING!
BUT HE DOESN'T KNOW ABOUT MAX. IT'S TAKING ALL MY WILLPOWER TO SLOW HIM DOWN--
M-M--
CAN HARDLY FORCE MYSELF TO SPEAK--
MAX! EMERGENCY PLAN A!
FWMMP
AAH!
THAT JUST MEANS "DO WHATEVER YOU CAN TO GET ME OUT OF THIS"!

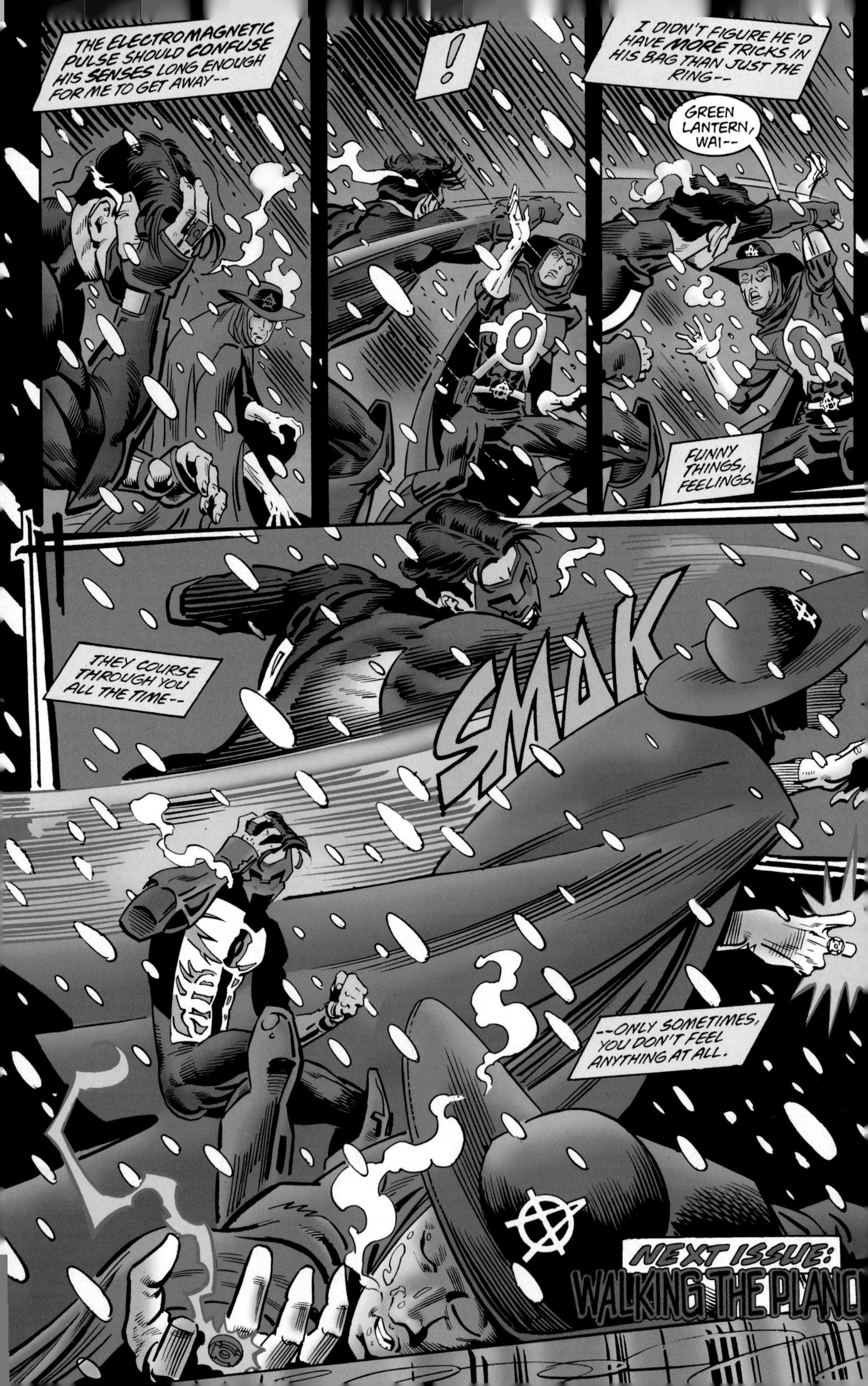
THE ELECTROMAGNETIC PULSE SHOULD CONFUSE HIS SENSES LONG ENOUGH FOR ME TO GET AWAY--
!
I DIDN'T FIGURE HE'D HAVE MORE TRICKS IN HIS BAG THAN JUST THE RING--
GREEN LANTERN, WAI--
FUNNY THINGS, FEELINGS.
THEY COURSE THROUGH YOU ALL THE TIME--
SMAK
--ONLY SOMETIMES, YOU DON'T FEEL ANYTHING AT ALL.
NEXT ISSUE:
WALKING THE PLANO

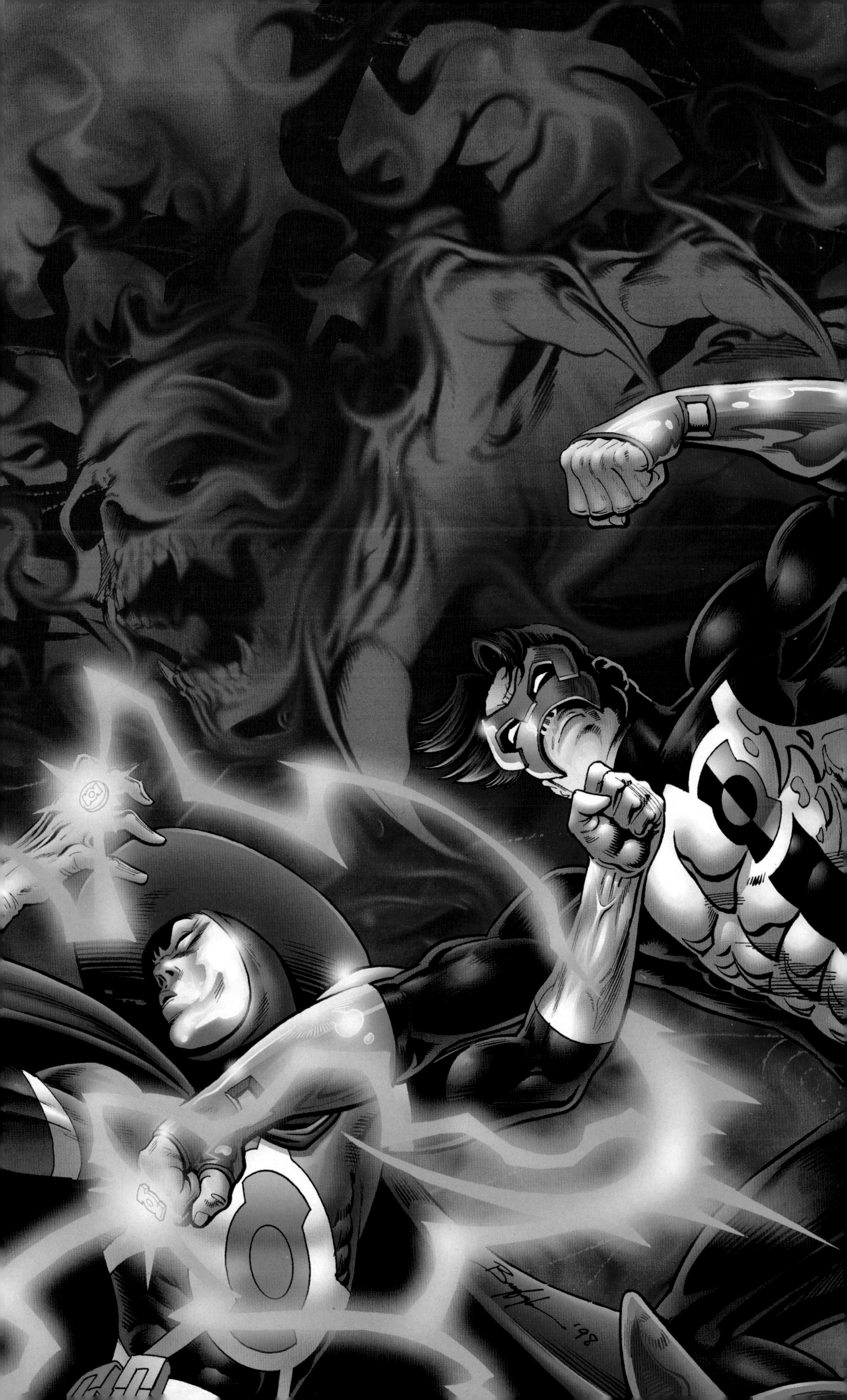

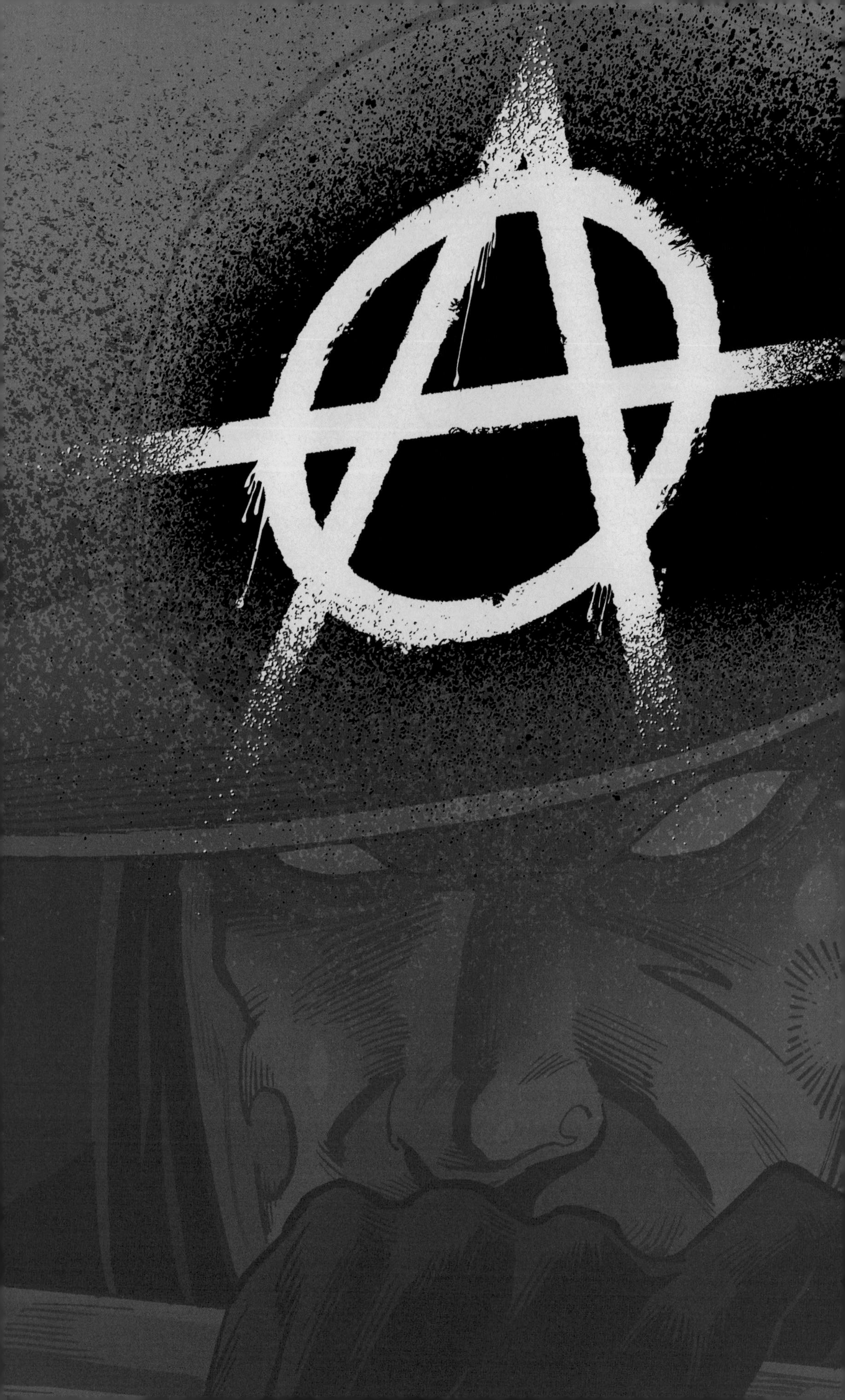

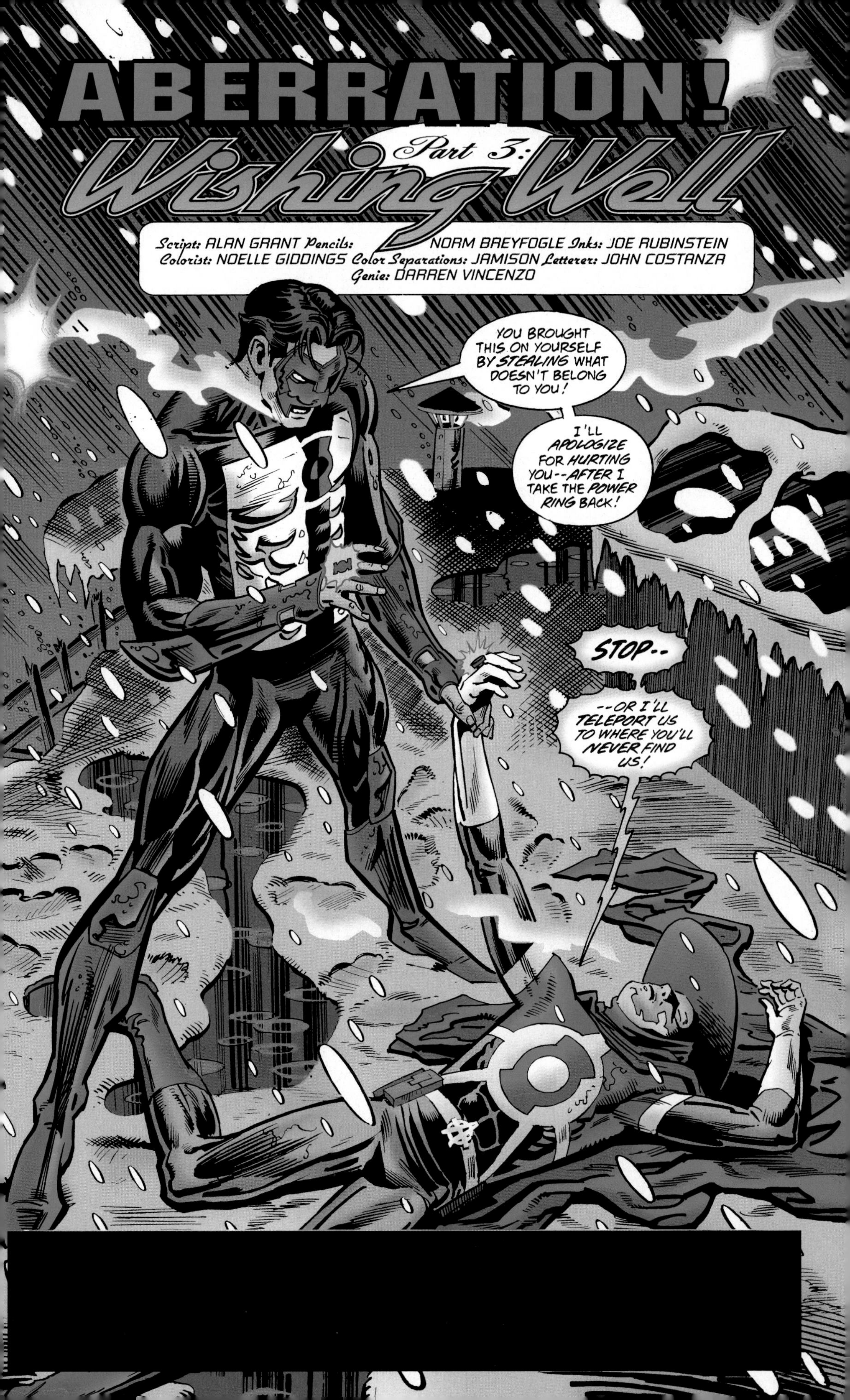
ABERRATION!
Part 3: Wishing Well
Script: ALAN GRANT Pencils: NORM BREYFOGLE Inks: JOE RUBINSTEIN
Colorist: NOELLE GIDDINGS Color Separations: JAMISON Letterer: JOHN COSTANZA
Genie: DARREN VINCENZO
YOU BROUGHT THIS ON YOURSELF BY STEALING WHAT DOESN'T BELONG TO YOU!
I'LL APOLOGIZE FOR HURTING YOU--AFTER I TAKE THE POWER RING BACK!
STOP--
--OR I'LL TELEPORT US TO WHERE YOU'LL NEVER FIND US!
[redacted]

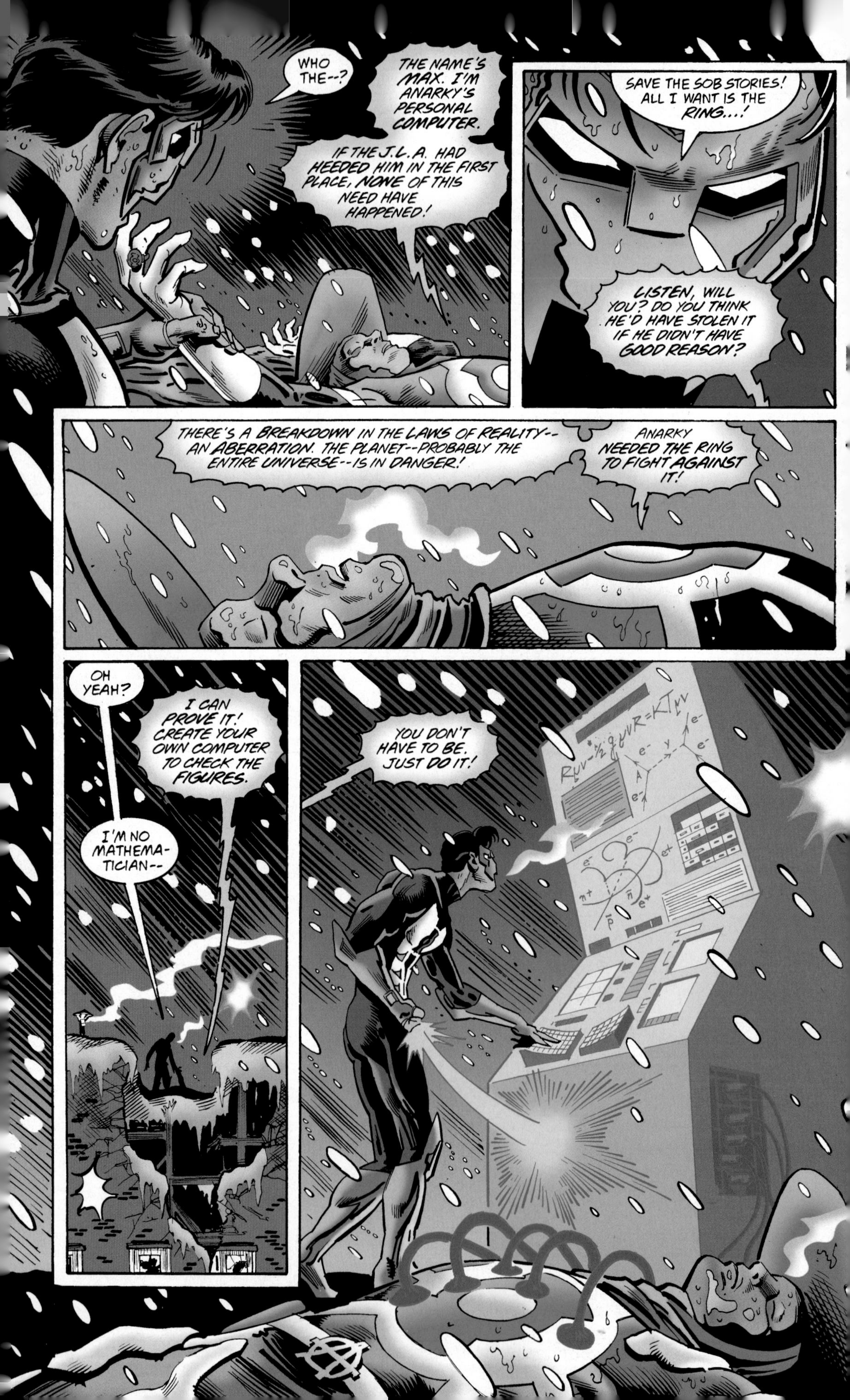

WHO THE--?
THE NAME'S MAX. I'M ANARKY'S PERSONAL COMPUTER.
IF THE J.L.A. HAD HEEDED HIM IN THE FIRST PLACE, NONE OF THIS NEED HAVE HAPPENED!
SAVE THE SOB STORIES! ALL I WANT IS THE RING...!
LISTEN, WILL YOU? DO YOU THINK HE'D HAVE STOLEN IT IF HE DIDN'T HAVE GOOD REASON?
THERE'S A BREAKDOWN IN THE LAWS OF REALITY--AN ABERRATION. THE PLANET--PROBABLY THE ENTIRE UNIVERSE--IS IN DANGER!
ANARKY NEEDED THE RING TO FIGHT AGAINST IT!
OH YEAH?
I CAN PROVE IT! CREATE YOUR OWN COMPUTER TO CHECK THE FIGURES.
I'M NO MATHEMATICIAN--
YOU DON'T HAVE TO BE. JUST DO IT!

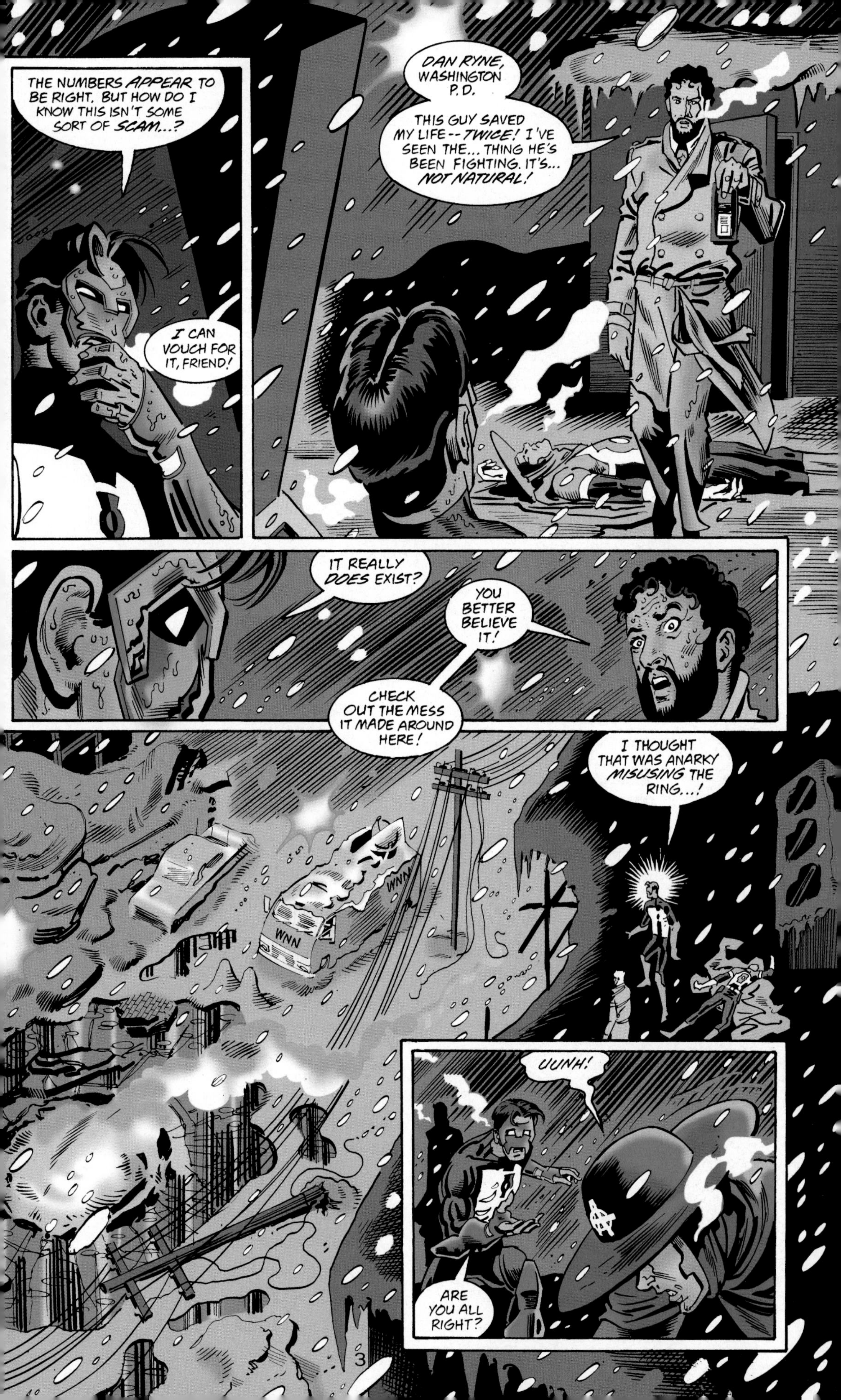
THE NUMBERS APPEAR TO BE RIGHT. BUT HOW DO I KNOW THIS ISN'T SOME SORT OF SCAM...?
I CAN VOUCH FOR IT, FRIEND!
DAN RYNE, WASHINGTON P.D.
THIS GUY SAVED MY LIFE--TWICE! I'VE SEEN THE... THING HE'S BEEN FIGHTING. IT'S... NOT NATURAL!
IT REALLY DOES EXIST?
YOU BETTER BELIEVE IT!
CHECK OUT THE MESS IT MADE AROUND HERE!
I THOUGHT THAT WAS ANARKY MISUSING THE RING...!
WNN
UUNH!
ARE YOU ALL RIGHT?

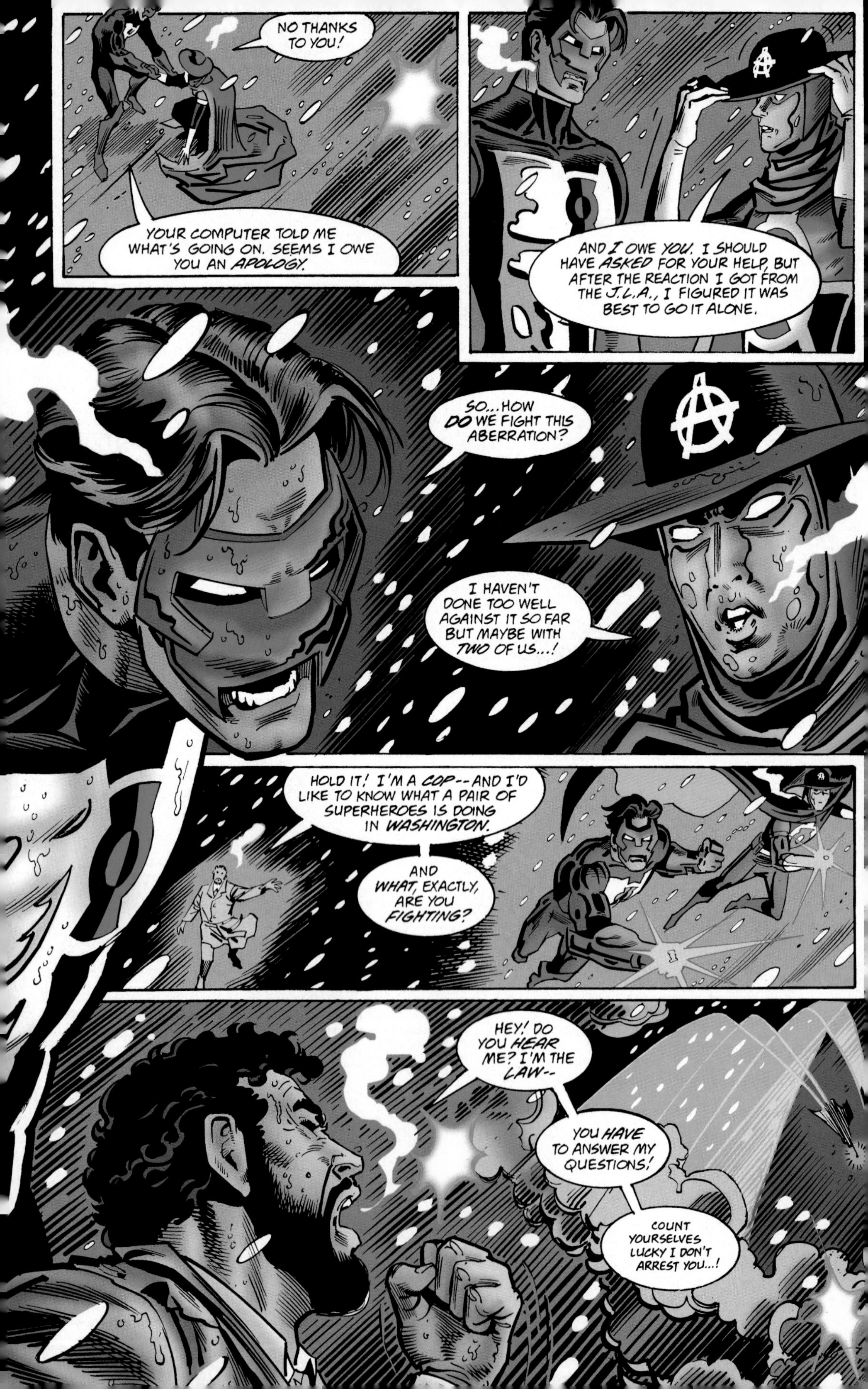
NO THANKS TO YOU!
YOUR COMPUTER TOLD ME WHAT'S GOING ON. SEEMS I OWE YOU AN APOLOGY.
AND I OWE YOU. I SHOULD HAVE ASKED FOR YOUR HELP, BUT AFTER THE REACTION I GOT FROM THE J.L.A., I FIGURED IT WAS BEST TO GO IT ALONE.
SO...HOW DO WE FIGHT THIS ABERRATION?
I HAVEN'T DONE TOO WELL AGAINST IT SO FAR BUT MAYBE WITH TWO OF US...!
HOLD IT! I'M A COP--AND I'D LIKE TO KNOW WHAT A PAIR OF SUPERHEROES IS DOING IN WASHINGTON.
AND WHAT, EXACTLY, ARE YOU FIGHTING?
HEY! DO YOU HEAR ME? I'M THE LAW--
YOU HAVE TO ANSWER MY QUESTIONS!
COUNT YOURSELVES LUCKY I DON'T ARREST YOU...!

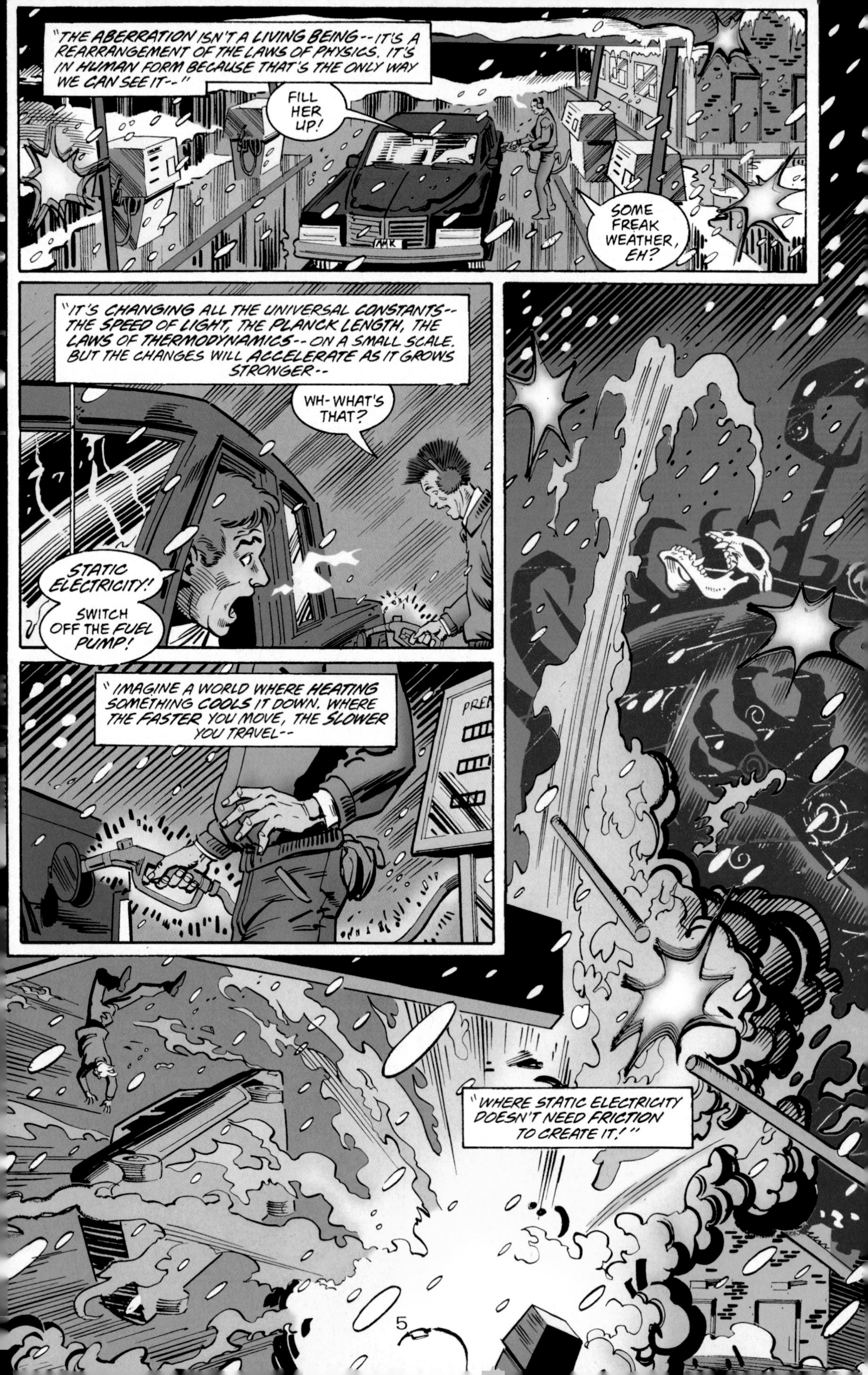
"THE ABERRATION ISN'T A LIVING BEING--IT'S A REARRANGEMENT OF THE LAWS OF PHYSICS. IT'S IN HUMAN FORM BECAUSE THAT'S THE ONLY WAY WE CAN SEE IT--"
FILL HER UP!
SOME FREAK WEATHER, EH?
"IT'S CHANGING ALL THE UNIVERSAL CONSTANTS--THE SPEED OF LIGHT, THE PLANCK LENGTH, THE LAWS OF THERMODYNAMICS--ON A SMALL SCALE. BUT THE CHANGES WILL ACCELERATE AS IT GROWS STRONGER--
WH-WHAT'S THAT?
STATIC ELECTRICITY!
SWITCH OFF THE FUEL PUMP!
"IMAGINE A WORLD WHERE HEATING SOMETHING COOLS IT DOWN. WHERE THE FASTER YOU MOVE, THE SLOWER YOU TRAVEL--
"WHERE STATIC ELECTRICITY DOESN'T NEED FRICTION TO CREATE IT!"

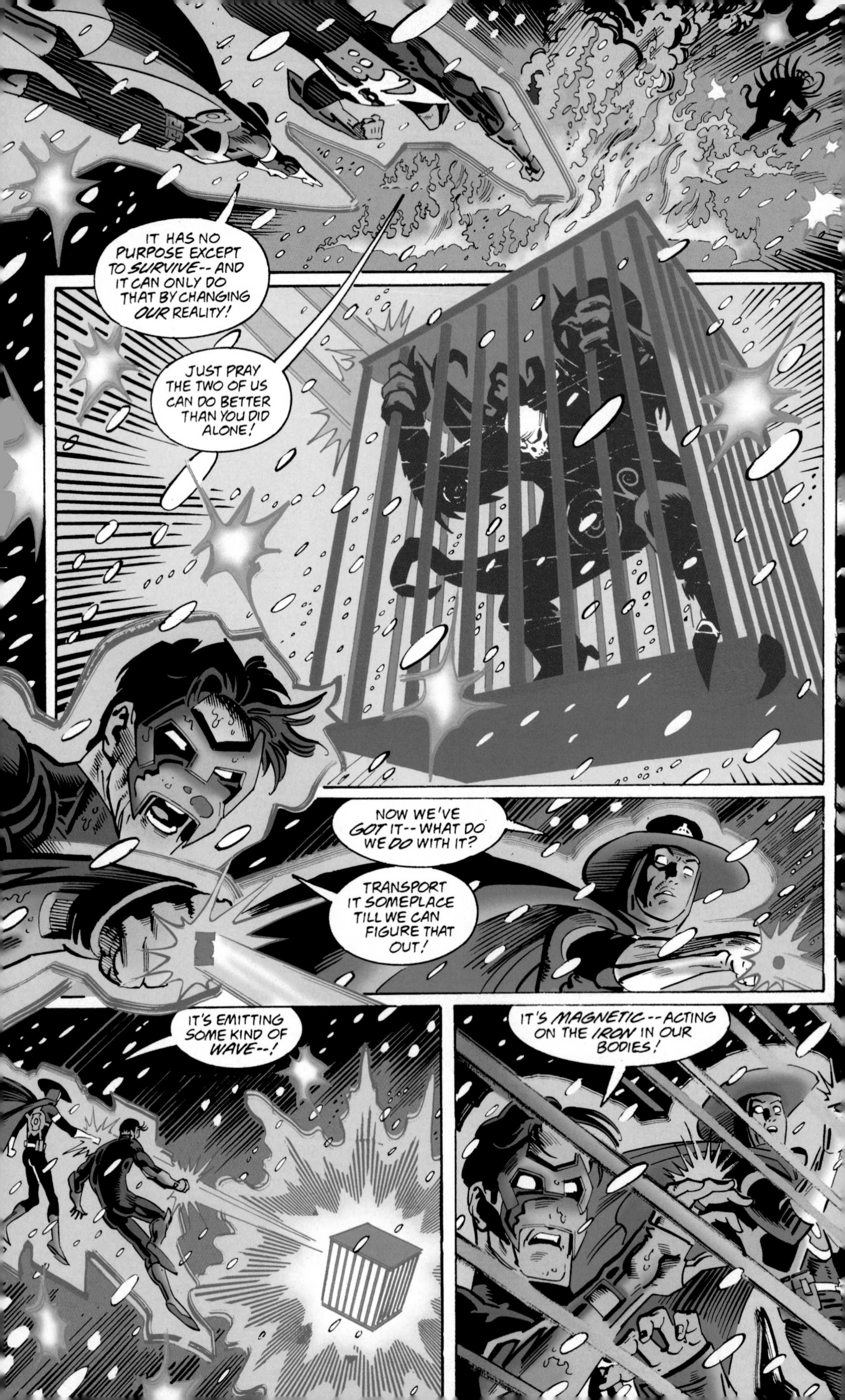
IT HAS NO PURPOSE EXCEPT TO SURVIVE-- AND IT CAN ONLY DO THAT BY CHANGING OUR REALITY!
JUST PRAY THE TWO OF US CAN DO BETTER THAN YOU DID ALONE!
NOW WE'VE GOT IT-- WHAT DO WE DO WITH IT?
TRANSPORT IT SOMEPLACE TILL WE CAN FIGURE THAT OUT!
IT'S EMITTING SOME KIND OF WAVE--!
IT'S MAGNETIC--ACTING ON THE IRON IN OUR BODIES!

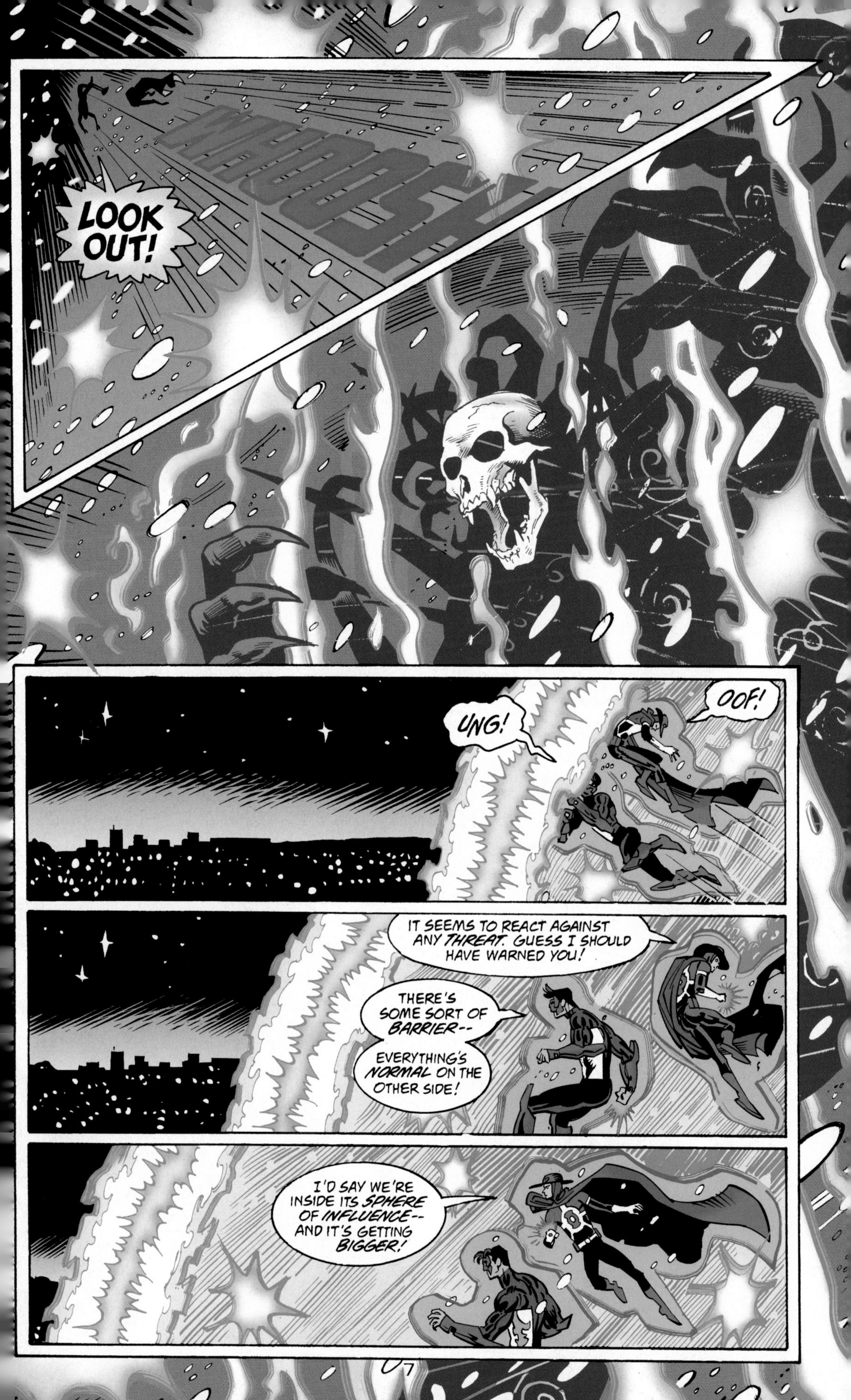
WHOOSH!
LOOK OUT!
UNG!
OOF!
IT SEEMS TO REACT AGAINST ANY THREAT. GUESS I SHOULD HAVE WARNED YOU!
THERE'S SOME SORT OF BARRIER--
EVERYTHING'S NORMAL ON THE OTHER SIDE!
I'D SAY WE'RE INSIDE ITS SPHERE OF INFLUENCE-- AND IT'S GETTING BIGGER!

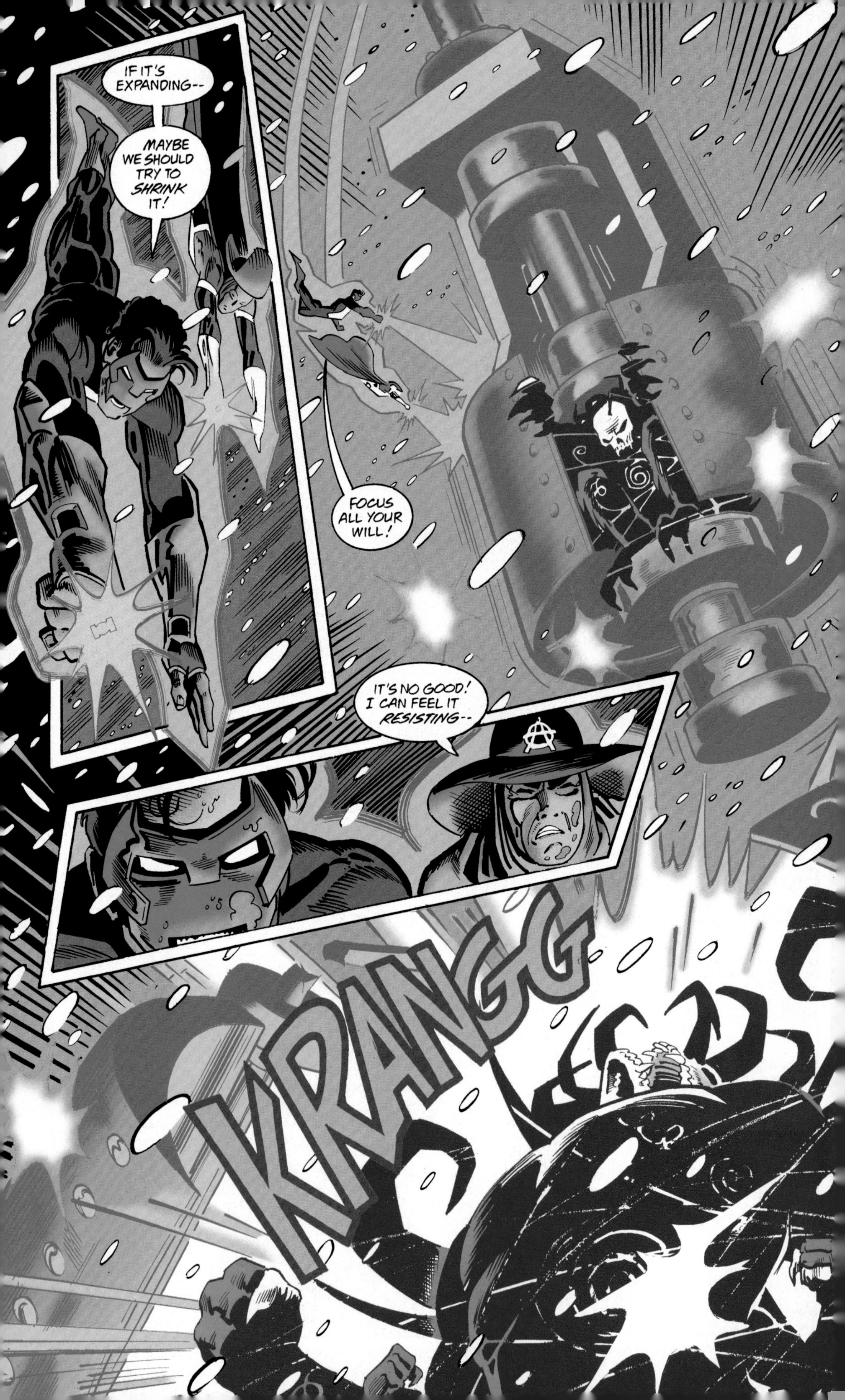
IF IT'S EXPANDING--
MAYBE WE SHOULD TRY TO SHRINK IT!
FOCUS ALL YOUR WILL!
IT'S NO GOOD! I CAN FEEL IT RESISTING--
KRANGG

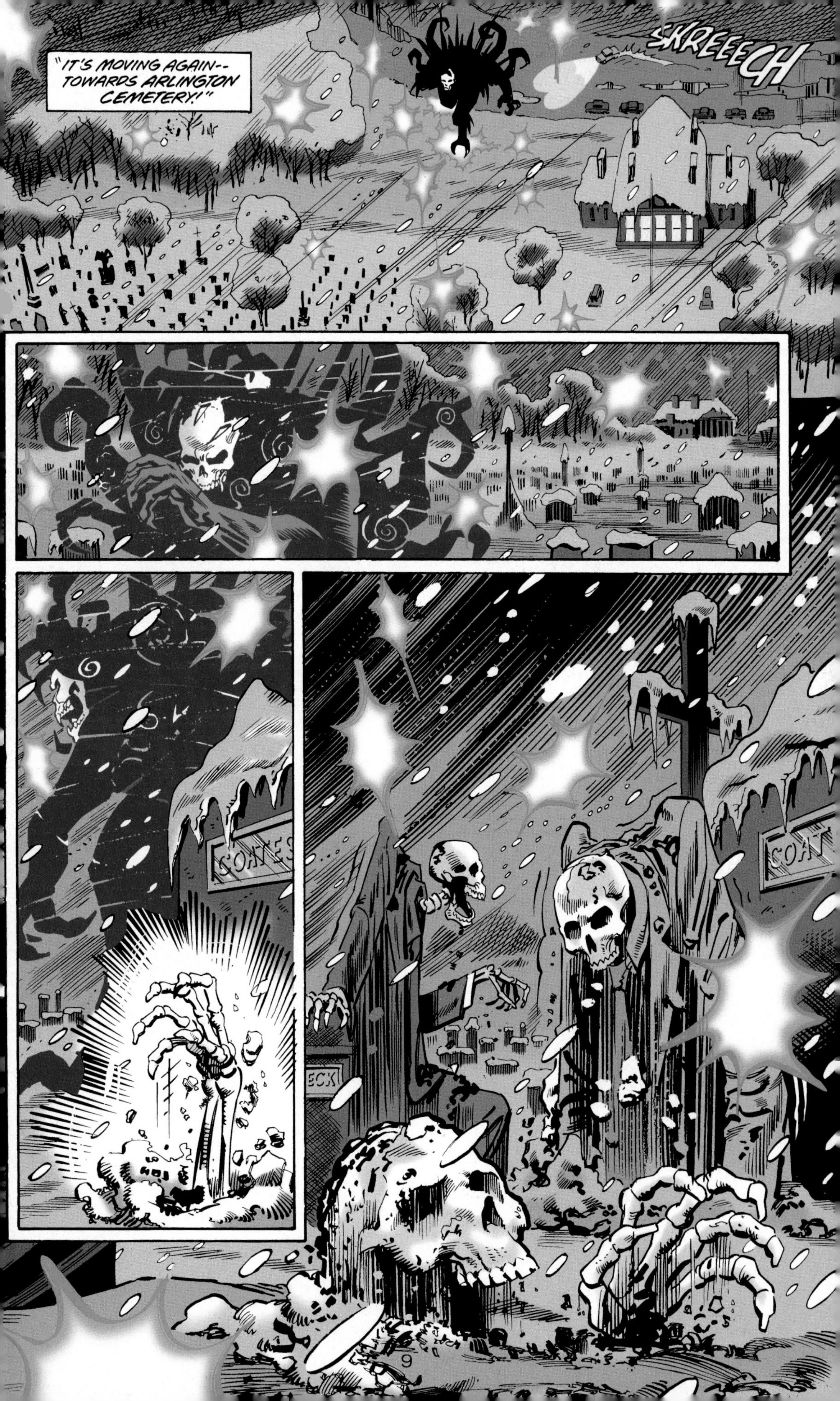
"IT'S MOVING AGAIN-- TOWARDS ARLINGTON CEMETERY!"
SKREEECH
COATES
COAT
ECK

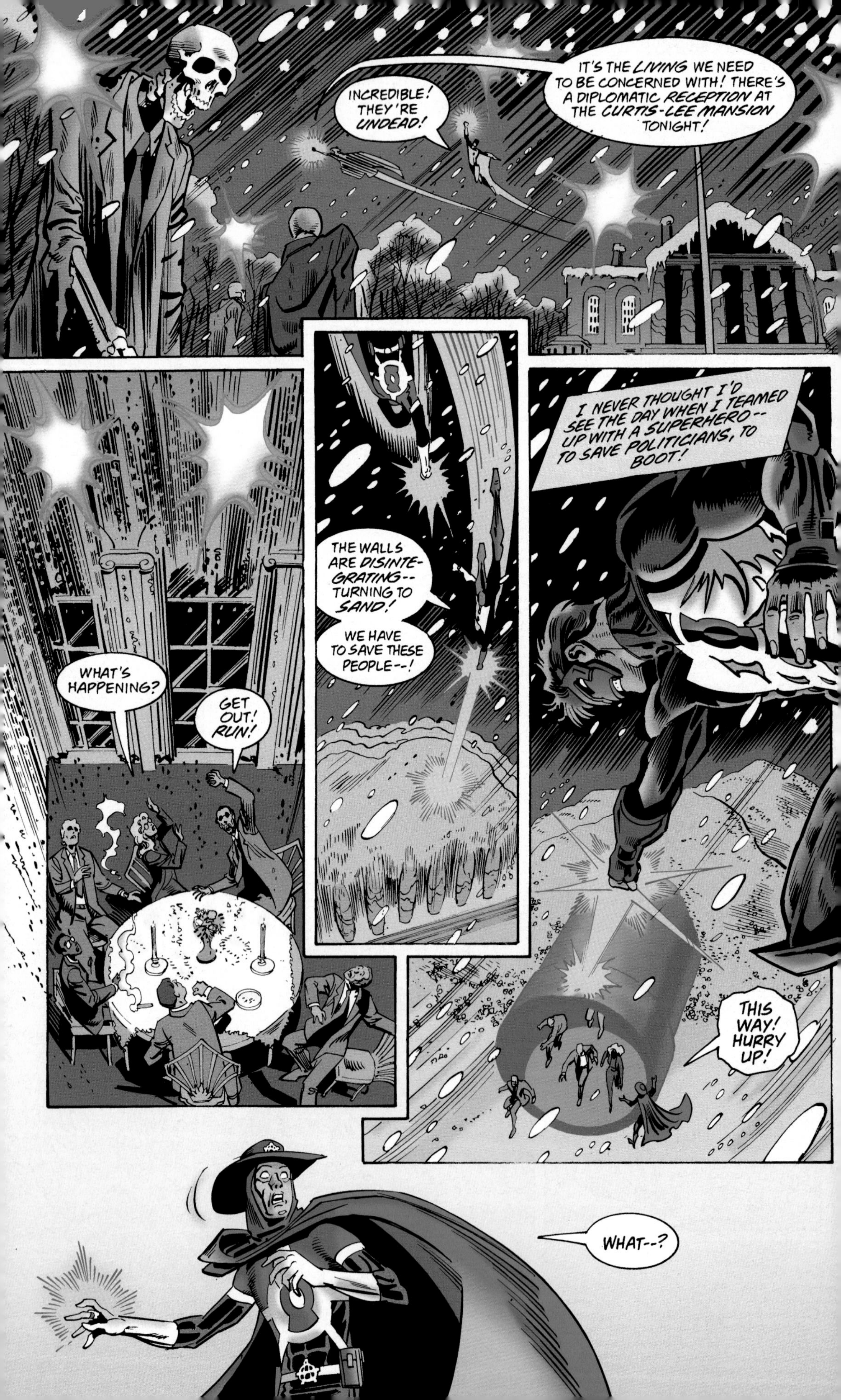

INCREDIBLE! THEY'RE UNDEAD!
IT'S THE LIVING WE NEED TO BE CONCERNED WITH! THERE'S A DIPLOMATIC RECEPTION AT THE CURTIS-LEE MANSION TONIGHT!
WHAT'S HAPPENING?
GET OUT! RUN!
THE WALLS ARE DISINTE-GRATING-- TURNING TO SAND!
WE HAVE TO SAVE THESE PEOPLE--!
I NEVER THOUGHT I'D SEE THE DAY WHEN I TEAMED UP WITH A SUPERHERO-- TO SAVE POLITICIANS, TO BOOT!
THIS WAY! HURRY UP!
WHAT--?

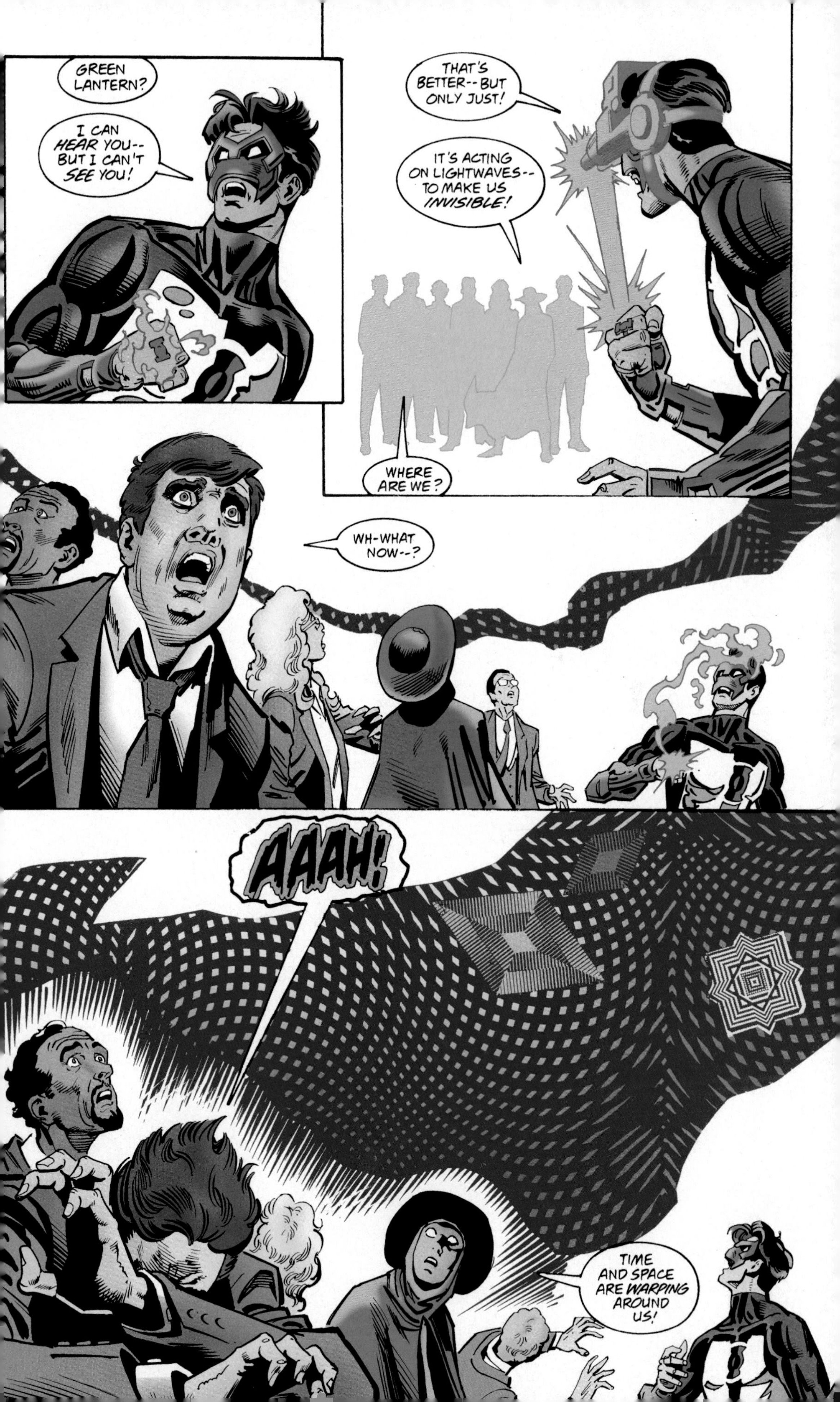
GREEN LANTERN?
I CAN HEAR YOU-- BUT I CAN'T SEE YOU!
THAT'S BETTER-- BUT ONLY JUST!
IT'S ACTING ON LIGHTWAVES-- TO MAKE US INVISIBLE!
WHERE ARE WE?
WH-WHAT NOW--?
AAAH!
TIME AND SPACE ARE WARPING AROUND US!

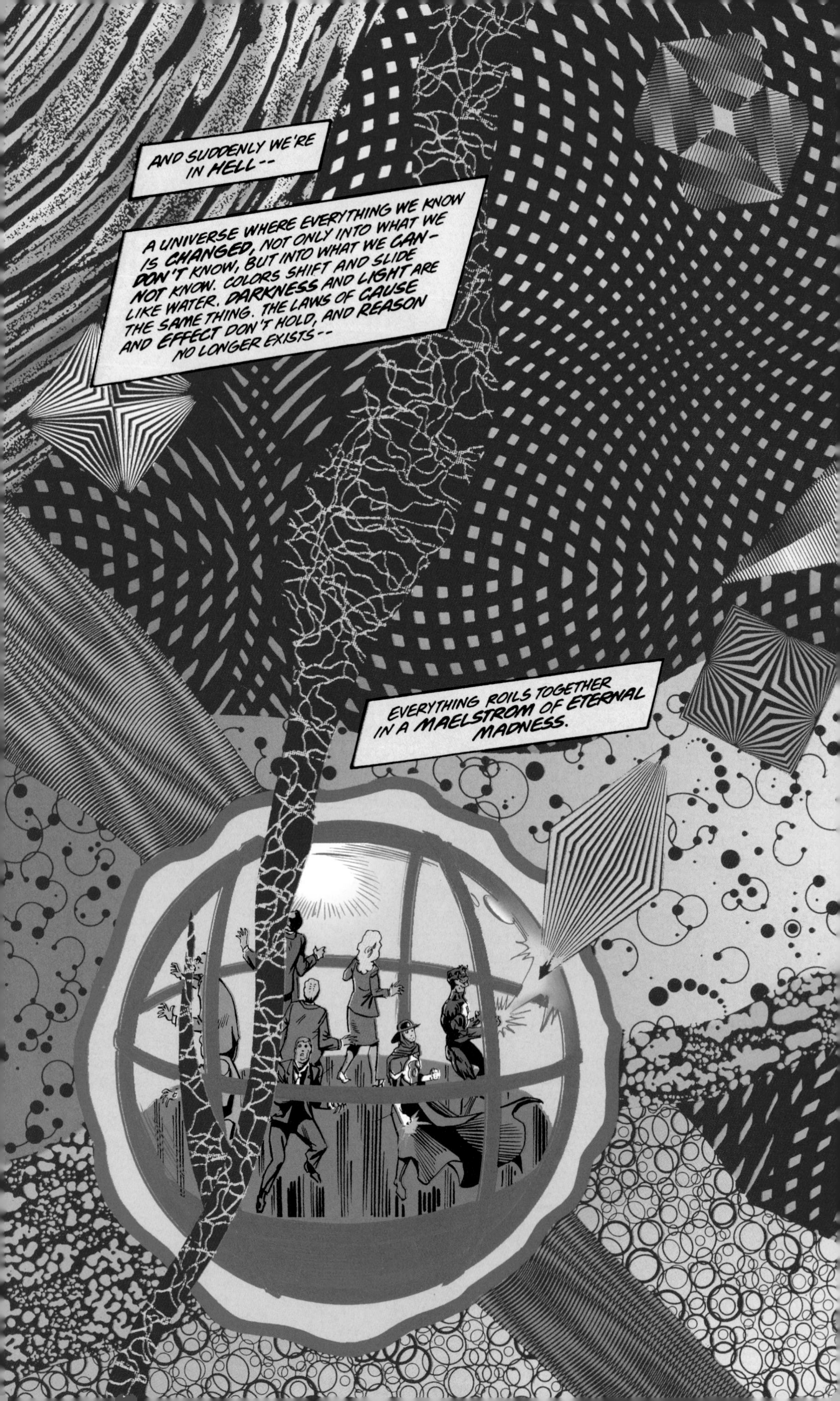
AND SUDDENLY WE'RE IN HELL--
A UNIVERSE WHERE EVERYTHING WE KNOW IS CHANGED, NOT ONLY INTO WHAT WE DON'T KNOW, BUT INTO WHAT WE CAN-NOT KNOW. COLORS SHIFT AND SLIDE LIKE WATER. DARKNESS AND LIGHT ARE THE SAME THING. THE LAWS OF CAUSE AND EFFECT DON'T HOLD, AND REASON NO LONGER EXISTS--
EVERYTHING ROILS TOGETHER IN A MAELSTROM OF ETERNAL MADNESS.

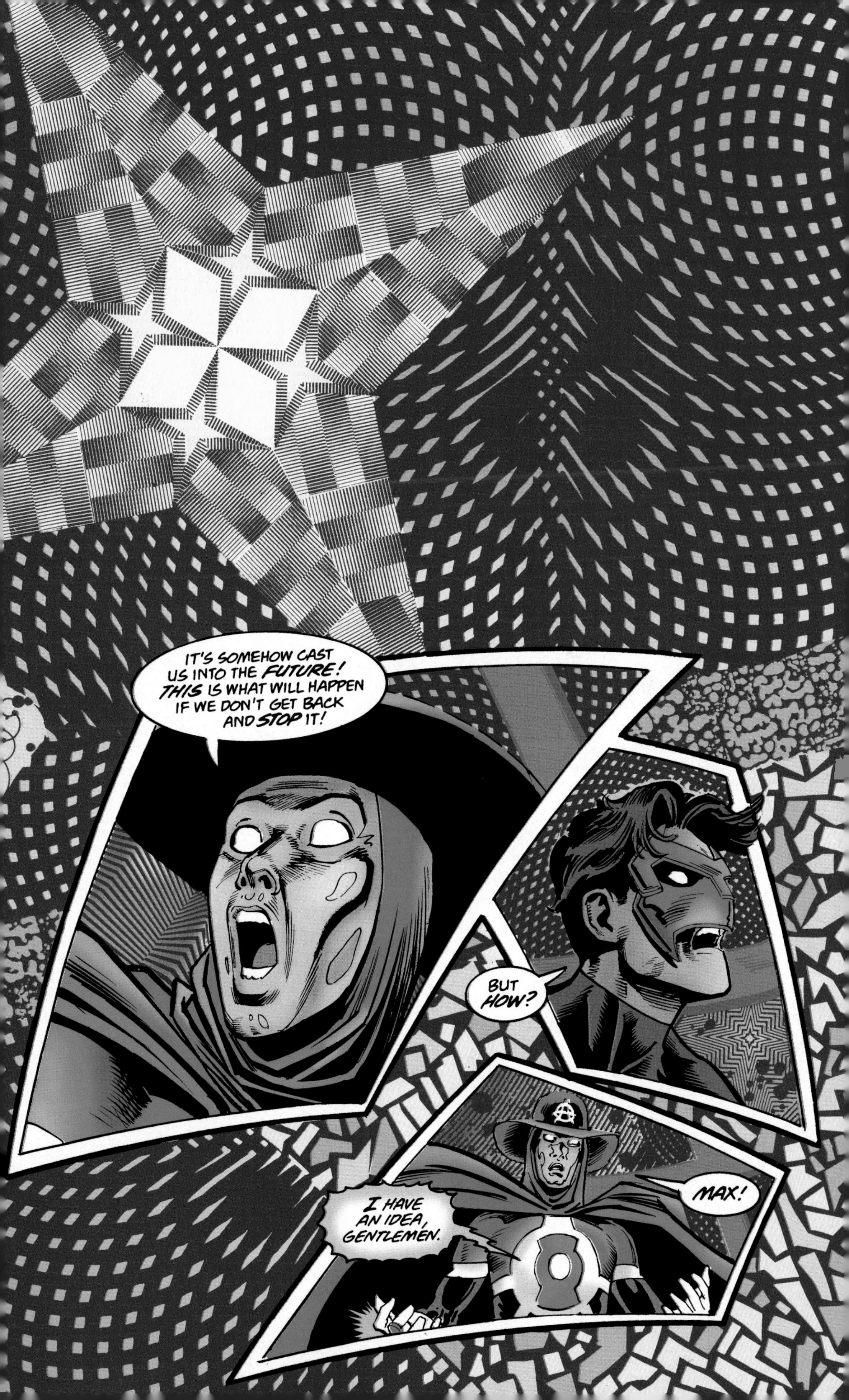
IT'S SOMEHOW CAST US INTO THE FUTURE! THIS IS WHAT WILL HAPPEN IF WE DON'T GET BACK AND STOP IT!
BUT HOW?
I HAVE AN IDEA, GENTLEMEN.
MAX!

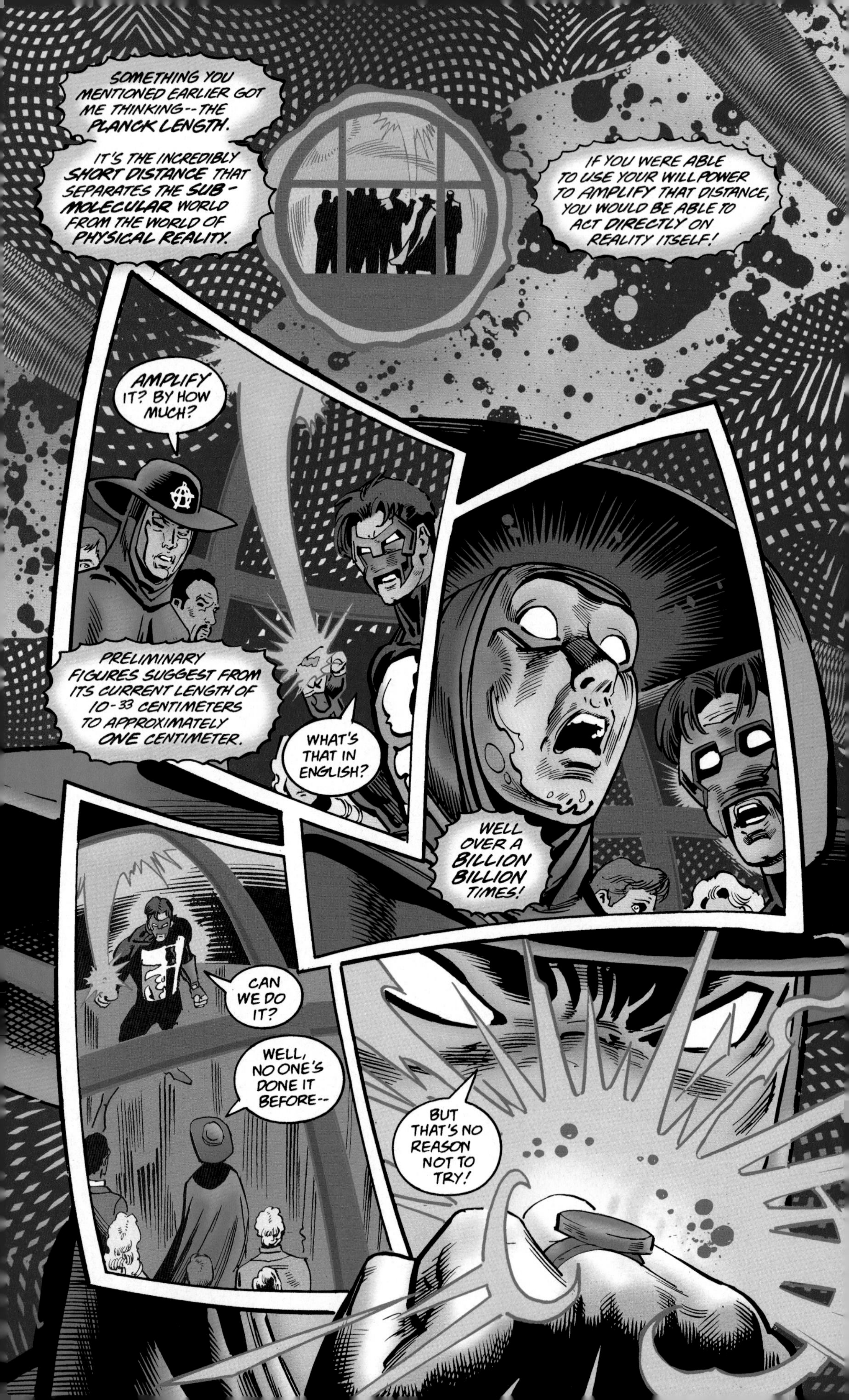
SOMETHING YOU MENTIONED EARLIER GOT ME THINKING--THE PLANCK LENGTH.
IT'S THE INCREDIBLY SHORT DISTANCE THAT SEPARATES THE SUB-MOLECULAR WORLD FROM THE WORLD OF PHYSICAL REALITY.
IF YOU WERE ABLE TO USE YOUR WILLPOWER TO AMPLIFY THAT DISTANCE, YOU WOULD BE ABLE TO ACT DIRECTLY ON REALITY ITSELF!
AMPLIFY IT? BY HOW MUCH?
PRELIMINARY FIGURES SUGGEST FROM ITS CURRENT LENGTH OF 10^{-33} CENTIMETERS TO APPROXIMATELY ONE CENTIMETER.
WHAT'S THAT IN ENGLISH?
WELL OVER A BILLION BILLION TIMES!
CAN WE DO IT?
WELL, NO ONE'S DONE IT BEFORE--
BUT THAT'S NO REASON NOT TO TRY!

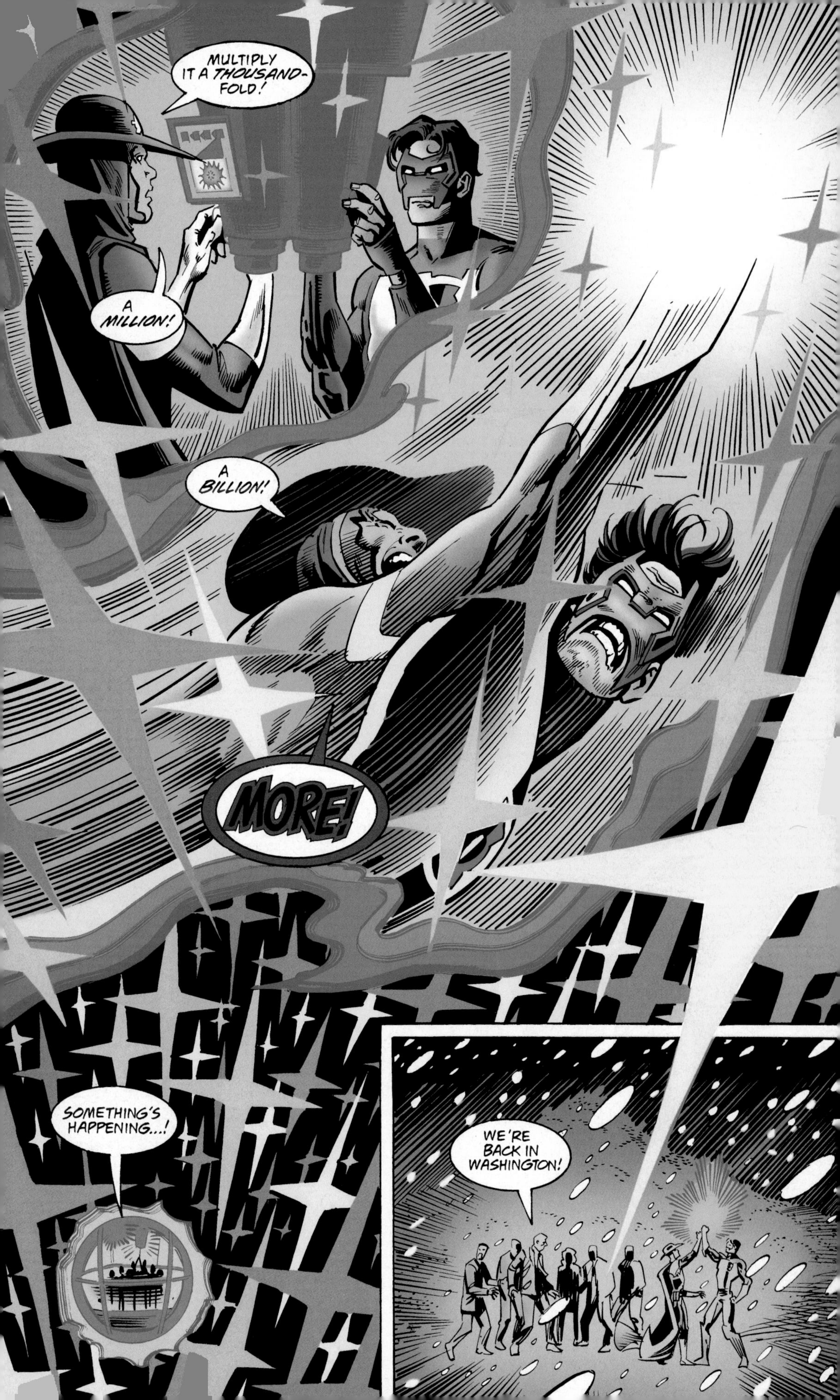
MULTIPLY IT A *THOUSAND*-FOLD!
A MILLION!
A BILLION!
MORE!
SOMETHING'S HAPPENING...!
WE'RE BACK IN WASHINGTON!

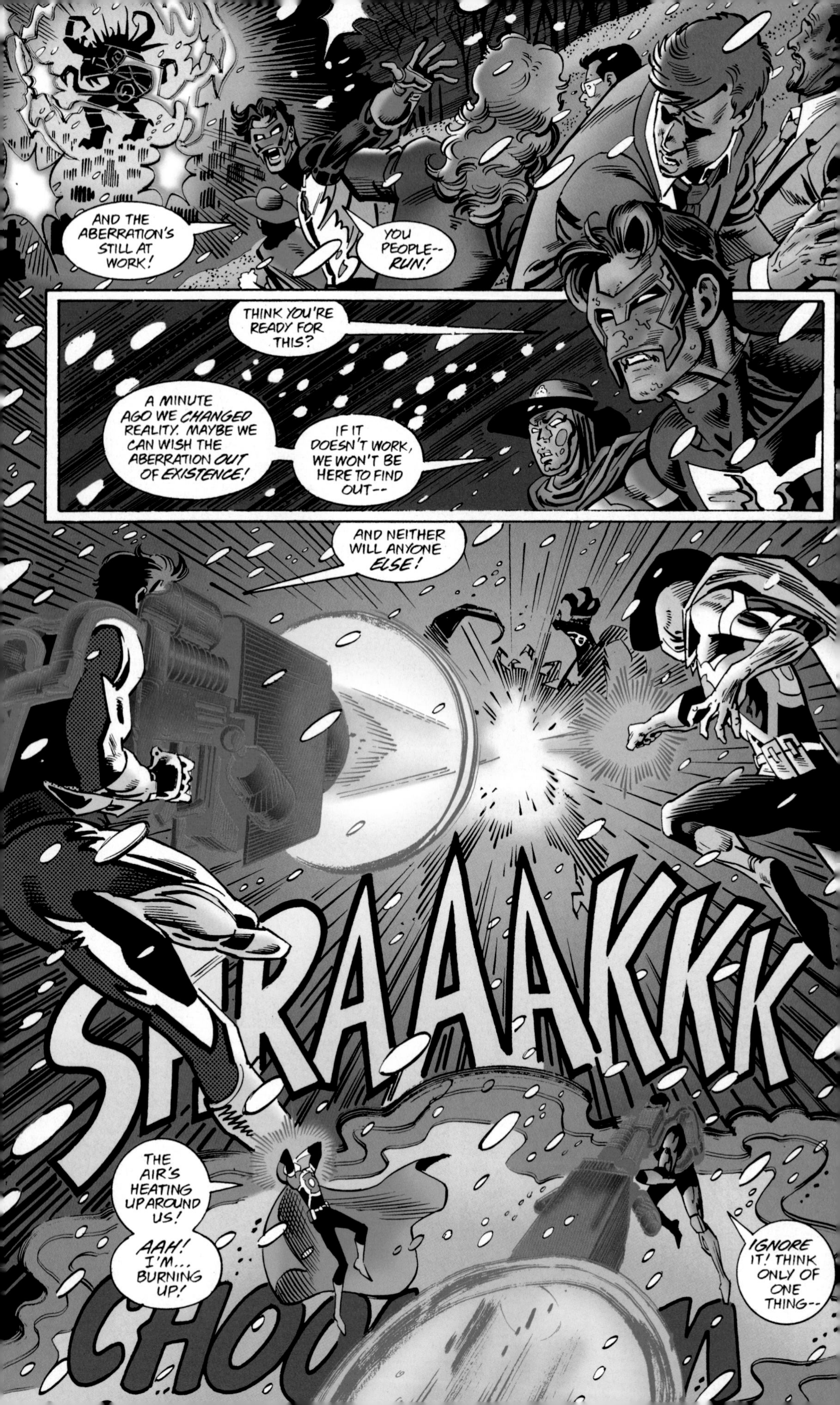
AND THE ABERRATION'S STILL AT WORK!
YOU PEOPLE-- RUN!
THINK YOU'RE READY FOR THIS?
A MINUTE AGO WE CHANGED REALITY. MAYBE WE CAN WISH THE ABERRATION OUT OF EXISTENCE!
IF IT DOESN'T WORK, WE WON'T BE HERE TO FIND OUT--
AND NEITHER WILL ANYONE ELSE!
SHRAAAKKK
THE AIR'S HEATING UP AROUND US!
AAH! I'M... BURNING UP!
IGNORE IT! THINK ONLY OF ONE THING--

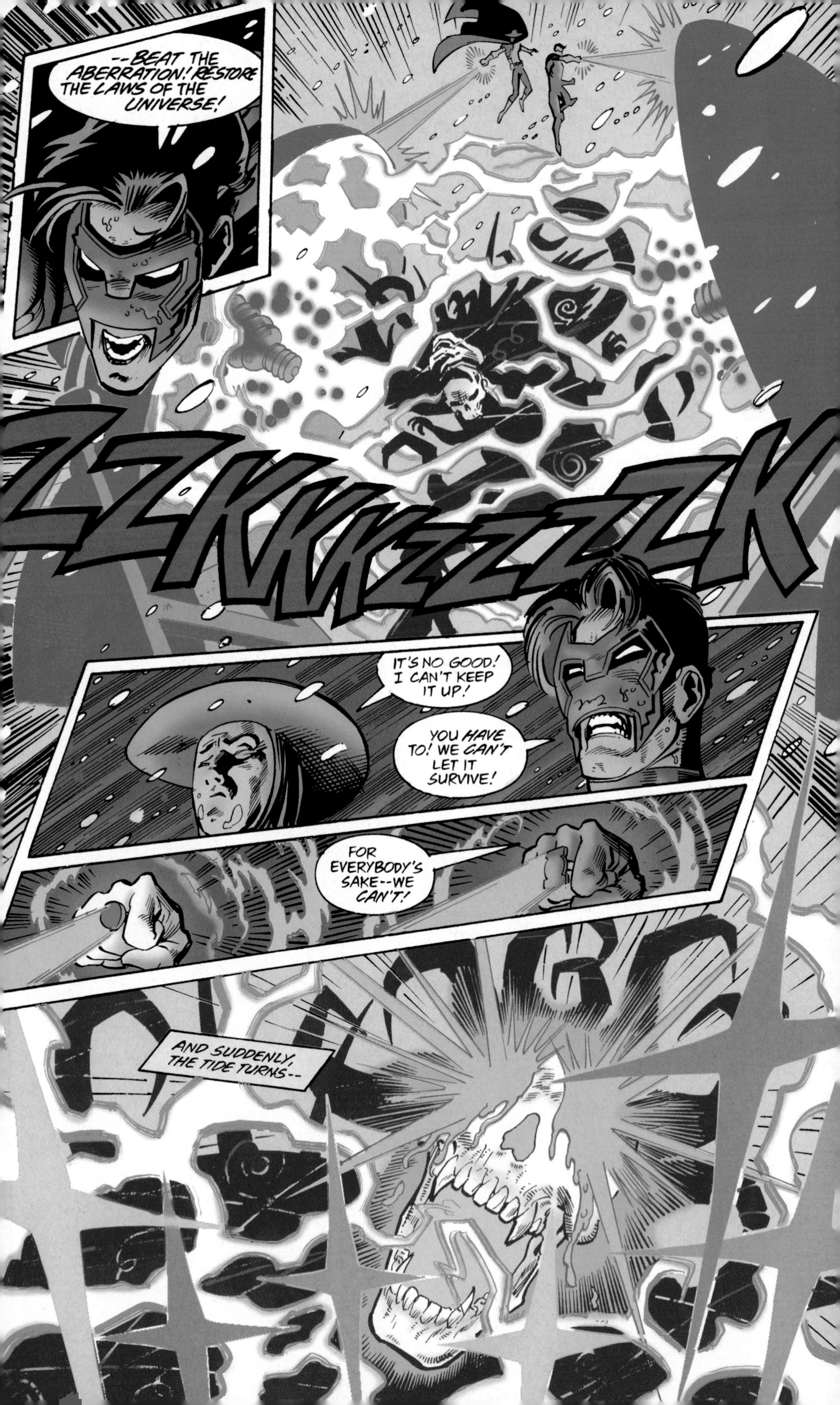
--BEAT THE ABERRATION! RESTORE THE LAWS OF THE UNIVERSE!
ZZKKKKZZZZK
IT'S NO GOOD! I CAN'T KEEP IT UP!
YOU HAVE TO! WE CAN'T LET IT SURVIVE!
FOR EVERYBODY'S SAKE--WE CAN'T!
AND SUDDENLY, THE TIDE TURNS--

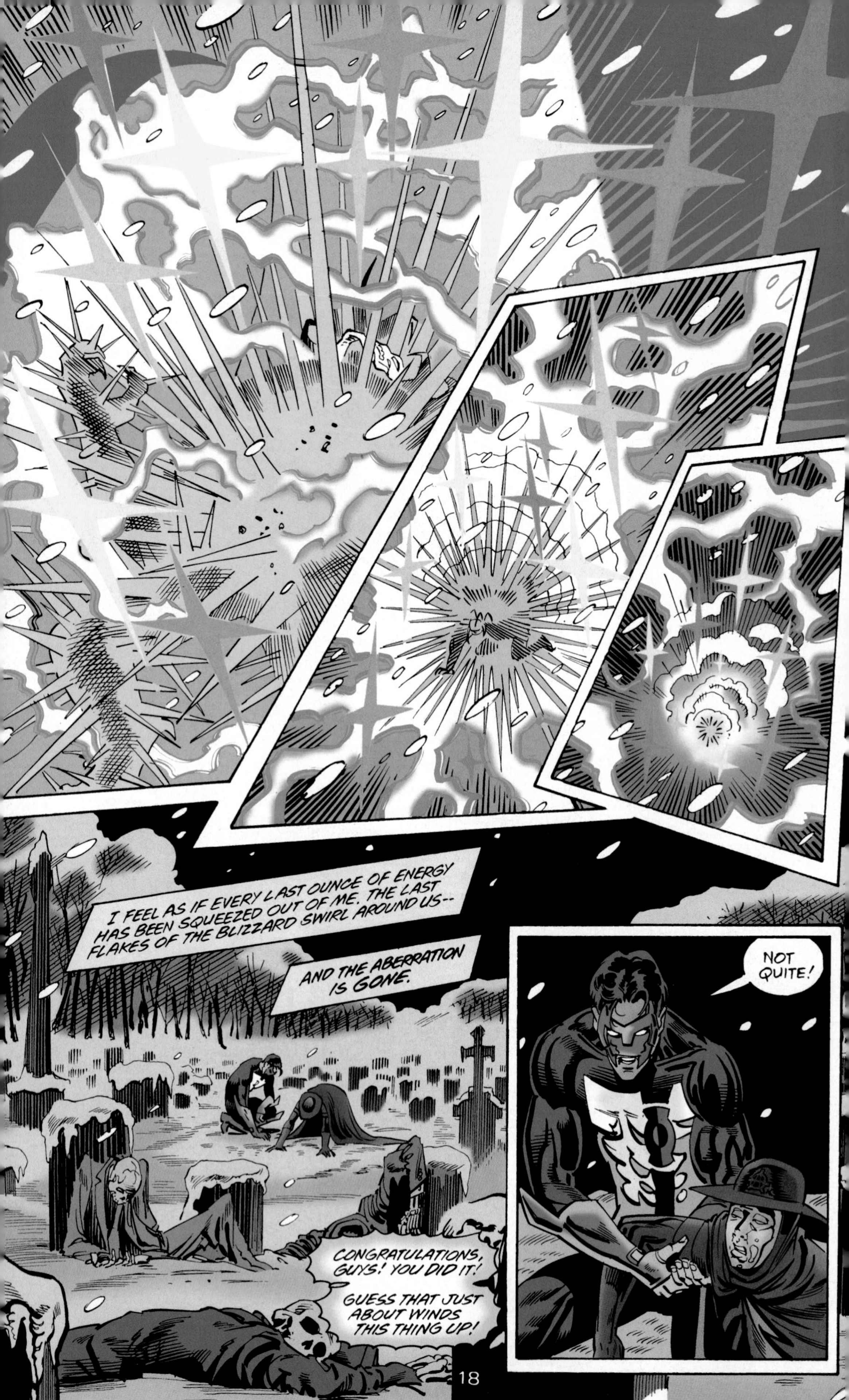
I FEEL AS IF EVERY LAST OUNCE OF ENERGY HAS BEEN SQUEEZED OUT OF ME. THE LAST FLAKES OF THE BLIZZARD SWIRL AROUND US--
AND THE ABERRATION IS GONE.
NOT QUITE!
CONGRATULATIONS, GUYS! YOU DID IT!
GUESS THAT JUST ABOUT WINDS THIS THING UP!

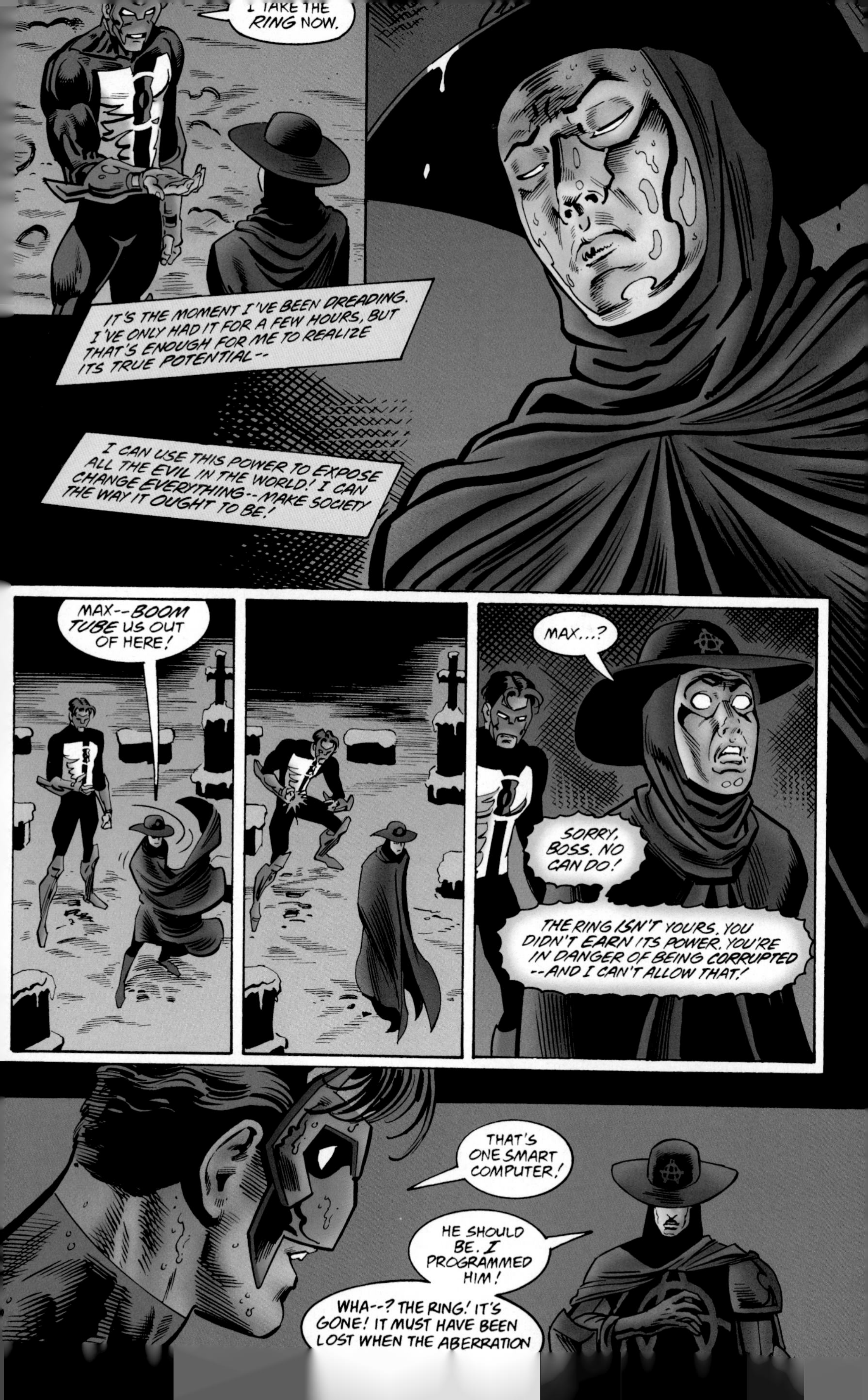
I TAKE THE RING NOW.
IT'S THE MOMENT I'VE BEEN DREADING. I'VE ONLY HAD IT FOR A FEW HOURS, BUT THAT'S ENOUGH FOR ME TO REALIZE ITS TRUE POTENTIAL--
I CAN USE THIS POWER TO EXPOSE ALL THE EVIL IN THE WORLD! I CAN CHANGE EVERYTHING--MAKE SOCIETY THE WAY IT OUGHT TO BE!
MAX--BOOM TUBE US OUT OF HERE!
MAX...?
SORRY, BOSS. NO CAN DO!
THE RING ISN'T YOURS. YOU DIDN'T EARN ITS POWER. YOU'RE IN DANGER OF BEING CORRUPTED --AND I CAN'T ALLOW THAT!
THAT'S ONE SMART COMPUTER!
HE SHOULD BE. I PROGRAMMED HIM!
WHA--? THE RING! IT'S GONE! IT MUST HAVE BEEN LOST WHEN THE ABERRATION

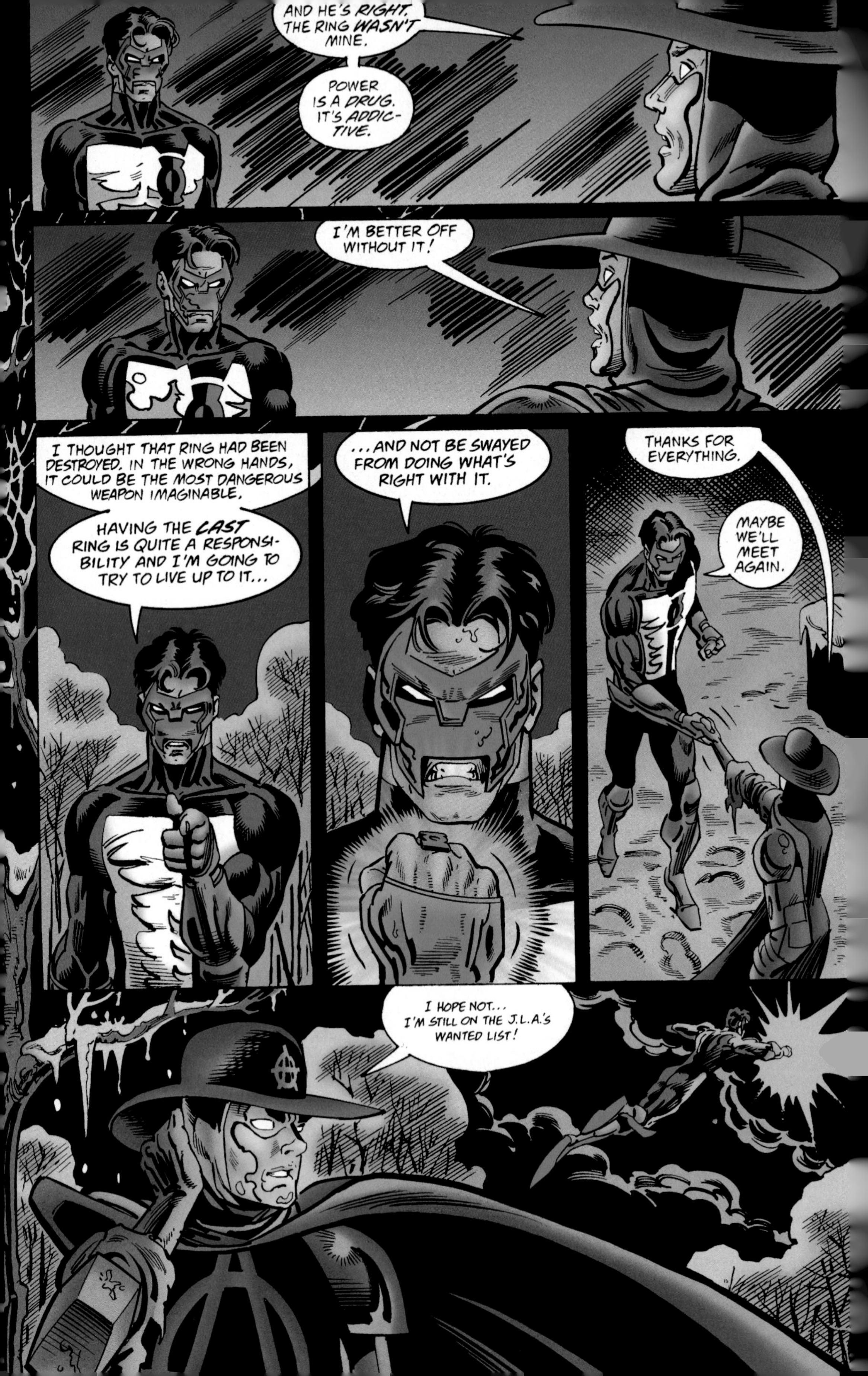
AND HE'S RIGHT. THE RING WASN'T MINE.
POWER IS A DRUG. IT'S ADDICTIVE.
I'M BETTER OFF WITHOUT IT!
I THOUGHT THAT RING HAD BEEN DESTROYED. IN THE WRONG HANDS, IT COULD BE THE MOST DANGEROUS WEAPON IMAGINABLE.
HAVING THE LAST RING IS QUITE A RESPONSIBILITY AND I'M GOING TO TRY TO LIVE UP TO IT...
...AND NOT BE SWAYED FROM DOING WHAT'S RIGHT WITH IT.
THANKS FOR EVERYTHING.
MAYBE WE'LL MEET AGAIN.
I HOPE NOT... I'M STILL ON THE J.L.A.'S WANTED LIST!

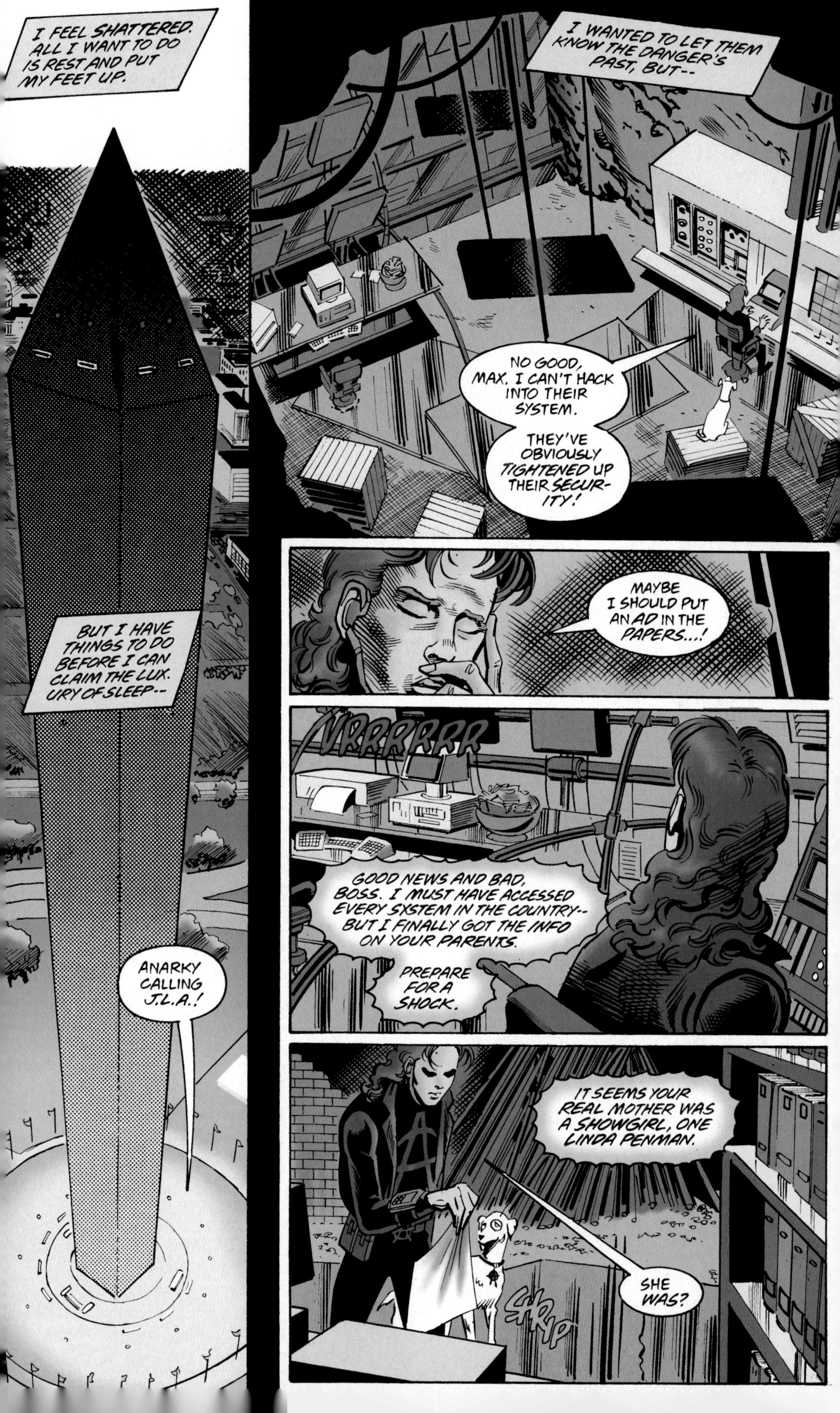
I FEEL SHATTERED. ALL I WANT TO DO IS REST AND PUT MY FEET UP.
BUT I HAVE THINGS TO DO BEFORE I CAN CLAIM THE LUX-URY OF SLEEP--
ANARKY CALLING J.L.A.!
I WANTED TO LET THEM KNOW THE DANGER'S PAST, BUT--
NO GOOD, MAX. I CAN'T HACK INTO THEIR SYSTEM.
THEY'VE OBVIOUSLY TIGHTENED UP THEIR SECUR-ITY!
MAYBE I SHOULD PUT AN AD IN THE PAPERS...!
VRRRRRR
GOOD NEWS AND BAD, BOSS. I MUST HAVE ACCESSED EVERY SYSTEM IN THE COUNTRY-- BUT I FINALLY GOT THE INFO ON YOUR PARENTS.
PREPARE FOR A SHOCK.
IT SEEMS YOUR REAL MOTHER WAS A SHOWGIRL, ONE LINDA PENMAN.
SHE WAS?
SHRIP

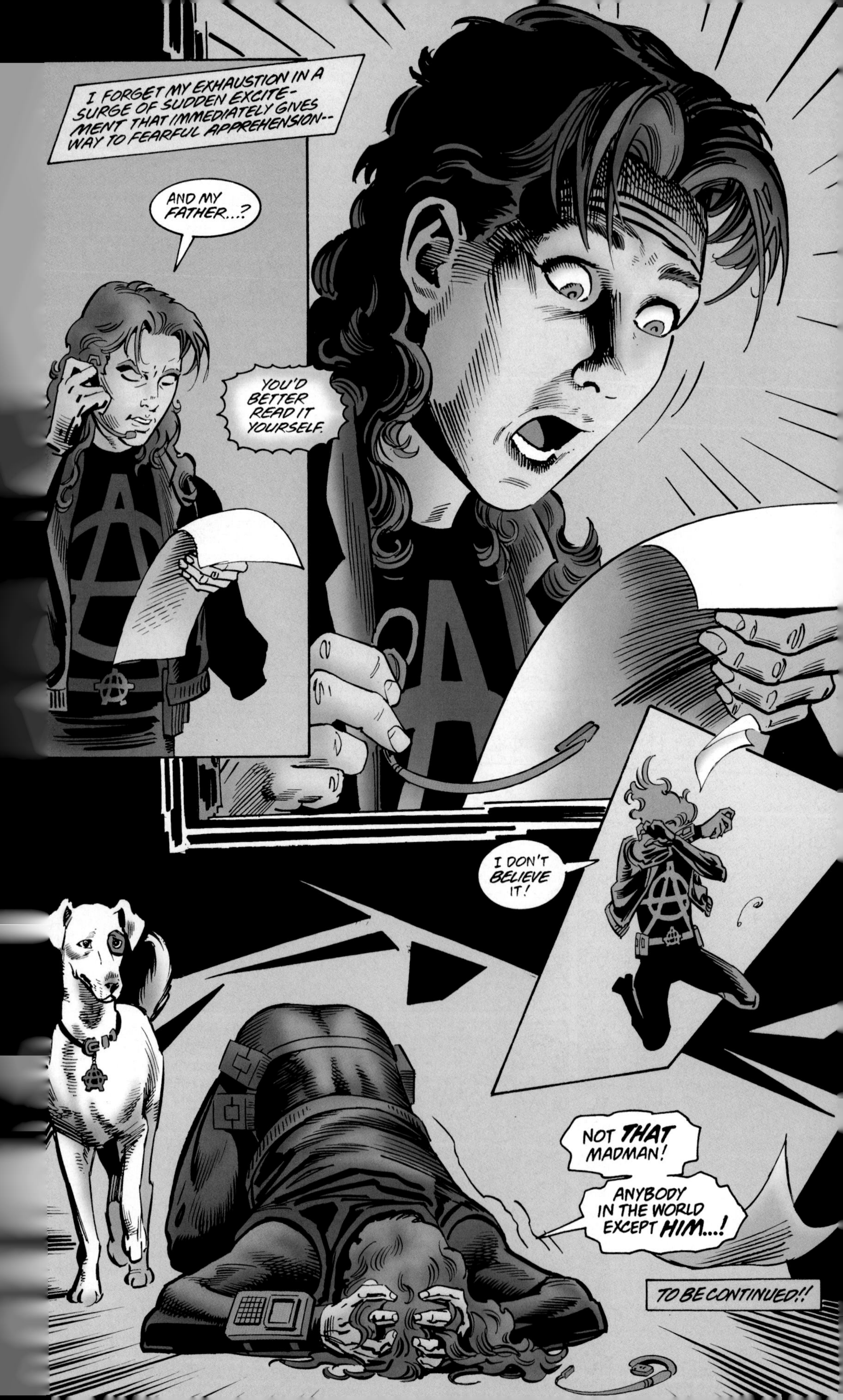
I FORGET MY EXHAUSTION IN A SURGE OF SUDDEN EXCITEMENT THAT IMMEDIATELY GIVES WAY TO FEARFUL APPREHENSION--
AND MY FATHER...?
YOU'D BETTER READ IT YOURSELF.
I DON'T BELIEVE IT!
NOT THAT MADMAN!
ANYBODY IN THE WORLD EXCEPT HIM...!
TO BE CONTINUED!!

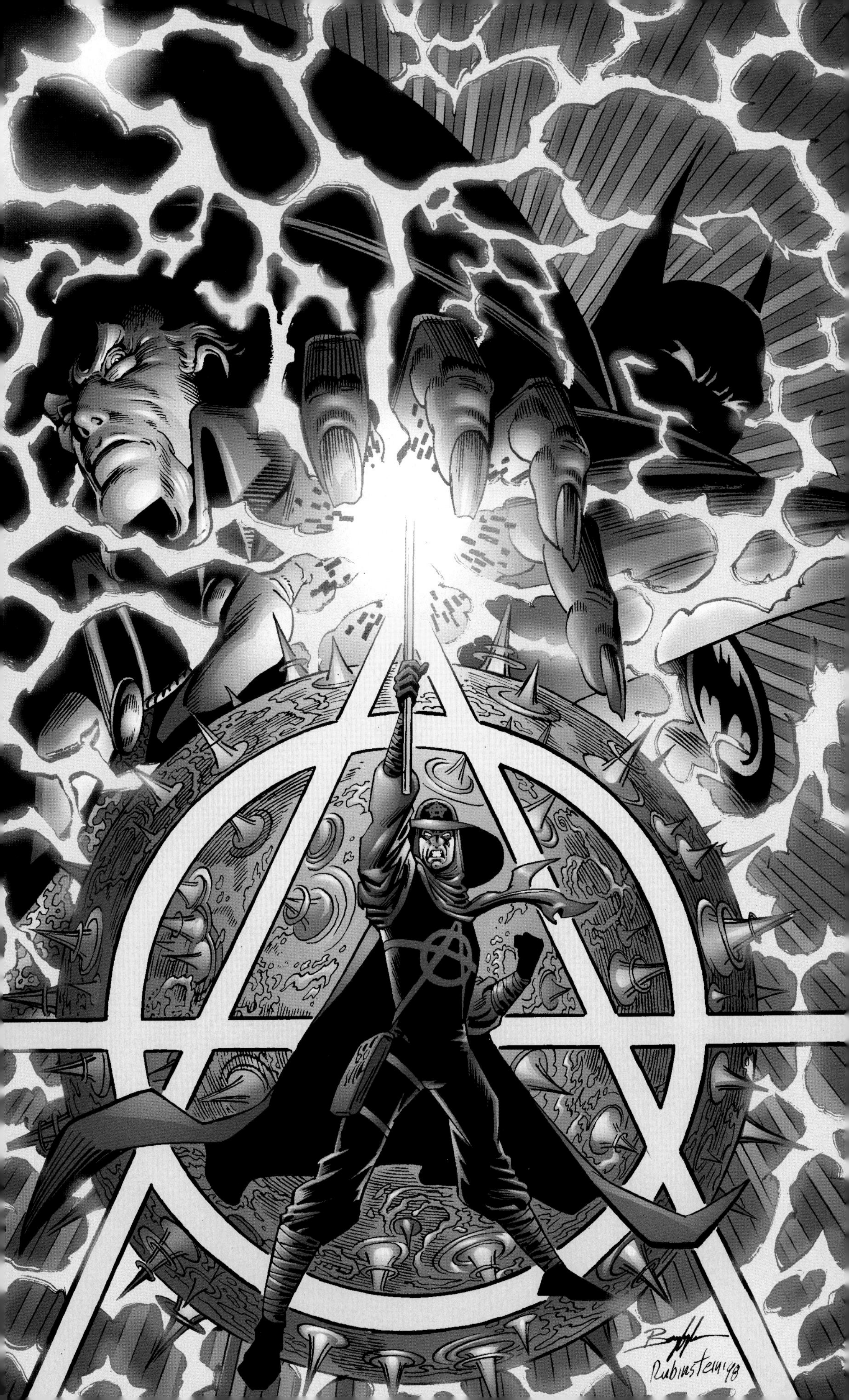
Rubinstein '98

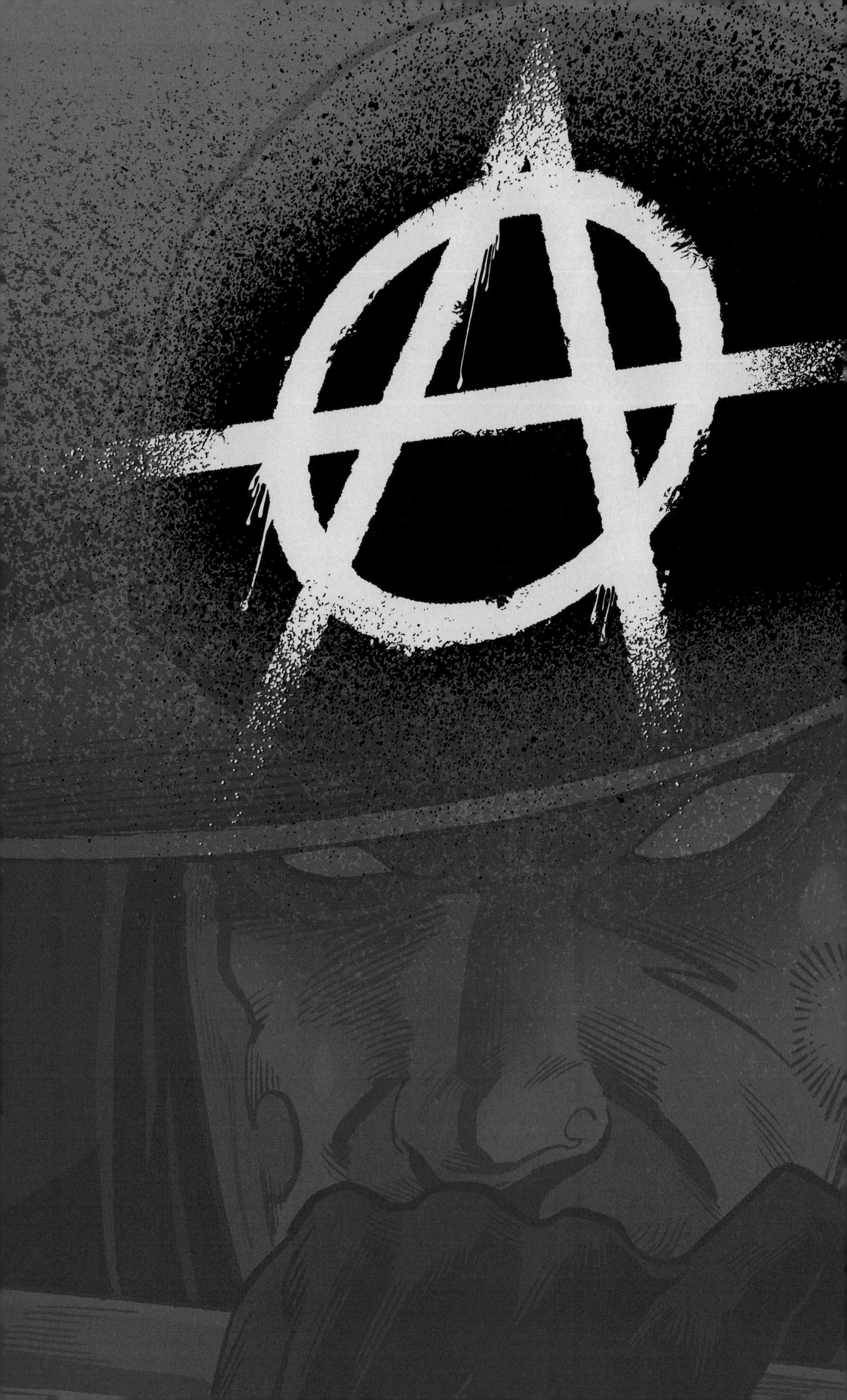

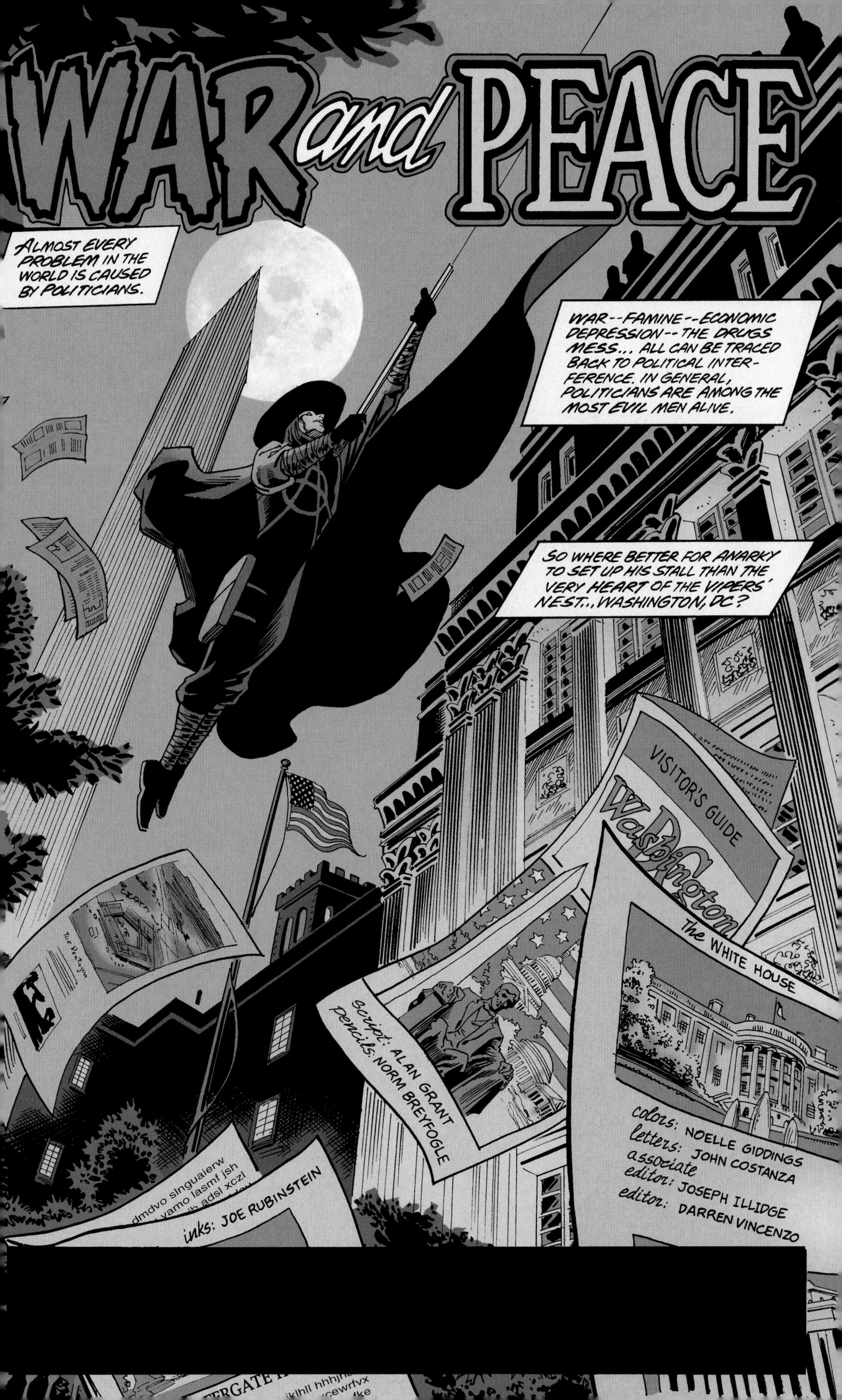

WAR and PEACE
ALMOST EVERY PROBLEM IN THE WORLD IS CAUSED BY POLITICIANS.
WAR--FAMINE--ECONOMIC DEPRESSION--THE DRUGS MESS... ALL CAN BE TRACED BACK TO POLITICAL INTERFERENCE. IN GENERAL, POLITICIANS ARE AMONG THE MOST EVIL MEN ALIVE.
SO WHERE BETTER FOR ANARKY TO SET UP HIS STALL THAN THE VERY HEART OF THE VIPERS' NEST... WASHINGTON, DC?
VISITOR'S GUIDE
Washington DC
The WHITE HOUSE
script: ALAN GRANT
pencils: NORM BREYFOGLE
inks: JOE RUBINSTEIN
colors: NOELLE GIDDINGS
letters: JOHN COSTANZA
associate editor: JOSEPH ILLIDGE
editor: DARREN VINCENZO

[redacted]

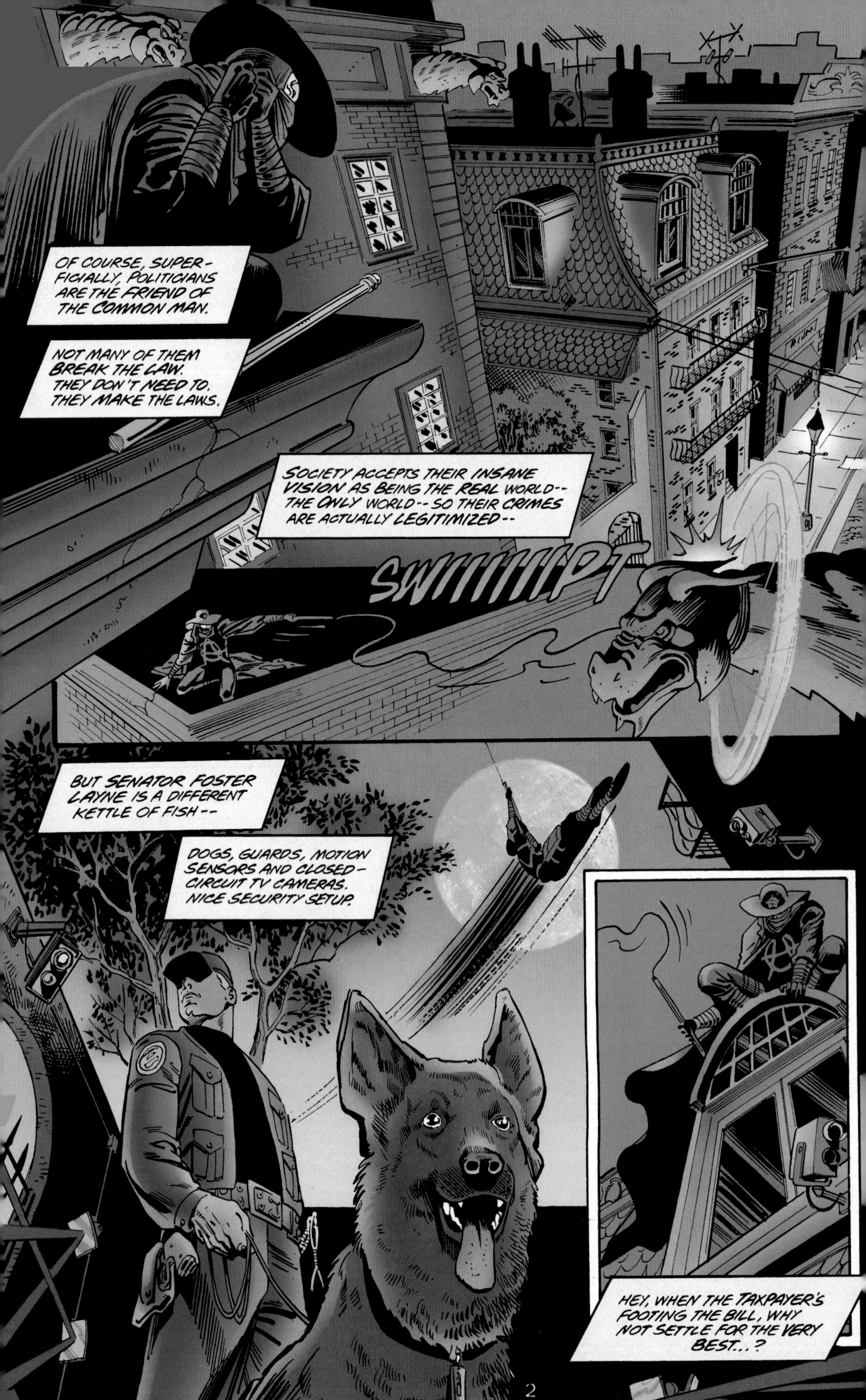
OF COURSE, SUPER-FICIALLY, POLITICIANS ARE THE FRIEND OF THE COMMON MAN.
NOT MANY OF THEM BREAK THE LAW. THEY DON'T NEED TO. THEY MAKE THE LAWS.
SOCIETY ACCEPTS THEIR INSANE VISION AS BEING THE REAL WORLD-- THE ONLY WORLD-- SO THEIR CRIMES ARE ACTUALLY LEGITIMIZED--
SWIIIIIIPT
BUT SENATOR FOSTER LAYNE IS A DIFFERENT KETTLE OF FISH--
DOGS, GUARDS, MOTION SENSORS AND CLOSED-CIRCUIT TV CAMERAS. NICE SECURITY SETUP.
HEY, WHEN THE TAXPAYER'S FOOTING THE BILL, WHY NOT SETTLE FOR THE VERY BEST...?

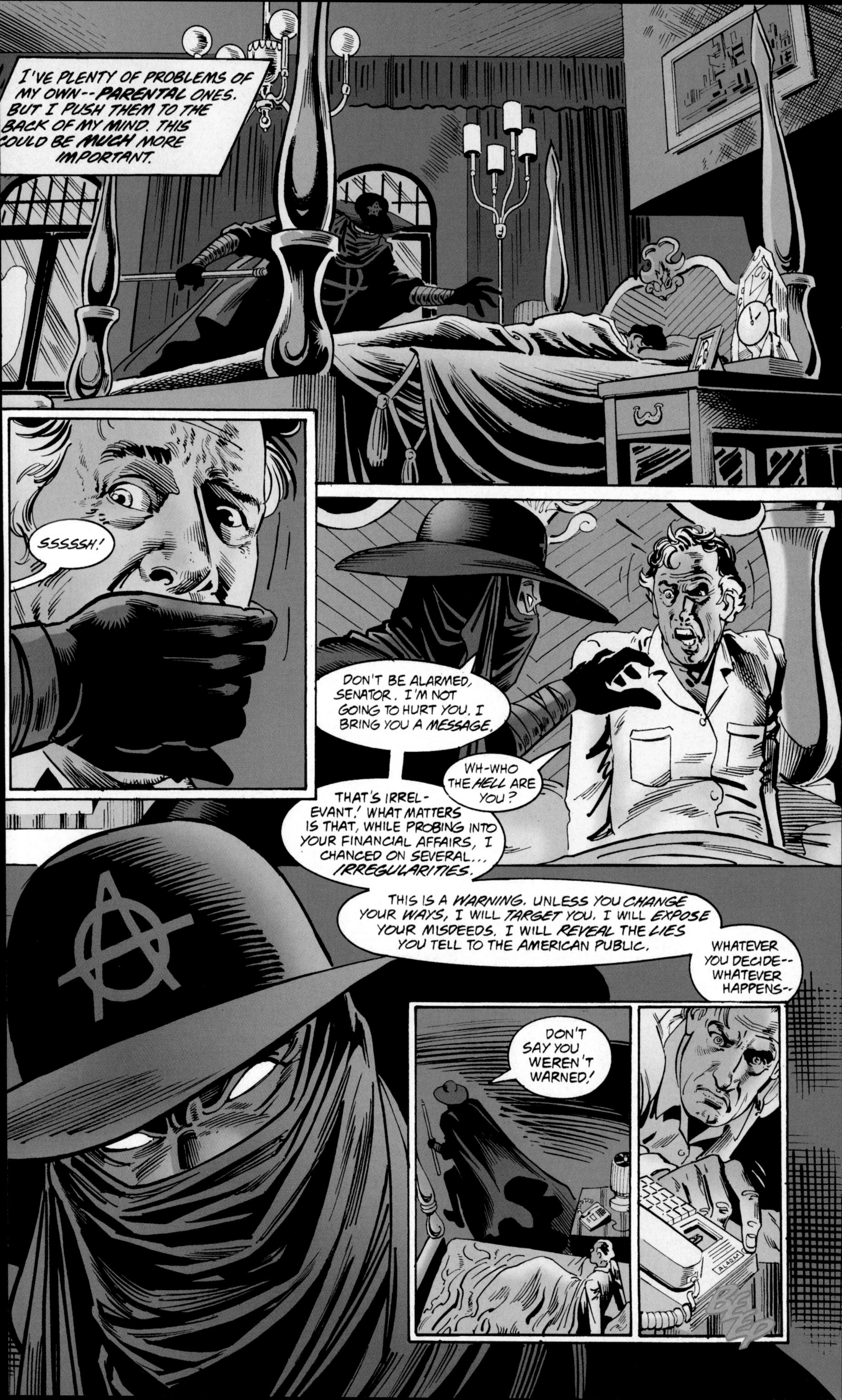

I'VE PLENTY OF PROBLEMS OF MY OWN--PARENTAL ONES. BUT I PUSH THEM TO THE BACK OF MY MIND. THIS COULD BE MUCH MORE IMPORTANT.
SSSSSH!
DON'T BE ALARMED, SENATOR. I'M NOT GOING TO HURT YOU. I BRING YOU A MESSAGE.
WH-WHO THE HELL ARE YOU?
THAT'S IRREL-EVANT! WHAT MATTERS IS THAT, WHILE PROBING INTO YOUR FINANCIAL AFFAIRS, I CHANCED ON SEVERAL... IRREGULARITIES.
THIS IS A WARNING. UNLESS YOU CHANGE YOUR WAYS, I WILL TARGET YOU. I WILL EXPOSE YOUR MISDEEDS. I WILL REVEAL THE LIES YOU TELL TO THE AMERICAN PUBLIC.
WHATEVER YOU DECIDE--WHATEVER HAPPENS--
DON'T SAY YOU WEREN'T WARNED!
ALARM
BEEP

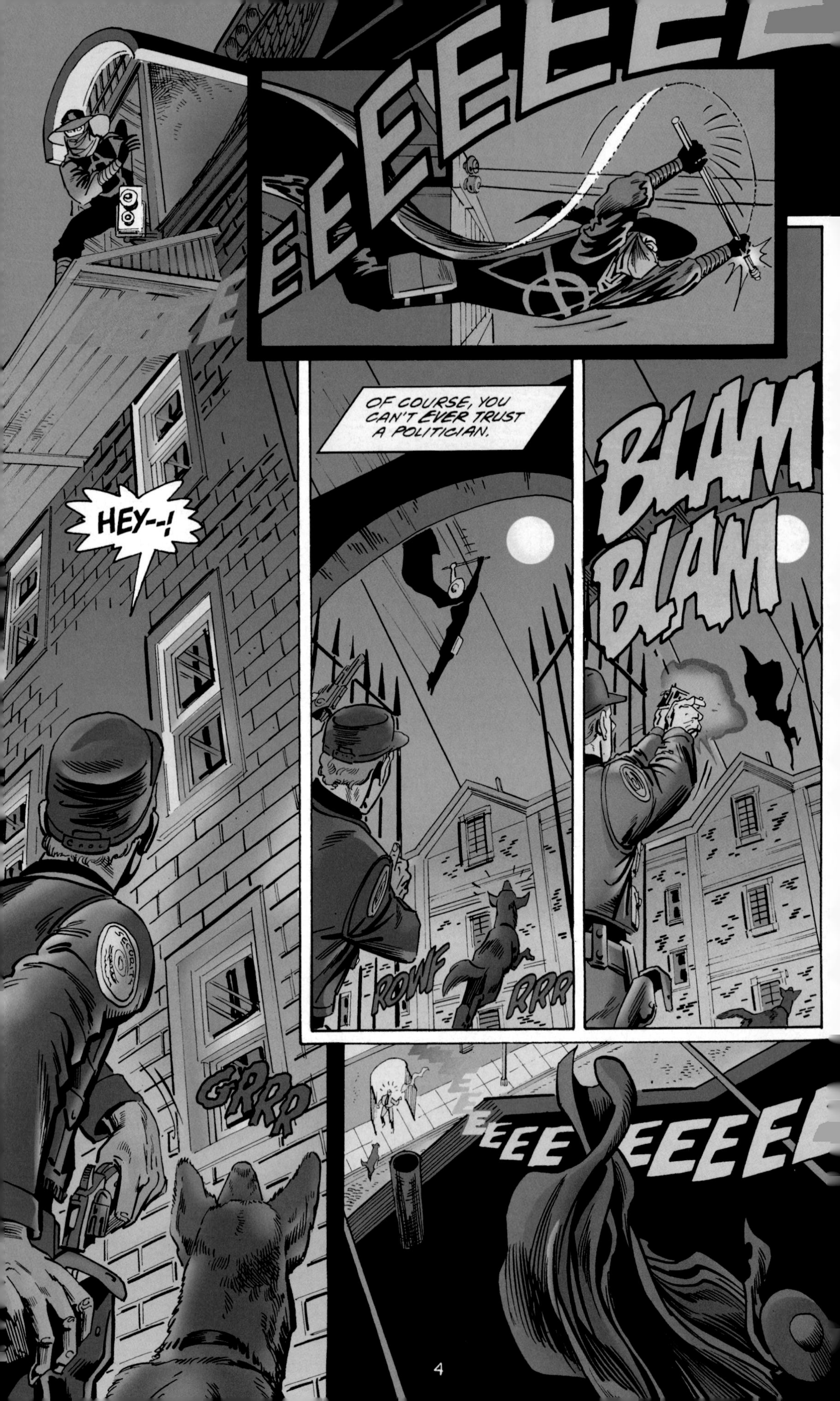
EEEEEEEE
OF COURSE, YOU CAN'T EVER TRUST A POLITICIAN.
BLAM BLAM
HEY--!
ROWF
RRR
GRRR
EEEEEEEEE

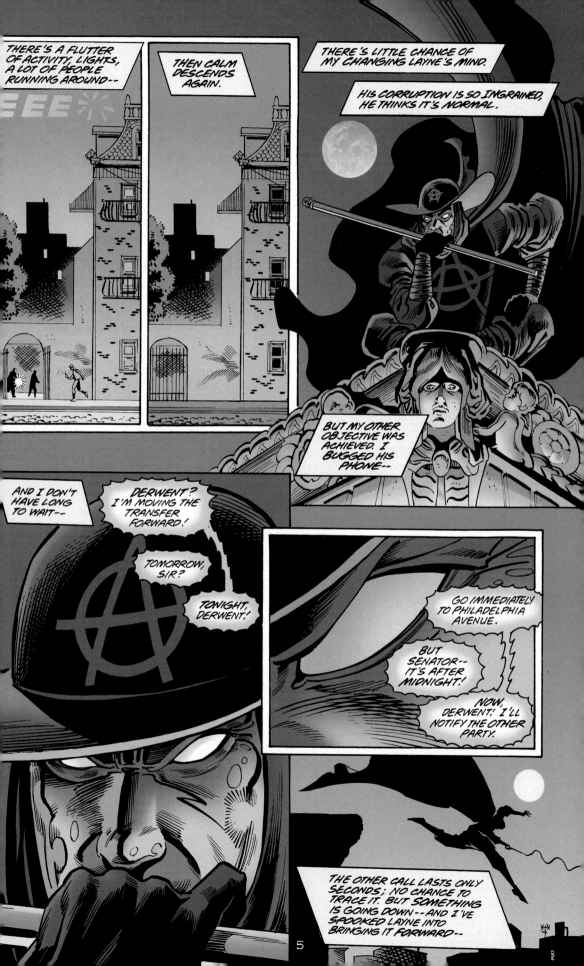

THERE'S A FLUTTER OF ACTIVITY, LIGHTS, A LOT OF PEOPLE RUNNING AROUND--

THEN CALM DESCENDS AGAIN.

THERE'S LITTLE CHANCE OF MY CHANGING LAYNE'S MIND.

HIS CORRUPTION IS SO INGRAINED, HE THINKS IT'S NORMAL.

BUT MY OTHER OBJECTIVE WAS ACHIEVED. I BUGGED HIS PHONE--

AND I DON'T HAVE LONG TO WAIT--

DERWENT? I'M MOVING THE TRANSFER FORWARD!

TOMORROW, SIR?

TONIGHT, DERWENT!

GO IMMEDIATELY TO PHILADELPHIA AVENUE.

BUT SENATOR-- IT'S AFTER MIDNIGHT!

NOW, DERWENT! I'LL NOTIFY THE OTHER PARTY.

THE OTHER CALL LASTS ONLY SECONDS; NO CHANCE TO TRACE IT. BUT SOMETHING IS GOING DOWN--AND I'VE SPOOKED LAYNE INTO BRINGING IT FORWARD--

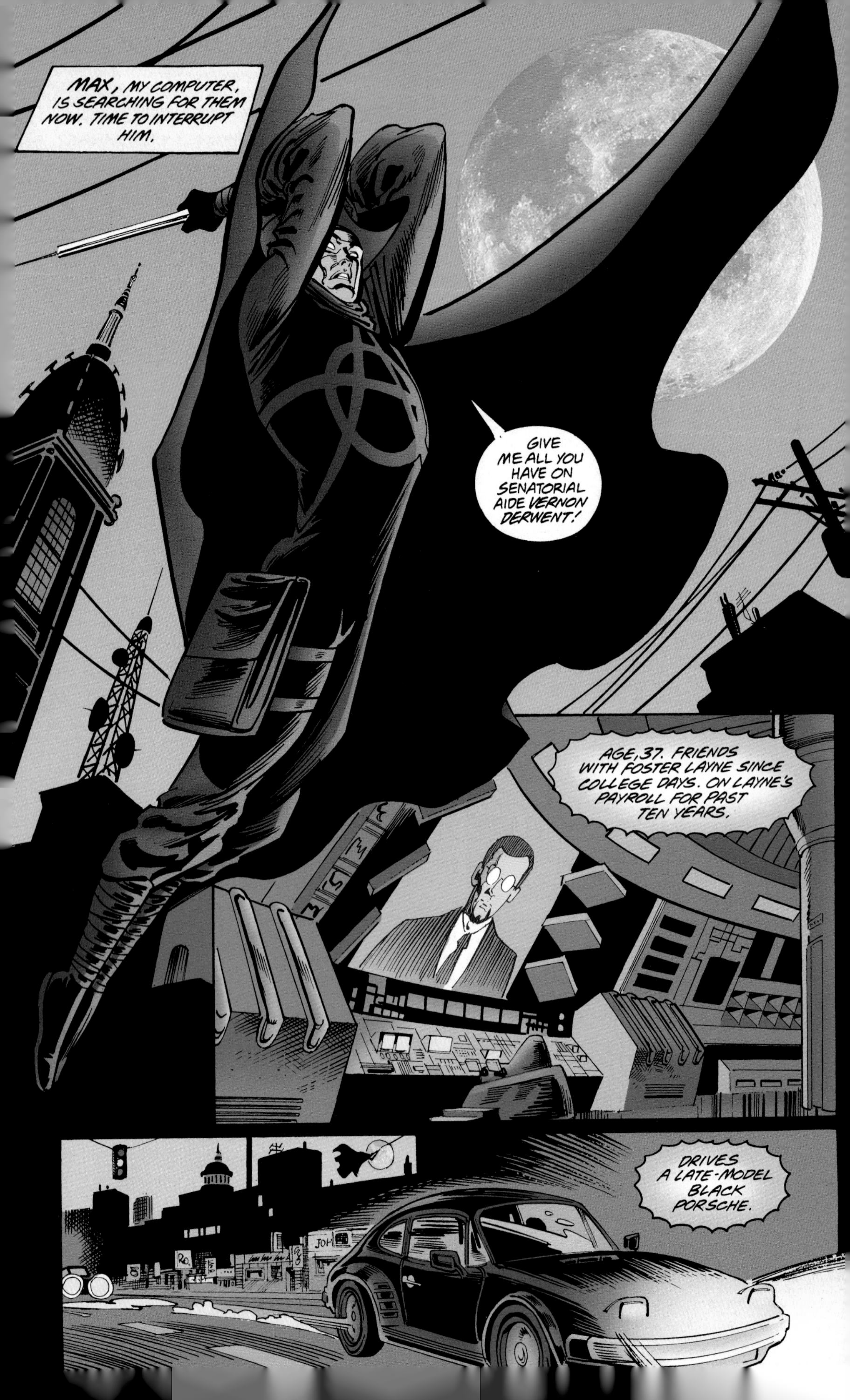
MAX, MY COMPUTER, IS SEARCHING FOR THEM NOW. TIME TO INTERRUPT HIM.
GIVE ME ALL YOU HAVE ON SENATORIAL AIDE VERNON DERWENT!
AGE, 37. FRIENDS WITH FOSTER LAYNE SINCE COLLEGE DAYS. ON LAYNE'S PAYROLL FOR PAST TEN YEARS.
DRIVES A LATE-MODEL BLACK PORSCHE.

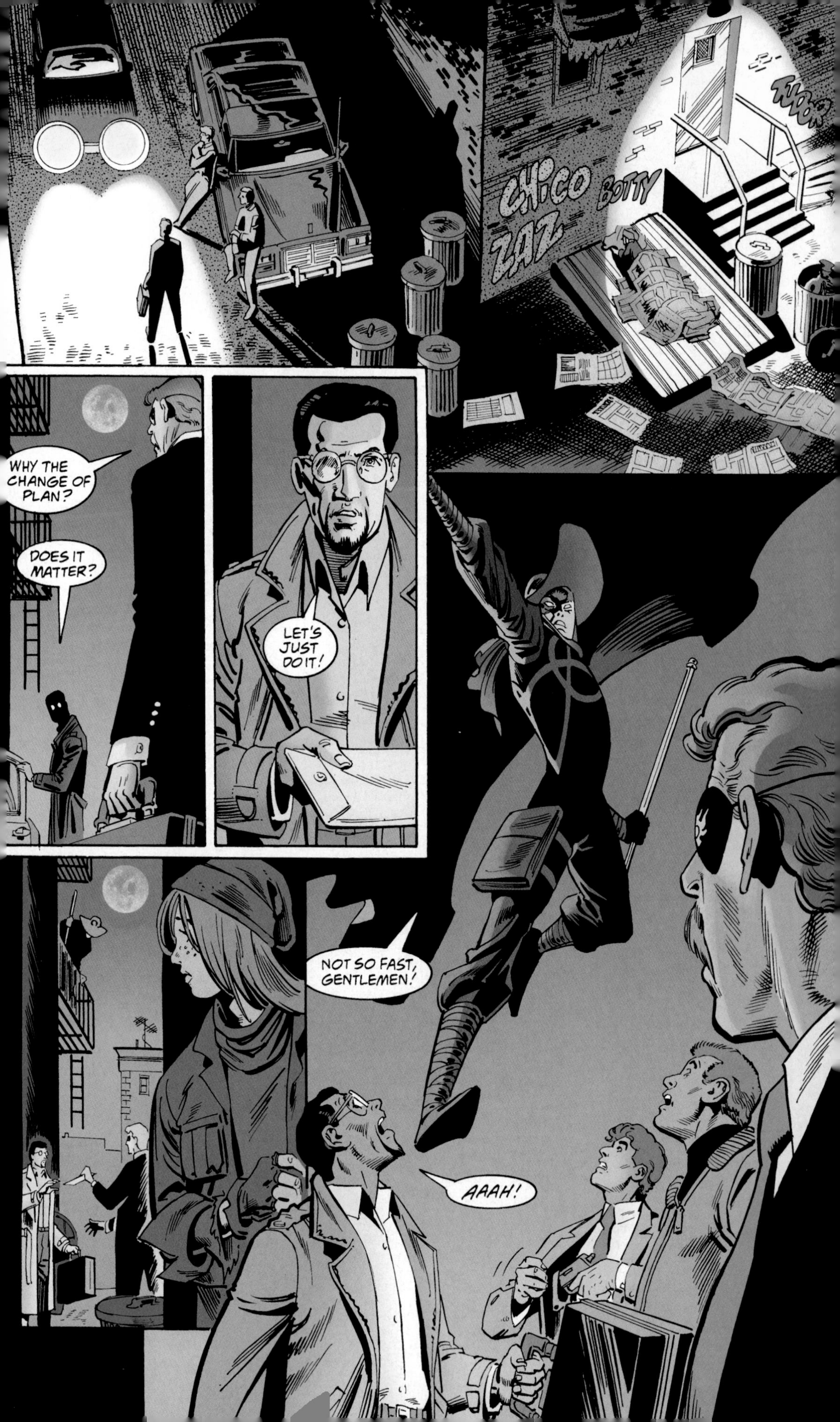
CHICO
ZAZ
BOTTY
TUDOR
WHY THE CHANGE OF PLAN?
DOES IT MATTER?
LET'S JUST DO IT!
NOT SO FAST, GENTLEMEN!
AAAH!

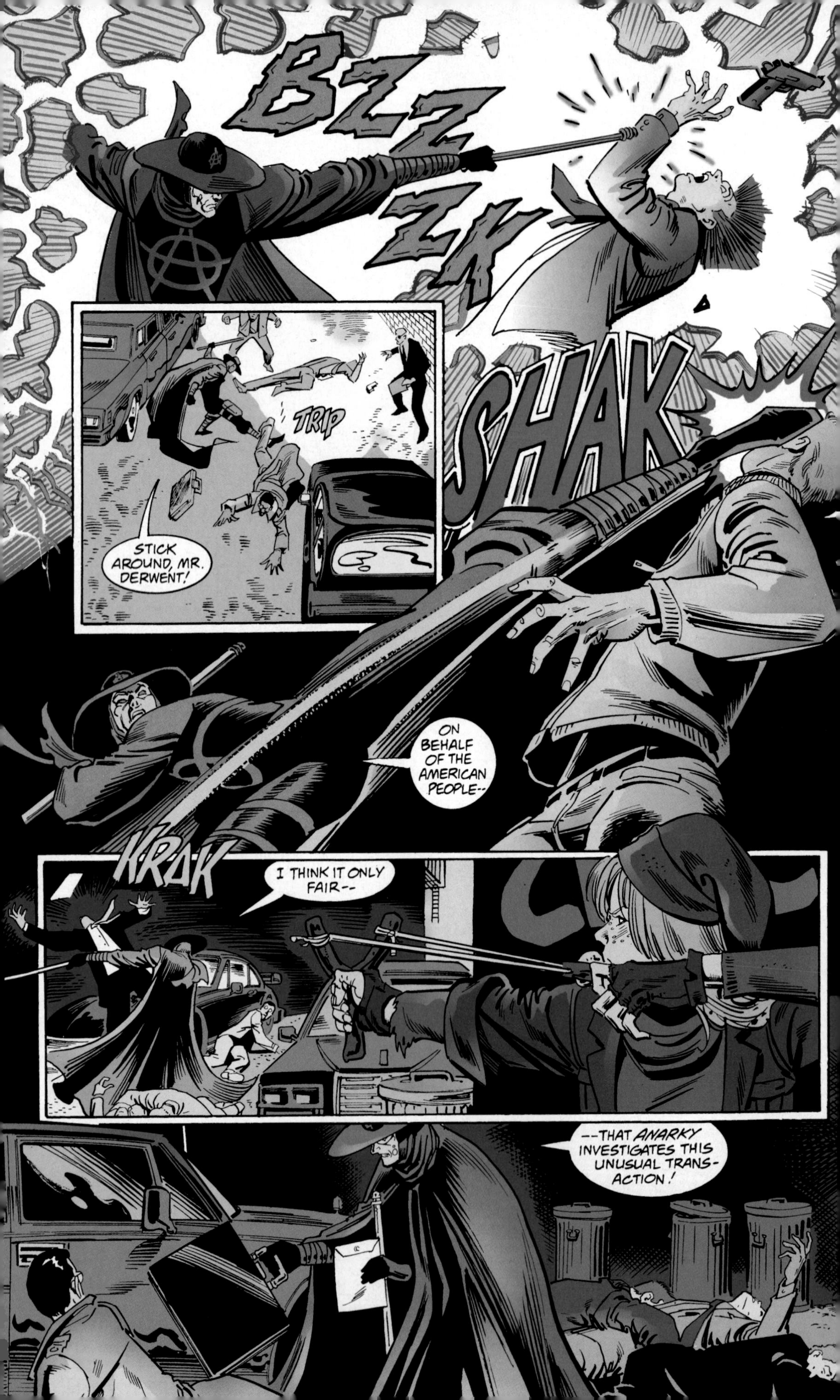
BZZZK
SHAK
TRIP
STICK AROUND, MR. DERWENT!
ON BEHALF OF THE AMERICAN PEOPLE--
KRAK
I THINK IT ONLY FAIR--
--THAT ANARKY INVESTIGATES THIS UNUSUAL TRANS-ACTION!

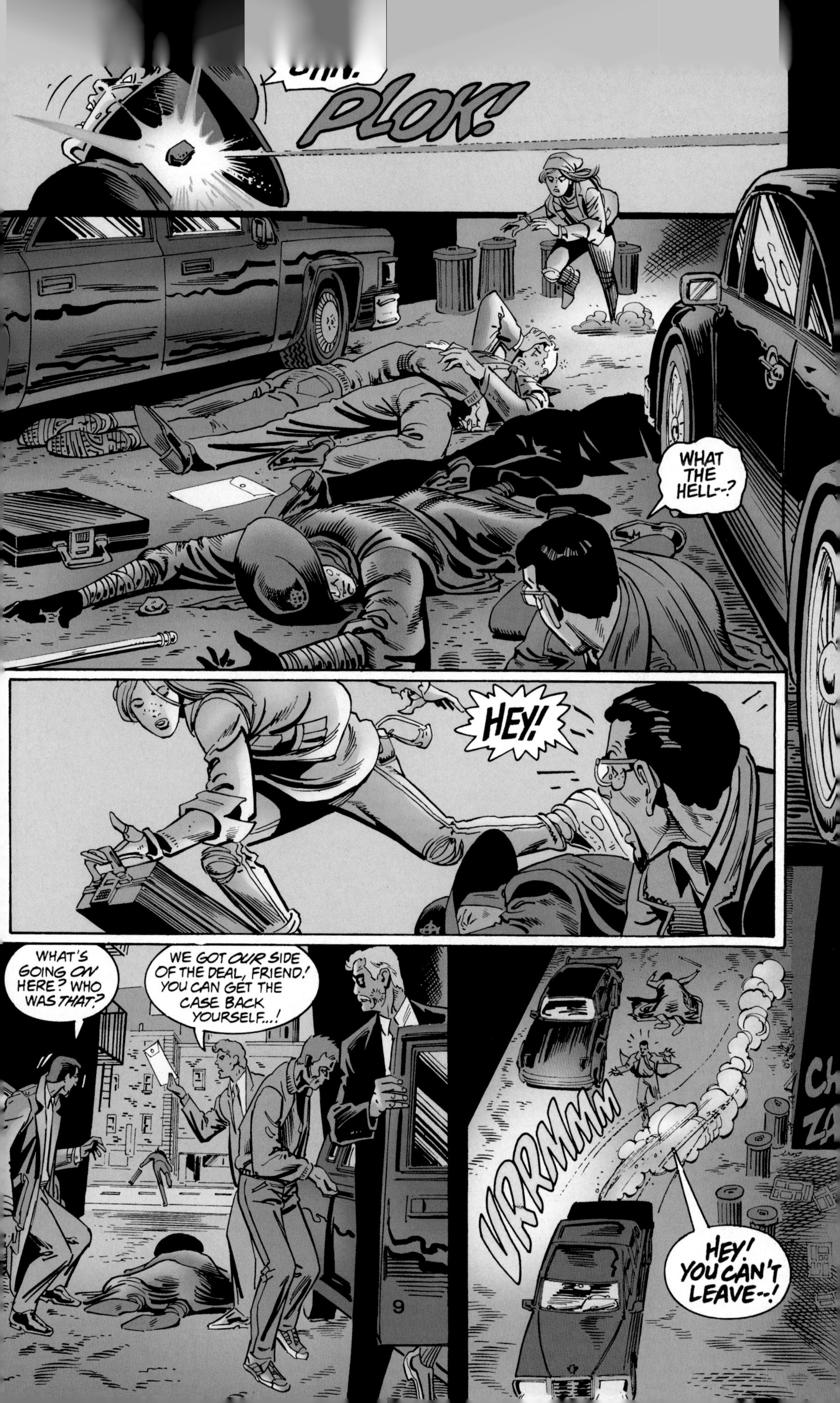

PLOK!
WHAT THE HELL--?
HEY!
WHAT'S GOING *ON* HERE? WHO WAS *THAT*?
WE GOT *OUR* SIDE OF THE DEAL, FRIEND! YOU CAN GET THE CASE BACK YOURSELF...!
VRRRMMMM
HEY! YOU CAN'T LEAVE--!

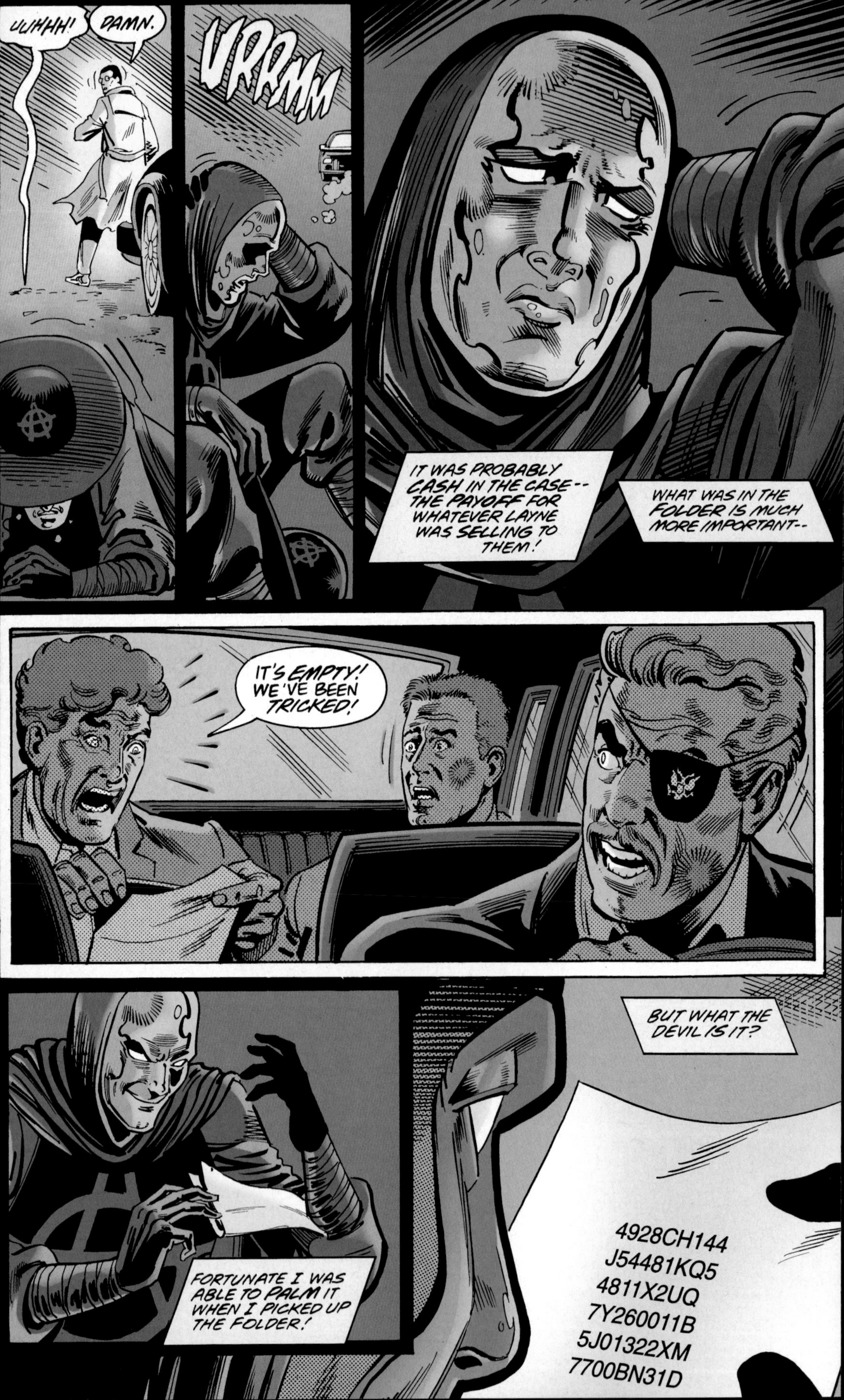
UUHHH!
DAMN.
VRRMM
IT WAS PROBABLY CASH IN THE CASE-- THE PAYOFF FOR WHATEVER LAYNE WAS SELLING TO THEM!
WHAT WAS IN THE FOLDER IS MUCH MORE IMPORTANT--
IT'S EMPTY! WE'VE BEEN TRICKED!
FORTUNATE I WAS ABLE TO PALM IT WHEN I PICKED UP THE FOLDER!
BUT WHAT THE DEVIL IS IT?
4928CH144
J54481KQ5
4811X2UQ
7Y260011B
5J01322XM
7700BN31D

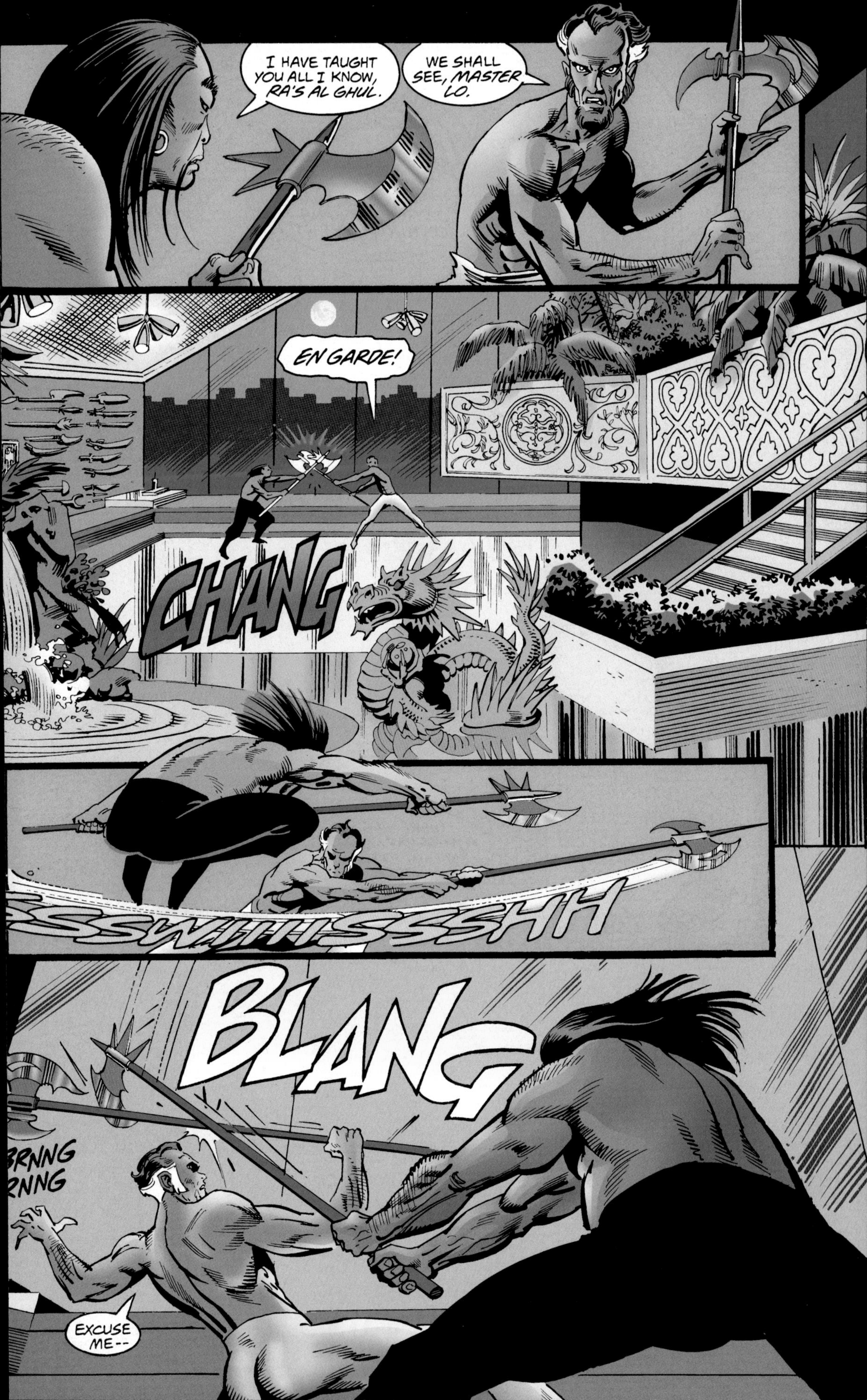
I HAVE TAUGHT YOU ALL I KNOW, RA'S AL GHUL.
WE SHALL SEE, MASTER LO.
EN GARDE!
CHANG
HHSSSSHHHWSS
BLANG
BRNNG
RNNG
EXCUSE ME--

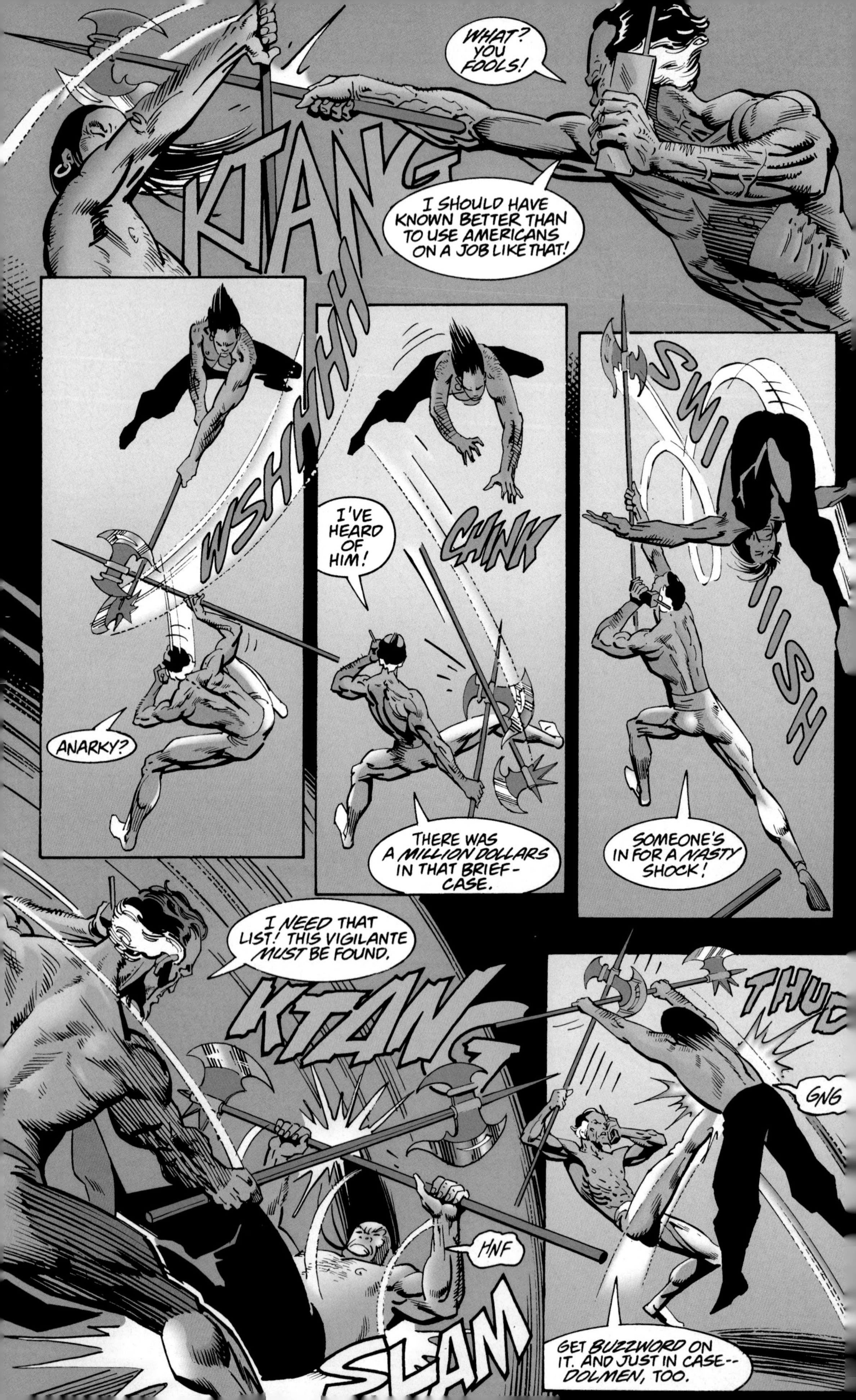
WHAT? YOU FOOLS!
KTANG
I SHOULD HAVE KNOWN BETTER THAN TO USE AMERICANS ON A JOB LIKE THAT!
WSHHHHH
ANARKY?
I'VE HEARD OF HIM!
CHINK
THERE WAS A MILLION DOLLARS IN THAT BRIEF-CASE.
SWIIIISH
SOMEONE'S IN FOR A NASTY SHOCK!
I NEED THAT LIST! THIS VIGILANTE MUST BE FOUND.
KTANG
HNF
SLAM
THUD
GNG
GET BUZZWORD ON IT. AND JUST IN CASE-- DOLMEN, TOO.

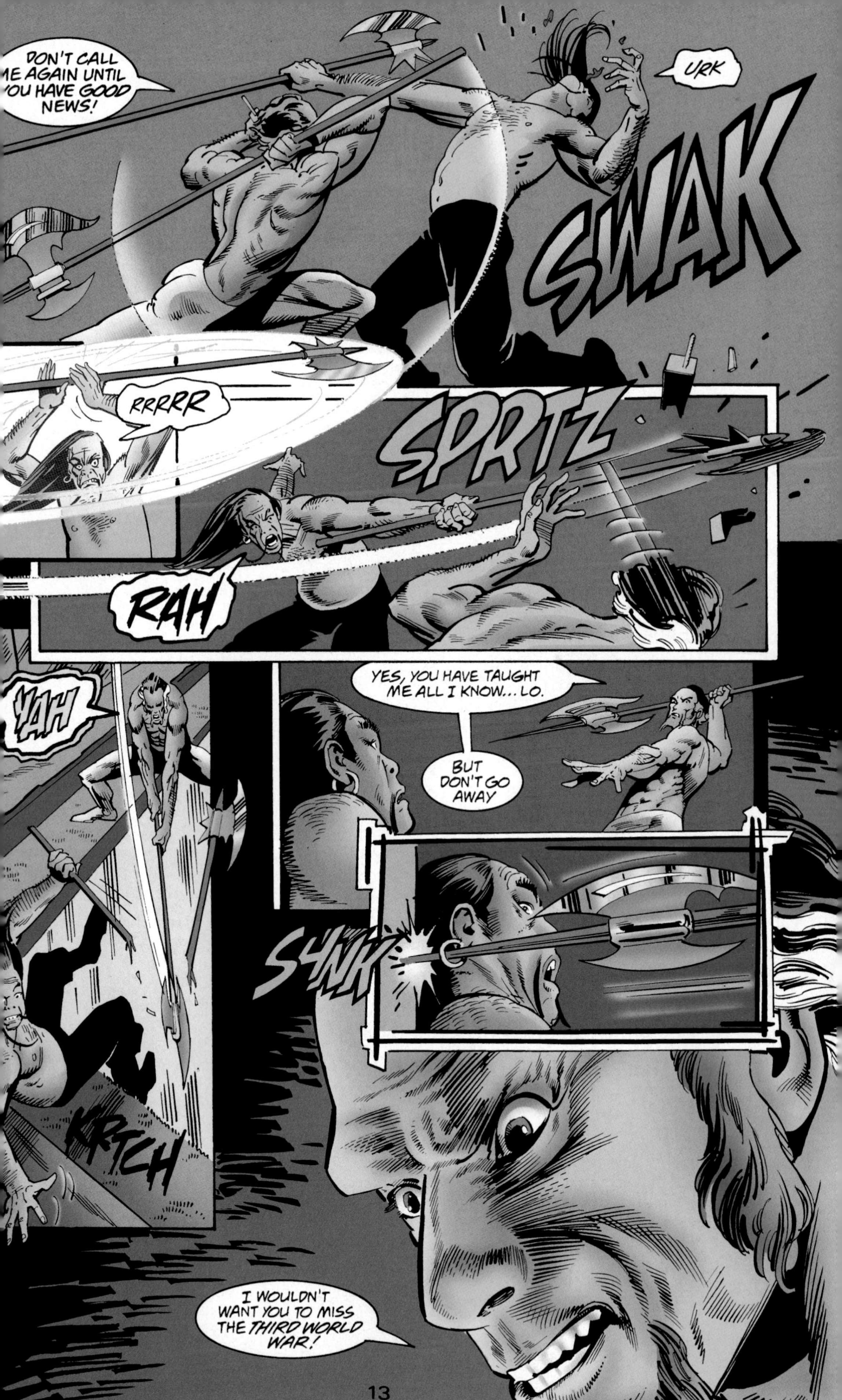
DON'T CALL ME AGAIN UNTIL YOU HAVE GOOD NEWS!
URK
SWAK
RRRRR
SPRTZ
RAH
YAH
YES, YOU HAVE TAUGHT ME ALL I KNOW... LO.
BUT DON'T GO AWAY
SHNK
KRTCH
I WOULDN'T WANT YOU TO MISS THE THIRD WORLD WAR!

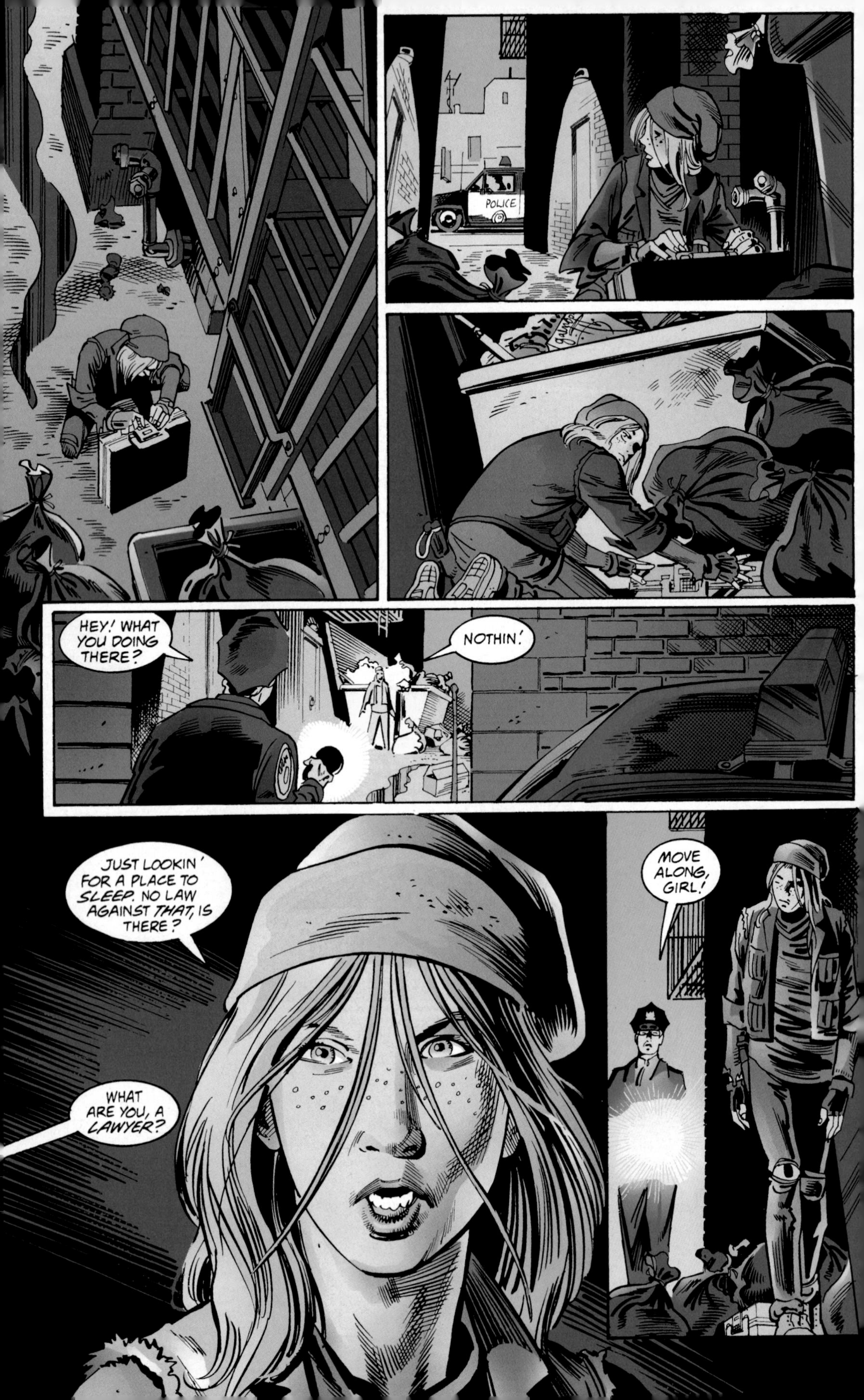

POLICE
HEY! WHAT YOU DOING THERE?
NOTHIN'!
JUST LOOKIN' FOR A PLACE TO SLEEP. NO LAW AGAINST THAT, IS THERE?
WHAT ARE YOU, A LAWYER?
MOVE ALONG, GIRL!

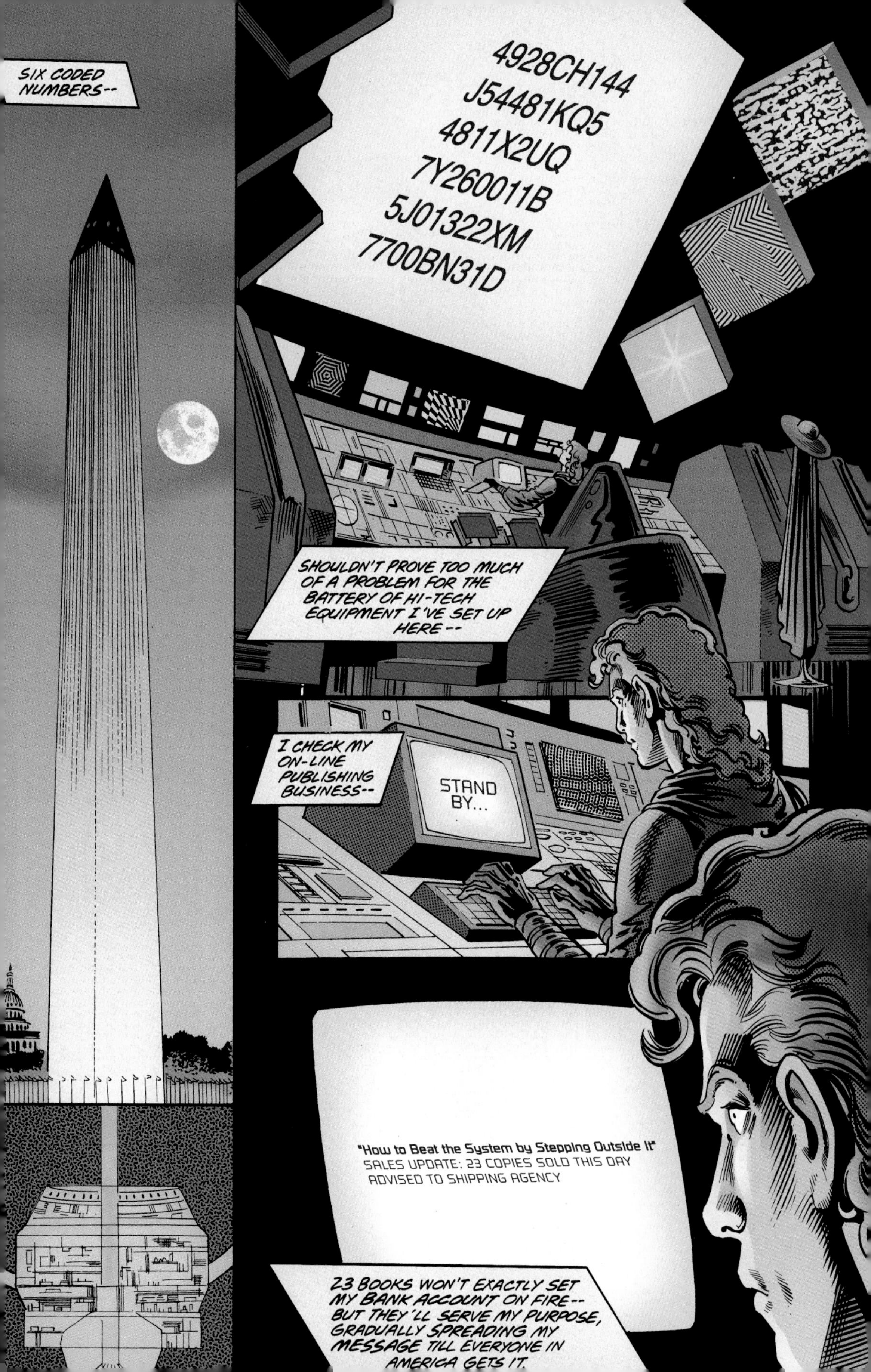
SIX CODED NUMBERS--
4928CH144
J54481KQ5
4811X2UQ
7Y260011B
5J01322XM
7700BN31D
SHOULDN'T PROVE TOO MUCH OF A PROBLEM FOR THE BATTERY OF HI-TECH EQUIPMENT I'VE SET UP HERE--
I CHECK MY ON-LINE PUBLISHING BUSINESS--
STAND BY...
"How to Beat the System by Stepping Outside It"
SALES UPDATE: 23 COPIES SOLD THIS DAY
ADVISED TO SHIPPING AGENCY
23 BOOKS WON'T EXACTLY SET MY BANK ACCOUNT ON FIRE-- BUT THEY'LL SERVE MY PURPOSE, GRADUALLY SPREADING MY MESSAGE TILL EVERYONE IN AMERICA GETS IT.

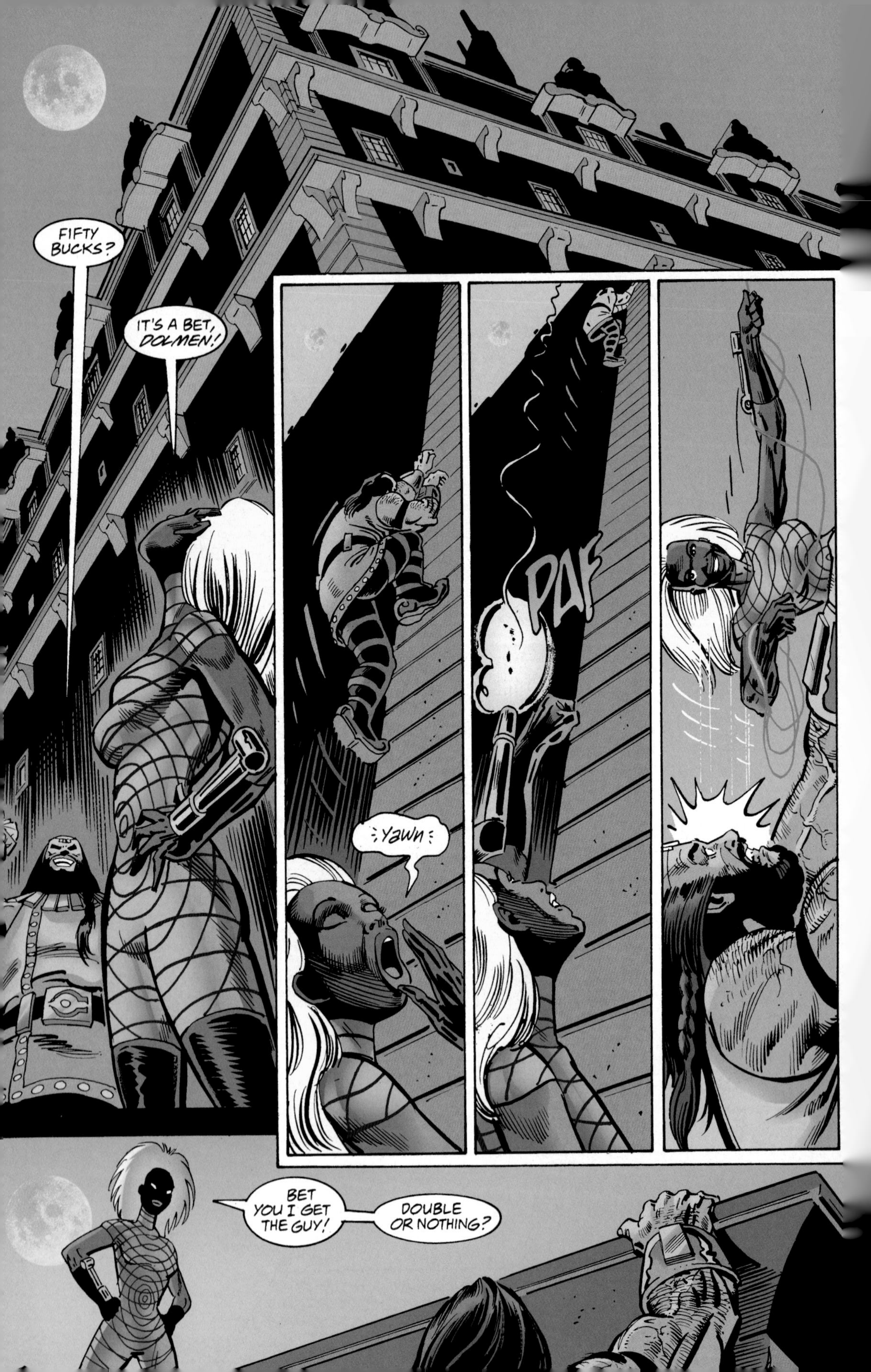
FIFTY BUCKS?
IT'S A BET, DOLMEN!
PAF
:YAWN:
BET YOU I GET THE GUY!
DOUBLE OR NOTHING?

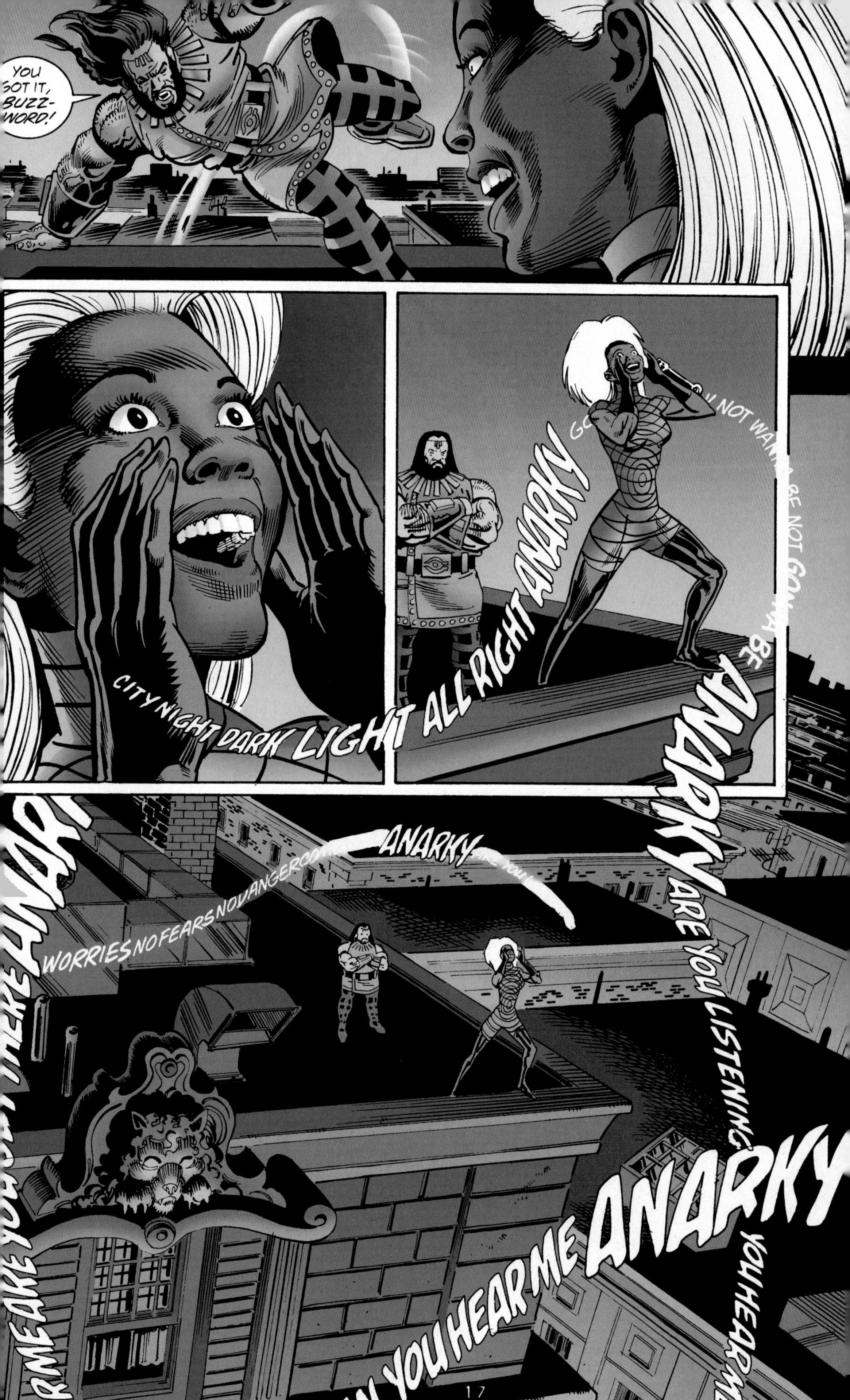

YOU GOT IT, BUZZ-WORD!
CITY NIGHT DARK LIGHT ALL RIGHT ANARKY
NOT GONNA BE ANARKY ARE YOU LISTENING
ANARKY
WORRIES NO FEARS NO DANGER
YOU HEAR ME ANARKY

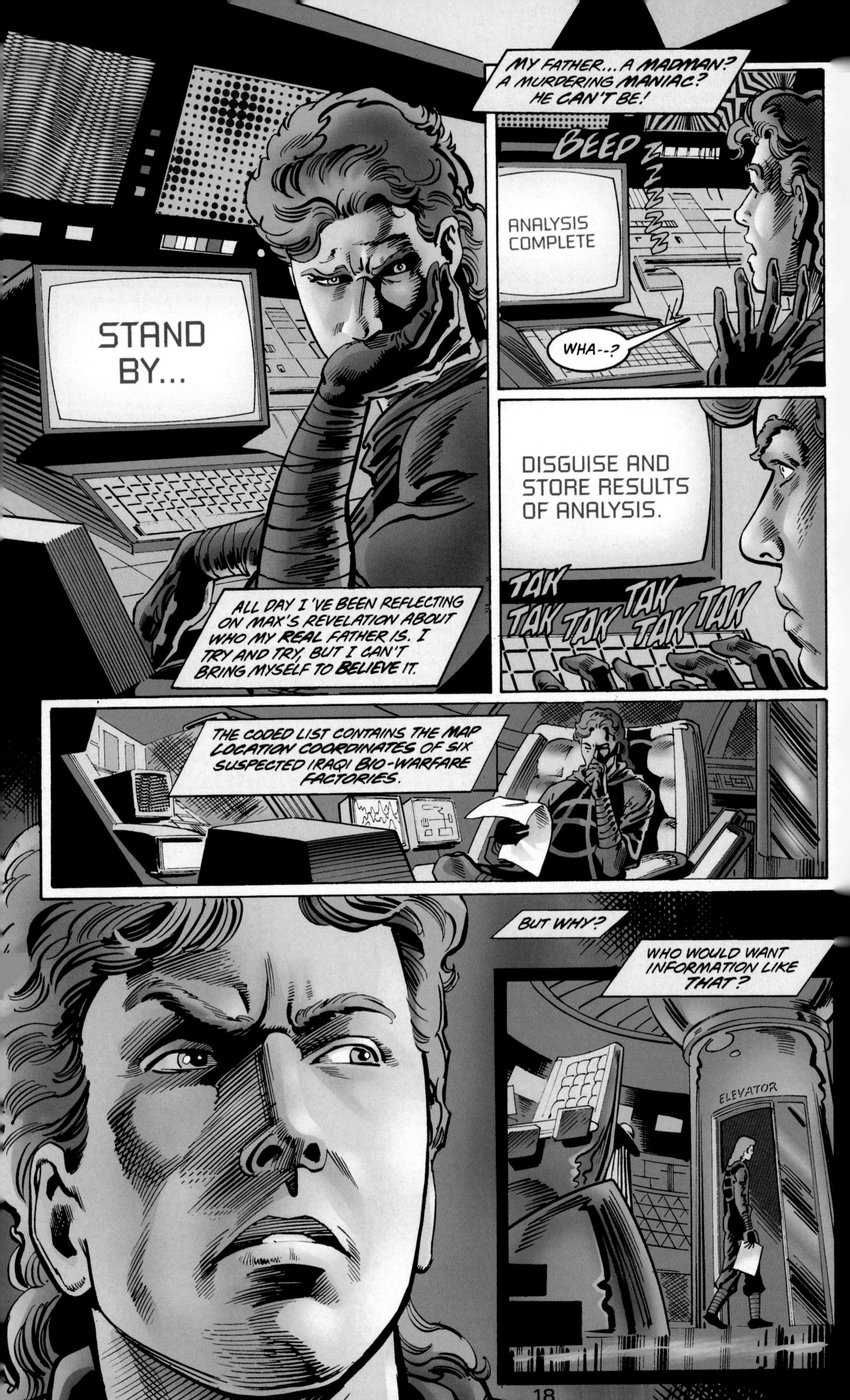
STAND BY...
ALL DAY I'VE BEEN REFLECTING ON MAX'S REVELATION ABOUT WHO MY REAL FATHER IS. I TRY AND TRY, BUT I CAN'T BRING MYSELF TO BELIEVE IT.
MY FATHER... A MADMAN? A MURDERING MANIAC? HE CAN'T BE!
BEEP
ANALYSIS COMPLETE
WHA--?
DISGUISE AND STORE RESULTS OF ANALYSIS.
TAK TAK TAK TAK TAK TAK
THE CODED LIST CONTAINS THE MAP LOCATION COORDINATES OF SIX SUSPECTED IRAQI BIO-WARFARE FACTORIES.
BUT WHY?
WHO WOULD WANT INFORMATION LIKE THAT?
ELEVATOR

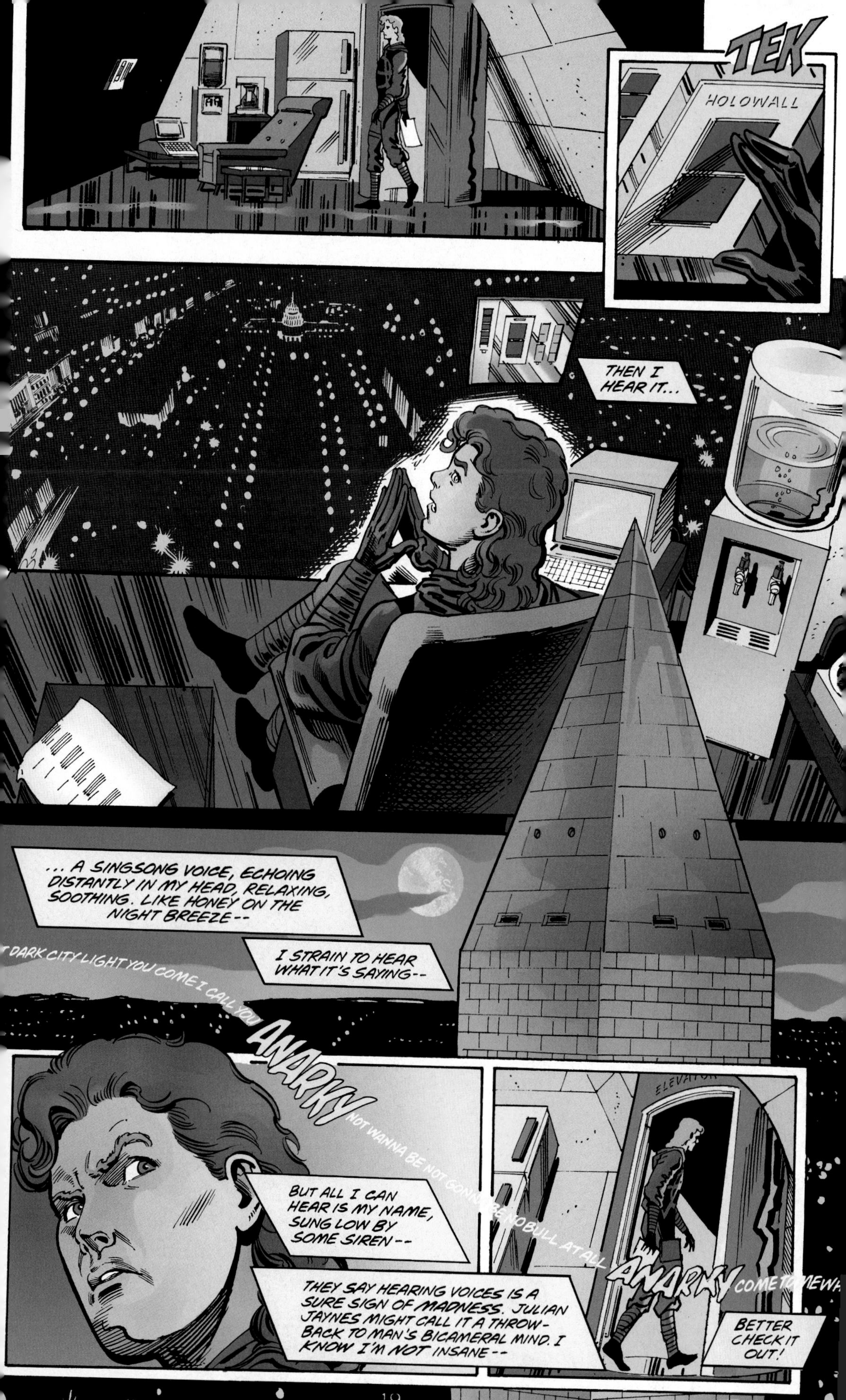
TEK
HOLOWALL
THEN I HEAR IT...
... A SINGSONG VOICE, ECHOING DISTANTLY IN MY HEAD, RELAXING, SOOTHING. LIKE HONEY ON THE NIGHT BREEZE--
I STRAIN TO HEAR WHAT IT'S SAYING--
DARK CITY LIGHT YOU COME I CALL YOU ANARKY NOT WANNA BE NOT GONN BE NO BULL AT ALL ANARKY COME TO ME
BUT ALL I CAN HEAR IS MY NAME, SUNG LOW BY SOME SIREN--
THEY SAY HEARING VOICES IS A SURE SIGN OF MADNESS. JULIAN JAYNES MIGHT CALL IT A THROW-BACK TO MAN'S BICAMERAL MIND. I KNOW I'M NOT INSANE--
ELEVATOR
BETTER CHECK IT OUT!

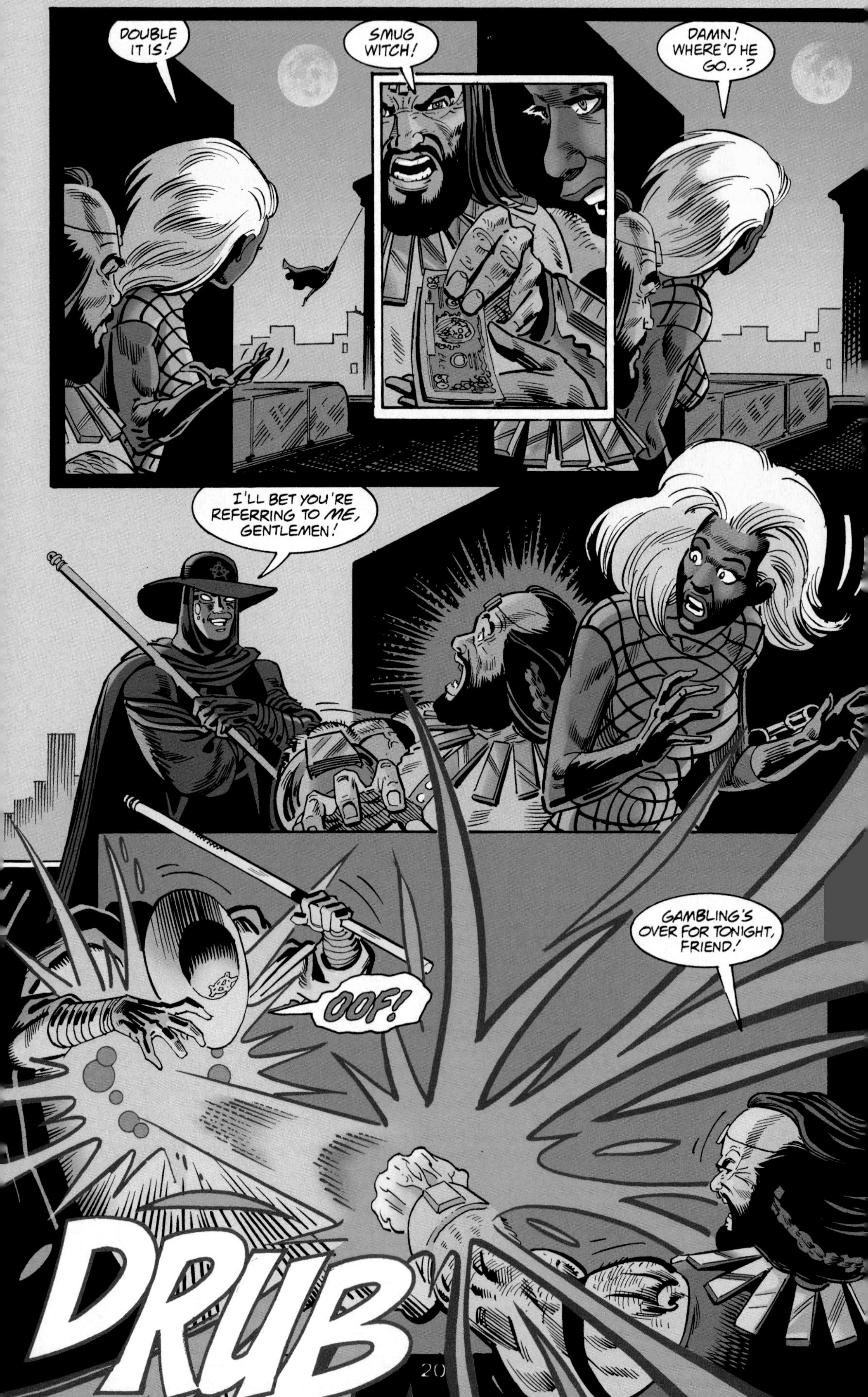
DOUBLE IT IS!
SMUG WITCH!
DAMN! WHERE'D HE GO...?
I'LL BET YOU'RE REFERRING TO ME, GENTLEMEN!
OOF!
GAMBLING'S OVER FOR TONIGHT, FRIEND!
DRUB

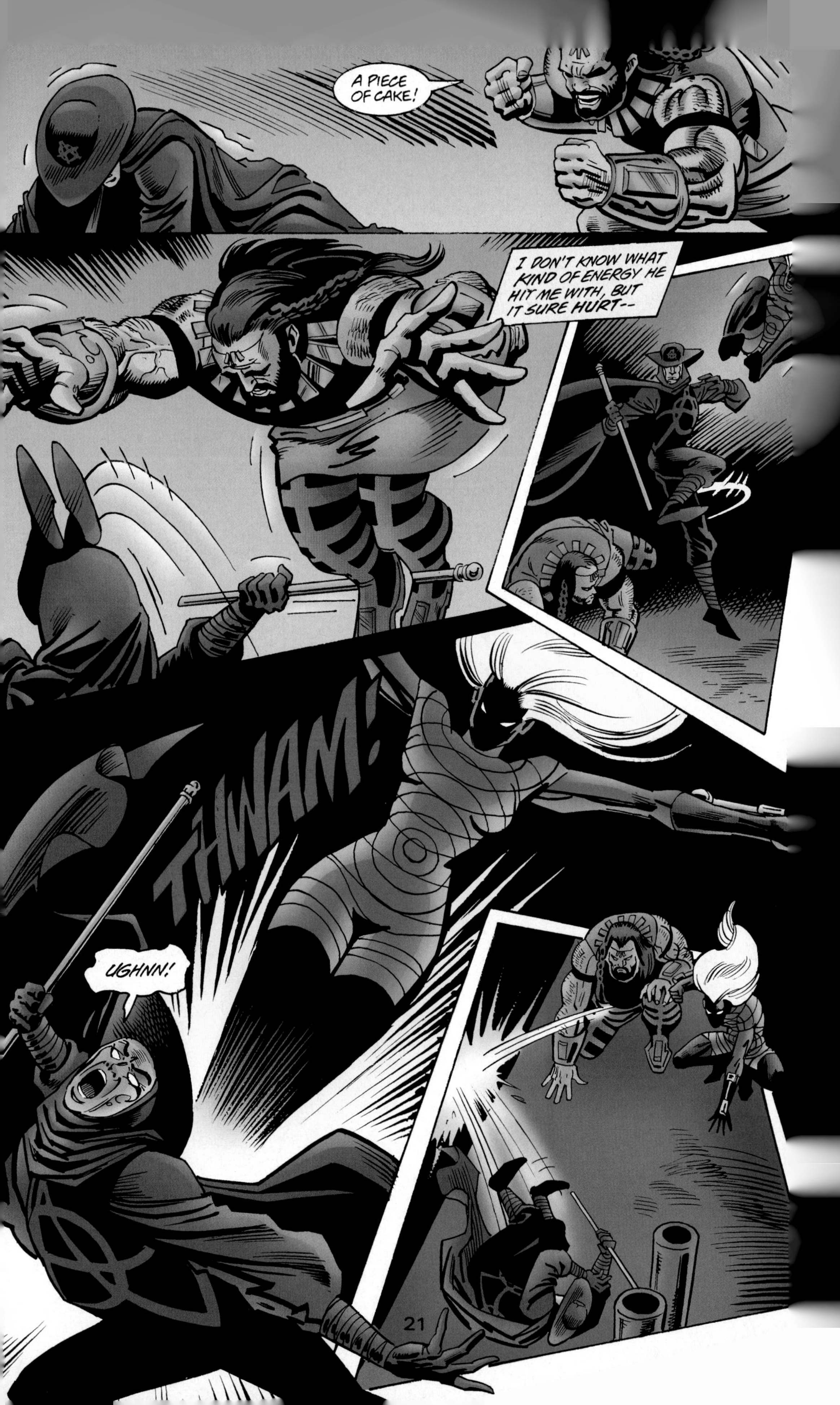
A PIECE OF CAKE!
I DON'T KNOW WHAT KIND OF ENERGY HE HIT ME WITH, BUT IT SURE HURT--
THWAM!
UGHNN!

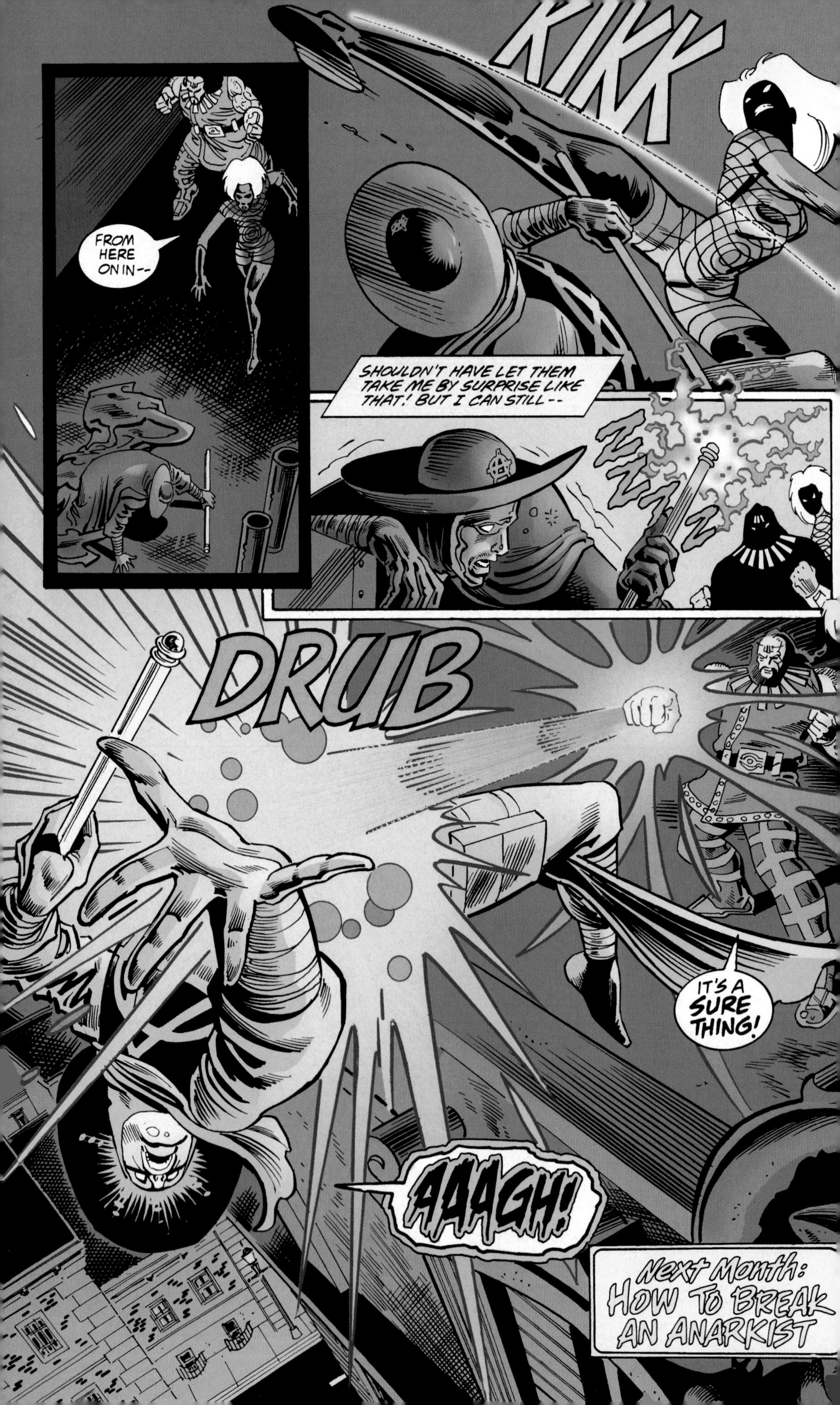
KIKK
FROM HERE ON IN--
SHOULDN'T HAVE LET THEM TAKE ME BY SURPRISE LIKE THAT! BUT I CAN STILL--
NNNAAAN
DRUB
IT'S A SURE THING!
AAAAGH!
Next Month:
HOW TO BREAK AN ANARKIST

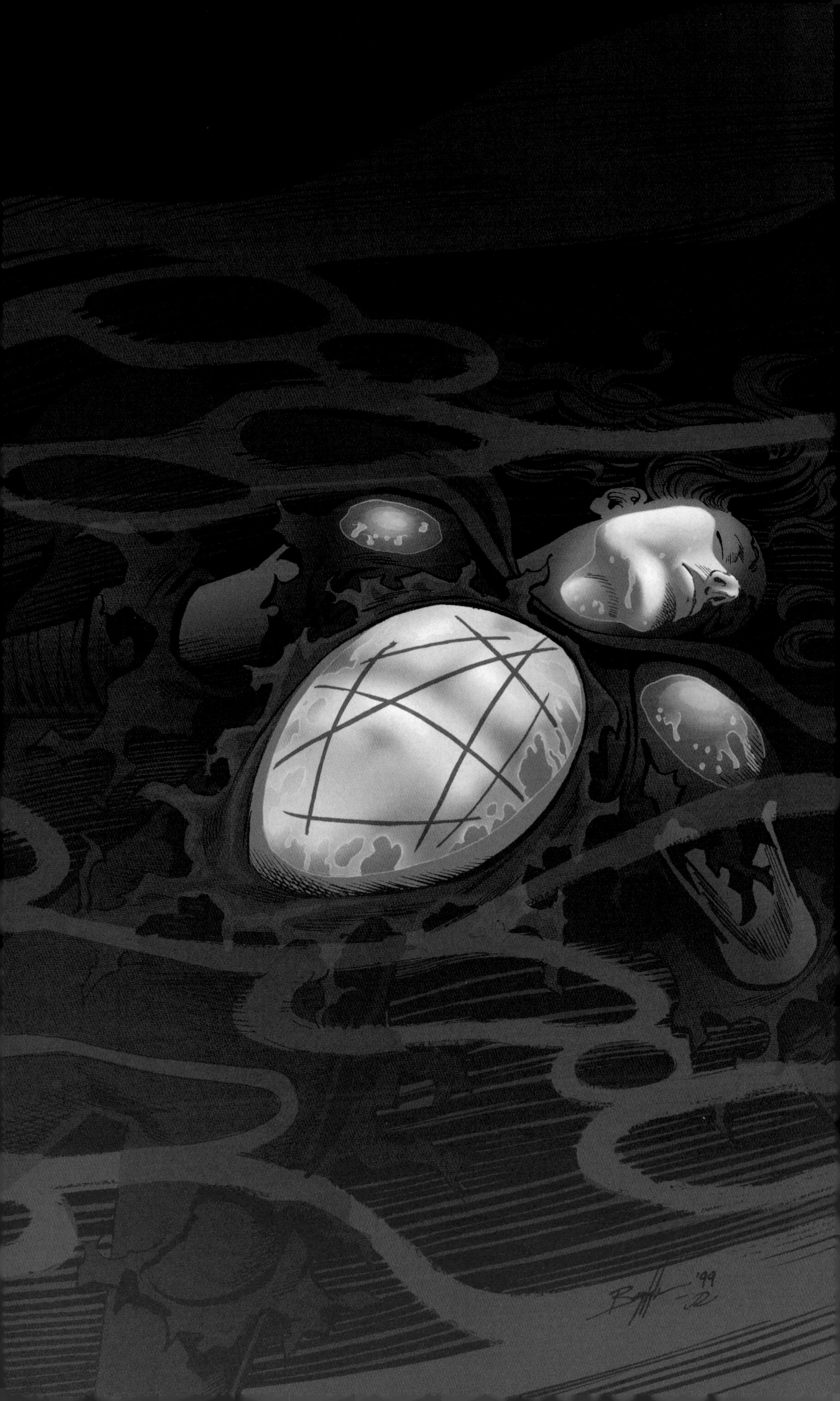

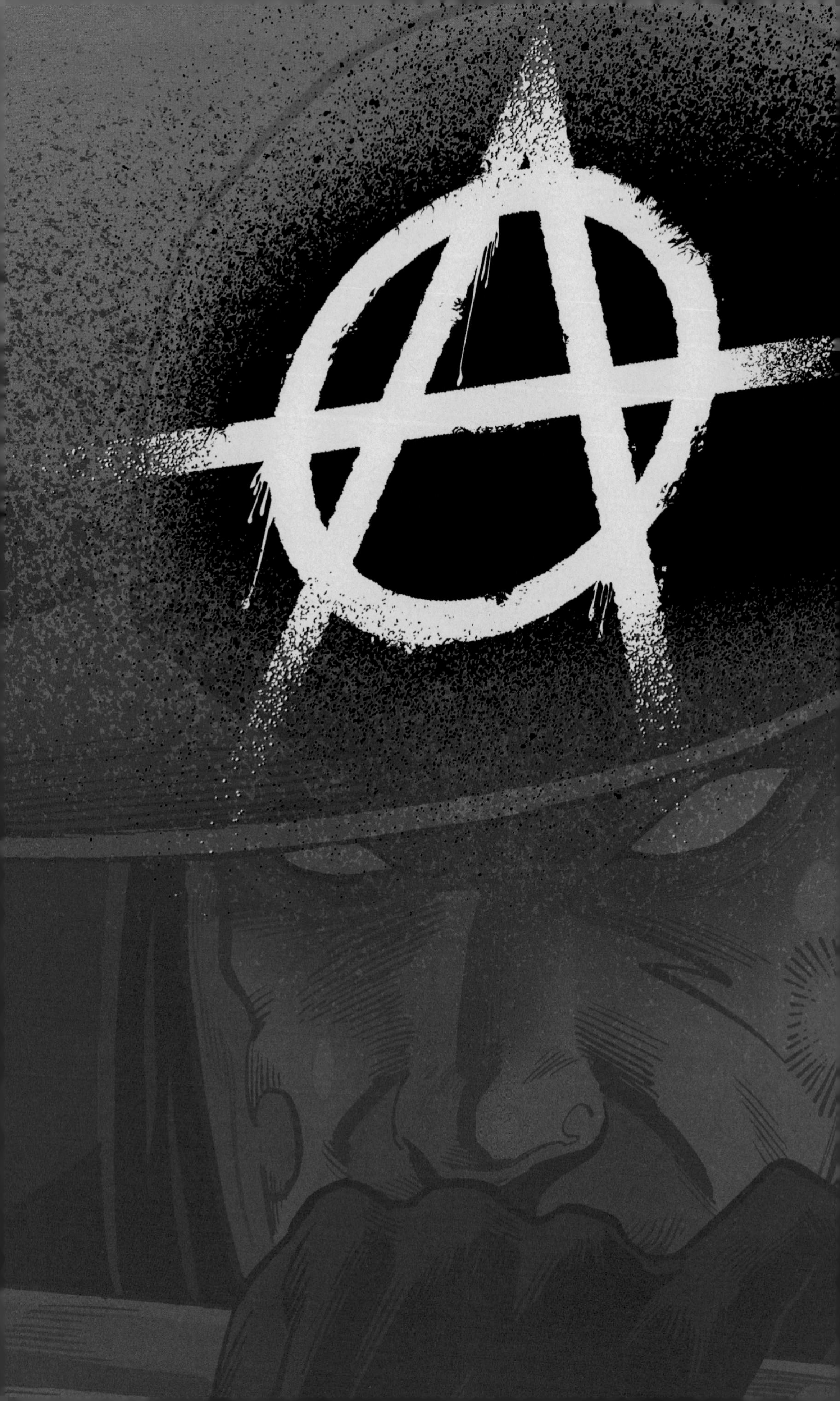

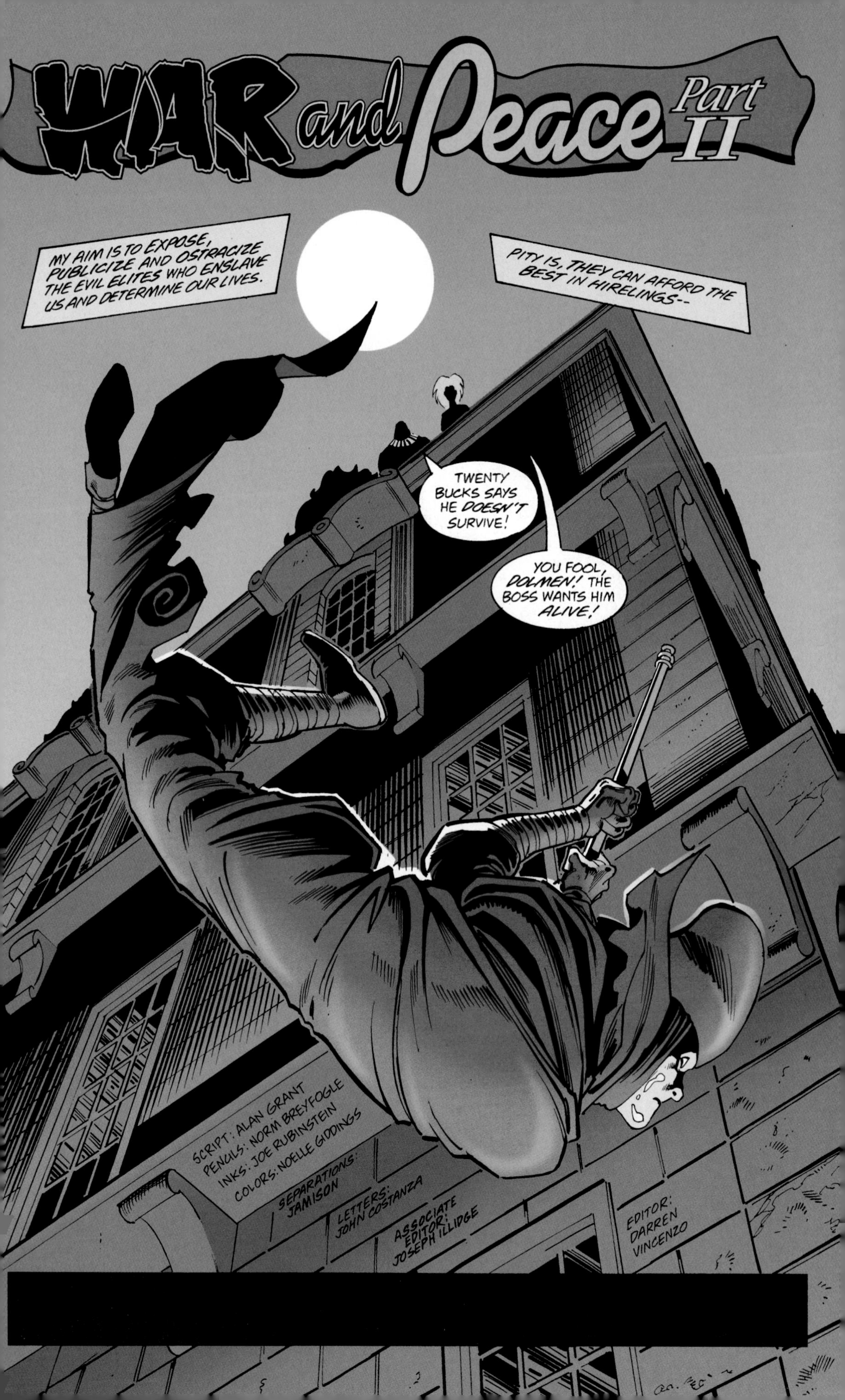

WAR and Peace Part II
MY AIM IS TO EXPOSE, PUBLICIZE AND OSTRACIZE THE EVIL ELITES WHO ENSLAVE US AND DETERMINE OUR LIVES.
PITY IS, THEY CAN AFFORD THE BEST IN HIRELINGS--
TWENTY BUCKS SAYS HE DOESN'T SURVIVE!
YOU FOOL, DOLMEN! THE BOSS WANTS HIM ALIVE!
SCRIPT: ALAN GRANT
PENCILS: NORM BREYFOGLE
INKS: JOE RUBINSTEIN
COLORS: NOELLE GIDDINGS
SEPARATIONS: JAMISON
LETTERS: JOHN COSTANZA
ASSOCIATE EDITOR: JOSEPH ILLIDGE
EDITOR: DARREN VINCENZO
[redacted]

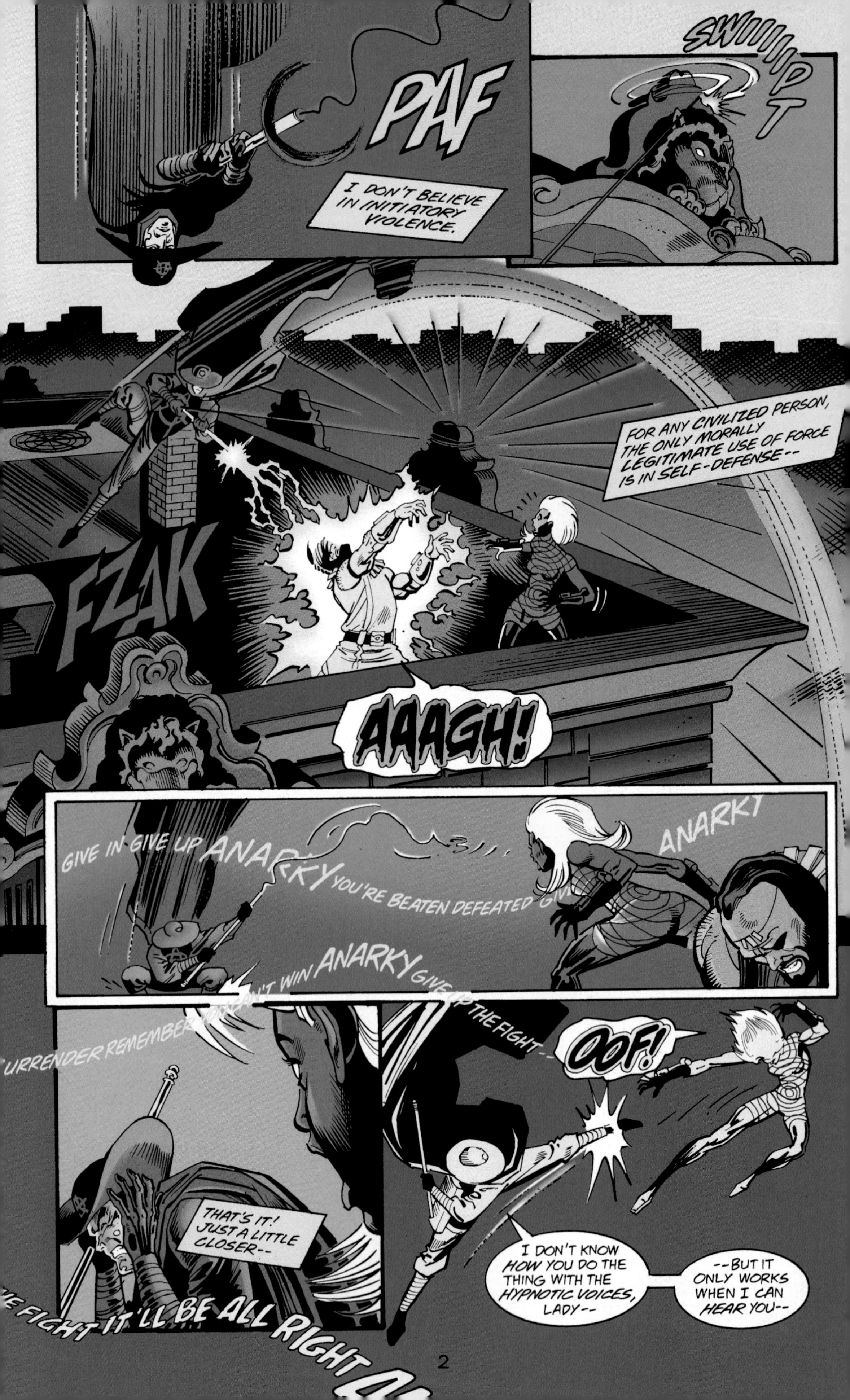
PAF
I DON'T BELIEVE IN INITIATORY VIOLENCE.
FOR ANY CIVILIZED PERSON, THE ONLY MORALLY LEGITIMATE USE OF FORCE IS IN SELF-DEFENSE--
FZAK
AAAGH!
GIVE IN GIVE UP ANARKY YOU'RE BEATEN DEFEATED
ANARKY
ANARKY GIVE UP THE FIGHT--
OOF!
THAT'S IT! JUST A LITTLE CLOSER--
IT'LL BE ALL RIGHT
I DON'T KNOW *HOW* YOU DO THE THING WITH THE *HYPNOTIC VOICES,* LADY--
--BUT IT ONLY WORKS WHEN I CAN *HEAR YOU*--

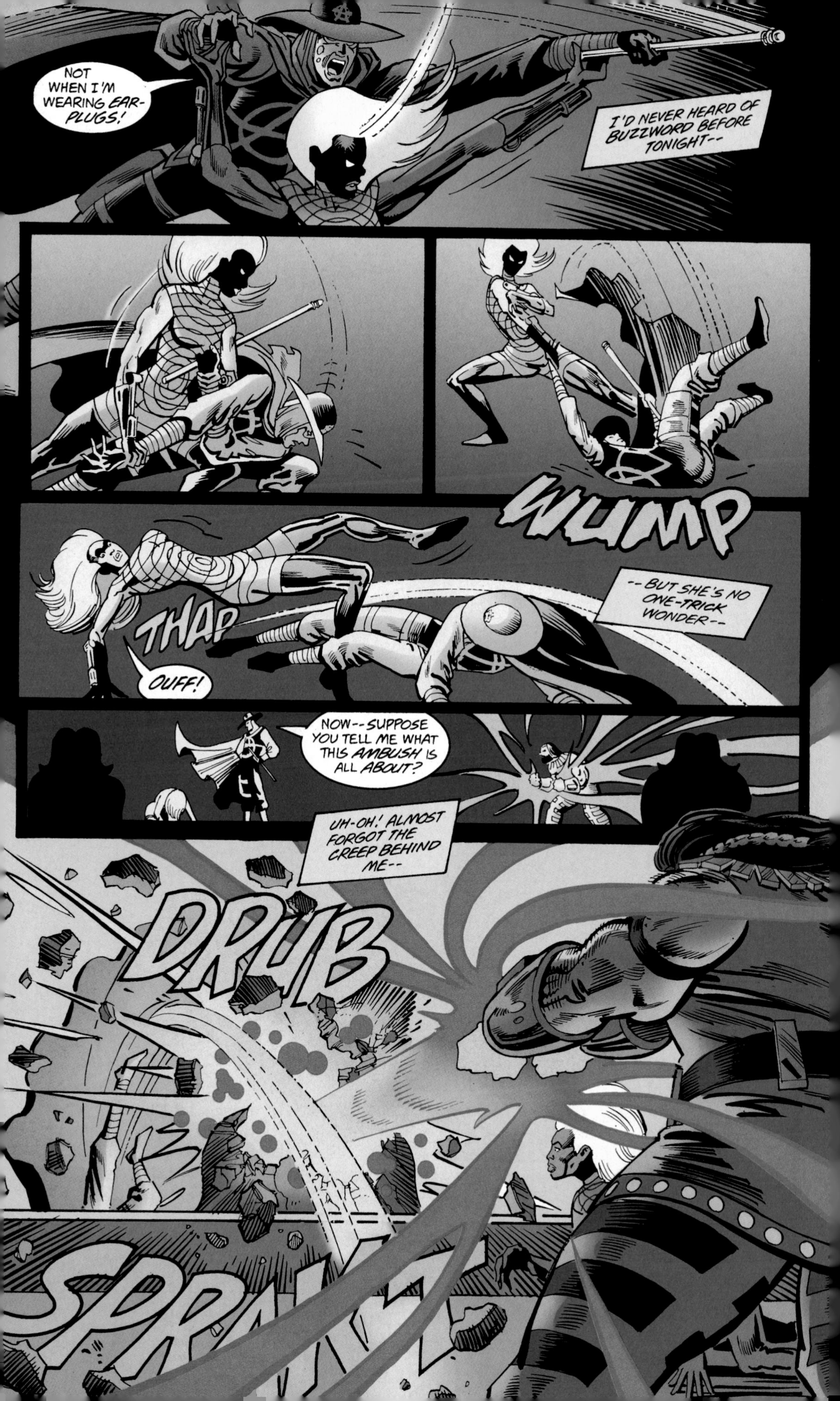
NOT WHEN I'M WEARING EAR-PLUGS!
I'D NEVER HEARD OF BUZZWORD BEFORE TONIGHT--
WUMP
THAP
--BUT SHE'S NO ONE-TRICK WONDER--
OUFF!
NOW--SUPPOSE YOU TELL ME WHAT THIS AMBUSH IS ALL ABOUT?
UH-OH! ALMOST FORGOT THE CREEP BEHIND ME--
DRUB

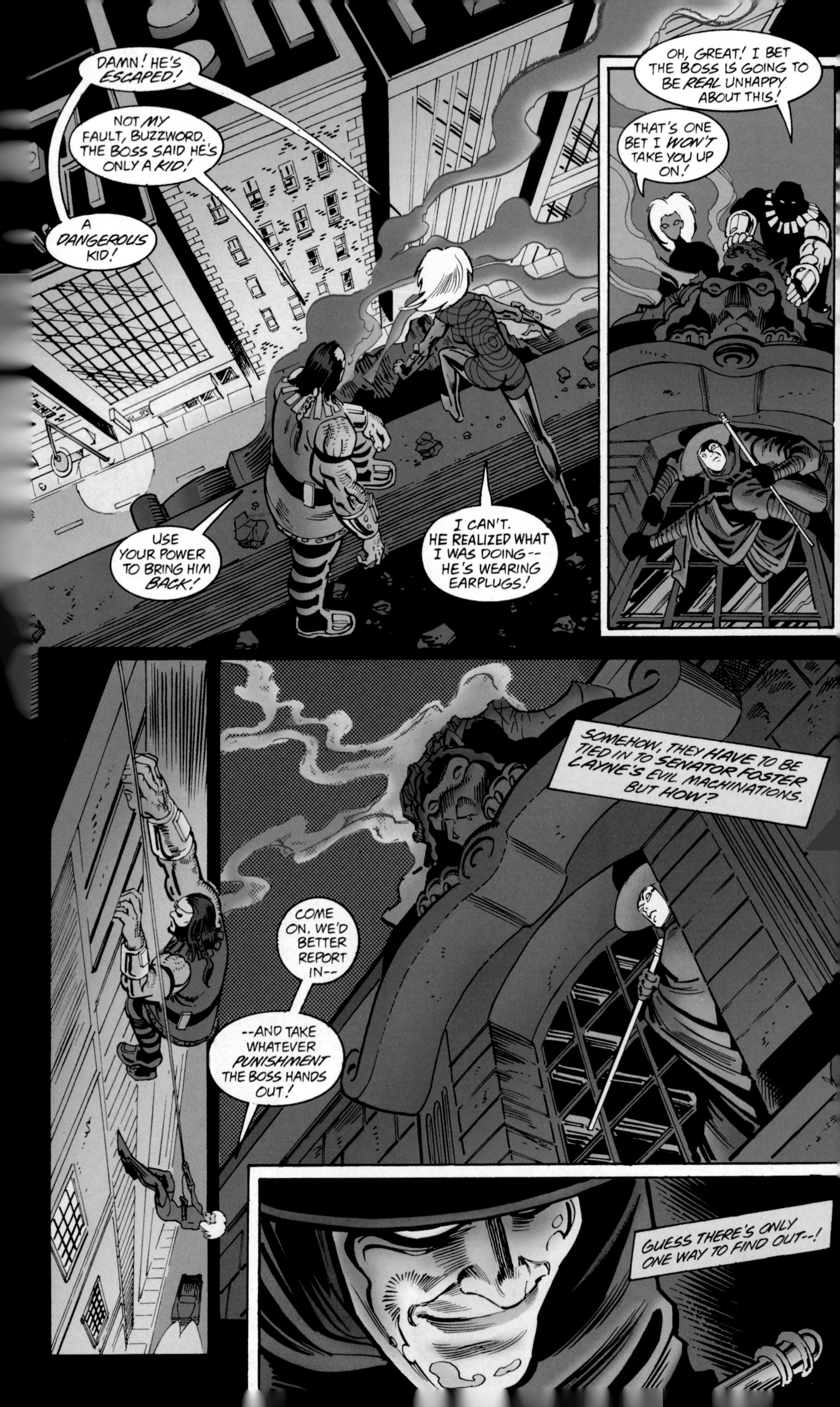
DAMN! HE'S ESCAPED!
NOT MY FAULT, BUZZWORD. THE BOSS SAID HE'S ONLY A KID!
A DANGEROUS KID!
USE YOUR POWER TO BRING HIM BACK!
I CAN'T. HE REALIZED WHAT I WAS DOING-- HE'S WEARING EARPLUGS!
OH, GREAT! I BET THE BOSS IS GOING TO BE REAL UNHAPPY ABOUT THIS!
THAT'S ONE BET I WON'T TAKE YOU UP ON!
SOMEHOW, THEY HAVE TO BE TIED IN TO SENATOR FOSTER LAYNE'S EVIL MACHINATIONS. BUT HOW?
COME ON. WE'D BETTER REPORT IN--
--AND TAKE WHATEVER PUNISHMENT THE BOSS HANDS OUT!
GUESS THERE'S ONLY ONE WAY TO FIND OUT--!

I DON'T *BELIEVE* THIS, DERWENT!

A SIMPLE HANDOVER-- AND *YOU!* LOUSED THE WHOLE THING UP!

IT WASN'T *ME*, SENATOR! SOME *COSTUMED HERO* MUSCLED IN ON US!

WITH A BIG *A-SYMBOL* ON HIS CHEST?

THAT'S *HIM!*

DAMN! HE CAME *HERE* FIRST --TO WARN ME, HE SAID. HE MUST HAVE BUGGED MY PHONE. GET SOMEBODY IN HERE TO MAKE A *SWEEP!*

THE SENATOR NEEDS TWO AGENTS-- WITH CLEANING EQUIPMENT.

SO... OUR ASSOCIATES HAVE THE *CODES*-- BUT THE *CASH* WAS STOLEN BY SOME CRUMMY STREET KID?

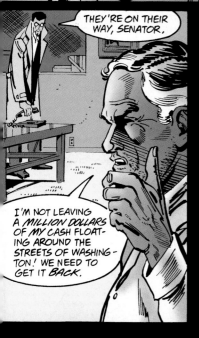

THEY'RE ON THEIR WAY, SENATOR.

I'M NOT LEAVING A *MILLION DOLLARS* OF MY CASH FLOATING AROUND THE STREETS OF WASHINGTON! WE NEED TO GET IT *BACK*.

IF ANYTHING *ELSE* GOES WRONG, WE SAY THE *VIGILANTE* STOLE THE CODES.

WHATEVER HAPPENS, WE BLAME IT ON *HIM!*

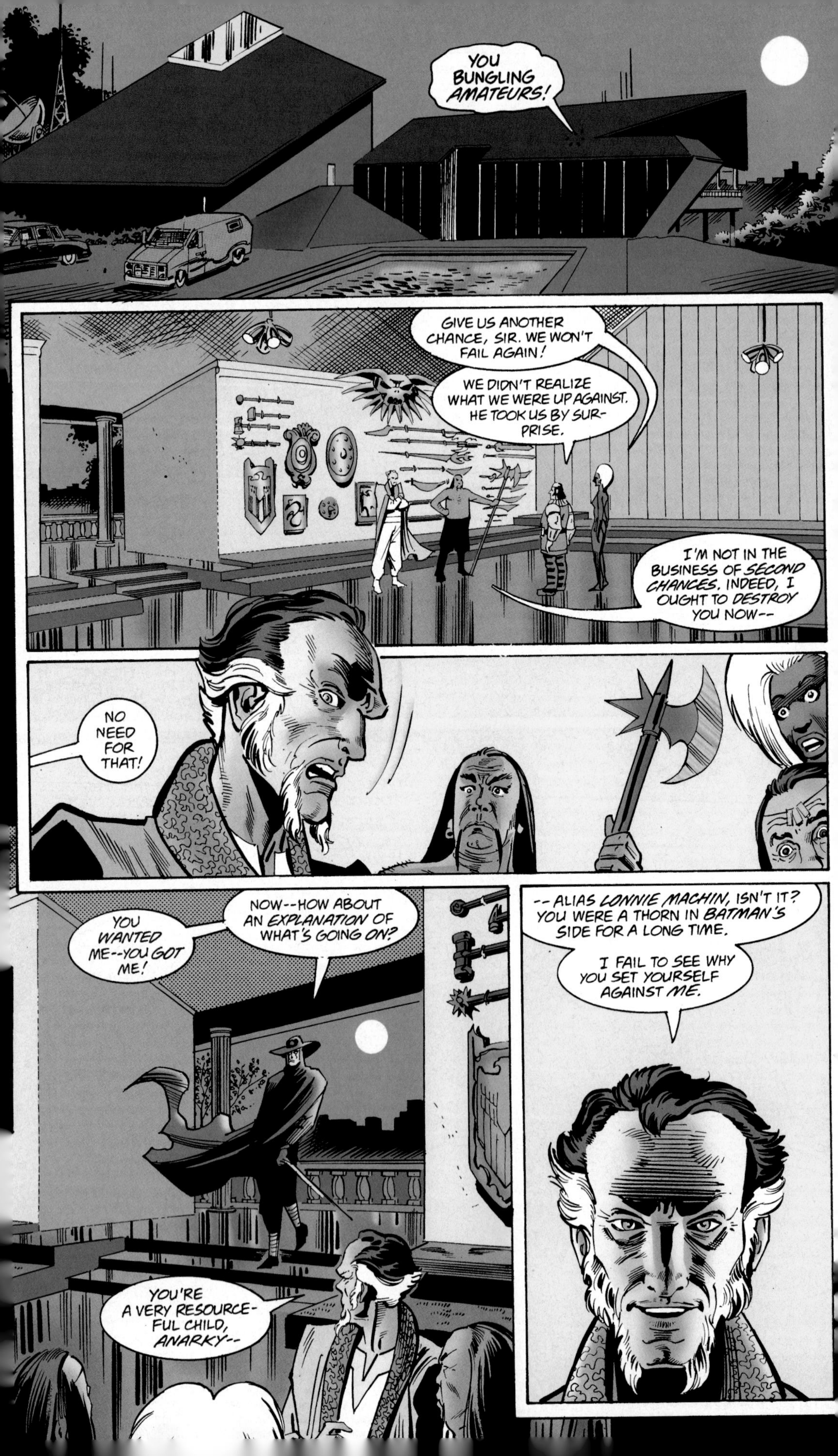
YOU BUNGLING AMATEURS!
GIVE US ANOTHER CHANCE, SIR. WE WON'T FAIL AGAIN!
WE DIDN'T REALIZE WHAT WE WERE UP AGAINST. HE TOOK US BY SURPRISE.
I'M NOT IN THE BUSINESS OF SECOND CHANCES. INDEED, I OUGHT TO DESTROY YOU NOW--
NO NEED FOR THAT!
YOU WANTED ME--YOU GOT ME!
NOW--HOW ABOUT AN EXPLANATION OF WHAT'S GOING ON?
YOU'RE A VERY RESOURCE-FUL CHILD, ANARKY--
--ALIAS LONNIE MACHIN, ISN'T IT? YOU WERE A THORN IN BATMAN'S SIDE FOR A LONG TIME.
I FAIL TO SEE WHY YOU SET YOURSELF AGAINST ME.

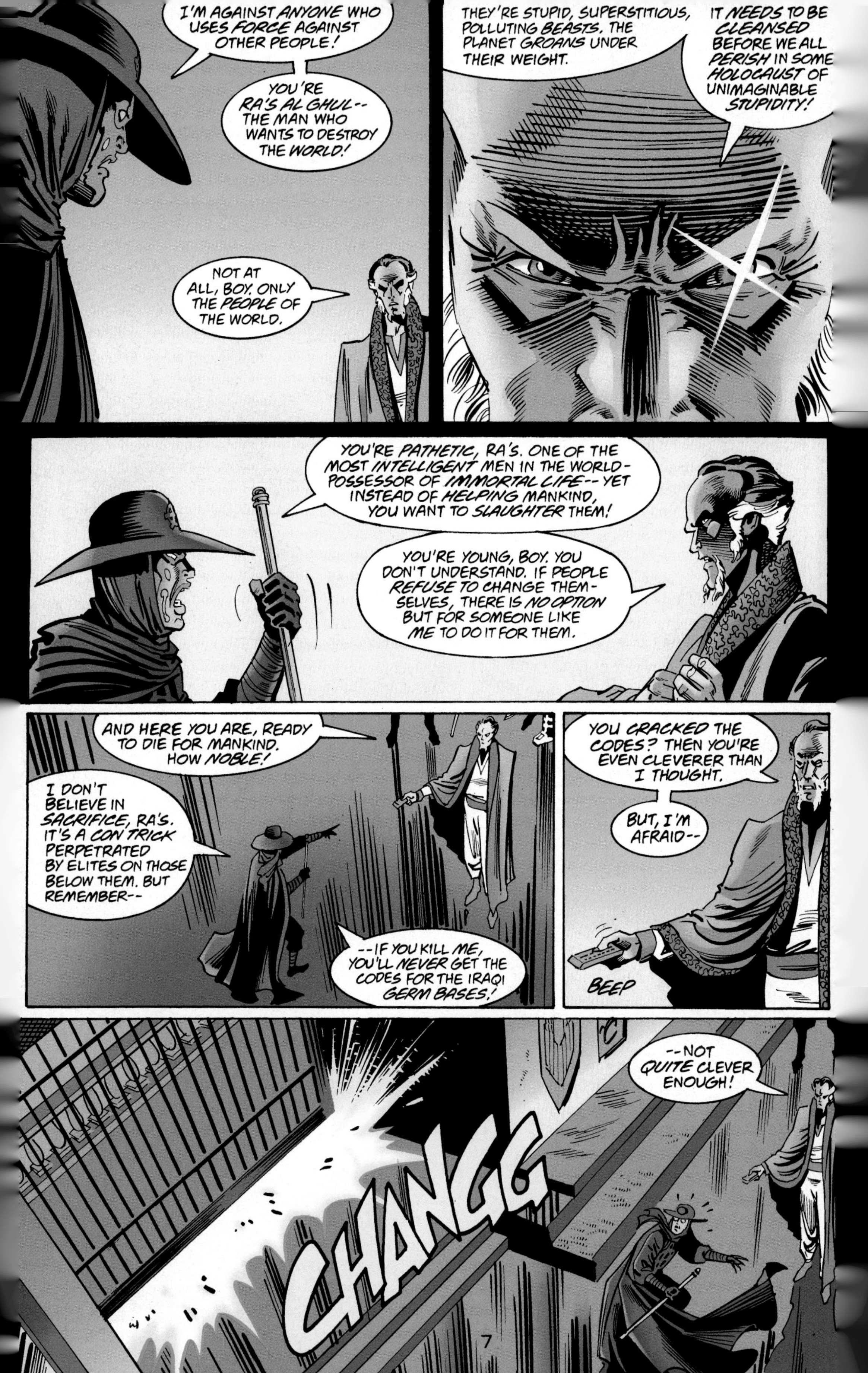
I'M AGAINST ANYONE WHO USES FORCE AGAINST OTHER PEOPLE!
YOU'RE RA'S AL GHUL-- THE MAN WHO WANTS TO DESTROY THE WORLD!
NOT AT ALL, BOY. ONLY THE PEOPLE OF THE WORLD.
THEY'RE STUPID, SUPERSTITIOUS, POLLUTING BEASTS. THE PLANET GROANS UNDER THEIR WEIGHT.
IT NEEDS TO BE CLEANSED BEFORE WE ALL PERISH IN SOME HOLOCAUST OF UNIMAGINABLE STUPIDITY!
YOU'RE PATHETIC, RA'S. ONE OF THE MOST INTELLIGENT MEN IN THE WORLD-POSSESSOR OF IMMORTAL LIFE-- YET INSTEAD OF HELPING MANKIND, YOU WANT TO SLAUGHTER THEM!
YOU'RE YOUNG, BOY. YOU DON'T UNDERSTAND. IF PEOPLE REFUSE TO CHANGE THEM-SELVES, THERE IS NO OPTION BUT FOR SOMEONE LIKE ME TO DO IT FOR THEM.
AND HERE YOU ARE, READY TO DIE FOR MANKIND. HOW NOBLE!
I DON'T BELIEVE IN SACRIFICE, RA'S. IT'S A CON TRICK PERPETRATED BY ELITES ON THOSE BELOW THEM. BUT REMEMBER--
--IF YOU KILL ME, YOU'LL NEVER GET THE CODES FOR THE IRAQI GERM BASES!
YOU CRACKED THE CODES? THEN YOU'RE EVEN CLEVERER THAN I THOUGHT.
BUT, I'M AFRAID--
BEEP
--NOT QUITE CLEVER ENOUGH!
CHANGG

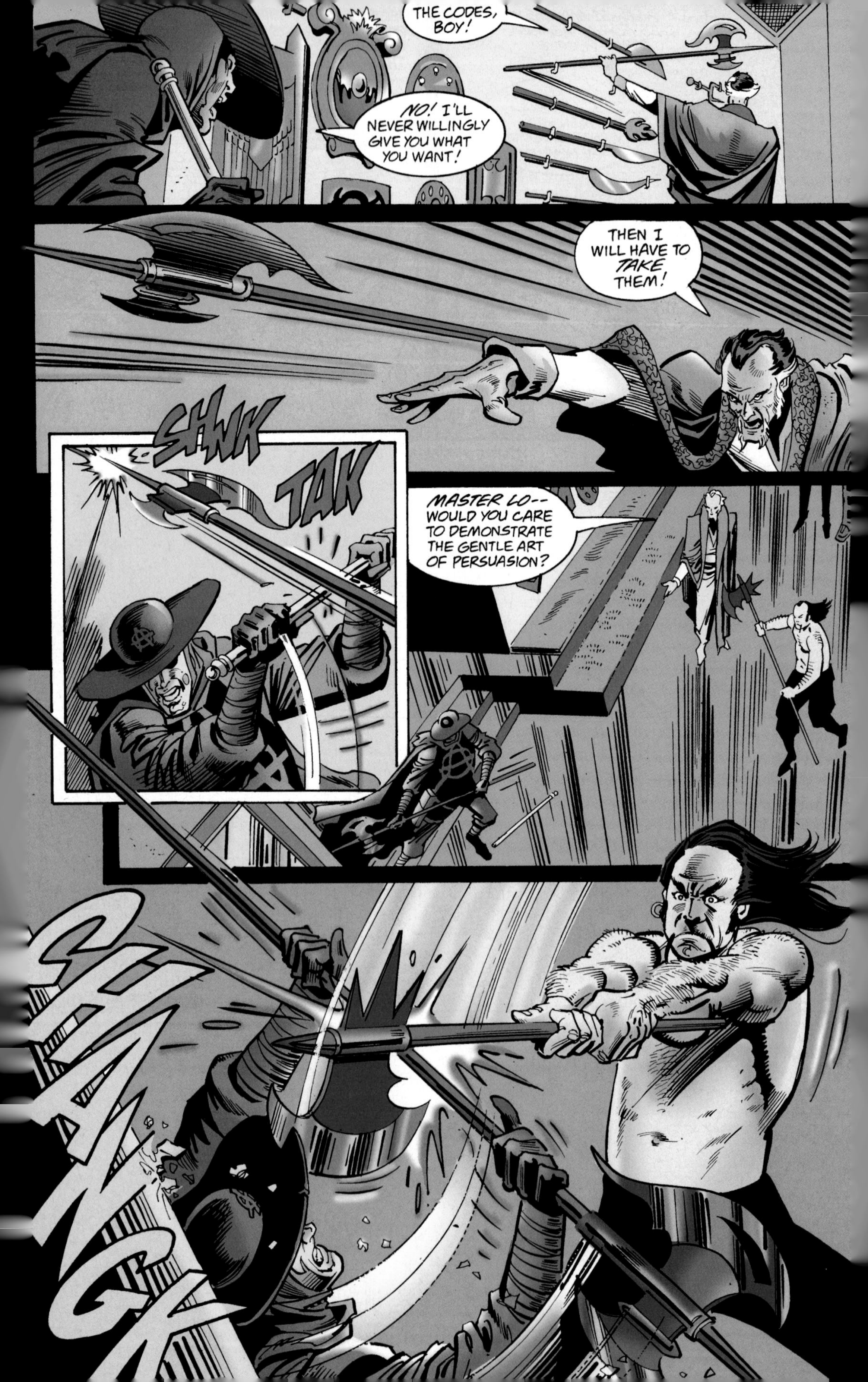
THE CODES, BOY!
NO! I'LL NEVER WILLINGLY GIVE YOU WHAT YOU WANT!
THEN I WILL HAVE TO TAKE THEM!
SHNK
TAK
MASTER LO-- WOULD YOU CARE TO DEMONSTRATE THE GENTLE ART OF PERSUASION?
CHANGK

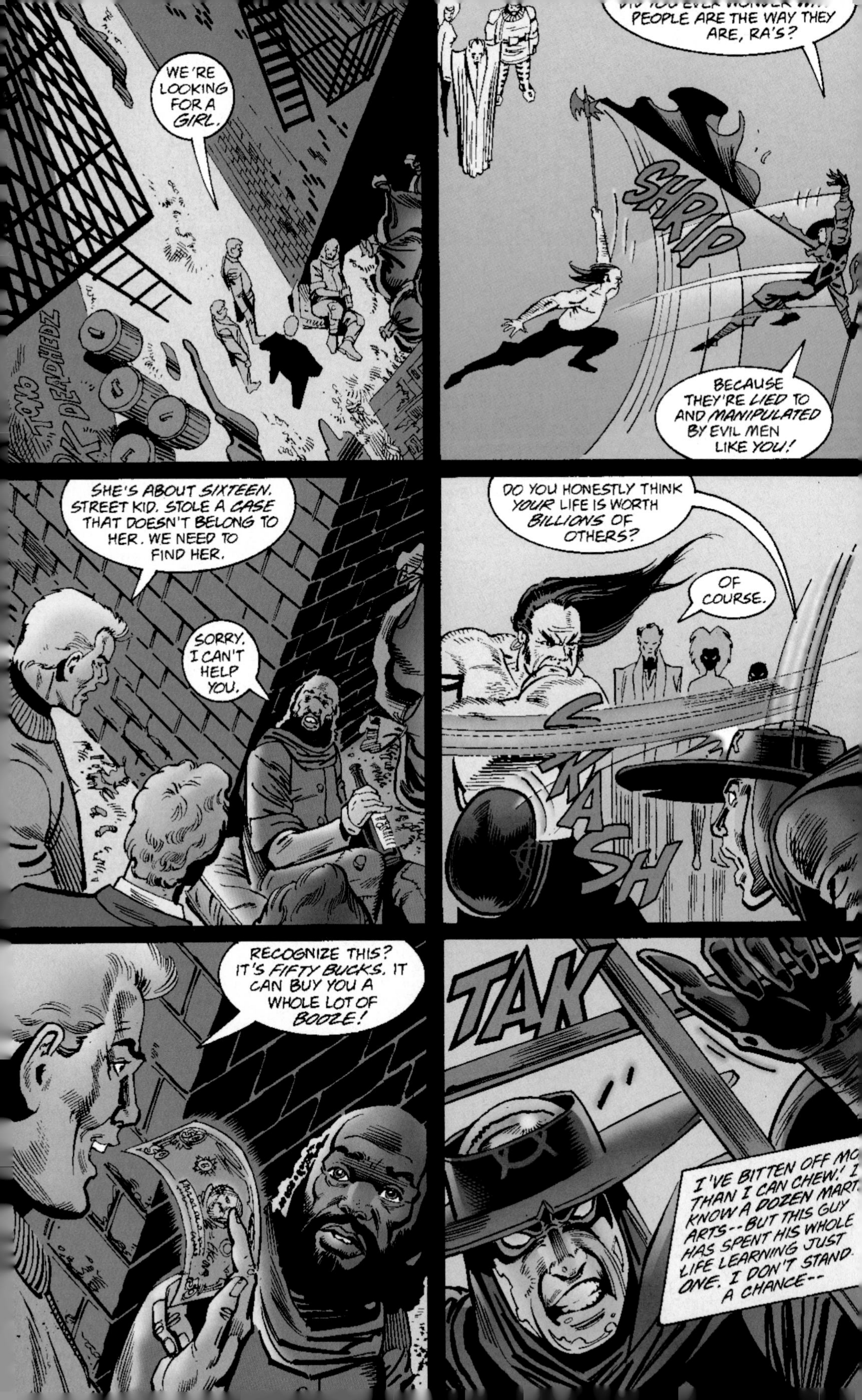
WE'RE LOOKING FOR A *GIRL*.
PEOPLE ARE THE WAY THEY ARE, RA'S?
SHRIP
BECAUSE THEY'RE *LIED* TO AND *MANIPULATED* BY EVIL MEN LIKE *YOU!*
SHE'S ABOUT *SIXTEEN*. STREET KID. STOLE A *CASE* THAT DOESN'T BELONG TO HER. WE NEED TO FIND HER.
SORRY. I CAN'T HELP YOU.
DO YOU HONESTLY THINK *YOUR* LIFE IS WORTH *BILLIONS* OF OTHERS?
OF COURSE.
KASH
RECOGNIZE THIS? IT'S *FIFTY BUCKS*. IT CAN BUY YOU A WHOLE LOT OF *BOOZE!*
TAK
I'VE BITTEN OFF MO THAN I CAN CHEW! I KNOW A DOZEN MART ARTS--BUT THIS GUY HAS SPENT HIS WHOLE LIFE LEARNING JUST ONE. I DON'T STAND A CHANCE--

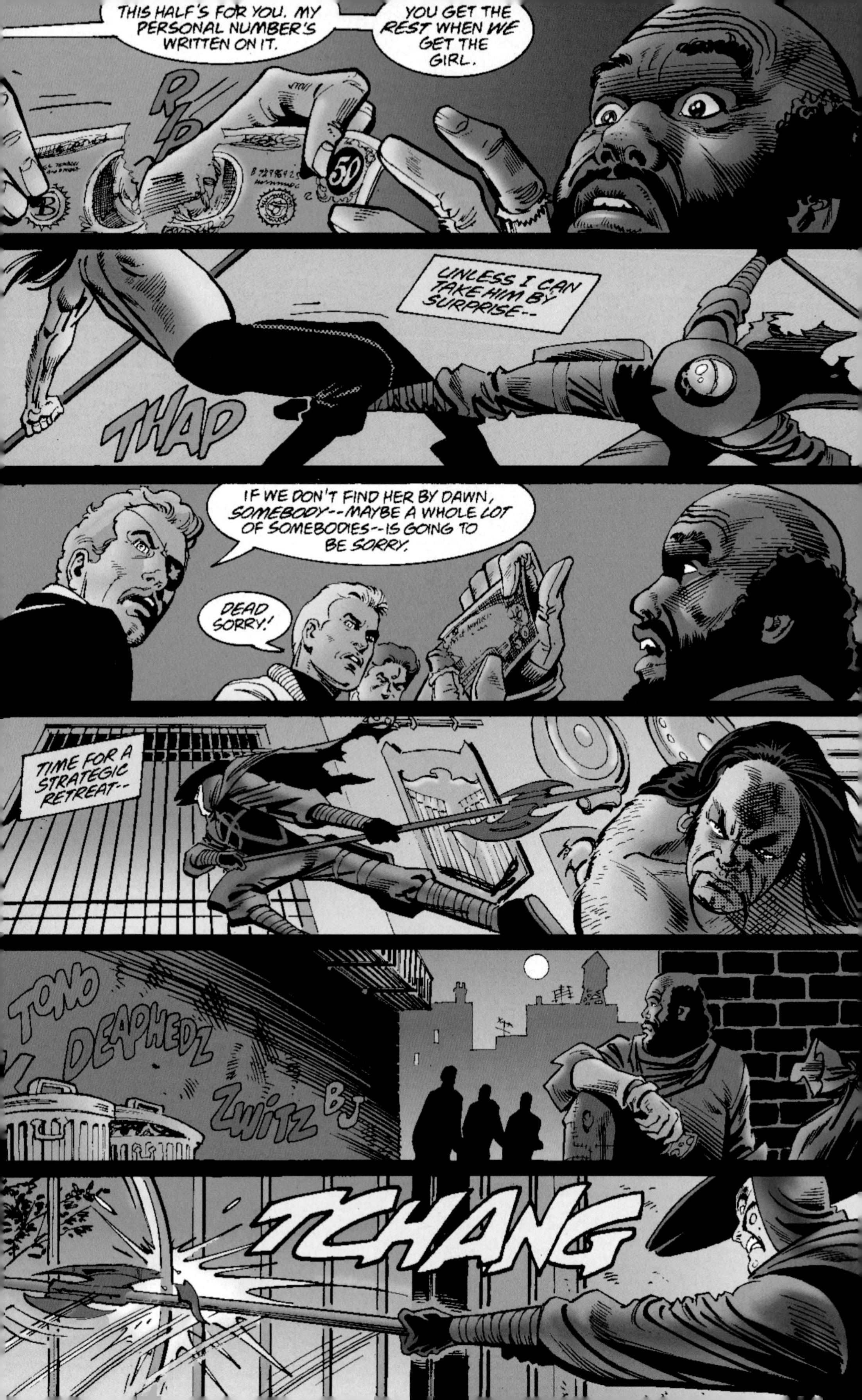
THIS HALF'S FOR YOU. MY PERSONAL NUMBER'S WRITTEN ON IT.
YOU GET THE REST WHEN WE GET THE GIRL.
RIP
UNLESS I CAN TAKE HIM BY SURPRISE--
THAP
IF WE DON'T FIND HER BY DAWN, SOMEBODY--MAYBE A WHOLE LOT OF SOMEBODIES--IS GOING TO BE SORRY.
DEAD SORRY!
TIME FOR A STRATEGIC RETREAT--
TONO
DEAPHEDZ
ZWITZ
BJ
TCHANG

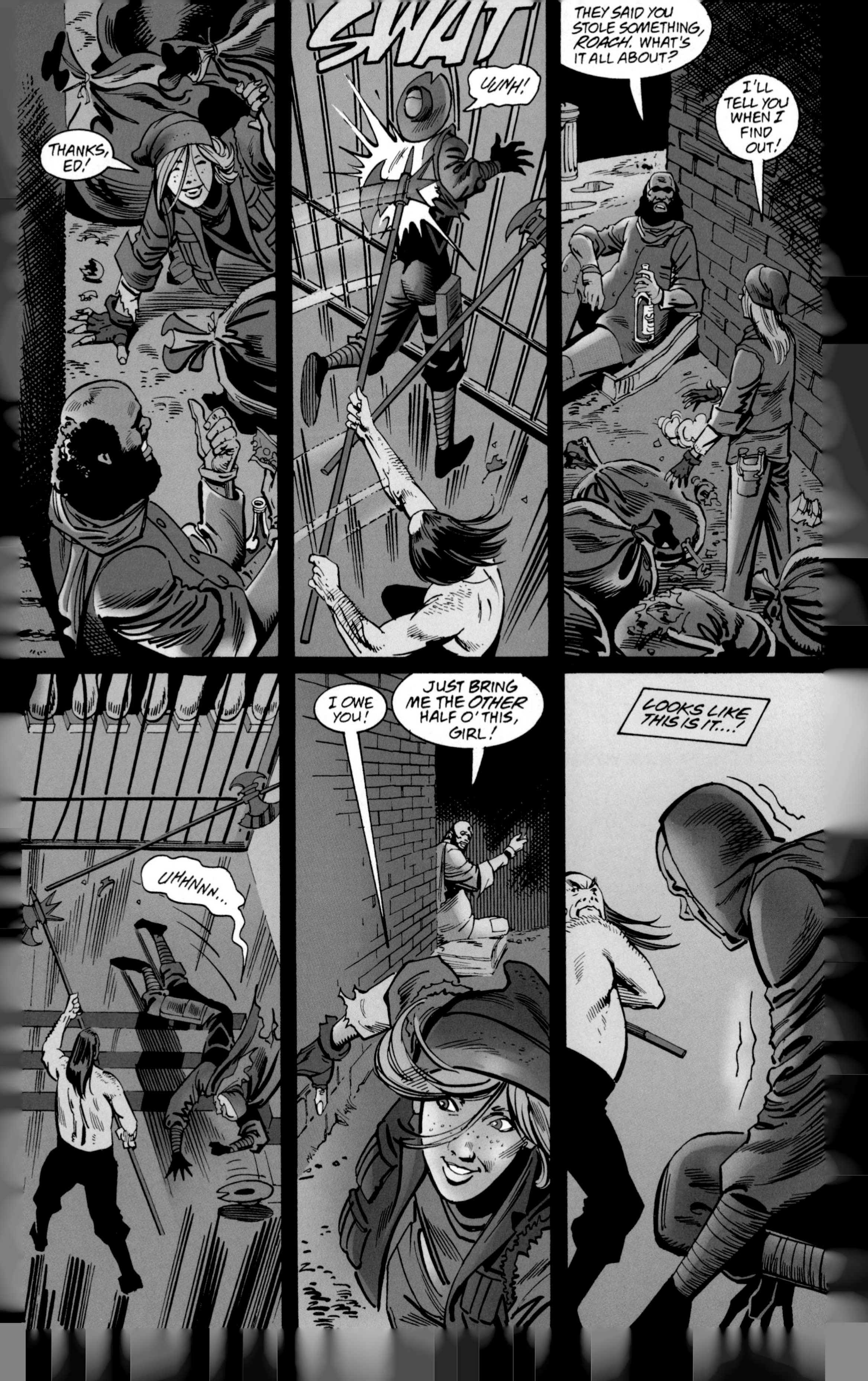

THANKS, ED!
SWAT
UUNH!
THEY SAID YOU STOLE SOMETHING, ROACH. WHAT'S IT ALL ABOUT?
I'LL TELL YOU WHEN I FIND OUT!
UHHNNN...
I OWE YOU!
JUST BRING ME THE OTHER HALF O' THIS, GIRL!
LOOKS LIKE THIS IS IT...!

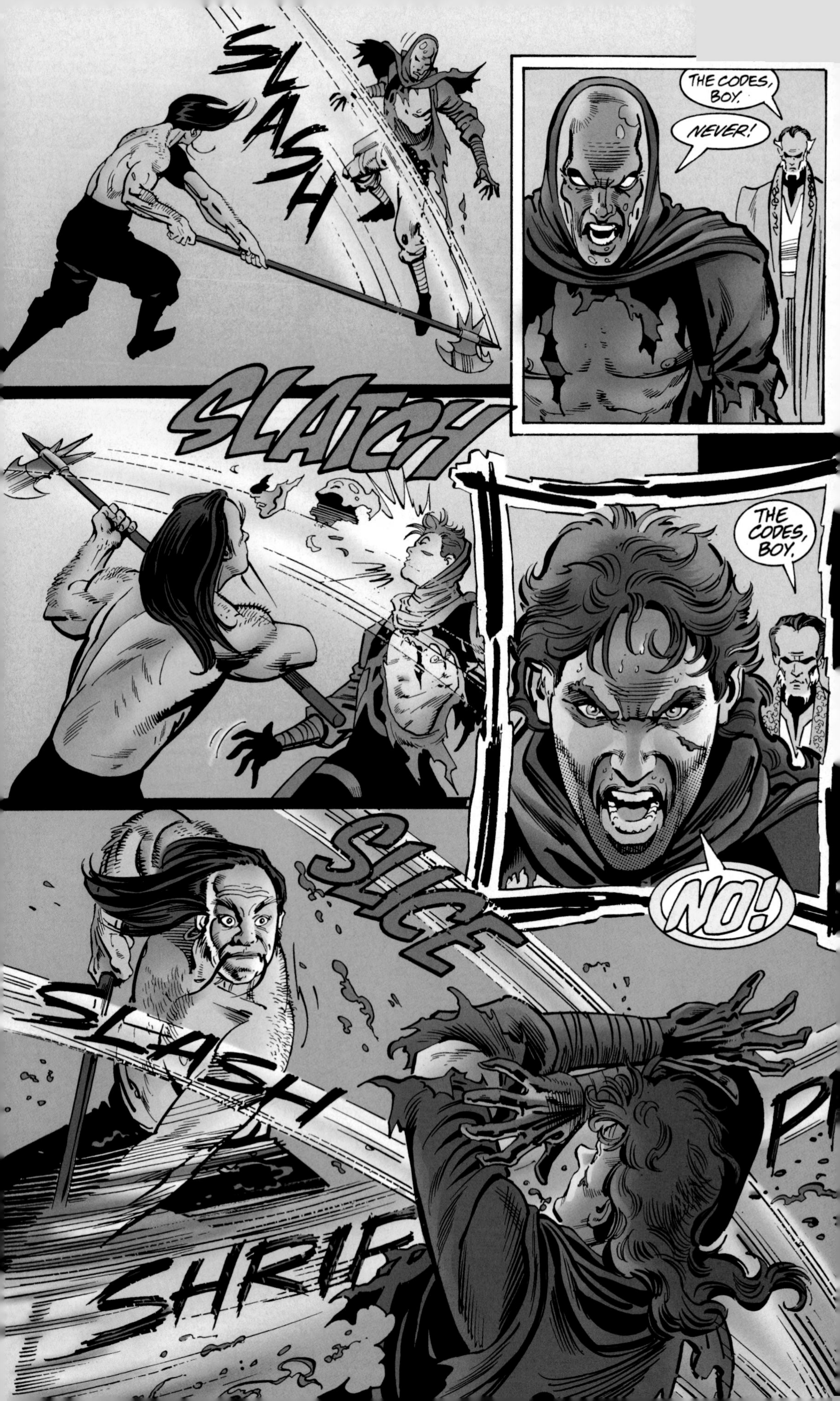

SLASH
THE CODES, BOY.
NEVER!
SLATCH
THE CODES, BOY.
NO!
SLICE
SLASH
SHRIE

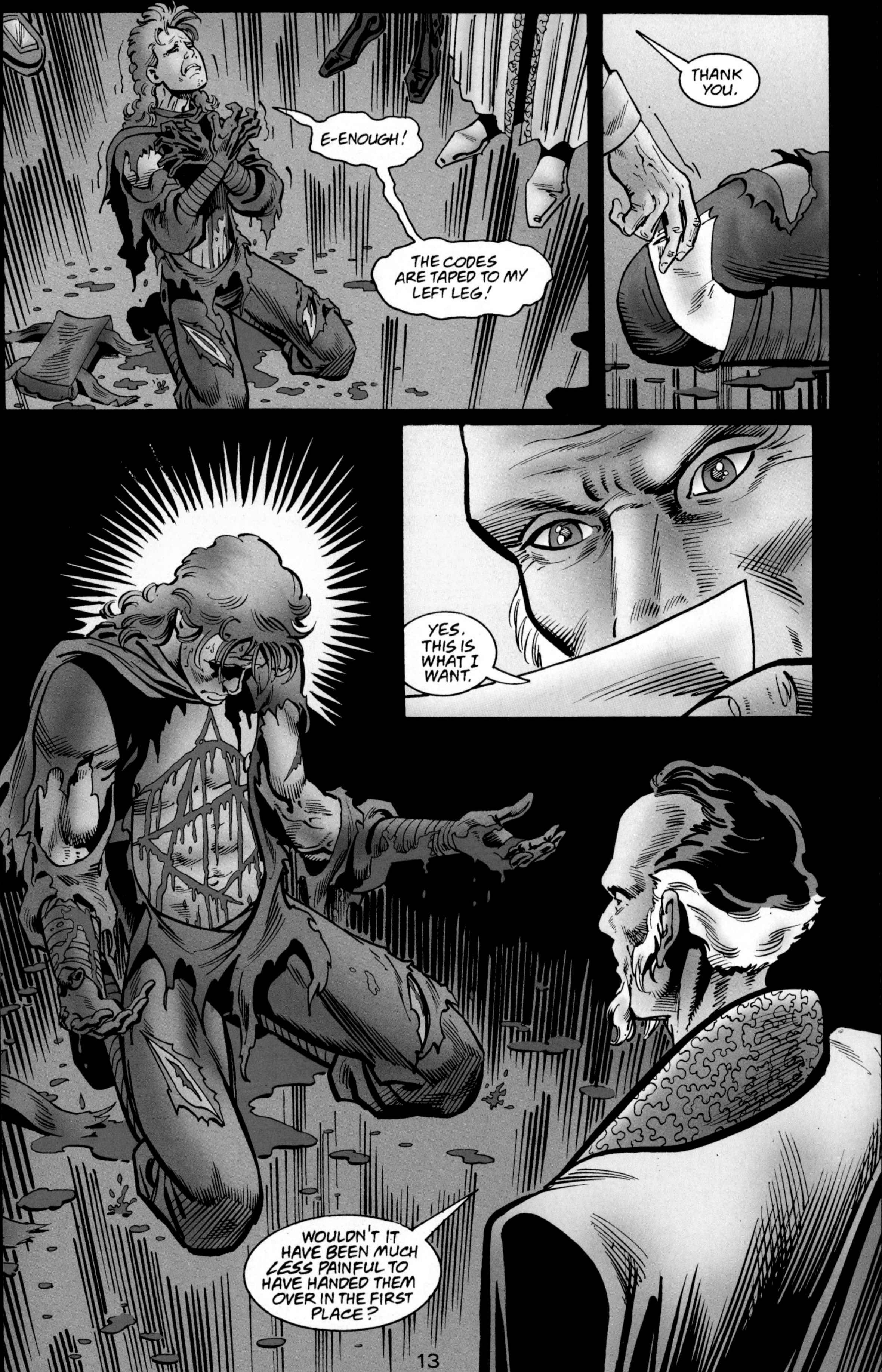
E-ENOUGH!
THE CODES ARE TAPED TO MY LEFT LEG!
THANK YOU.
YES. THIS IS WHAT I WANT.
WOULDN'T IT HAVE BEEN MUCH LESS PAINFUL TO HAVE HANDED THEM OVER IN THE FIRST PLACE?

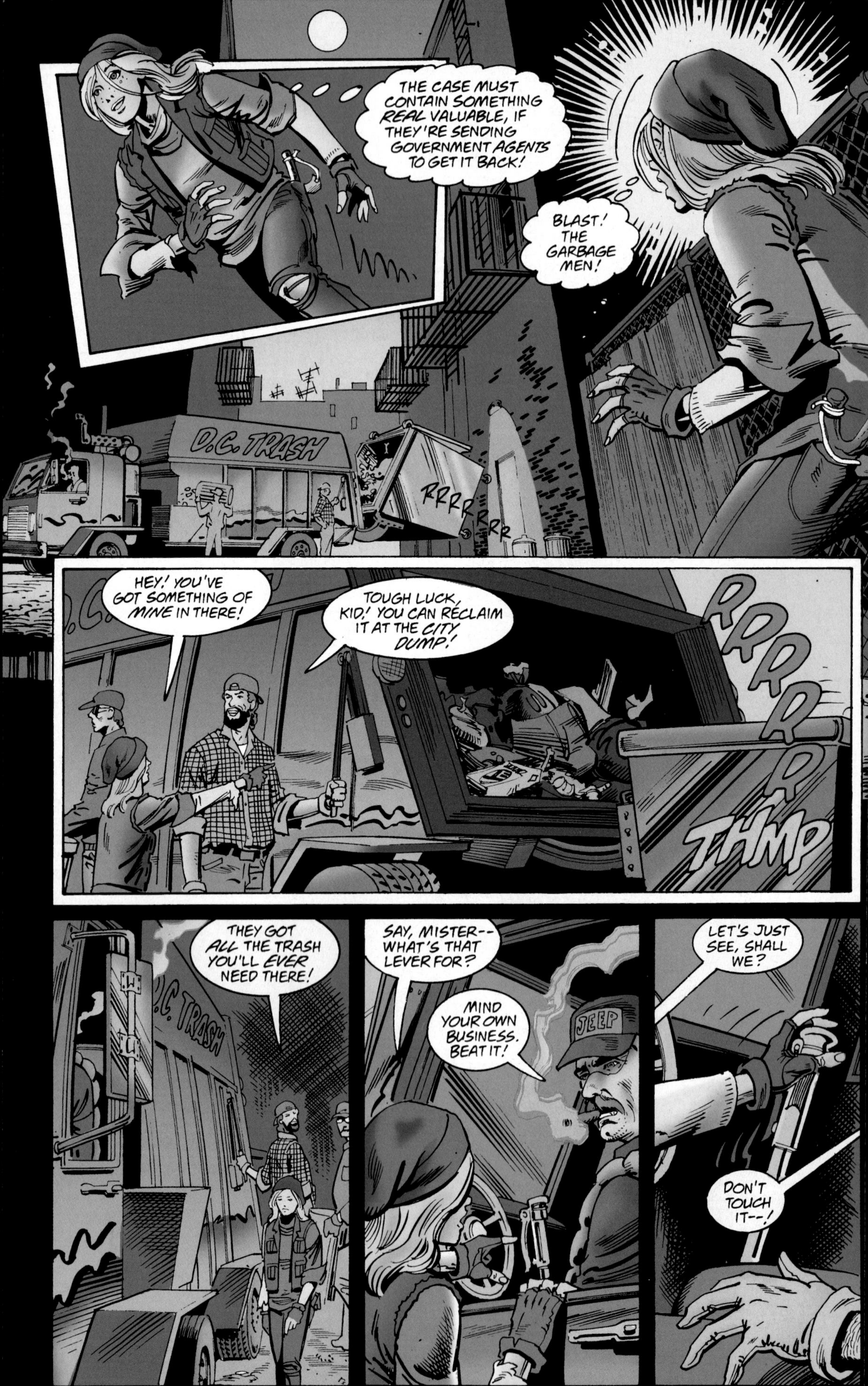
THE CASE MUST CONTAIN SOMETHING REAL VALUABLE, IF THEY'RE SENDING GOVERNMENT AGENTS TO GET IT BACK!
BLAST! THE GARBAGE MEN!
D.C. TRASH
RRRRRRR
HEY! YOU'VE GOT SOMETHING OF MINE IN THERE!
TOUGH LUCK, KID! YOU CAN RECLAIM IT AT THE CITY DUMP!
RRRRRR
THMP
THEY GOT ALL THE TRASH YOU'LL EVER NEED THERE!
D.C. TRASH
SAY, MISTER-- WHAT'S THAT LEVER FOR?
MIND YOUR OWN BUSINESS. BEAT IT!
JEEP
LET'S JUST SEE, SHALL WE?
DON'T TOUCH IT--!

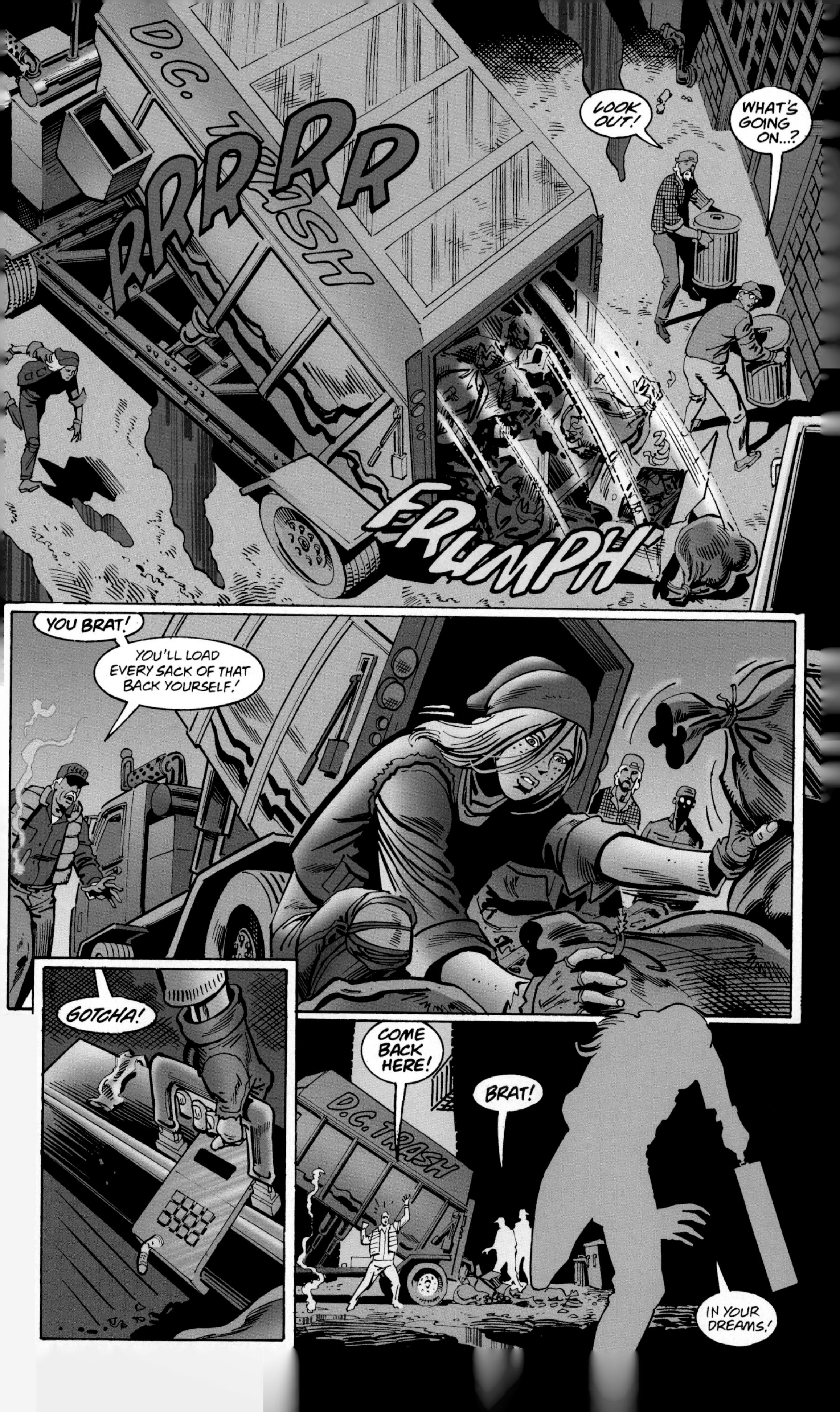
RRRRR
D.C. TRASH
LOOK OUT!
WHAT'S GOING ON...?
FRUMPH
YOU BRAT!
YOU'LL LOAD EVERY SACK OF THAT BACK YOURSELF!
GOTCHA!
COME BACK HERE!
D.C. TRASH
BRAT!
IN YOUR DREAMS!

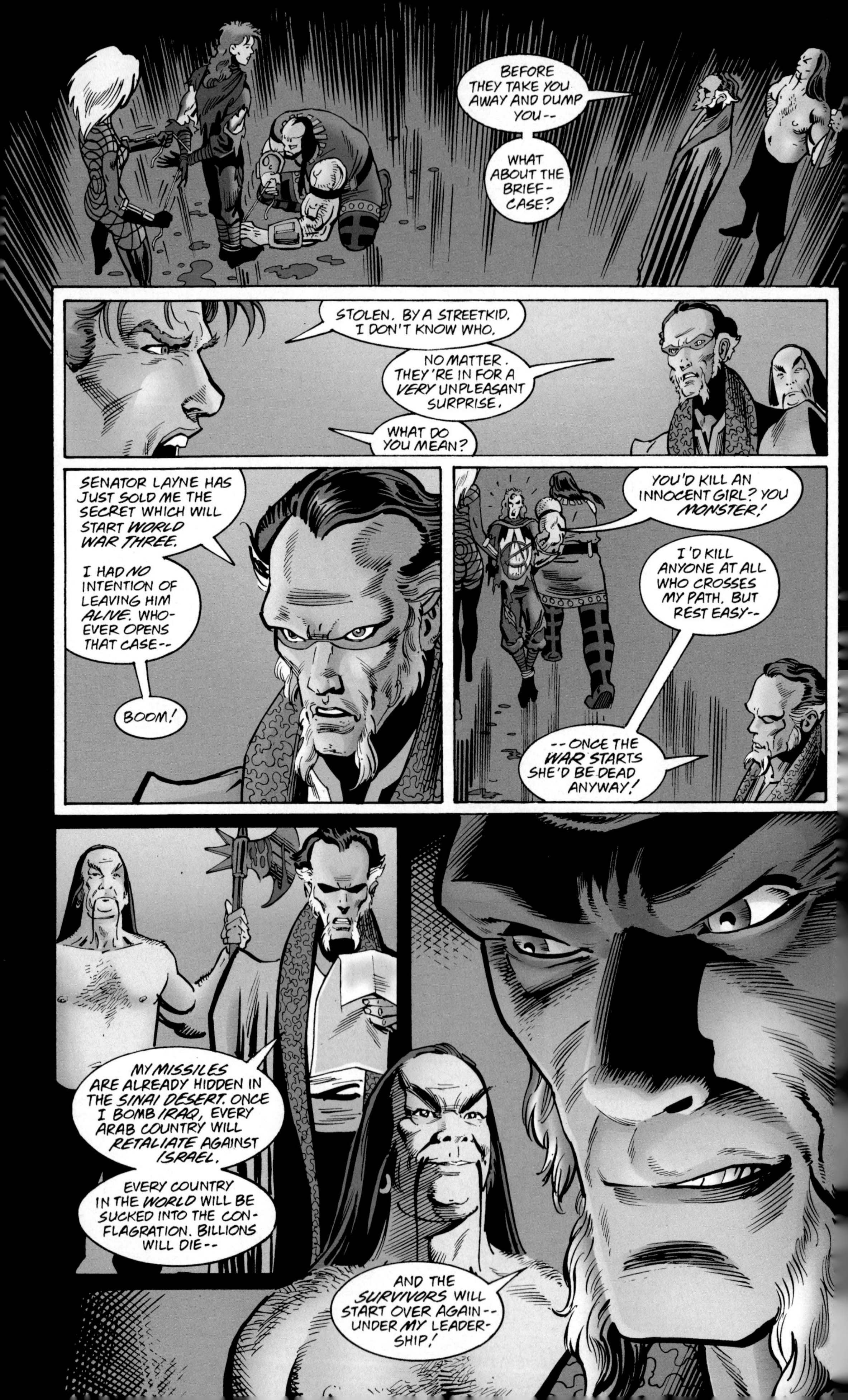
BEFORE THEY TAKE YOU AWAY AND DUMP YOU--
WHAT ABOUT THE BRIEF-CASE?
STOLEN. BY A STREETKID. I DON'T KNOW WHO.
NO MATTER. THEY'RE IN FOR A VERY UNPLEASANT SURPRISE.
WHAT DO YOU MEAN?
SENATOR LAYNE HAS JUST SOLD ME THE SECRET WHICH WILL START WORLD WAR THREE.
I HAD NO INTENTION OF LEAVING HIM ALIVE. WHO-EVER OPENS THAT CASE--
BOOM!
YOU'D KILL AN INNOCENT GIRL? YOU MONSTER!
I'D KILL ANYONE AT ALL WHO CROSSES MY PATH. BUT REST EASY--
--ONCE THE WAR STARTS SHE'D BE DEAD ANYWAY!
MY MISSILES ARE ALREADY HIDDEN IN THE SINAI DESERT. ONCE I BOMB IRAQ, EVERY ARAB COUNTRY WILL RETALIATE AGAINST ISRAEL.
EVERY COUNTRY IN THE WORLD WILL BE SUCKED INTO THE CON-FLAGRATION. BILLIONS WILL DIE--
AND THE SURVIVORS WILL START OVER AGAIN--UNDER MY LEADER-SHIP!

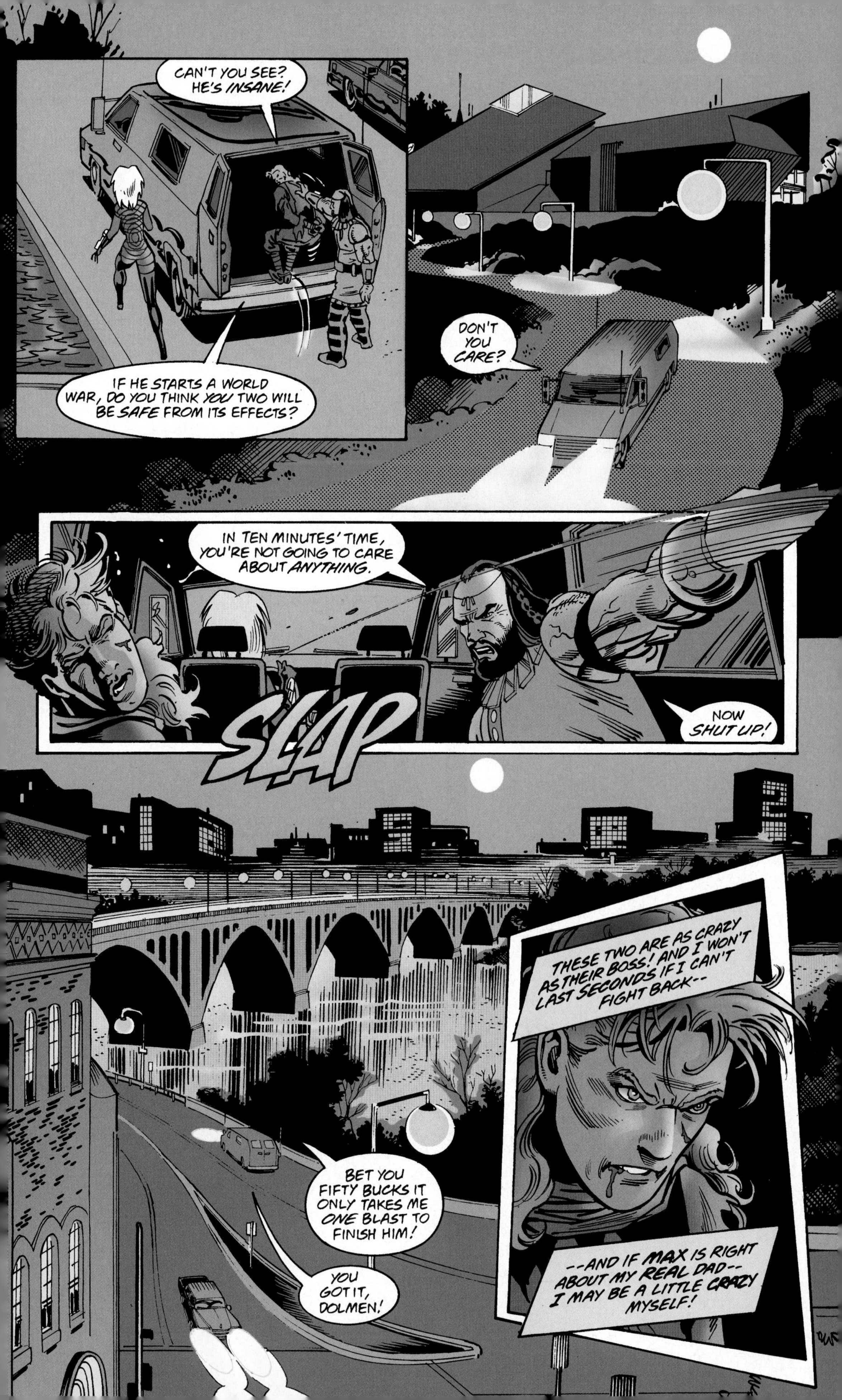

CAN'T YOU SEE? HE'S INSANE!
IF HE STARTS A WORLD WAR, DO YOU THINK YOU TWO WILL BE SAFE FROM ITS EFFECTS?
DON'T YOU CARE?
IN TEN MINUTES' TIME, YOU'RE NOT GOING TO CARE ABOUT ANYTHING.
SLAP
NOW SHUT UP!
BET YOU FIFTY BUCKS IT ONLY TAKES ME ONE BLAST TO FINISH HIM!
YOU GOT IT, DOLMEN!
THESE TWO ARE AS CRAZY AS THEIR BOSS! AND I WON'T LAST SECONDS IF I CAN'T FIGHT BACK--
--AND IF MAX IS RIGHT ABOUT MY REAL DAD-- I MAY BE A LITTLE CRAZY MYSELF!

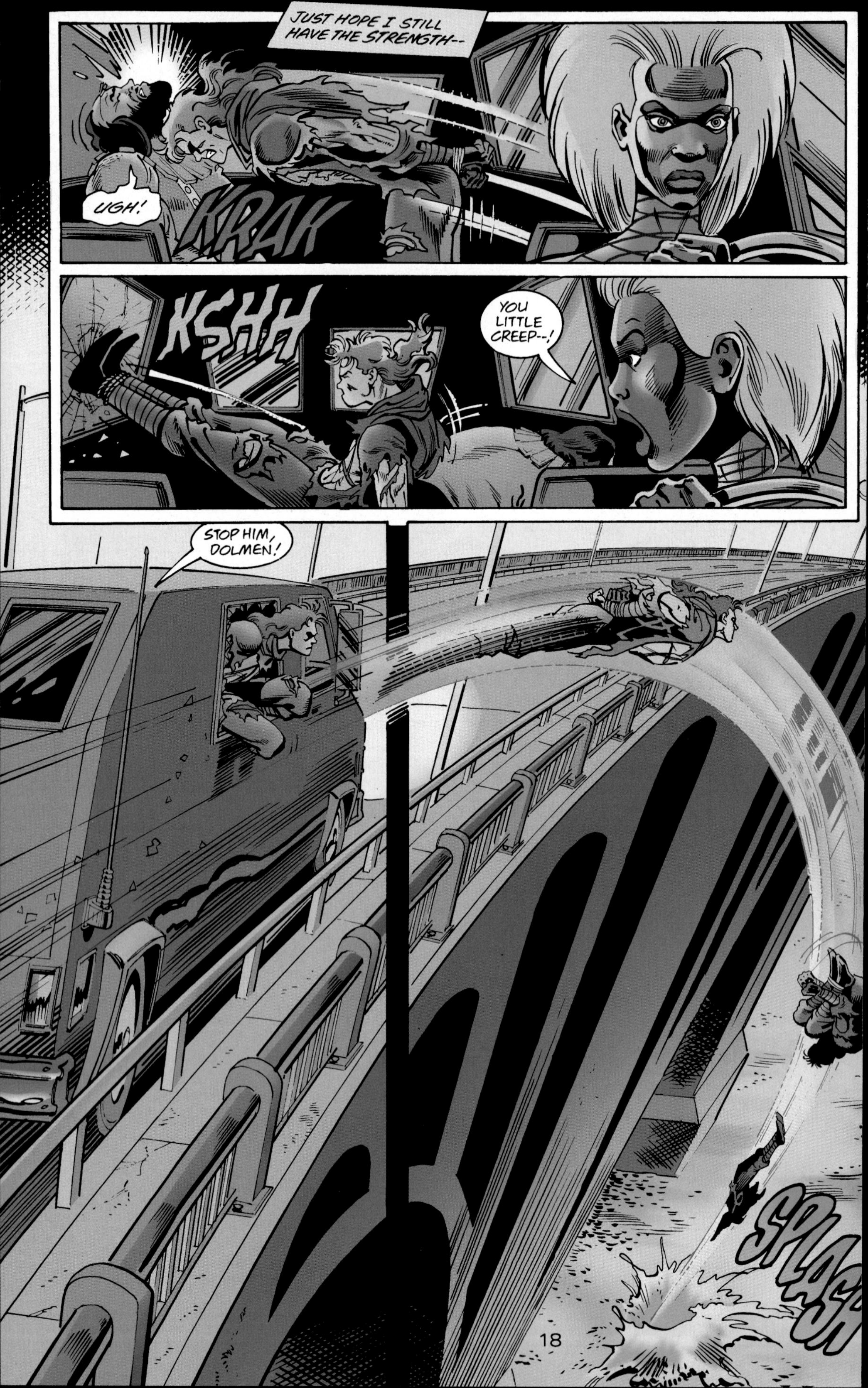
JUST HOPE I STILL HAVE THE STRENGTH--
UGH!
KRAK
KSHH
YOU LITTLE CREEP--!
STOP HIM, DOLMEN!
SPLASH

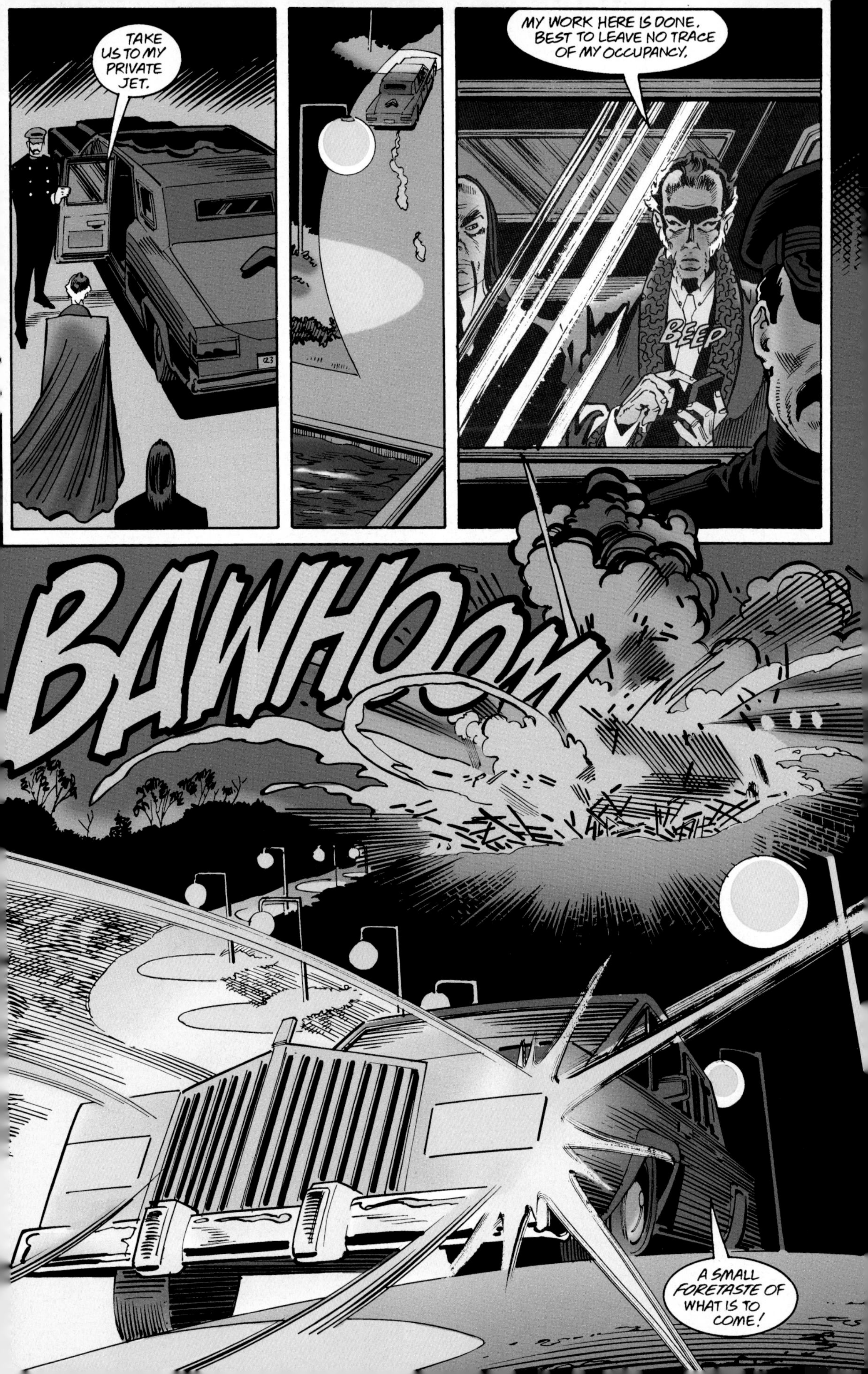
TAKE US TO MY PRIVATE JET.
MY WORK HERE IS DONE. BEST TO LEAVE NO TRACE OF MY OCCUPANCY.
BEEP
BAWHOOM
A SMALL FORETASTE OF WHAT IS TO COME!

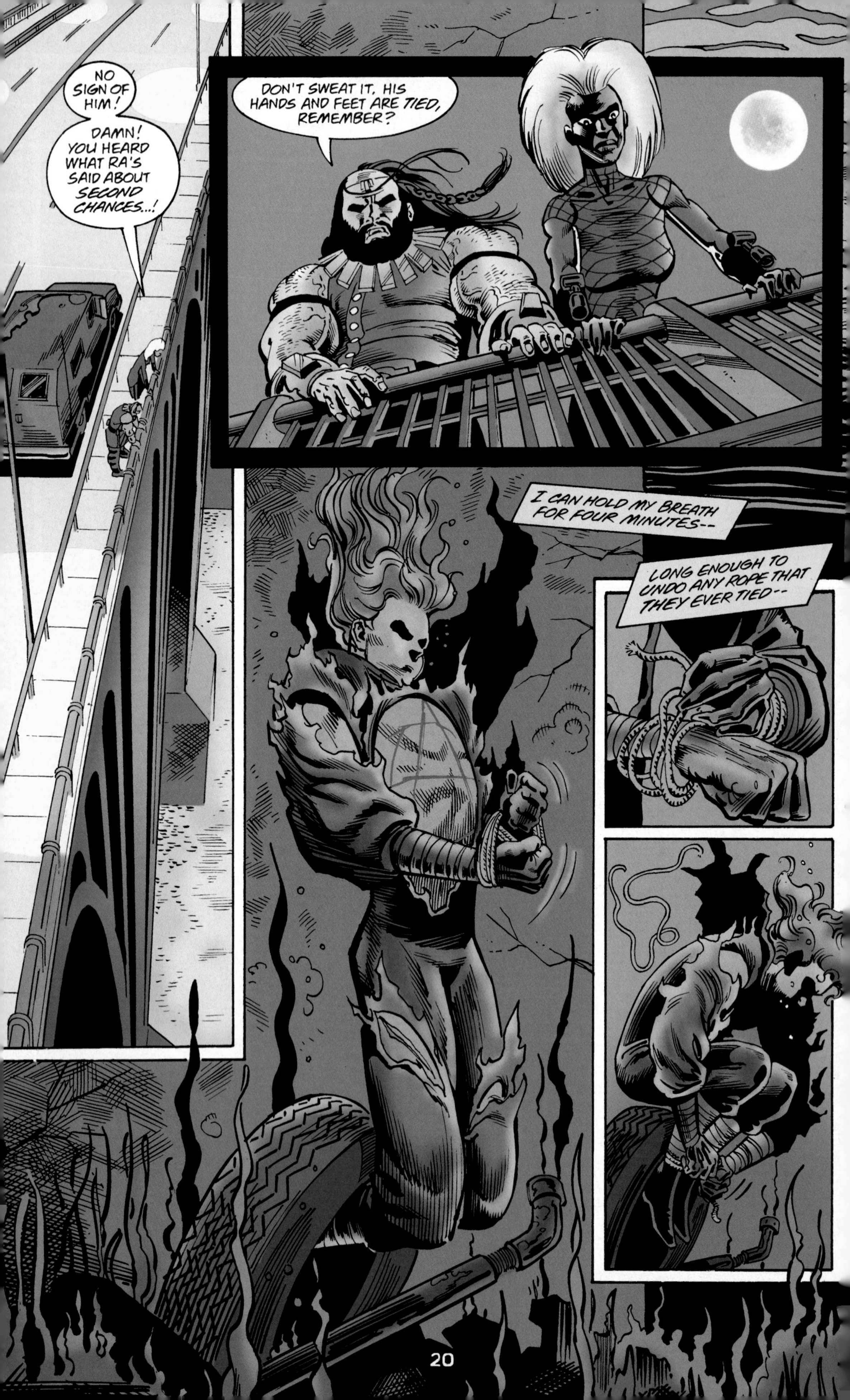
NO SIGN OF HIM!
DAMN! YOU HEARD WHAT RA'S SAID ABOUT SECOND CHANCES...!
DON'T SWEAT IT, HIS HANDS AND FEET ARE TIED, REMEMBER?
I CAN HOLD MY BREATH FOR FOUR MINUTES--
LONG ENOUGH TO UNDO ANY ROPE THAT THEY EVER TIED--

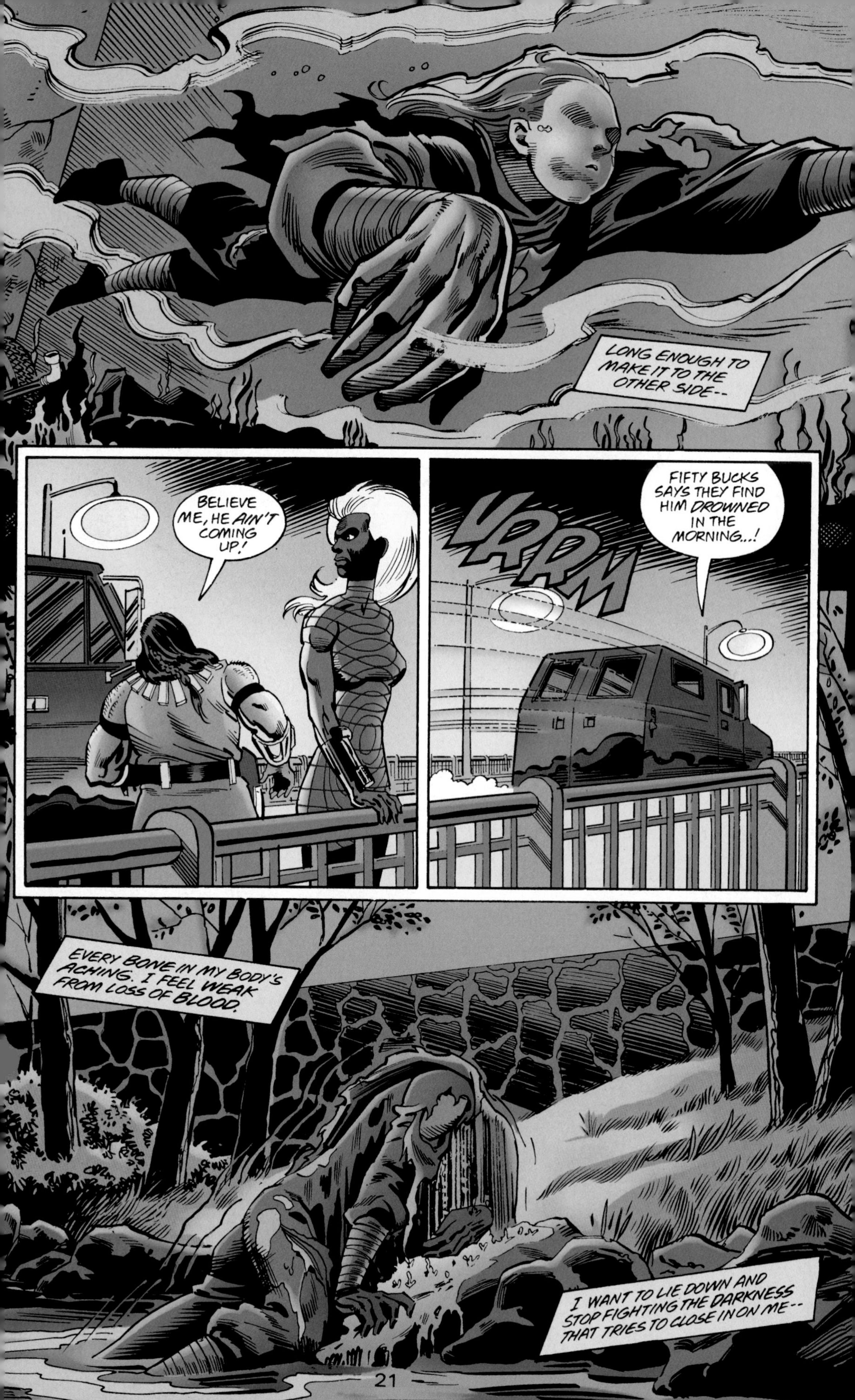
LONG ENOUGH TO MAKE IT TO THE OTHER SIDE--
BELIEVE ME, HE AIN'T COMING UP!
URRM
FIFTY BUCKS SAYS THEY FIND HIM DROWNED IN THE MORNING...!
EVERY BONE IN MY BODY'S ACHING. I FEEL WEAK FROM LOSS OF BLOOD.
I WANT TO LIE DOWN AND STOP FIGHTING THE DARKNESS THAT TRIES TO CLOSE IN ON ME--

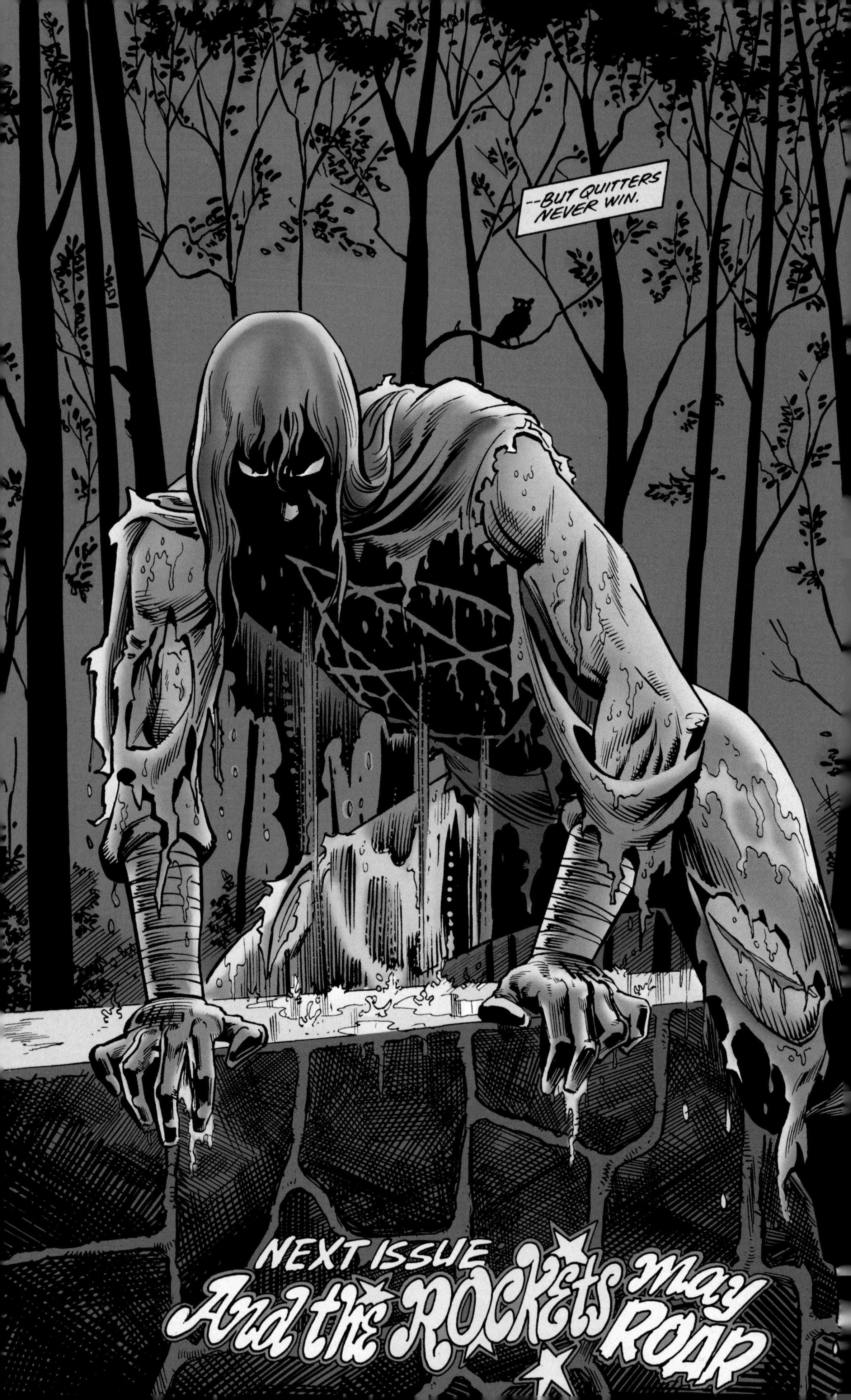
--BUT QUITTERS NEVER WIN.
NEXT ISSUE
And the ROCKETS may ROAR

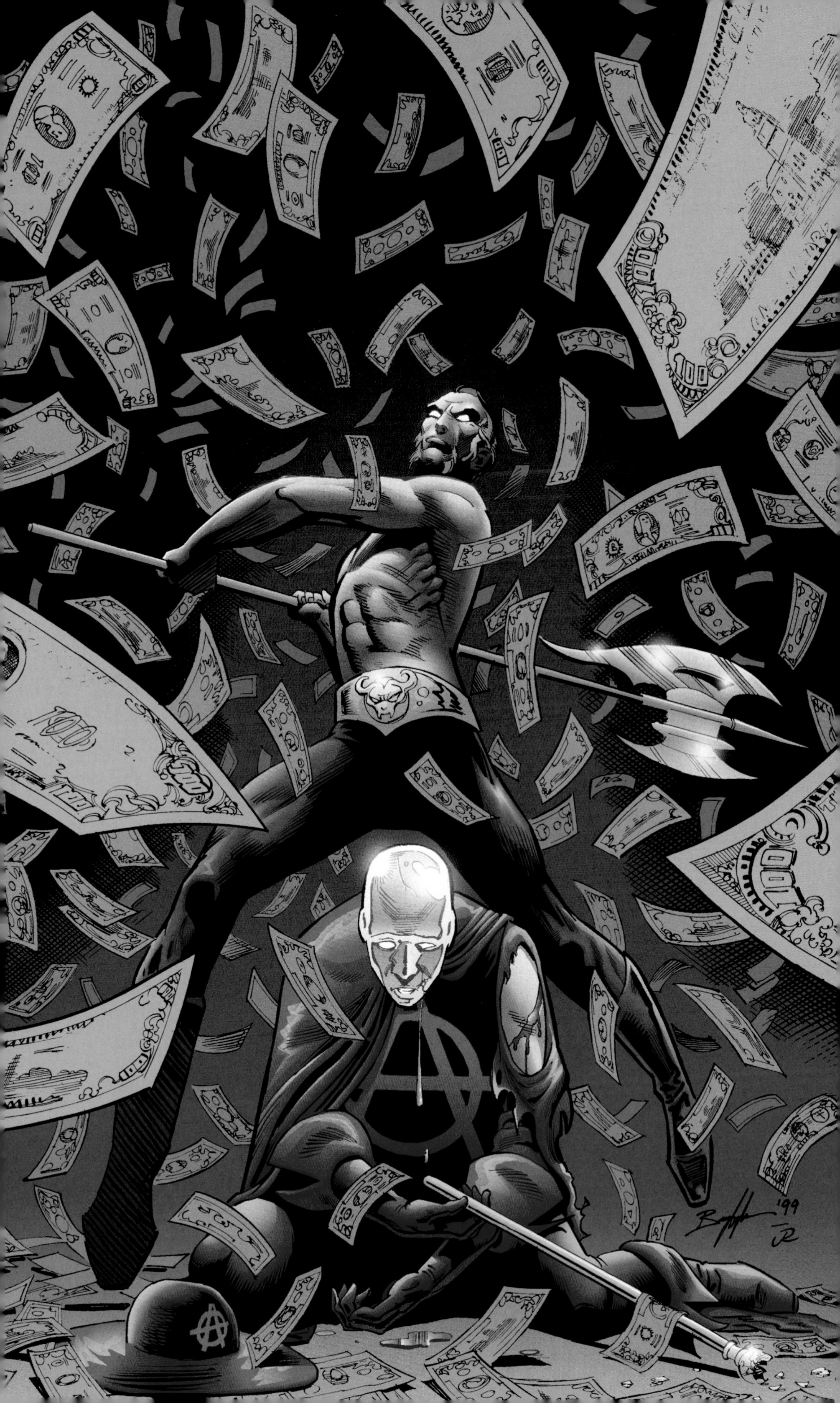

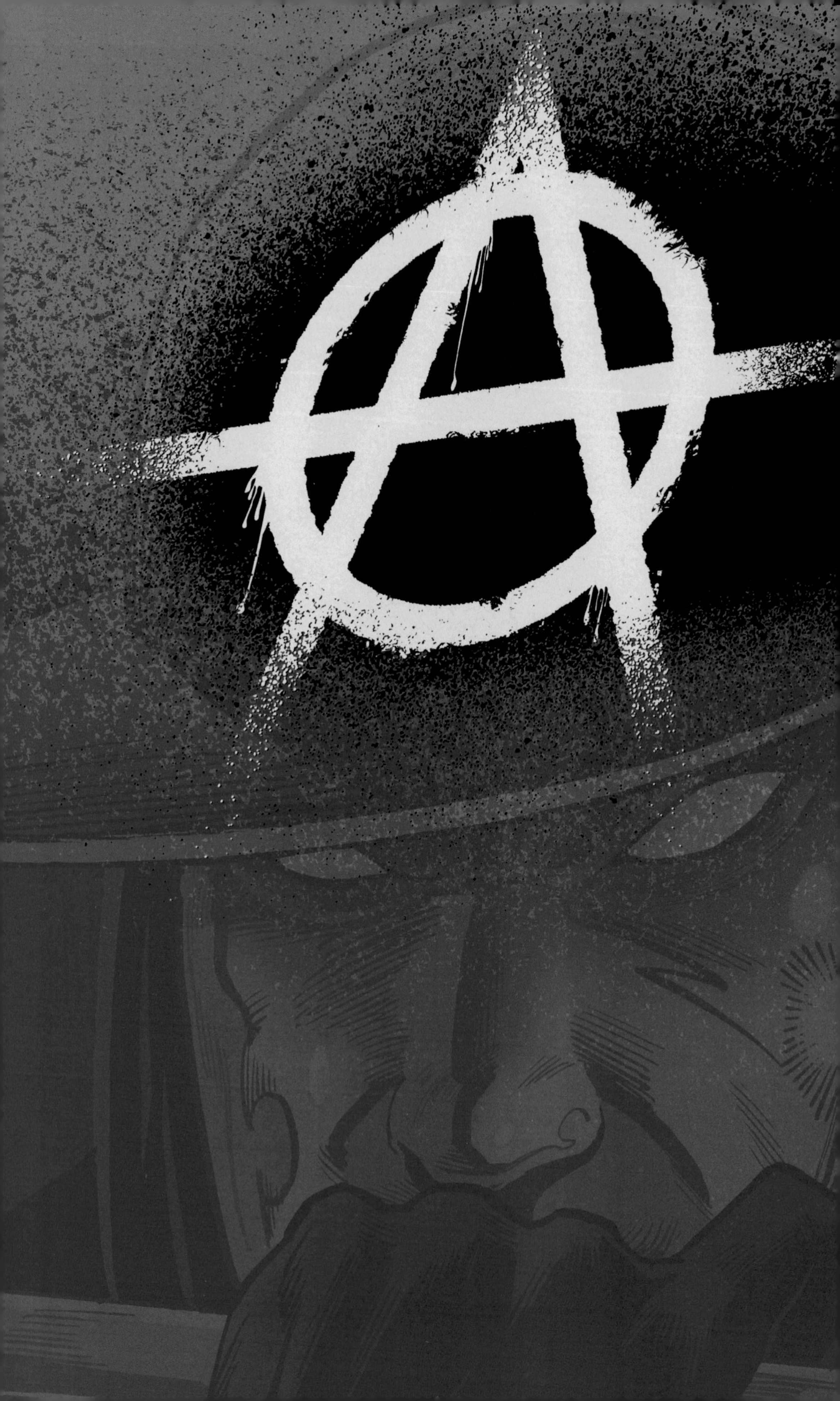

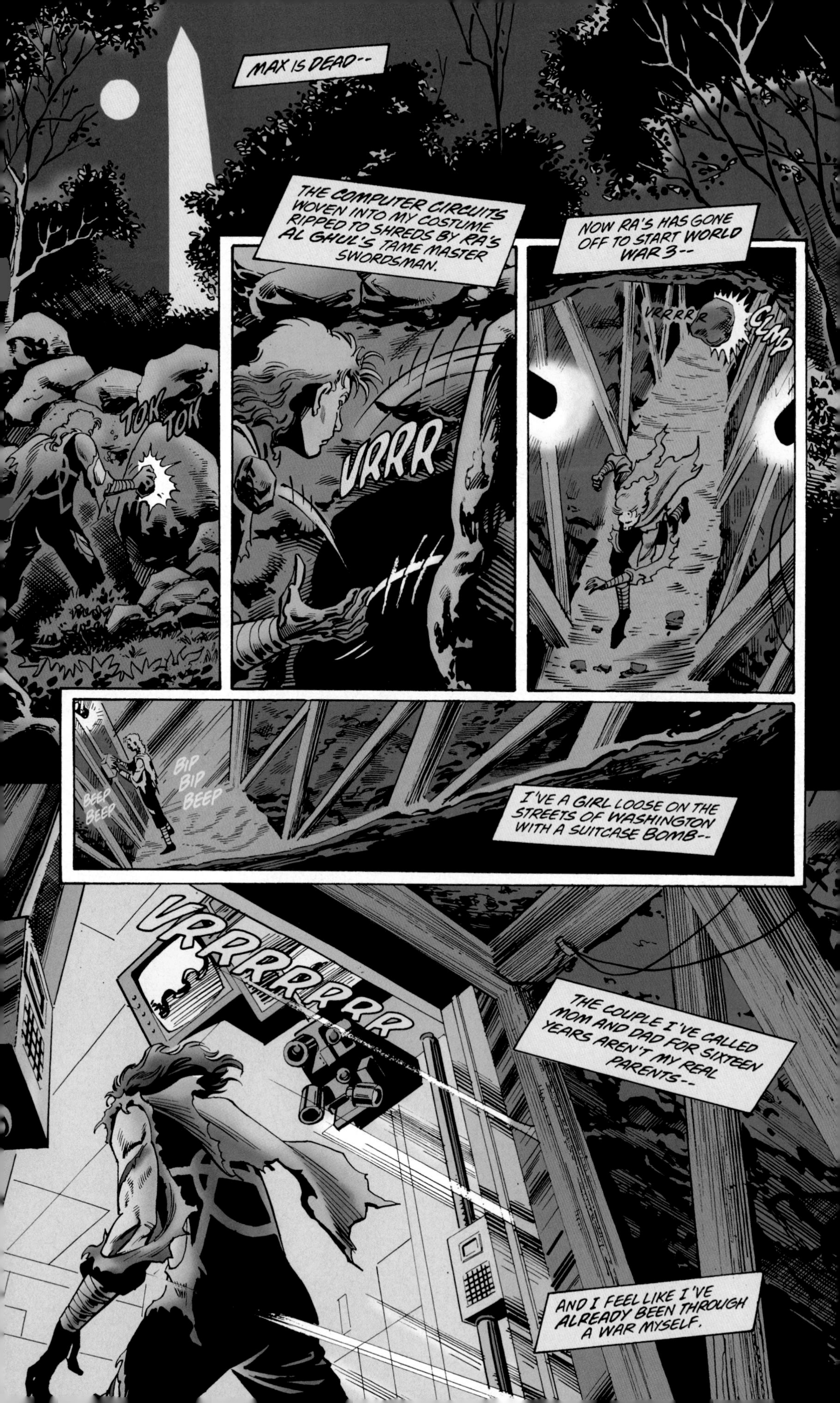
MAX IS DEAD--
TOK TOK
THE COMPUTER CIRCUITS WOVEN INTO MY COSTUME RIPPED TO SHREDS BY RA'S AL GHUL'S TAME MASTER SWORDSMAN.
VRRR
NOW RA'S HAS GONE OFF TO START WORLD WAR 3--
VRRRRR
CLMP
BIP BIP BEEP
BEEP BEEP
I'VE A GIRL LOOSE ON THE STREETS OF WASHINGTON WITH A SUITCASE BOMB--
VRRRRRRRR
THE COUPLE I'VE CALLED MOM AND DAD FOR SIXTEEN YEARS AREN'T MY REAL PARENTS--
AND I FEEL LIKE I'VE ALREADY BEEN THROUGH A WAR MYSELF.

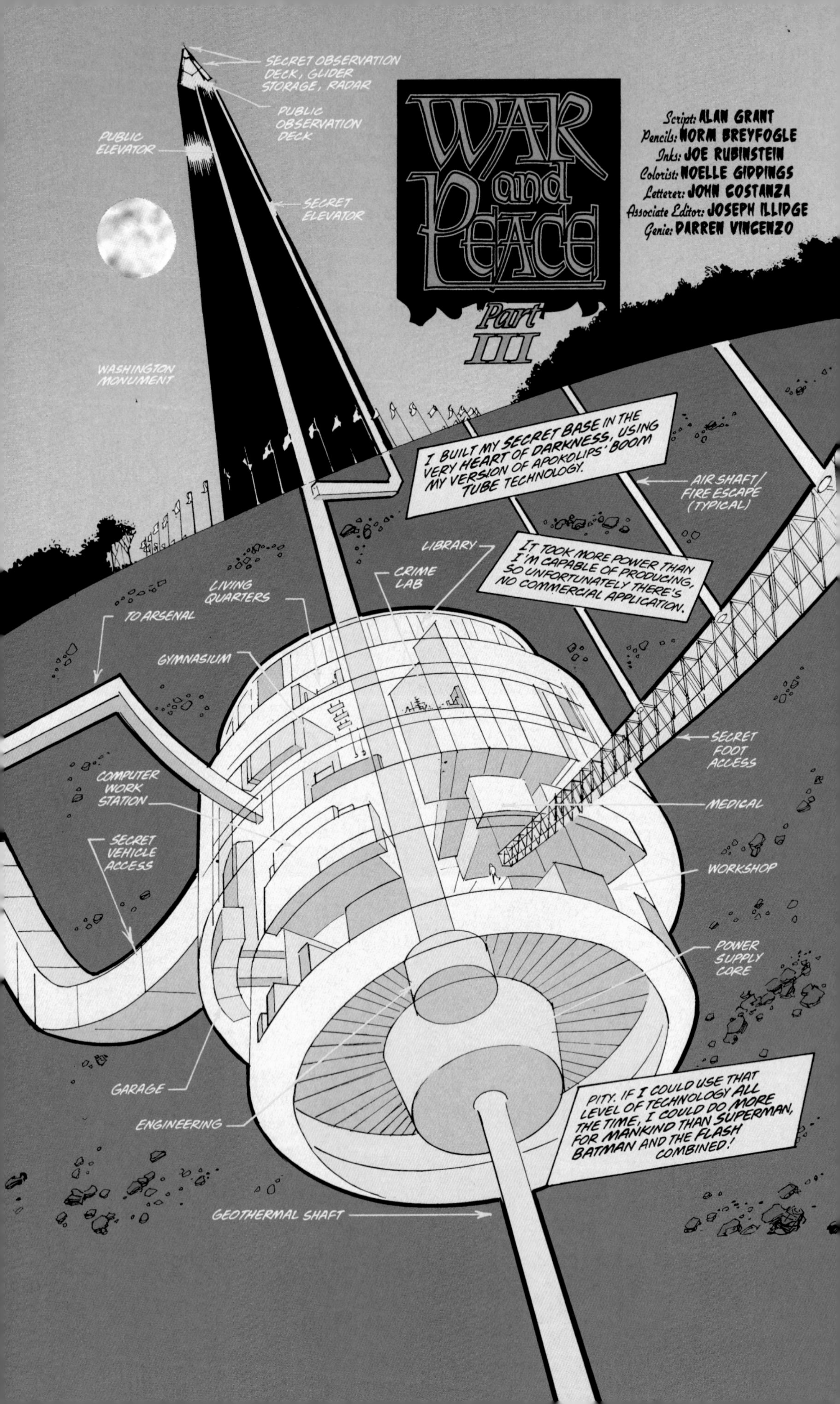
WAR and PEACE
Part III
Script: ALAN GRANT
Pencils: NORM BREYFOGLE
Inks: JOE RUBINSTEIN
Colorist: NOELLE GIDDINGS
Letterer: JOHN COSTANZA
Associate Editor: JOSEPH ILLIDGE
Genie: DARREN VINCENZO
SECRET OBSERVATION DECK, GLIDER STORAGE, RADAR
PUBLIC OBSERVATION DECK
PUBLIC ELEVATOR
SECRET ELEVATOR
WASHINGTON MONUMENT
I BUILT MY SECRET BASE IN THE VERY HEART OF DARKNESS, USING MY VERSION OF APOKOLIPS' BOOM TUBE TECHNOLOGY.
AIR SHAFT/ FIRE ESCAPE (TYPICAL)
LIBRARY
IT TOOK MORE POWER THAN I'M CAPABLE OF PRODUCING, SO UNFORTUNATELY THERE'S NO COMMERCIAL APPLICATION.
CRIME LAB
LIVING QUARTERS
TO ARSENAL
GYMNASIUM
SECRET FOOT ACCESS
COMPUTER WORK STATION
MEDICAL
SECRET VEHICLE ACCESS
WORKSHOP
POWER SUPPLY CORE
GARAGE
PITY. IF I COULD USE THAT LEVEL OF TECHNOLOGY ALL THE TIME, I COULD DO MORE FOR MANKIND THAN SUPERMAN, BATMAN AND THE FLASH COMBINED!
ENGINEERING
GEOTHERMAL SHAFT

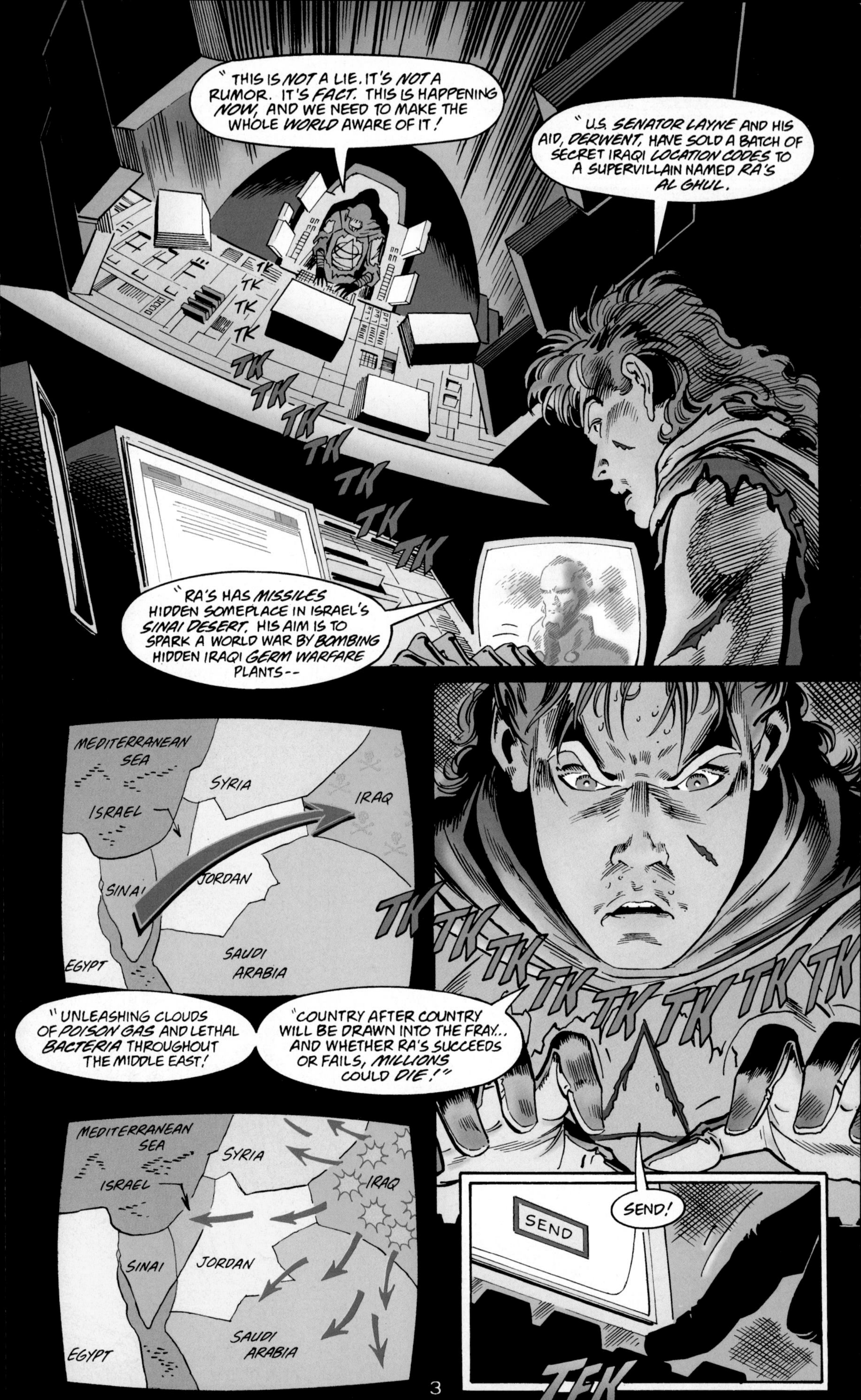
"THIS IS NOT A LIE. IT'S NOT A RUMOR. IT'S FACT. THIS IS HAPPENING NOW, AND WE NEED TO MAKE THE WHOLE WORLD AWARE OF IT!
"U.S. SENATOR LAYNE AND HIS AID, DERWENT, HAVE SOLD A BATCH OF SECRET IRAQI LOCATION CODES TO A SUPERVILLAIN NAMED RA'S AL GHUL.
TK TK TK TK TK TK TK TK TK TK TK
"RA'S HAS MISSILES HIDDEN SOMEPLACE IN ISRAEL'S SINAI DESERT. HIS AIM IS TO SPARK A WORLD WAR BY BOMBING HIDDEN IRAQI GERM WARFARE PLANTS--
MEDITERRANEAN SEA
SYRIA
IRAQ
ISRAEL
JORDAN
SINAI
EGYPT
SAUDI ARABIA
TK TK TK TK TK TK TK TK TK
"UNLEASHING CLOUDS OF POISON GAS AND LETHAL BACTERIA THROUGHOUT THE MIDDLE EAST!
"COUNTRY AFTER COUNTRY WILL BE DRAWN INTO THE FRAY... AND WHETHER RA'S SUCCEEDS OR FAILS, MILLIONS COULD DIE!"
MEDITERRANEAN SEA
SYRIA
ISRAEL
IRAQ
SINAI
JORDAN
SAUDI ARABIA
EGYPT
SEND!
SEND
TEK

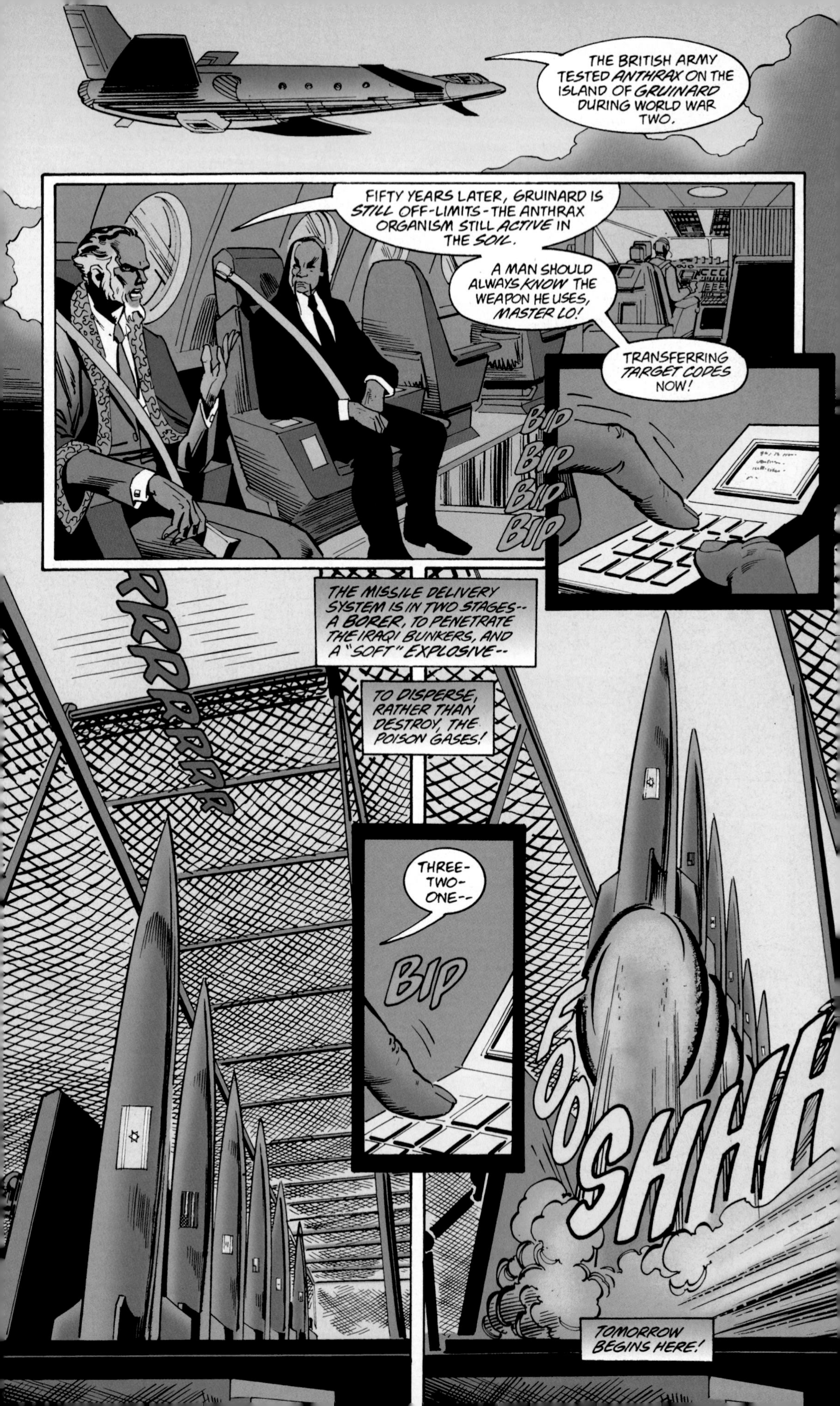
THE BRITISH ARMY TESTED ANTHRAX ON THE ISLAND OF GRUINARD DURING WORLD WAR TWO.
FIFTY YEARS LATER, GRUINARD IS STILL OFF-LIMITS - THE ANTHRAX ORGANISM STILL ACTIVE IN THE SOIL.
A MAN SHOULD ALWAYS KNOW THE WEAPON HE USES, MASTER LO!
TRANSFERRING TARGET CODES NOW!
BIP BIP BIP BIP
RRRRRRRR
THE MISSILE DELIVERY SYSTEM IS IN TWO STAGES-- A BORER, TO PENETRATE THE IRAQI BUNKERS, AND A "SOFT" EXPLOSIVE--
TO DISPERSE, RATHER THAN DESTROY, THE POISON GASES!
THREE-TWO-ONE--
BIP
FOOOSHHH
TOMORROW BEGINS HERE!

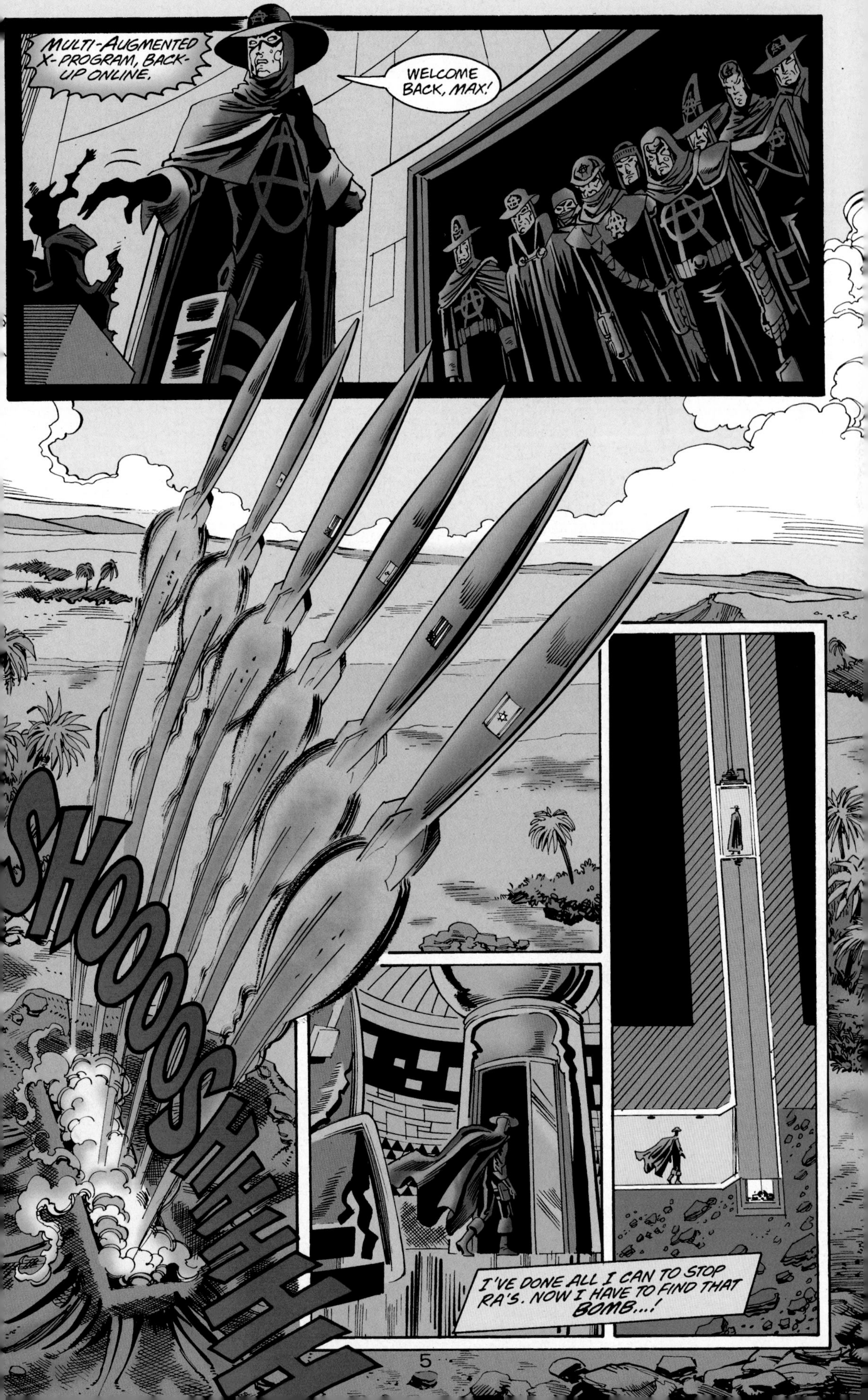
MULTI-AUGMENTED X-PROGRAM, BACK-UP ONLINE.
WELCOME BACK, MAX!
SHOOOOOSHHHHHH
I'VE DONE ALL I CAN TO STOP RA'S. NOW I HAVE TO FIND THAT BOMB...!

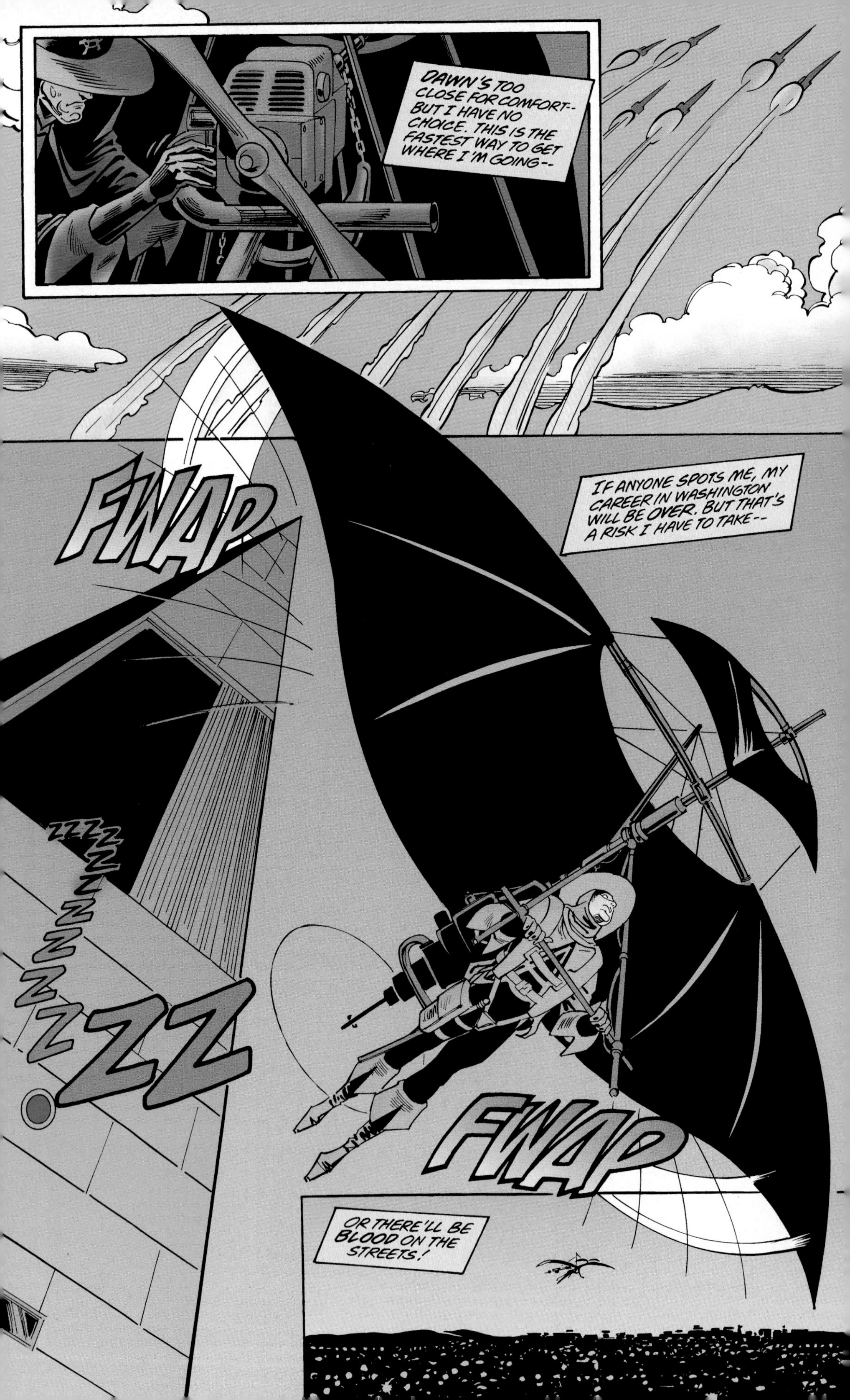
DAWN'S TOO CLOSE FOR COMFORT-- BUT I HAVE NO CHOICE. THIS IS THE FASTEST WAY TO GET WHERE I'M GOING--
FWAP
IF ANYONE SPOTS ME, MY CAREER IN WASHINGTON WILL BE OVER. BUT THAT'S A RISK I HAVE TO TAKE--
ZZZZZZZZZZZZ
FWAP
OR THERE'LL BE BLOOD ON THE STREETS!

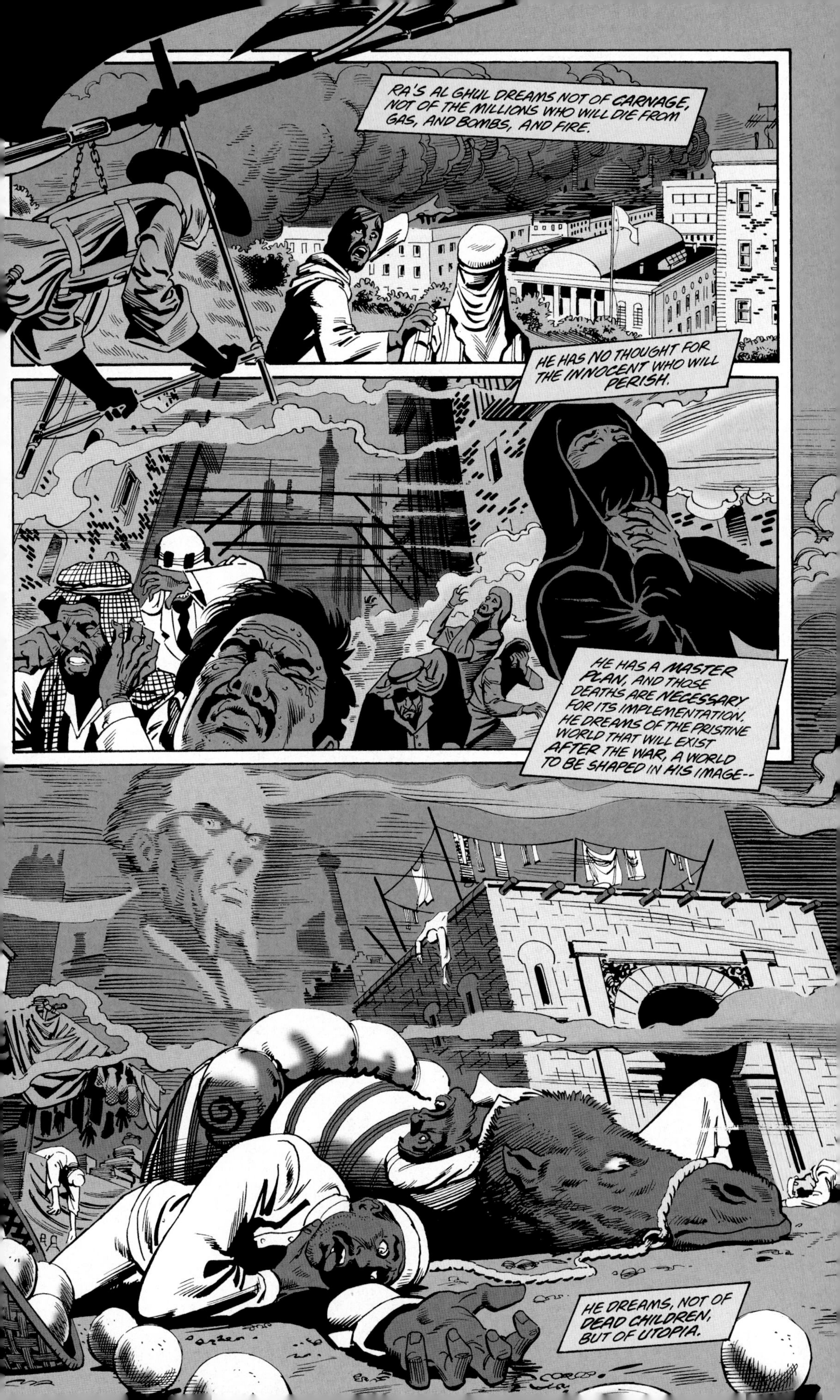
RA'S AL GHUL DREAMS NOT OF CARNAGE, NOT OF THE MILLIONS WHO WILL DIE FROM GAS, AND BOMBS, AND FIRE.
HE HAS NO THOUGHT FOR THE INNOCENT WHO WILL PERISH.
HE HAS A MASTER PLAN, AND THOSE DEATHS ARE NECESSARY FOR ITS IMPLEMENTATION. HE DREAMS OF THE PRISTINE WORLD THAT WILL EXIST AFTER THE WAR, A WORLD TO BE SHAPED IN HIS IMAGE--
HE DREAMS, NOT OF DEAD CHILDREN, BUT OF UTOPIA.

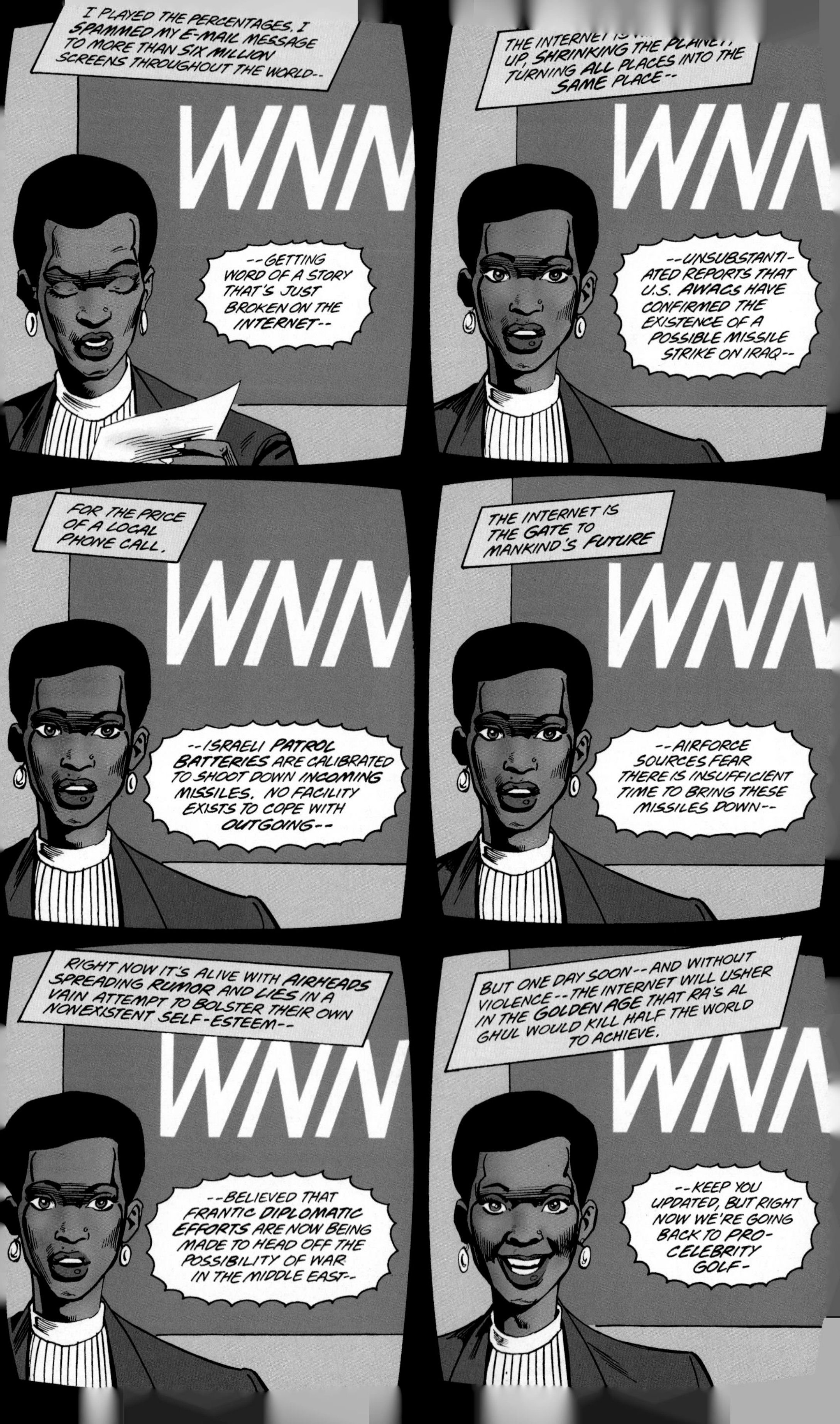
I PLAYED THE PERCENTAGES. I SPAMMED MY E-MAIL MESSAGE TO MORE THAN SIX MILLION SCREENS THROUGHOUT THE WORLD--
WNN
--GETTING WORD OF A STORY THAT'S JUST BROKEN ON THE INTERNET--
THE INTERNET IS
UP, SHRINKING THE
TURNING ALL PLACES INTO THE SAME PLACE--
WNN
--UNSUBSTANTIATED REPORTS THAT U.S. AWACS HAVE CONFIRMED THE EXISTENCE OF A POSSIBLE MISSILE STRIKE ON IRAQ--
FOR THE PRICE OF A LOCAL PHONE CALL.
WNN
--ISRAELI PATROL BATTERIES ARE CALIBRATED TO SHOOT DOWN INCOMING MISSILES. NO FACILITY EXISTS TO COPE WITH OUTGOING--
THE INTERNET IS THE GATE TO MANKIND'S FUTURE
WNN
--AIRFORCE SOURCES FEAR THERE IS INSUFFICIENT TIME TO BRING THESE MISSILES DOWN--
RIGHT NOW IT'S ALIVE WITH AIRHEADS SPREADING RUMOR AND LIES IN A VAIN ATTEMPT TO BOLSTER THEIR OWN NONEXISTENT SELF-ESTEEM--
WNN
--BELIEVED THAT FRANTIC DIPLOMATIC EFFORTS ARE NOW BEING MADE TO HEAD OFF THE POSSIBILITY OF WAR IN THE MIDDLE EAST--
BUT ONE DAY SOON--AND WITHOUT VIOLENCE--THE INTERNET WILL USHER IN THE GOLDEN AGE THAT RA'S AL GHUL WOULD KILL HALF THE WORLD TO ACHIEVE.
WNN
--KEEP YOU UPDATED, BUT RIGHT NOW WE'RE GOING BACK TO PRO-CELEBRITY GOLF-

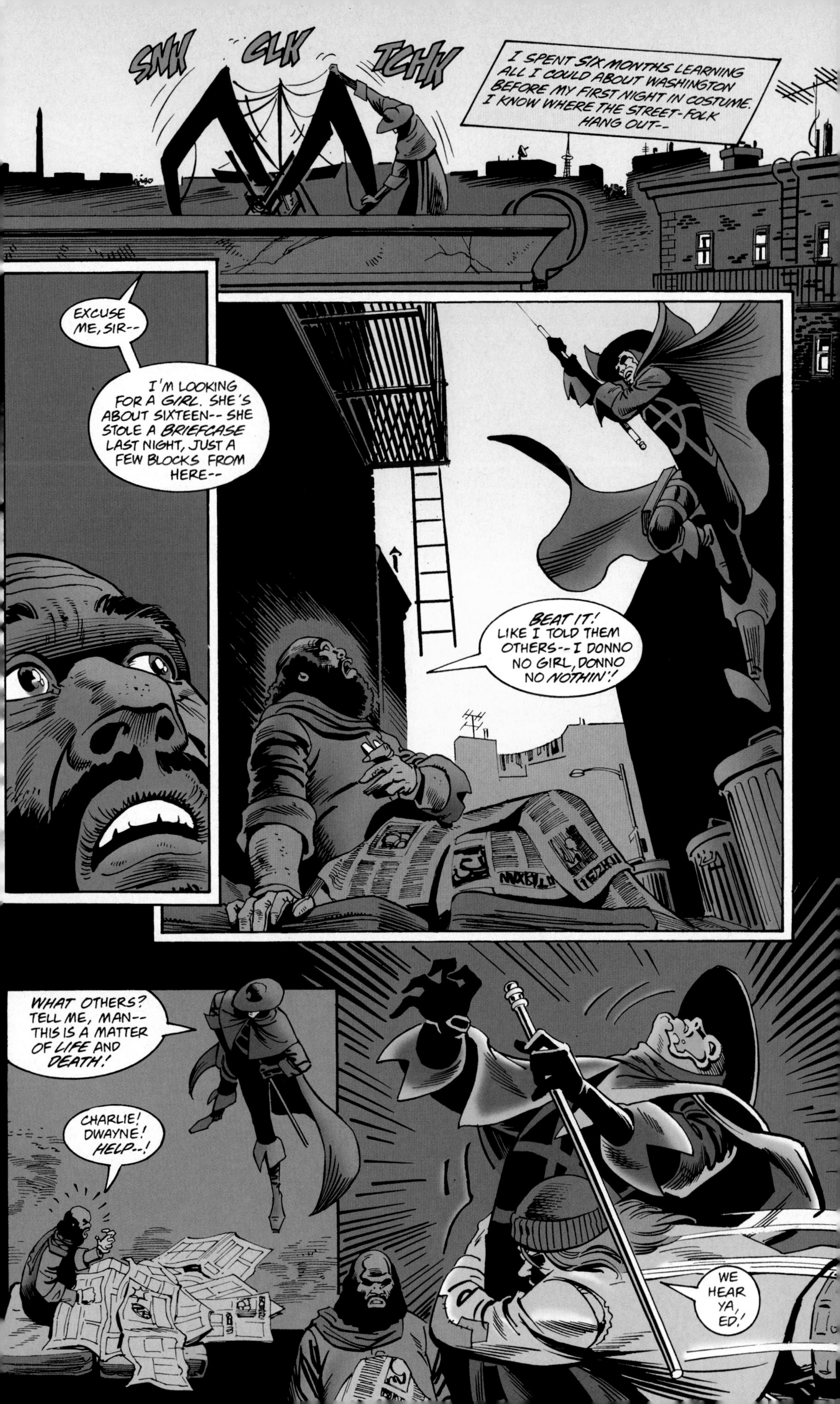
SNK
CLK
TCHK
I SPENT SIX MONTHS LEARNING ALL I COULD ABOUT WASHINGTON BEFORE MY FIRST NIGHT IN COSTUME. I KNOW WHERE THE STREET-FOLK HANG OUT--
EXCUSE ME, SIR--
I'M LOOKING FOR A GIRL. SHE'S ABOUT SIXTEEN-- SHE STOLE A BRIEFCASE LAST NIGHT, JUST A FEW BLOCKS FROM HERE--
BEAT IT! LIKE I TOLD THEM OTHERS-- I DONNO NO GIRL, DONNO NO NOTHIN'!
WHAT OTHERS? TELL ME, MAN-- THIS IS A MATTER OF LIFE AND DEATH!
CHARLIE! DWAYNE! HELP--!
WE HEAR YA, ED!

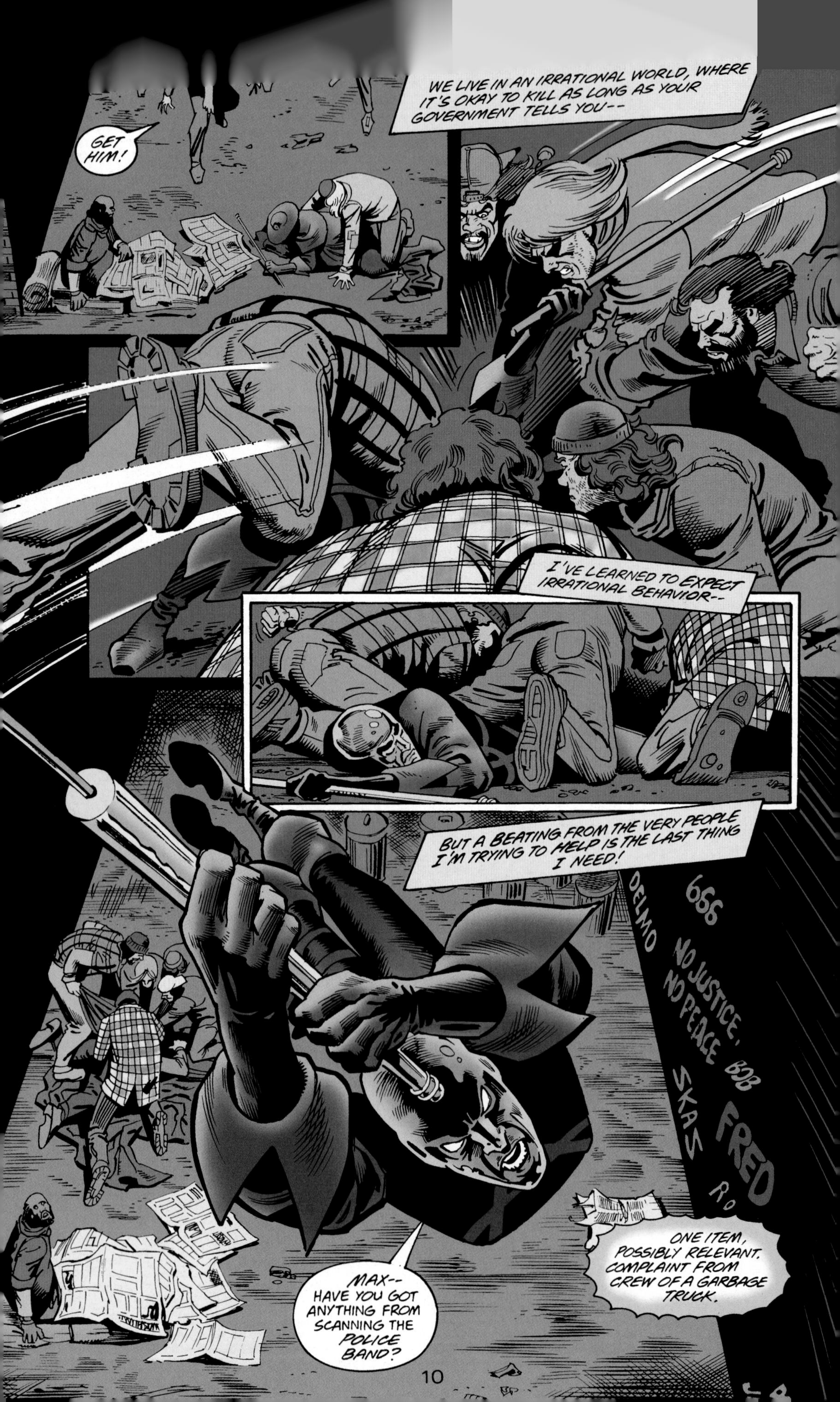

WE LIVE IN AN IRRATIONAL WORLD, WHERE IT'S OKAY TO KILL AS LONG AS YOUR GOVERNMENT TELLS YOU--
GET HIM!
I'VE LEARNED TO EXPECT IRRATIONAL BEHAVIOR--
BUT A BEATING FROM THE VERY PEOPLE I'M TRYING TO HELP IS THE LAST THING I NEED!
666
DELMO
NO JUSTICE, NO PEACE
BOB
SKAS
FRED
MAX-- HAVE YOU GOT ANYTHING FROM SCANNING THE POLICE BAND?
ONE ITEM, POSSIBLY RELEVANT. COMPLAINT FROM CREW OF A GARBAGE TRUCK.

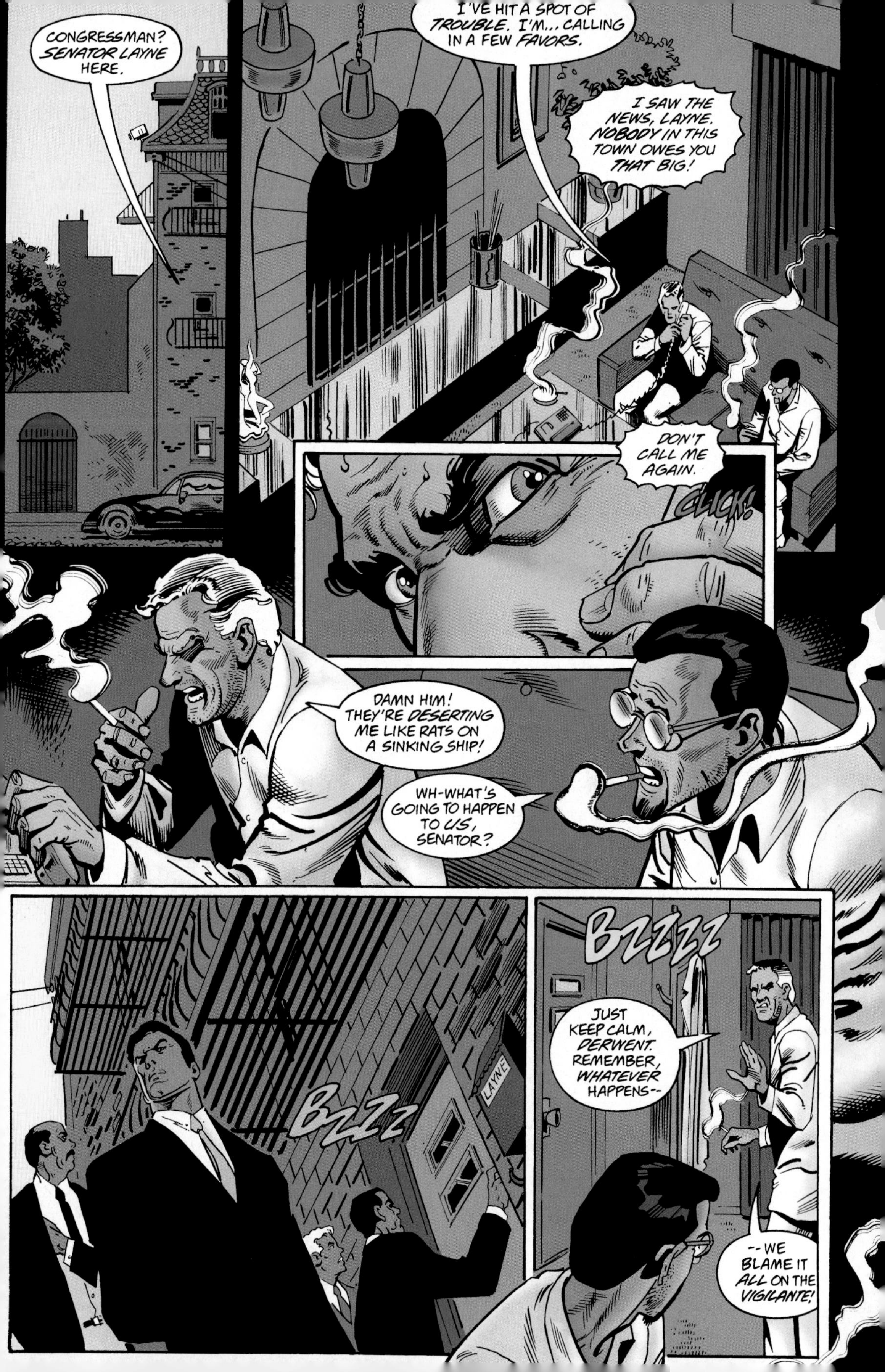
CONGRESSMAN? SENATOR LAYNE HERE.
I'VE HIT A SPOT OF TROUBLE. I'M... CALLING IN A FEW FAVORS.
I SAW THE NEWS, LAYNE. NOBODY IN THIS TOWN OWES YOU THAT BIG!
DON'T CALL ME AGAIN.
CLICK!
DAMN HIM! THEY'RE DESERTING ME LIKE RATS ON A SINKING SHIP!
WH-WHAT'S GOING TO HAPPEN TO US, SENATOR?
LAYNE
BZZZ
BZZZZ
JUST KEEP CALM, DERWENT. REMEMBER, WHATEVER HAPPENS--
--WE BLAME IT ALL ON THE VIGILANTE!

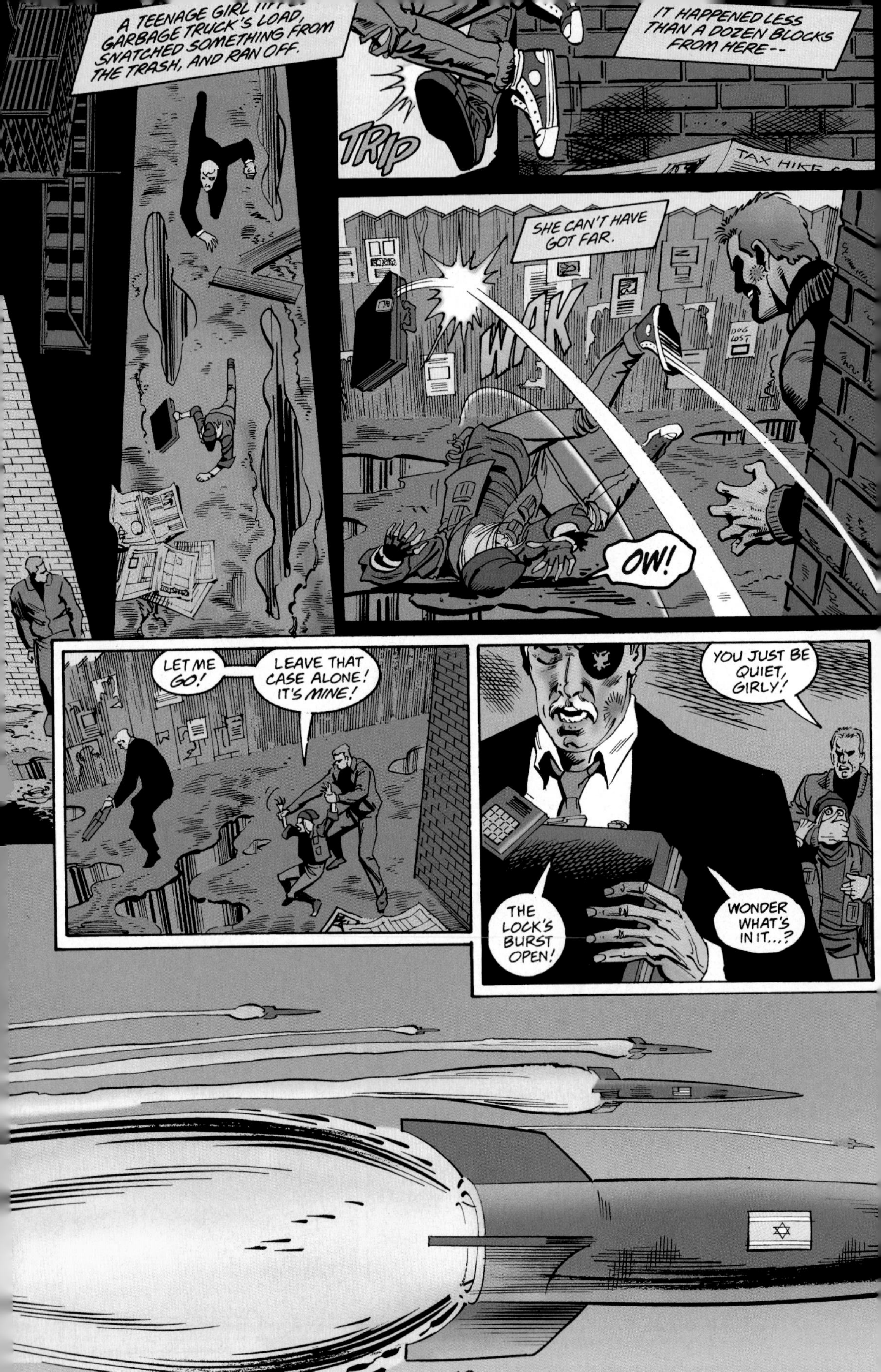

A TEENAGE GIRL ... GARBAGE TRUCK'S LOAD, SNATCHED SOMETHING FROM THE TRASH, AND RAN OFF.
IT HAPPENED LESS THAN A DOZEN BLOCKS FROM HERE--
TRIP
TAX HIKE
SHE CAN'T HAVE GOT FAR.
WAK
DOG LOST
OW!
LET ME GO!
LEAVE THAT CASE ALONE! IT'S MINE!
YOU JUST BE QUIET, GIRLY!
THE LOCK'S BURST OPEN!
WONDER WHAT'S IN IT...?

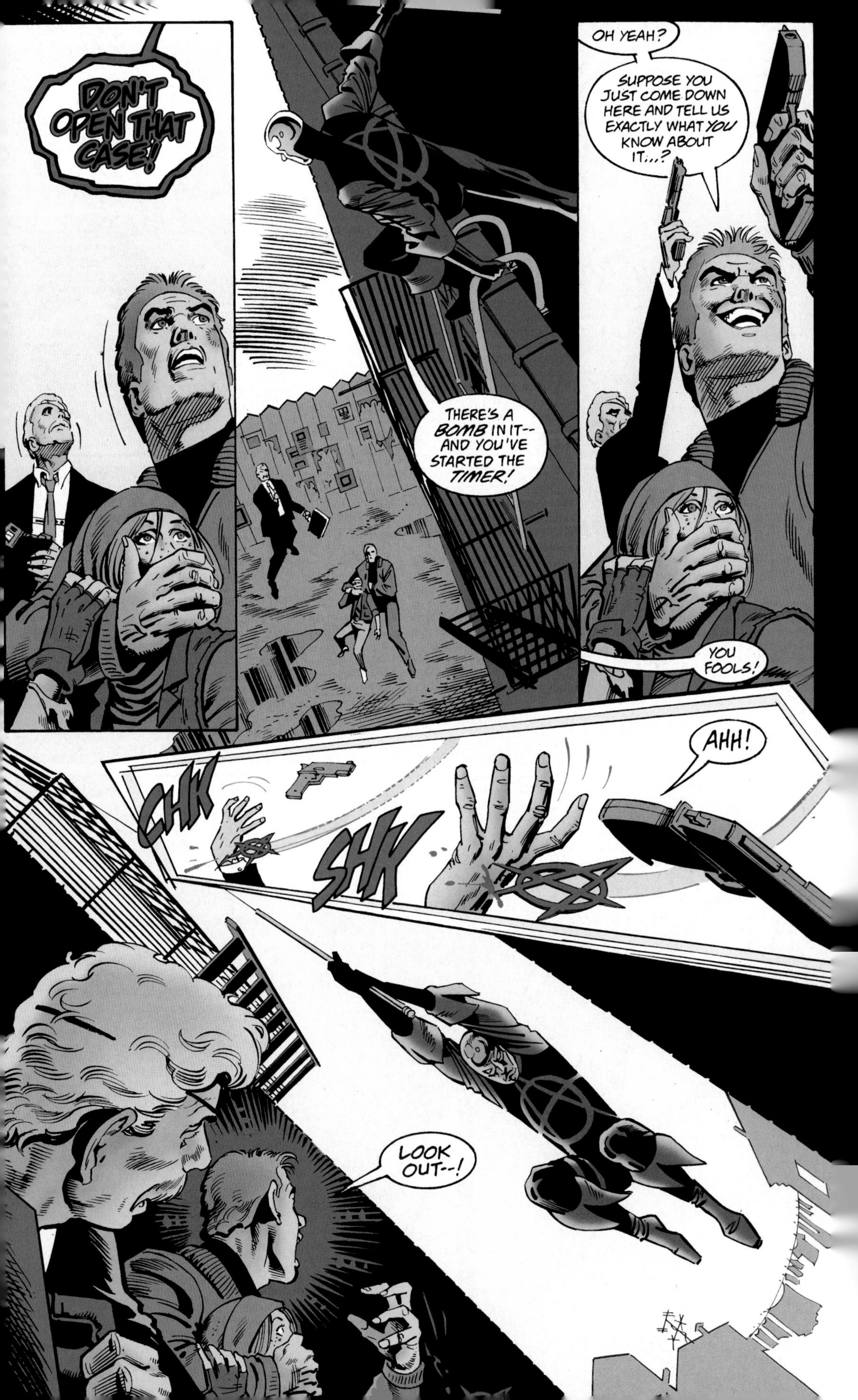
DON'T OPEN THAT CASE!
THERE'S A BOMB IN IT-- AND YOU'VE STARTED THE TIMER!
OH YEAH?
SUPPOSE YOU JUST COME DOWN HERE AND TELL US EXACTLY WHAT YOU KNOW ABOUT IT...?
YOU FOOLS!
AHH!
CHK
SHK
LOOK OUT--!

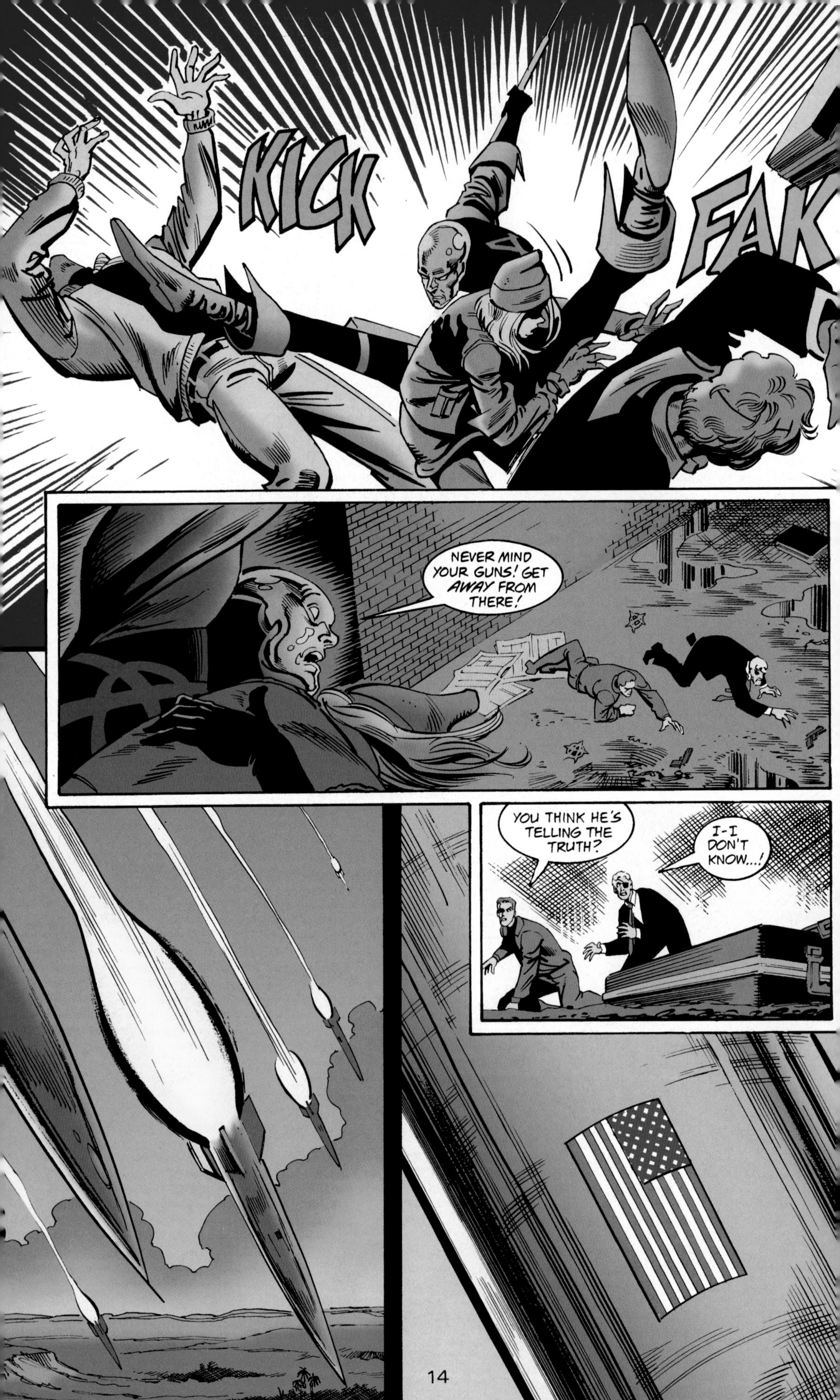
KICK
FAK
NEVER MIND YOUR GUNS! GET AWAY FROM THERE!
YOU THINK HE'S TELLING THE TRUTH?
I-I DON'T KNOW...!

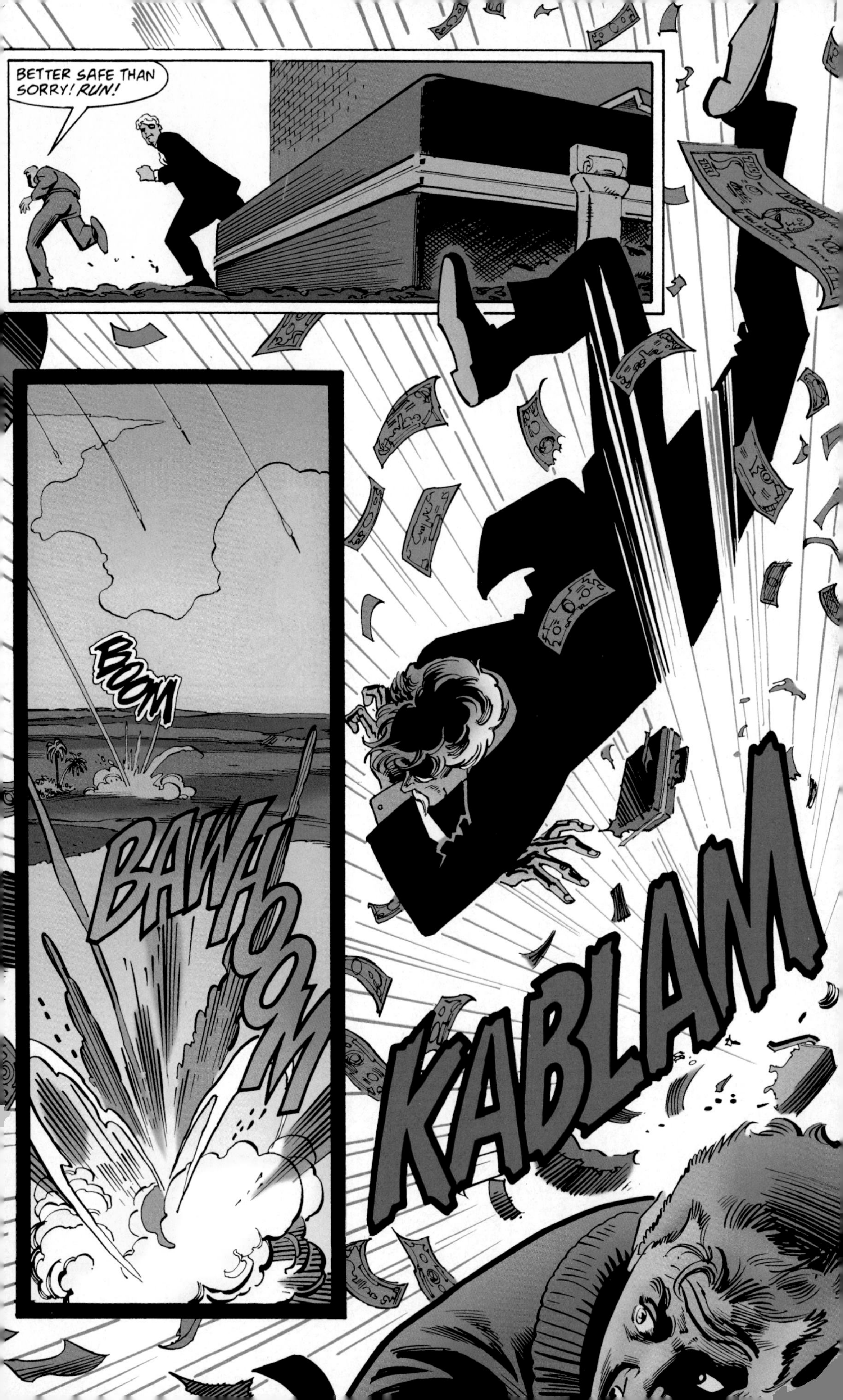
BETTER SAFE THAN SORRY! RUN!
BOOM
BAWHOOM
KABLAM

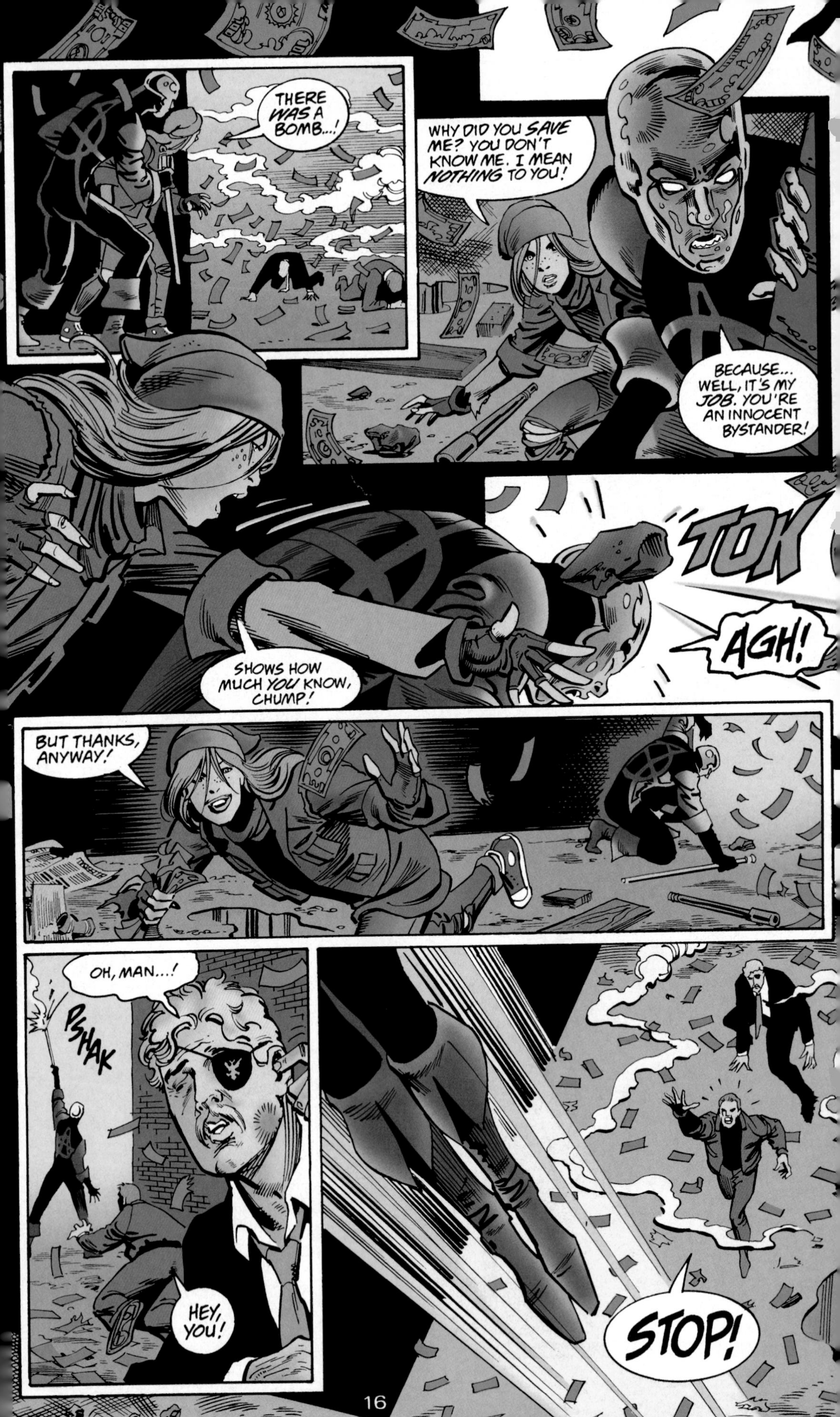
THERE WAS A BOMB...!
WHY DID YOU SAVE ME? YOU DON'T KNOW ME. I MEAN NOTHING TO YOU!
BECAUSE... WELL, IT'S MY JOB. YOU'RE AN INNOCENT BYSTANDER!
SHOWS HOW MUCH YOU KNOW, CHUMP!
TOK
AGH!
BUT THANKS, ANYWAY!
OH, MAN...!
PSHAK
HEY, YOU!
STOP!

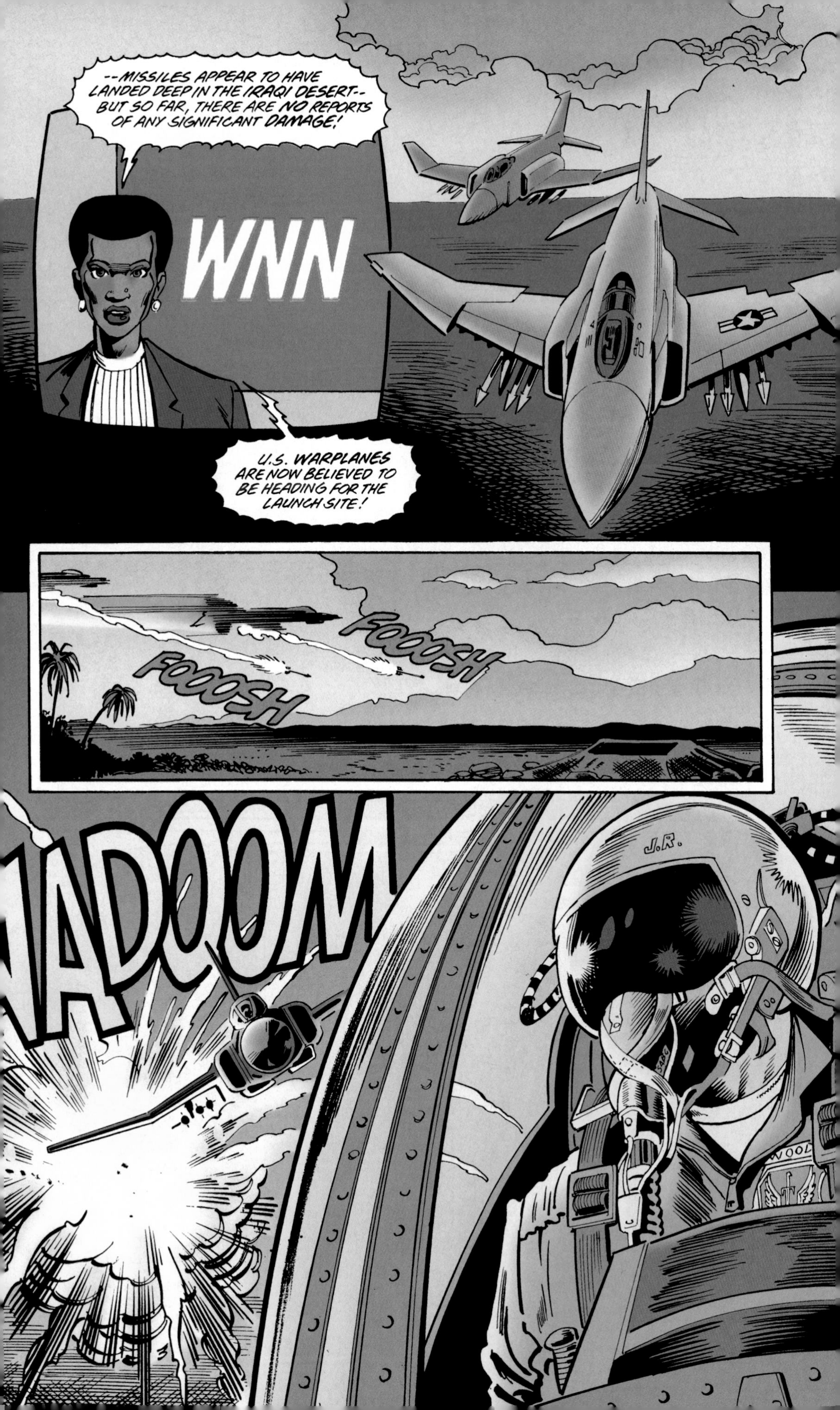
--MISSILES APPEAR TO HAVE LANDED DEEP IN THE IRAQI DESERT-- BUT SO FAR, THERE ARE NO REPORTS OF ANY SIGNIFICANT DAMAGE!
WNN
U.S. WARPLANES ARE NOW BELIEVED TO BE HEADING FOR THE LAUNCH SITE!
FOOOSH
FOOOSH
ADOOM
J.R.

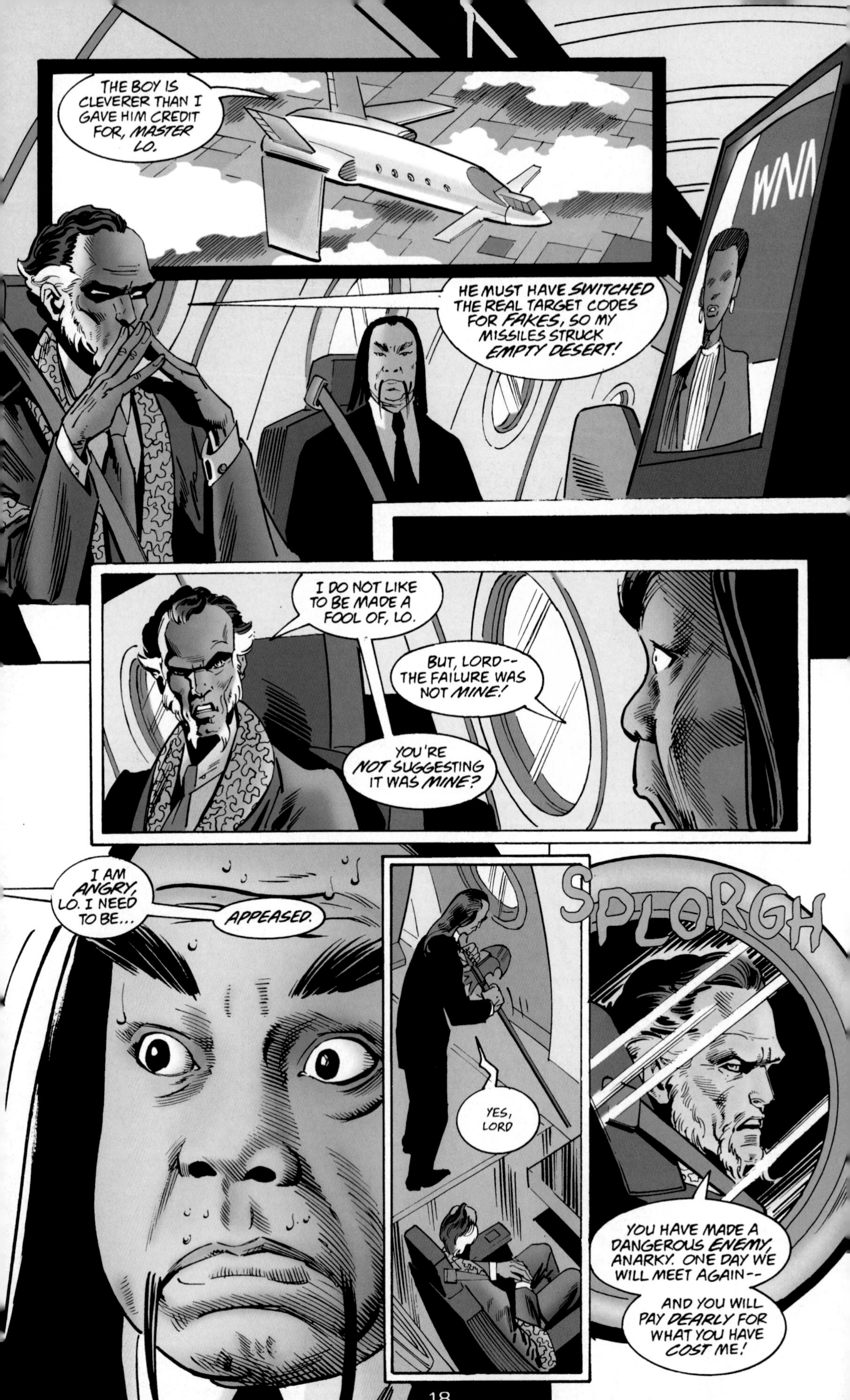
THE BOY IS CLEVERER THAN I GAVE HIM CREDIT FOR, MASTER LO.
WNN
HE MUST HAVE SWITCHED THE REAL TARGET CODES FOR FAKES, SO MY MISSILES STRUCK EMPTY DESERT!
I DO NOT LIKE TO BE MADE A FOOL OF, LO.
BUT, LORD-- THE FAILURE WAS NOT MINE!
YOU'RE NOT SUGGESTING IT WAS MINE?
I AM ANGRY, LO. I NEED TO BE...
APPEASED.
YES, LORD
SPLORGH
YOU HAVE MADE A DANGEROUS ENEMY, ANARKY. ONE DAY WE WILL MEET AGAIN--
AND YOU WILL PAY DEARLY FOR WHAT YOU HAVE COST ME!

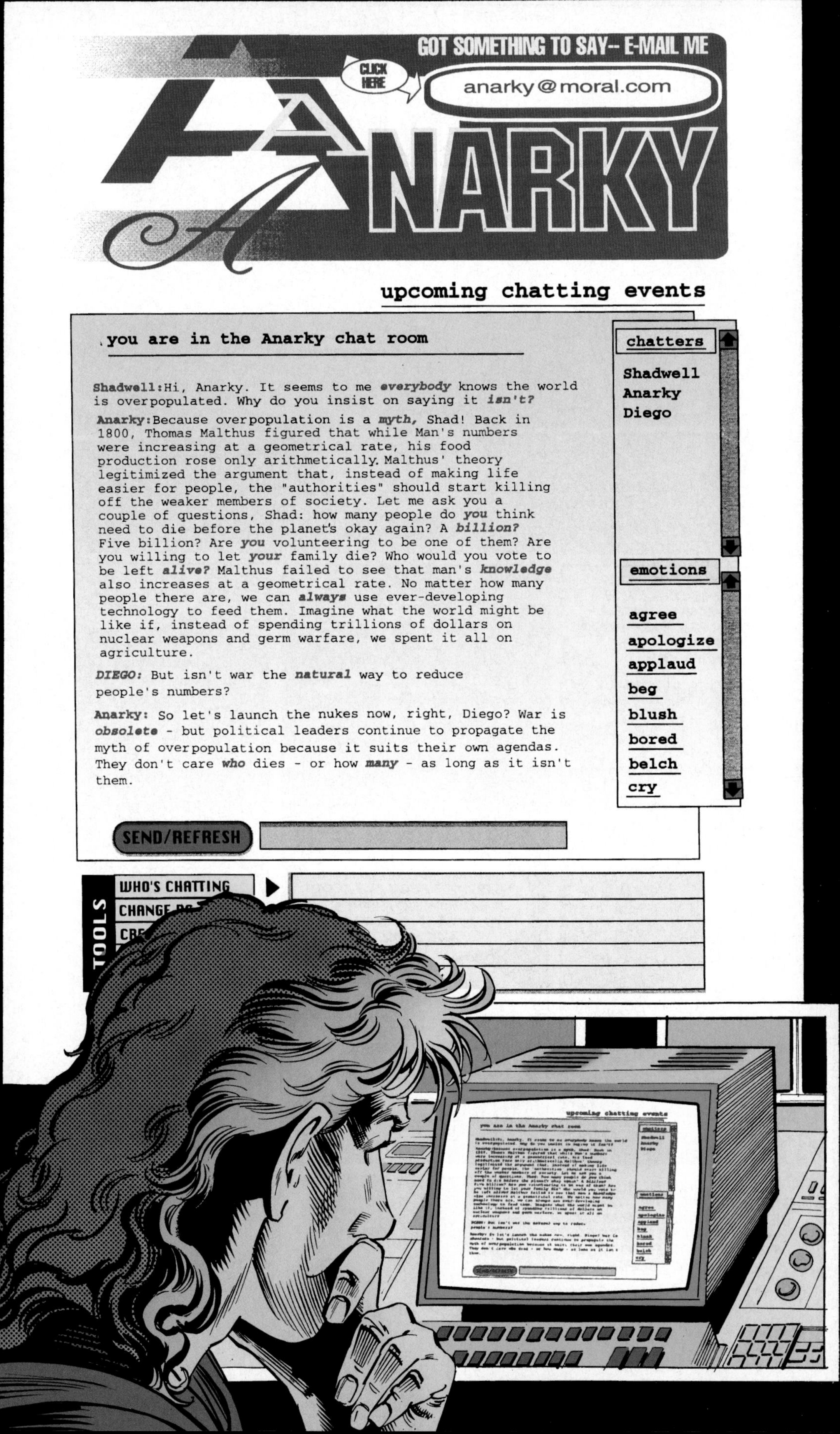
GOT SOMETHING TO SAY-- E-MAIL ME
CLICK HERE
anarky@moral.com
ANARKY
upcoming chatting events
you are in the Anarky chat room
Shadwell: Hi, Anarky. It seems to me everybody knows the world is overpopulated. Why do you insist on saying it isn't?
Anarky: Because overpopulation is a myth, Shad! Back in 1800, Thomas Malthus figured that while Man's numbers were increasing at a geometrical rate, his food production rose only arithmetically. Malthus' theory legitimized the argument that, instead of making life easier for people, the "authorities" should start killing off the weaker members of society. Let me ask you a couple of questions, Shad: how many people do you think need to die before the planet's okay again? A billion? Five billion? Are you volunteering to be one of them? Are you willing to let your family die? Who would you vote to be left alive? Malthus failed to see that man's knowledge also increases at a geometrical rate. No matter how many people there are, we can always use ever-developing technology to feed them. Imagine what the world might be like if, instead of spending trillions of dollars on nuclear weapons and germ warfare, we spent it all on agriculture.
DIEGO: But isn't war the natural way to reduce people's numbers?
Anarky: So let's launch the nukes now, right, Diego? War is obsolete - but political leaders continue to propagate the myth of overpopulation because it suits their own agendas. They don't care who dies - or how many - as long as it isn't them.
chatters
Shadwell
Anarky
Diego
emotions
agree
apologize
applaud
beg
blush
bored
belch
cry
SEND/REFRESH
TOOLS
WHO'S CHATTING

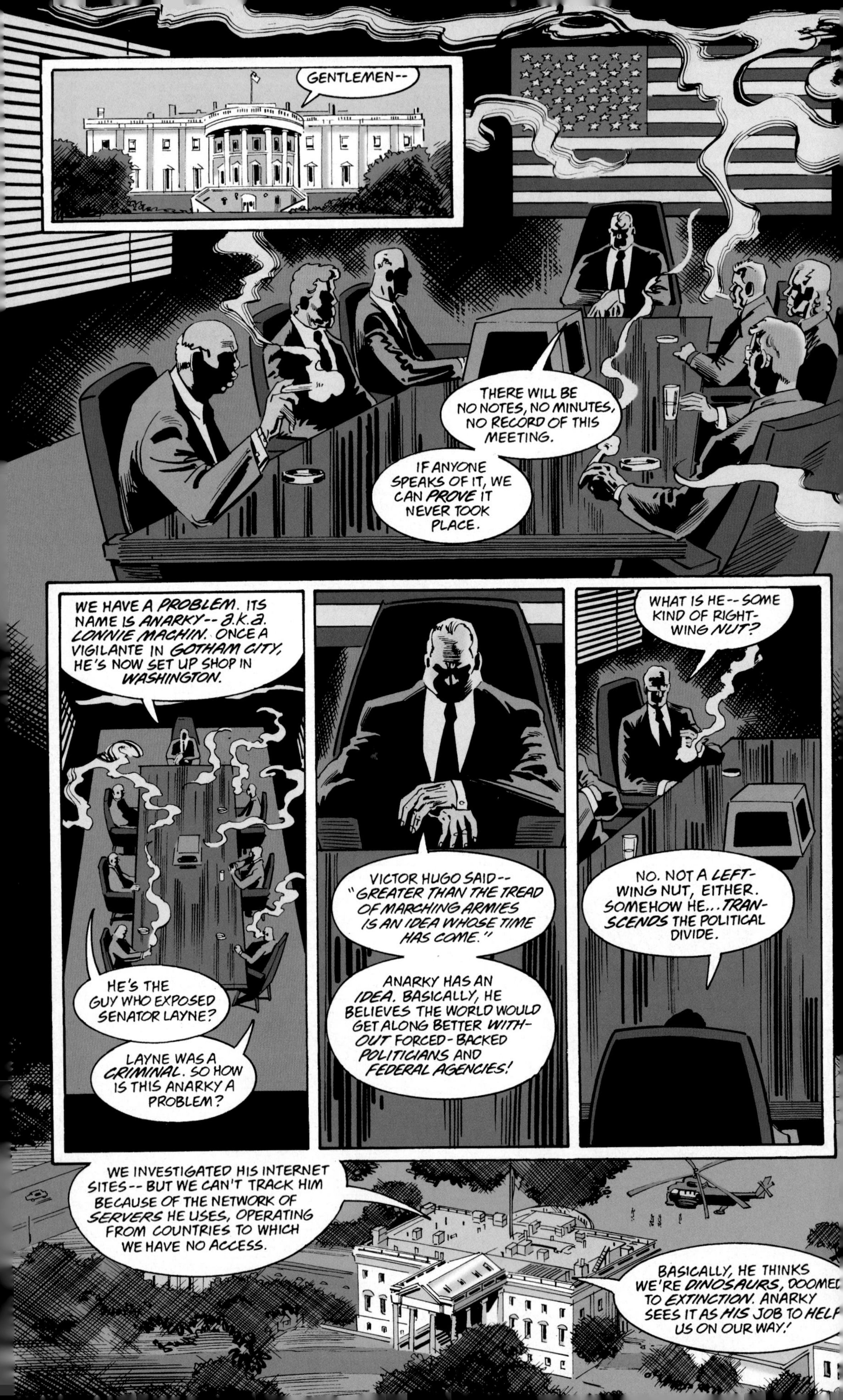
GENTLEMEN--
THERE WILL BE NO NOTES, NO MINUTES, NO RECORD OF THIS MEETING.
IF ANYONE SPEAKS OF IT, WE CAN PROVE IT NEVER TOOK PLACE.
WE HAVE A PROBLEM. ITS NAME IS ANARKY-- a.k.a. LONNIE MACHIN. ONCE A VIGILANTE IN GOTHAM CITY, HE'S NOW SET UP SHOP IN WASHINGTON.
HE'S THE GUY WHO EXPOSED SENATOR LAYNE?
LAYNE WAS A CRIMINAL. SO HOW IS THIS ANARKY A PROBLEM?
VICTOR HUGO SAID-- "GREATER THAN THE TREAD OF MARCHING ARMIES IS AN IDEA WHOSE TIME HAS COME."
ANARKY HAS AN IDEA. BASICALLY, HE BELIEVES THE WORLD WOULD GET ALONG BETTER WITH-OUT FORCED-BACKED POLITICIANS AND FEDERAL AGENCIES!
WHAT IS HE--SOME KIND OF RIGHT-WING NUT?
NO. NOT A LEFT-WING NUT, EITHER. SOMEHOW HE...TRAN-SCENDS THE POLITICAL DIVIDE.
WE INVESTIGATED HIS INTERNET SITES-- BUT WE CAN'T TRACK HIM BECAUSE OF THE NETWORK OF SERVERS HE USES, OPERATING FROM COUNTRIES TO WHICH WE HAVE NO ACCESS.
BASICALLY, HE THINKS WE'RE DINOSAURS, DOOMED TO EXTINCTION. ANARKY SEES IT AS HIS JOB TO HELP US ON OUR WAY!

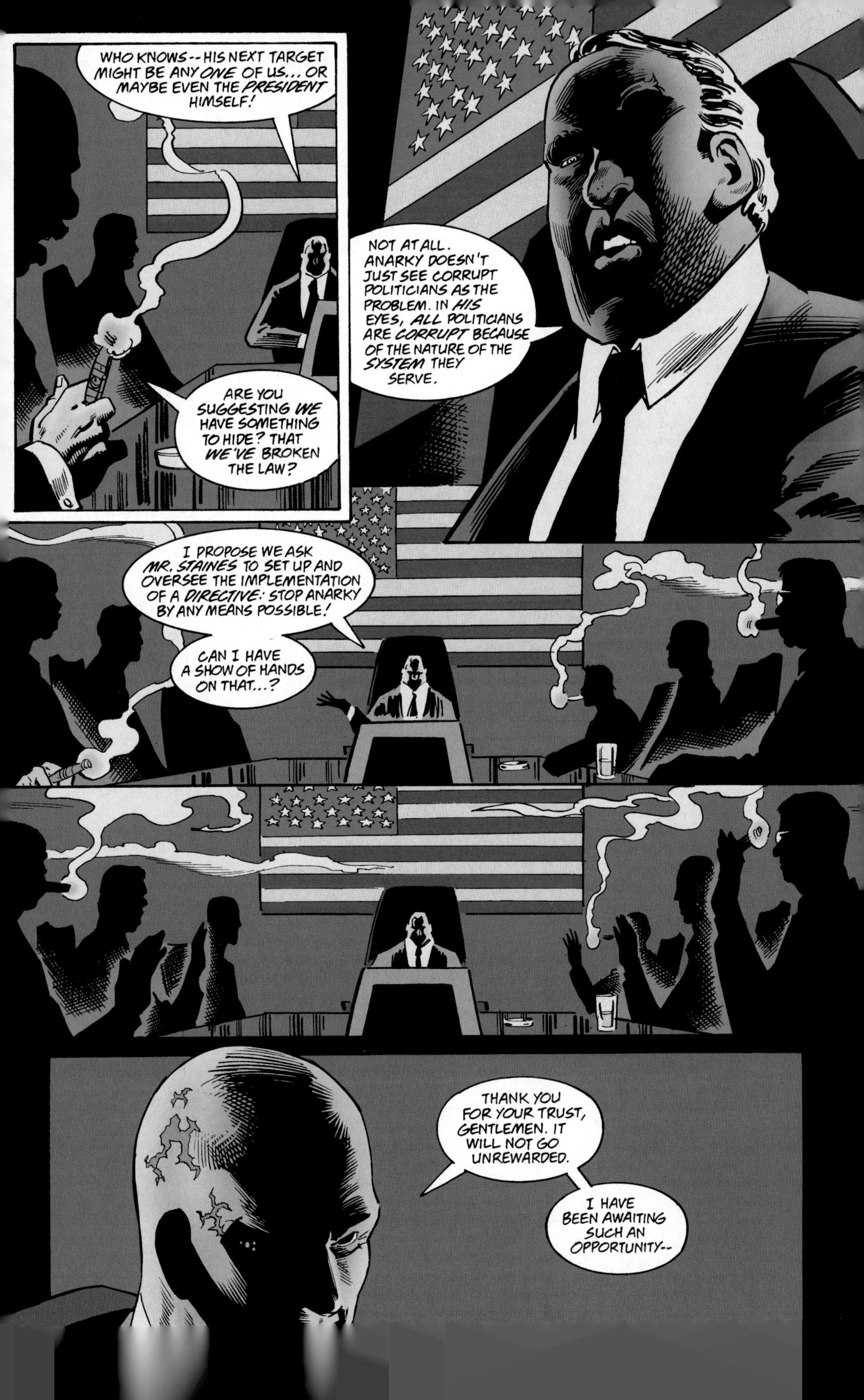
WHO KNOWS--HIS NEXT TARGET MIGHT BE ANY ONE OF US... OR MAYBE EVEN THE PRESIDENT HIMSELF!
ARE YOU SUGGESTING WE HAVE SOMETHING TO HIDE? THAT WE'VE BROKEN THE LAW?
NOT AT ALL. ANARKY DOESN'T JUST SEE CORRUPT POLITICIANS AS THE PROBLEM. IN HIS EYES, ALL POLITICIANS ARE CORRUPT BECAUSE OF THE NATURE OF THE SYSTEM THEY SERVE.
I PROPOSE WE ASK MR. STAINES TO SET UP AND OVERSEE THE IMPLEMENTATION OF A DIRECTIVE: STOP ANARKY BY ANY MEANS POSSIBLE!
CAN I HAVE A SHOW OF HANDS ON THAT...?
THANK YOU FOR YOUR TRUST, GENTLEMEN. IT WILL NOT GO UNREWARDED.
I HAVE BEEN AWAITING SUCH AN OPPORTUNITY--

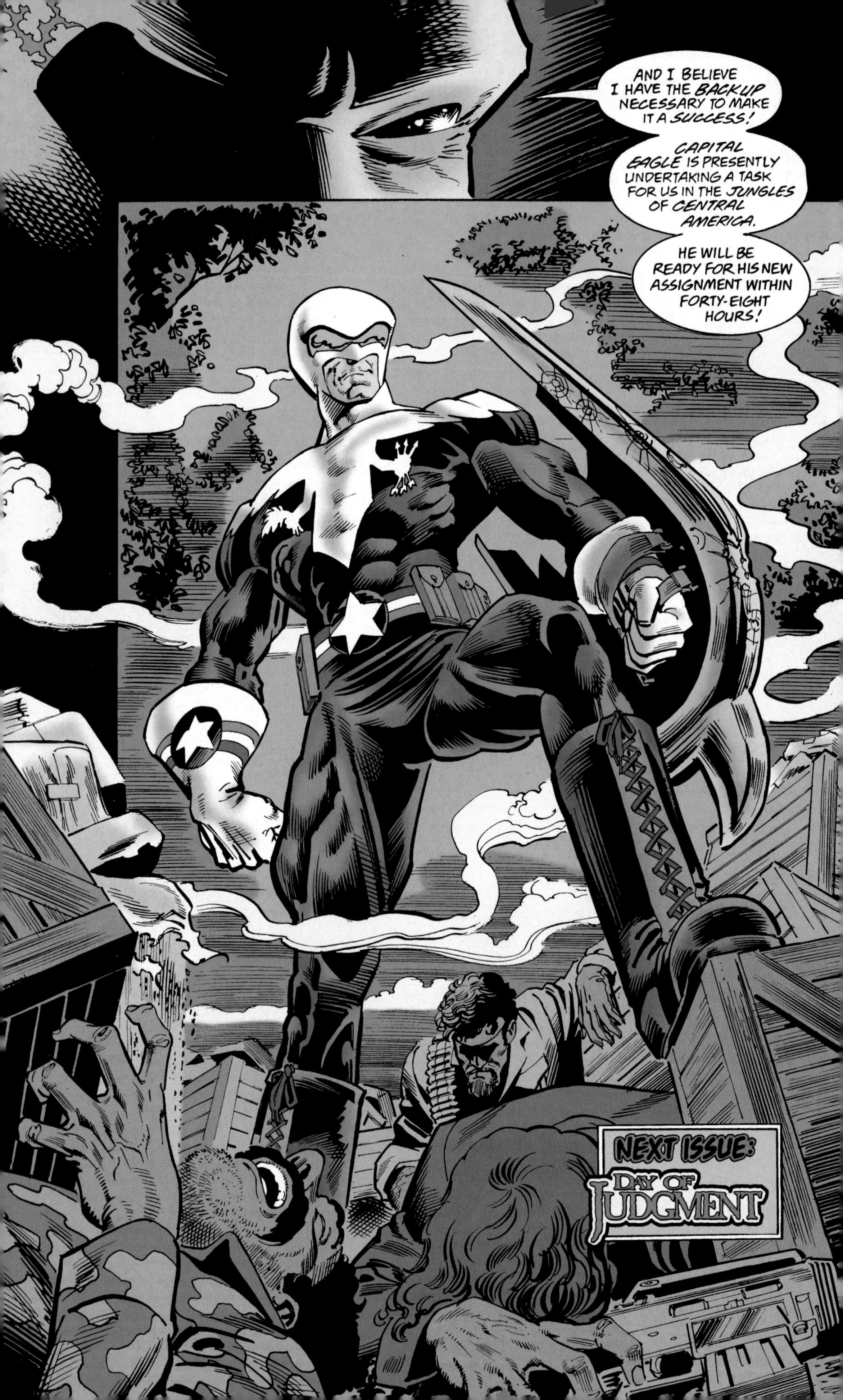
AND I BELIEVE I HAVE THE BACKUP NECESSARY TO MAKE IT A SUCCESS!
CAPITAL EAGLE IS PRESENTLY UNDERTAKING A TASK FOR US IN THE JUNGLES OF CENTRAL AMERICA.
HE WILL BE READY FOR HIS NEW ASSIGNMENT WITHIN FORTY-EIGHT HOURS!
NEXT ISSUE: DAY OF JUDGMENT

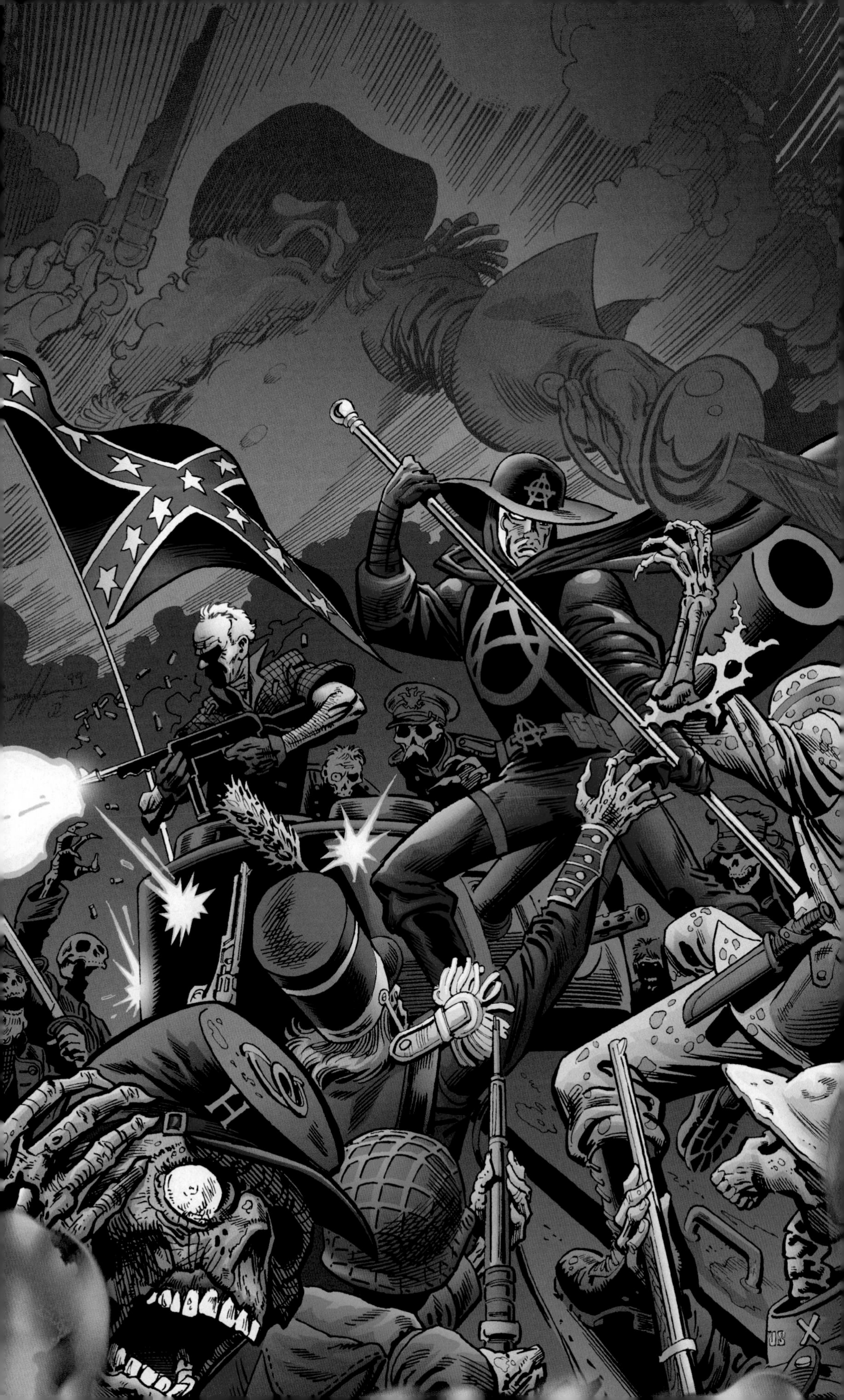

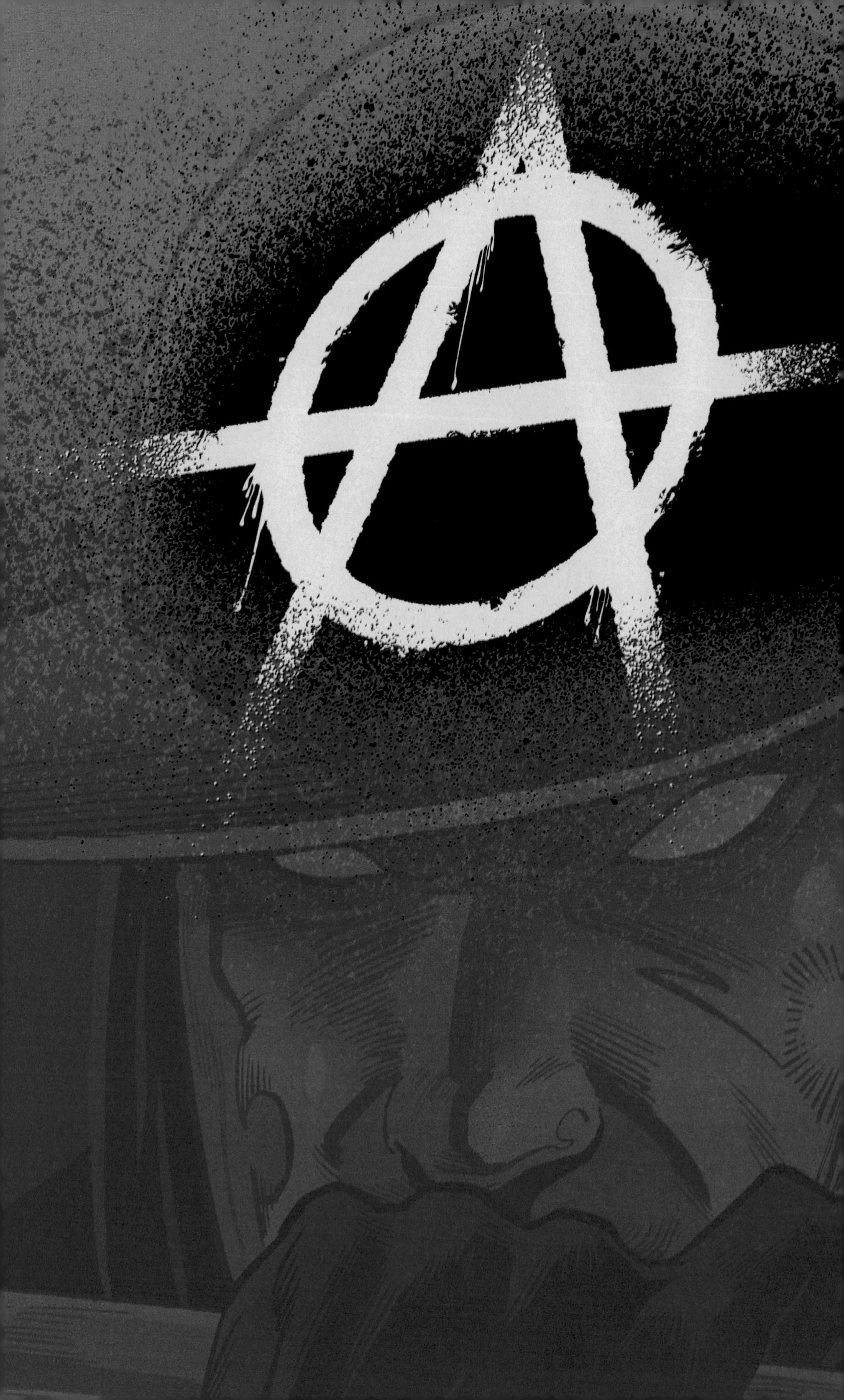

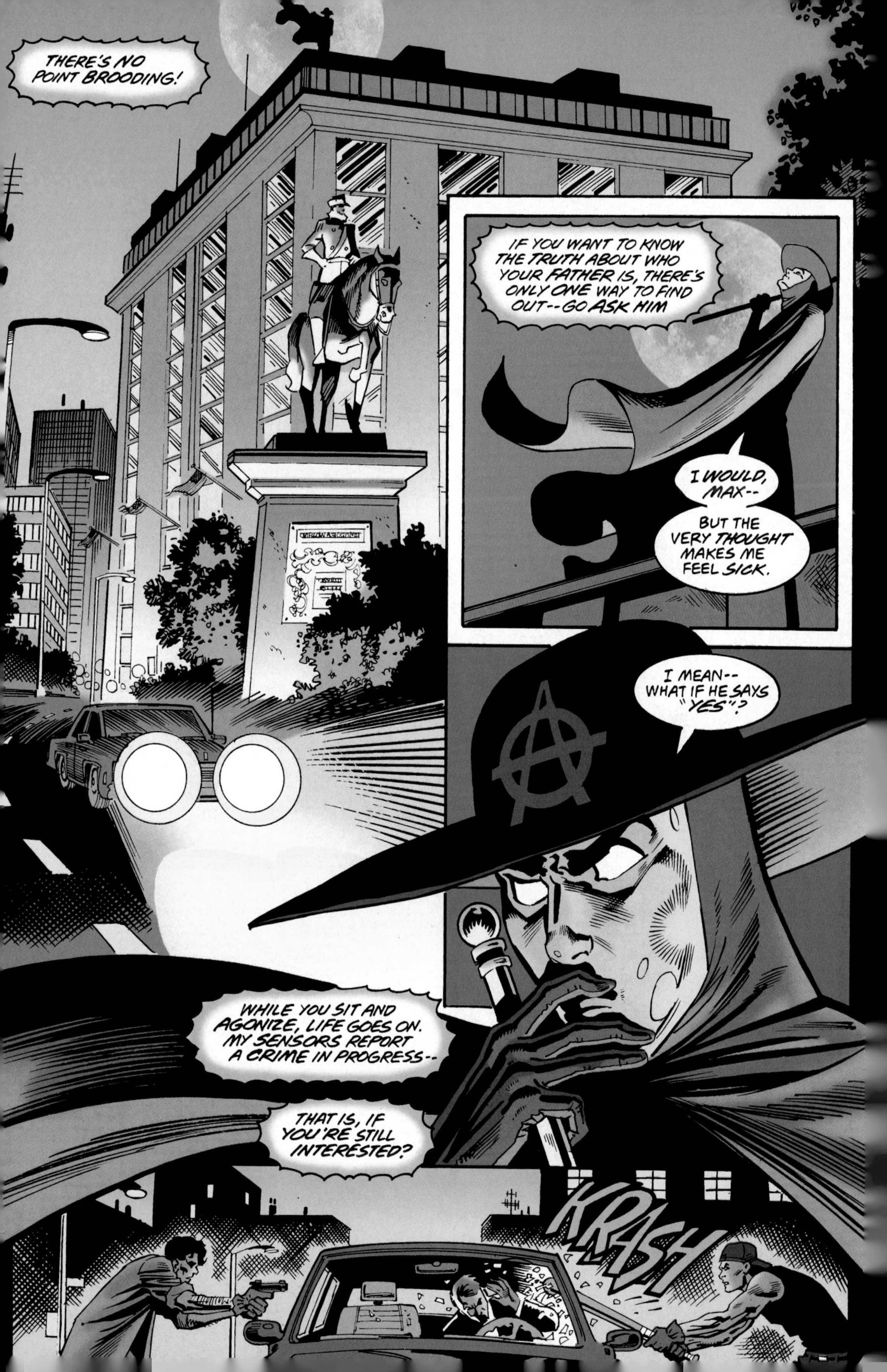
THERE'S NO POINT BROODING!
IF YOU WANT TO KNOW THE TRUTH ABOUT WHO YOUR FATHER IS, THERE'S ONLY ONE WAY TO FIND OUT--GO ASK HIM
I WOULD, MAX--
BUT THE VERY THOUGHT MAKES ME FEEL SICK.
I MEAN-- WHAT IF HE SAYS "YES"?
WHILE YOU SIT AND AGONIZE, LIFE GOES ON. MY SENSORS REPORT A CRIME IN PROGRESS--
THAT IS, IF YOU'RE STILL INTERESTED?
KRASH

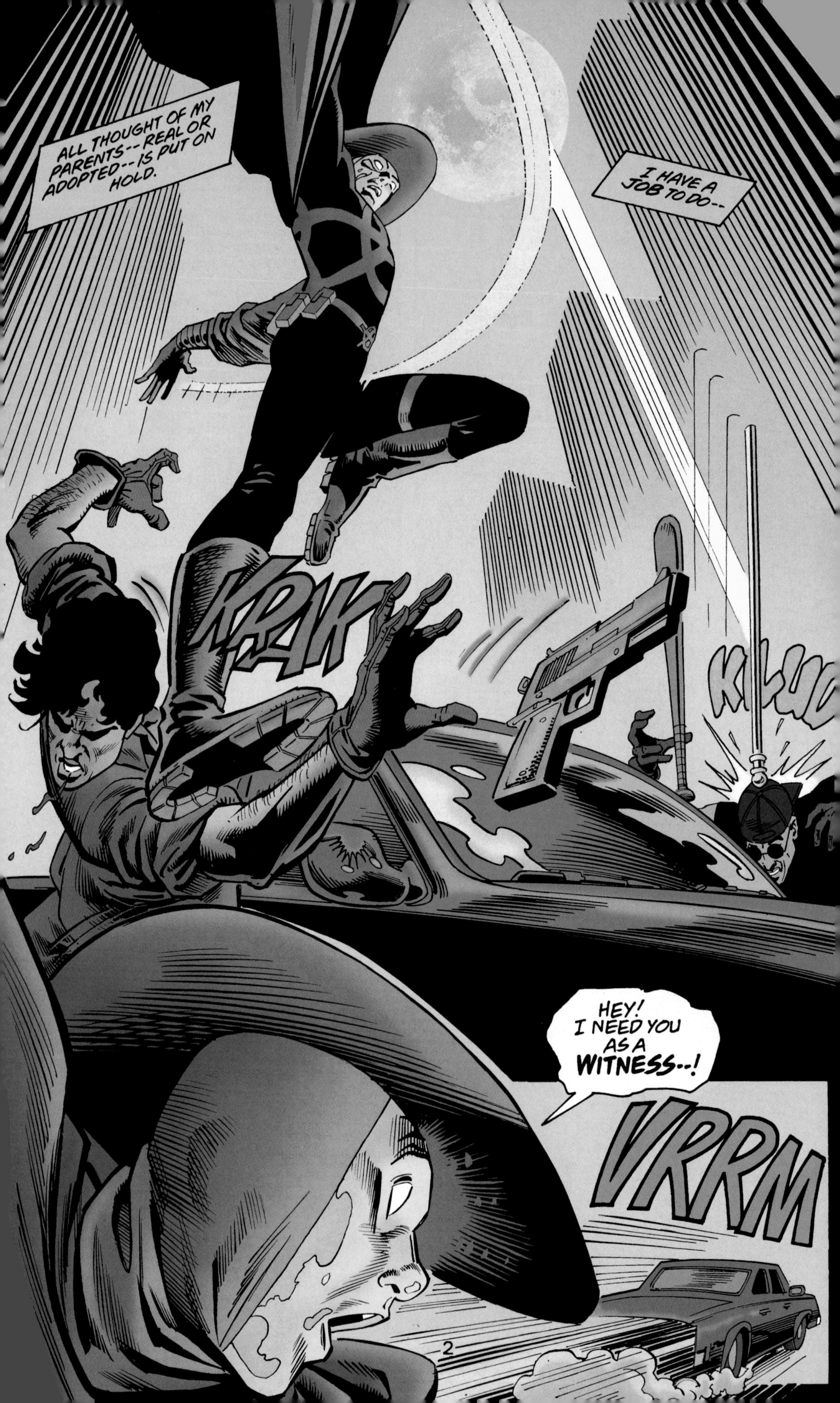
ALL THOUGHT OF MY PARENTS--REAL OR ADOPTED--IS PUT ON HOLD.
I HAVE A JOB TO DO--
KRAK
KLUD
HEY! I NEED YOU AS A WITNESS--!
VRRM
2

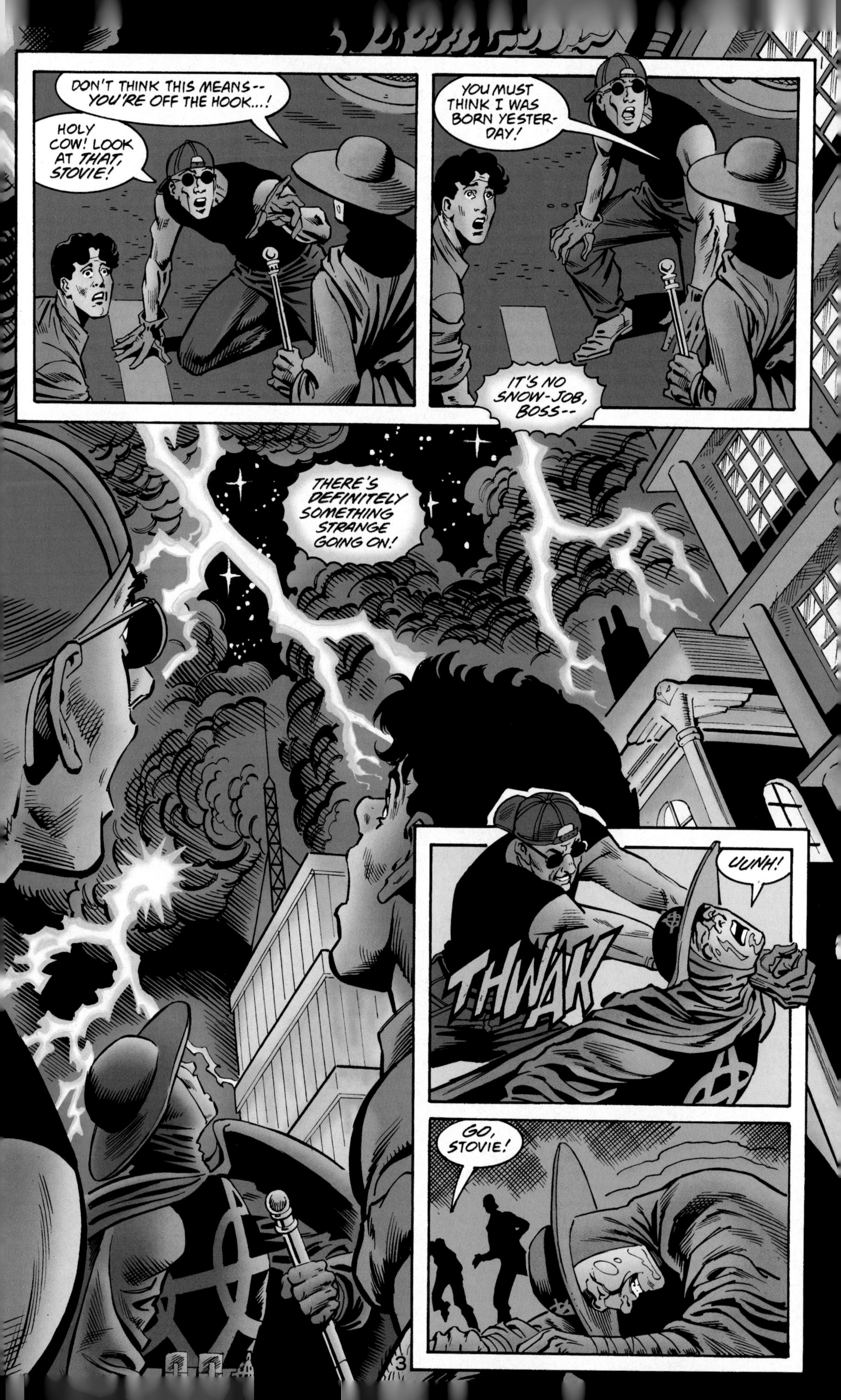

DON'T THINK THIS MEANS-- YOU'RE OFF THE HOOK...!
HOLY COW! LOOK AT THAT, STOVIE!
YOU MUST THINK I WAS BORN YESTER-DAY!
IT'S NO SNOW-JOB, BOSS--
THERE'S DEFINITELY SOMETHING STRANGE GOING ON!
UUNH!
THWAK
GO, STOVIE!

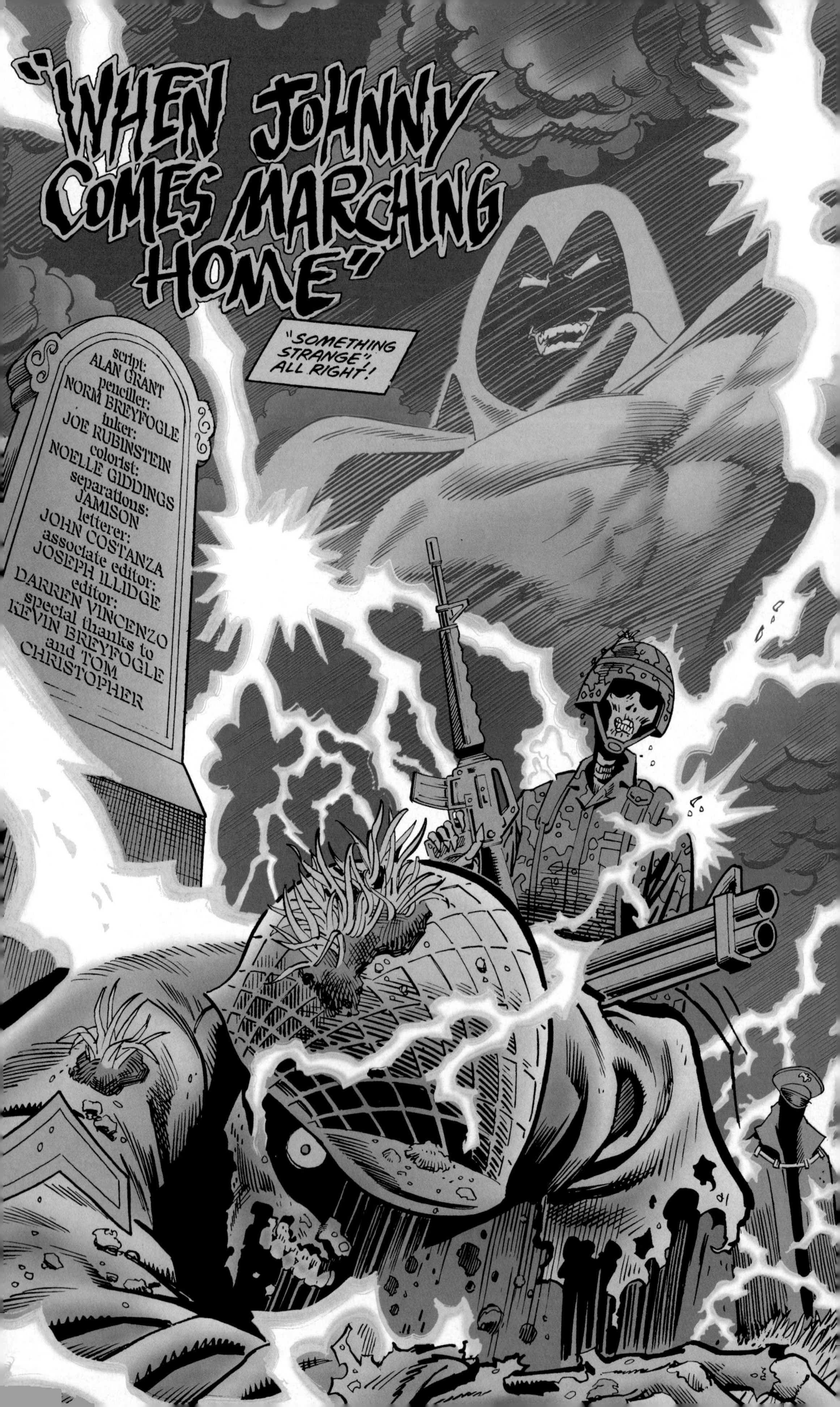
"WHEN JOHNNY COMES MARCHING HOME"
"SOMETHING STRANGE", ALL RIGHT!
script: ALAN GRANT
penciller: NORM BREYFOGLE
inker: JOE RUBINSTEIN
colorist: NOELLE GIDDINGS
separations: JAMISON
letterer: JOHN COSTANZA
associate editor: JOSEPH ILLIDGE
editor: DARREN VINCENZO
special thanks to KEVIN BREYFOGLE and TOM CHRISTOPHER

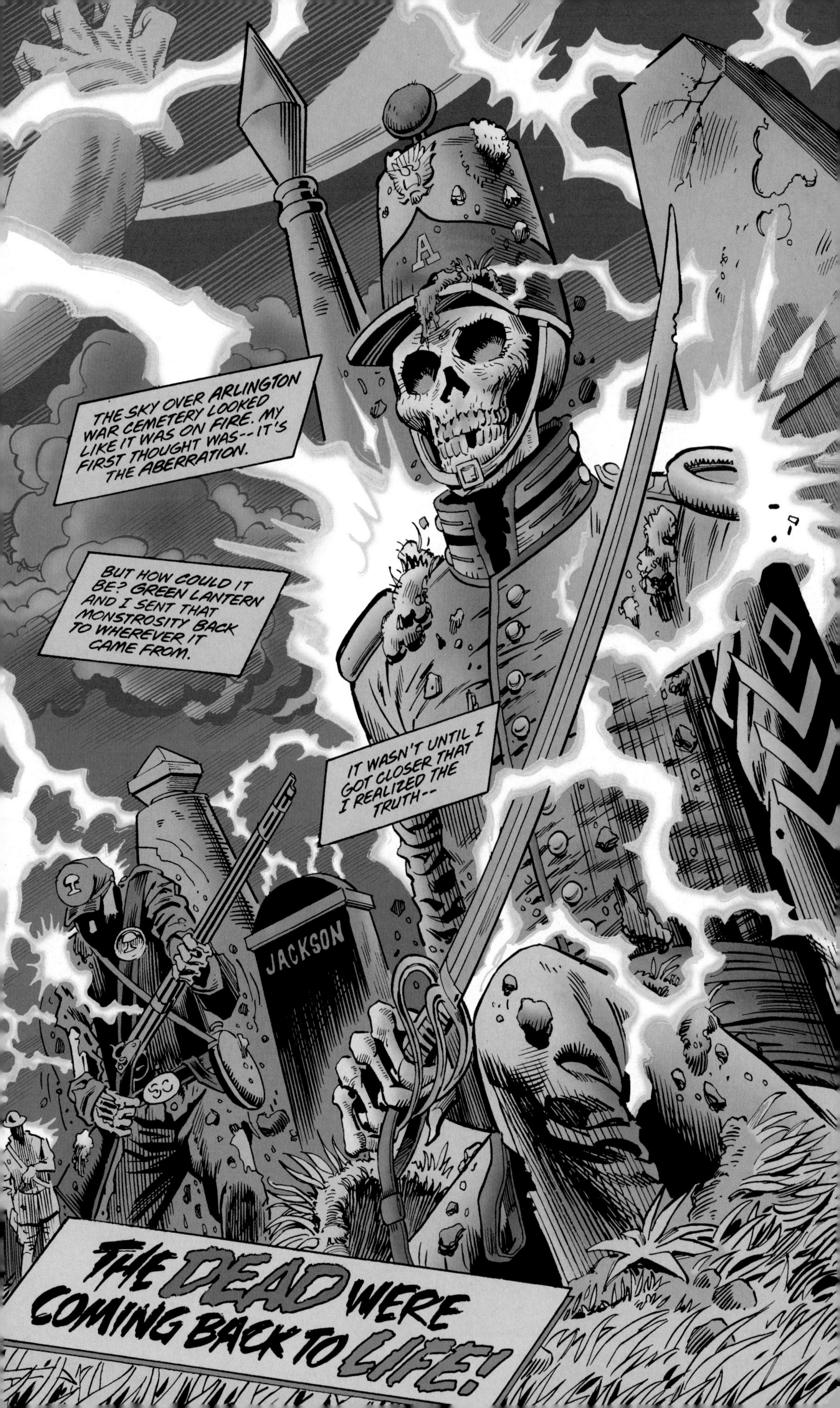
THE SKY OVER ARLINGTON WAR CEMETERY LOOKED LIKE IT WAS ON FIRE. MY FIRST THOUGHT WAS-- IT'S THE ABERRATION.
BUT HOW COULD IT BE? GREEN LANTERN AND I SENT THAT MONSTROSITY BACK TO WHEREVER IT CAME FROM.
IT WASN'T UNTIL I GOT CLOSER THAT I REALIZED THE TRUTH--
JACKSON
THE DEAD WERE COMING BACK TO LIFE!

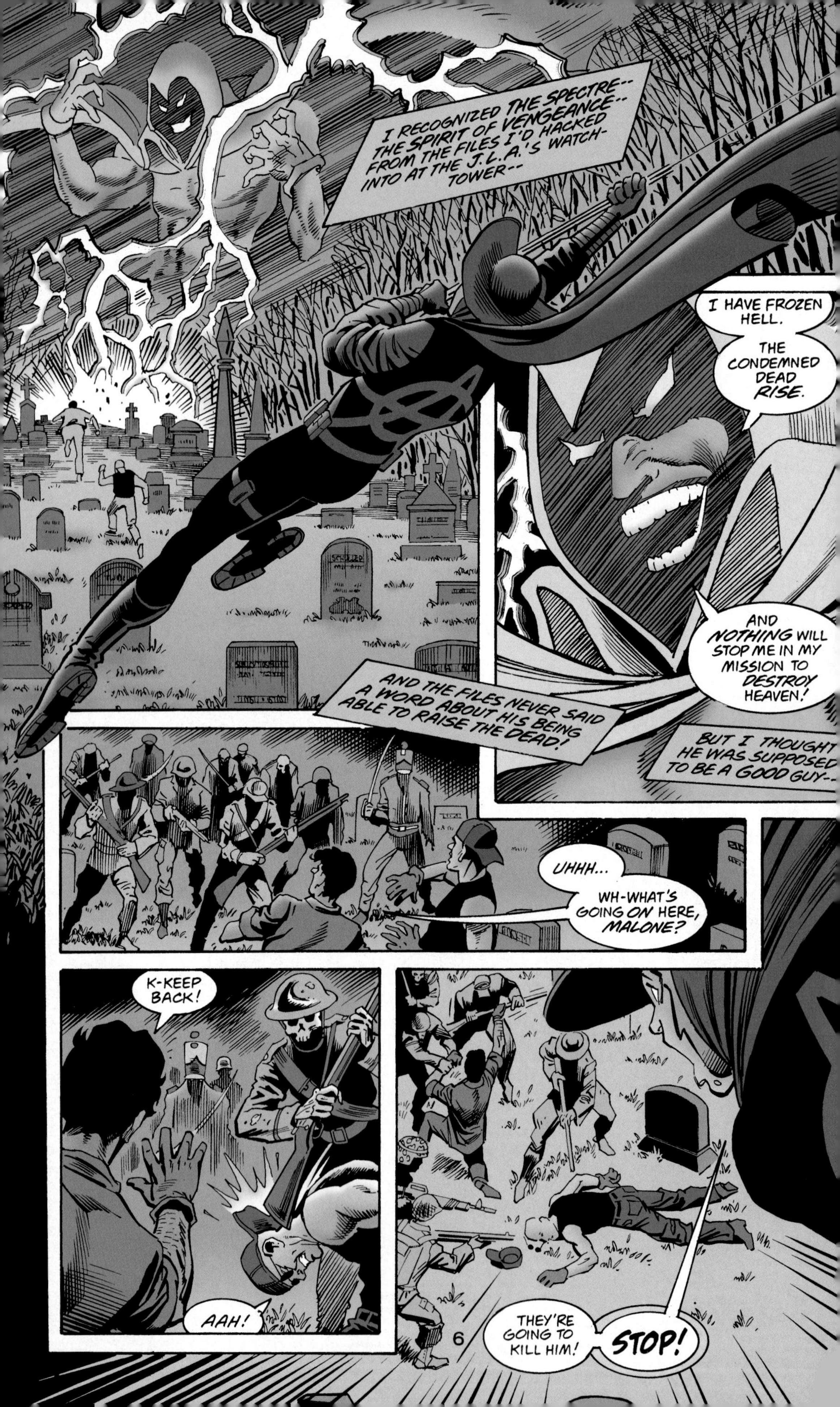
I RECOGNIZED THE SPECTRE-- THE SPIRIT OF VENGEANCE-- FROM THE FILES I'D HACKED INTO AT THE J.L.A.'S WATCH-TOWER--
I HAVE FROZEN HELL.
THE CONDEMNED DEAD RISE.
AND NOTHING WILL STOP ME IN MY MISSION TO DESTROY HEAVEN!
AND THE FILES NEVER SAID A WORD ABOUT HIS BEING ABLE TO RAISE THE DEAD!
BUT I THOUGHT HE WAS SUPPOSED TO BE A GOOD GUY--
UHHH...
WH-WHAT'S GOING ON HERE, MALONE?
K-KEEP BACK!
AAH!
THEY'RE GOING TO KILL HIM!
STOP!

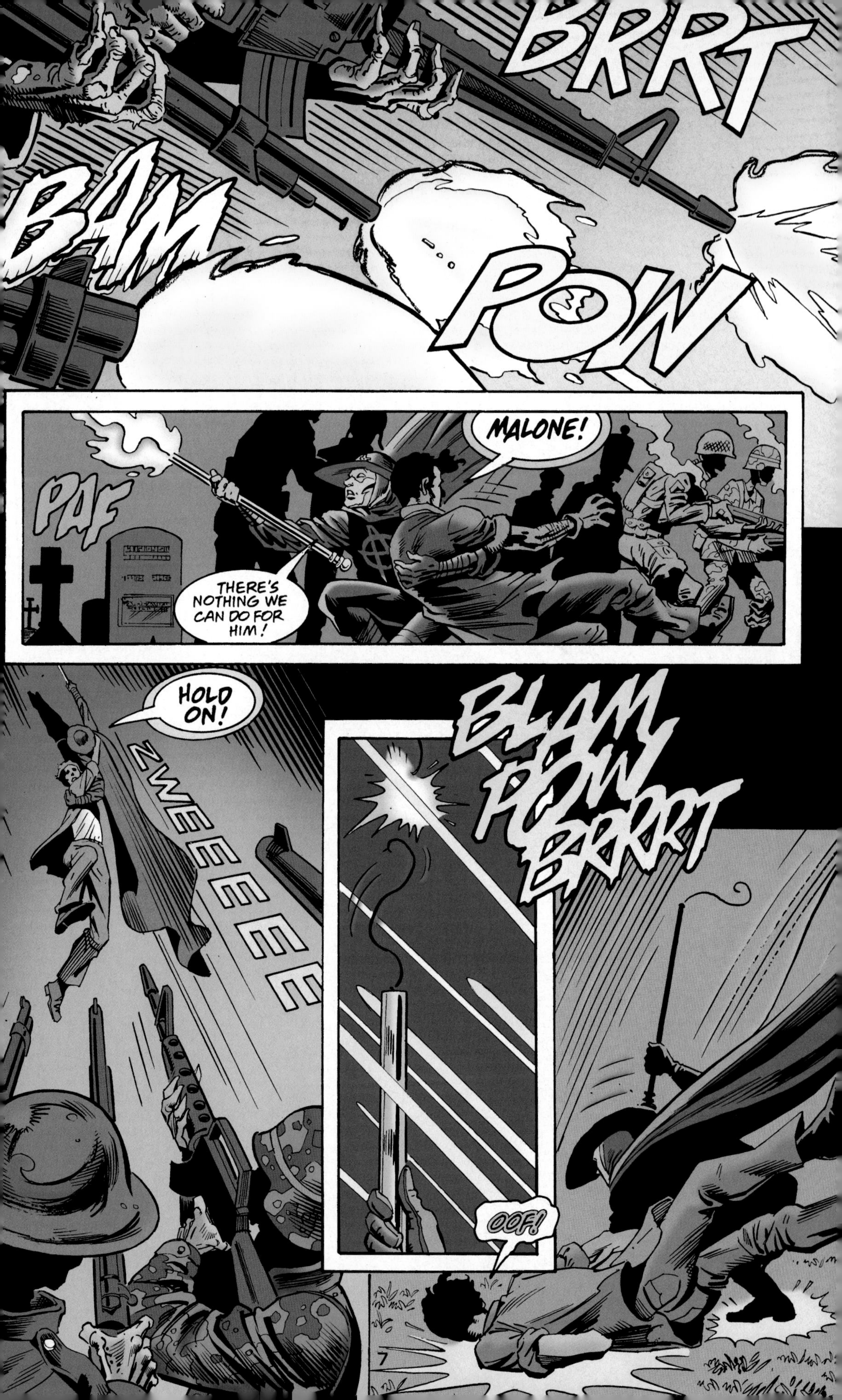
BRRT
BAM
POW
PAF
MALONE!
THERE'S NOTHING WE CAN DO FOR HIM!
HOLD ON!
ZWEEEEE
BLAM
POW
BRRRT
OOF!
7

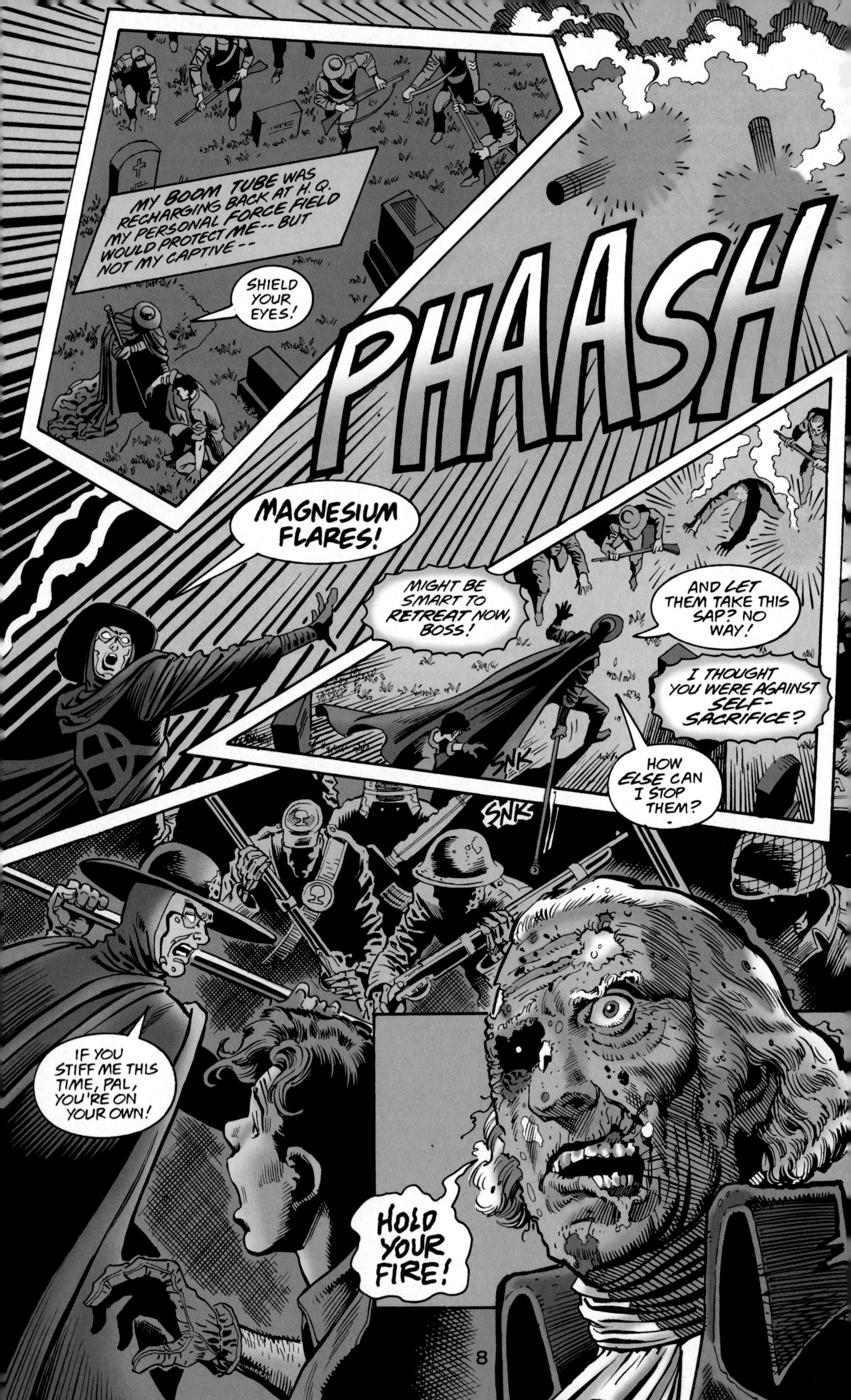
MY BOOM TUBE WAS RECHARGING BACK AT H.Q. MY PERSONAL FORCE FIELD WOULD PROTECT ME-- BUT NOT MY CAPTIVE--
SHIELD YOUR EYES!
PHAASH
MAGNESIUM FLARES!
MIGHT BE SMART TO RETREAT NOW, BOSS!
AND LET THEM TAKE THIS SAP? NO WAY!
I THOUGHT YOU WERE AGAINST SELF-SACRIFICE?
HOW ELSE CAN I STOP THEM?
SNK
SNK
IF YOU STIFF ME THIS TIME, PAL, YOU'RE ON YOUR OWN!
HOLD YOUR FIRE!

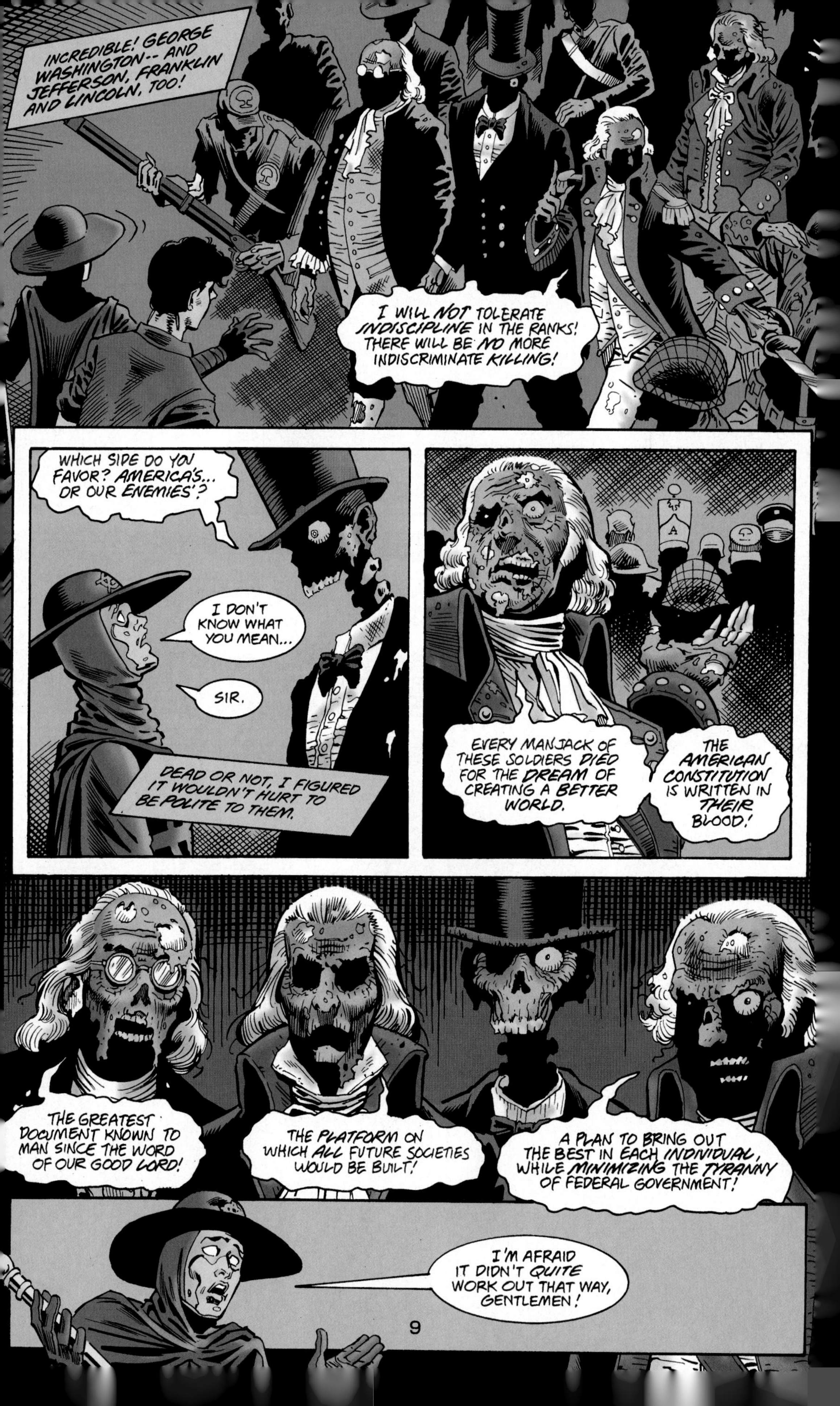
INCREDIBLE! GEORGE WASHINGTON-- AND JEFFERSON, FRANKLIN AND LINCOLN, TOO!
I WILL NOT TOLERATE INDISCIPLINE IN THE RANKS! THERE WILL BE NO MORE INDISCRIMINATE KILLING!
WHICH SIDE DO YOU FAVOR? AMERICA'S... OR OUR ENEMIES'?
I DON'T KNOW WHAT YOU MEAN...
SIR.
DEAD OR NOT, I FIGURED IT WOULDN'T HURT TO BE POLITE TO THEM.
EVERY MANJACK OF THESE SOLDIERS DIED FOR THE DREAM OF CREATING A BETTER WORLD.
THE AMERICAN CONSTITUTION IS WRITTEN IN THEIR BLOOD!
THE GREATEST DOCUMENT KNOWN TO MAN SINCE THE WORD OF OUR GOOD LORD!
THE PLATFORM ON WHICH ALL FUTURE SOCIETIES WOULD BE BUILT!
A PLAN TO BRING OUT THE BEST IN EACH INDIVIDUAL, WHILE MINIMIZING THE TYRANNY OF FEDERAL GOVERNMENT!
I'M AFRAID IT DIDN'T QUITE WORK OUT THAT WAY, GENTLEMEN!

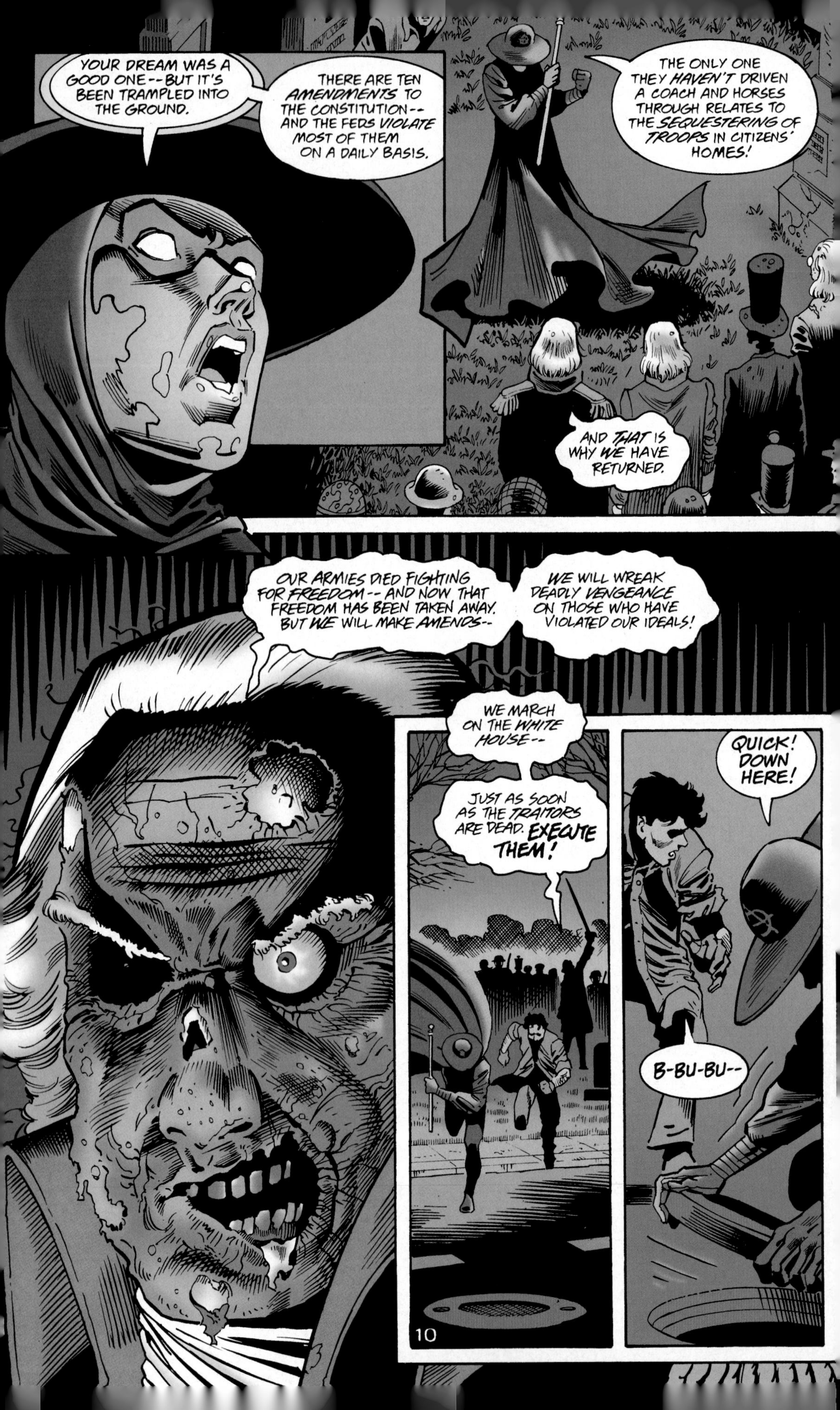
YOUR DREAM WAS A GOOD ONE--BUT IT'S BEEN TRAMPLED INTO THE GROUND.
THERE ARE TEN AMENDMENTS TO THE CONSTITUTION--AND THE FEDS VIOLATE MOST OF THEM ON A DAILY BASIS.
THE ONLY ONE THEY HAVEN'T DRIVEN A COACH AND HORSES THROUGH RELATES TO THE SEQUESTERING OF TROOPS IN CITIZENS' HOMES!
AND THAT IS WHY WE HAVE RETURNED.
OUR ARMIES DIED FIGHTING FOR FREEDOM--AND NOW THAT FREEDOM HAS BEEN TAKEN AWAY. BUT WE WILL MAKE AMENDS--
WE WILL WREAK DEADLY VENGEANCE ON THOSE WHO HAVE VIOLATED OUR IDEALS!
WE MARCH ON THE WHITE HOUSE--
JUST AS SOON AS THE TRAITORS ARE DEAD. EXECUTE THEM!
QUICK! DOWN HERE!
B-BU-BU--

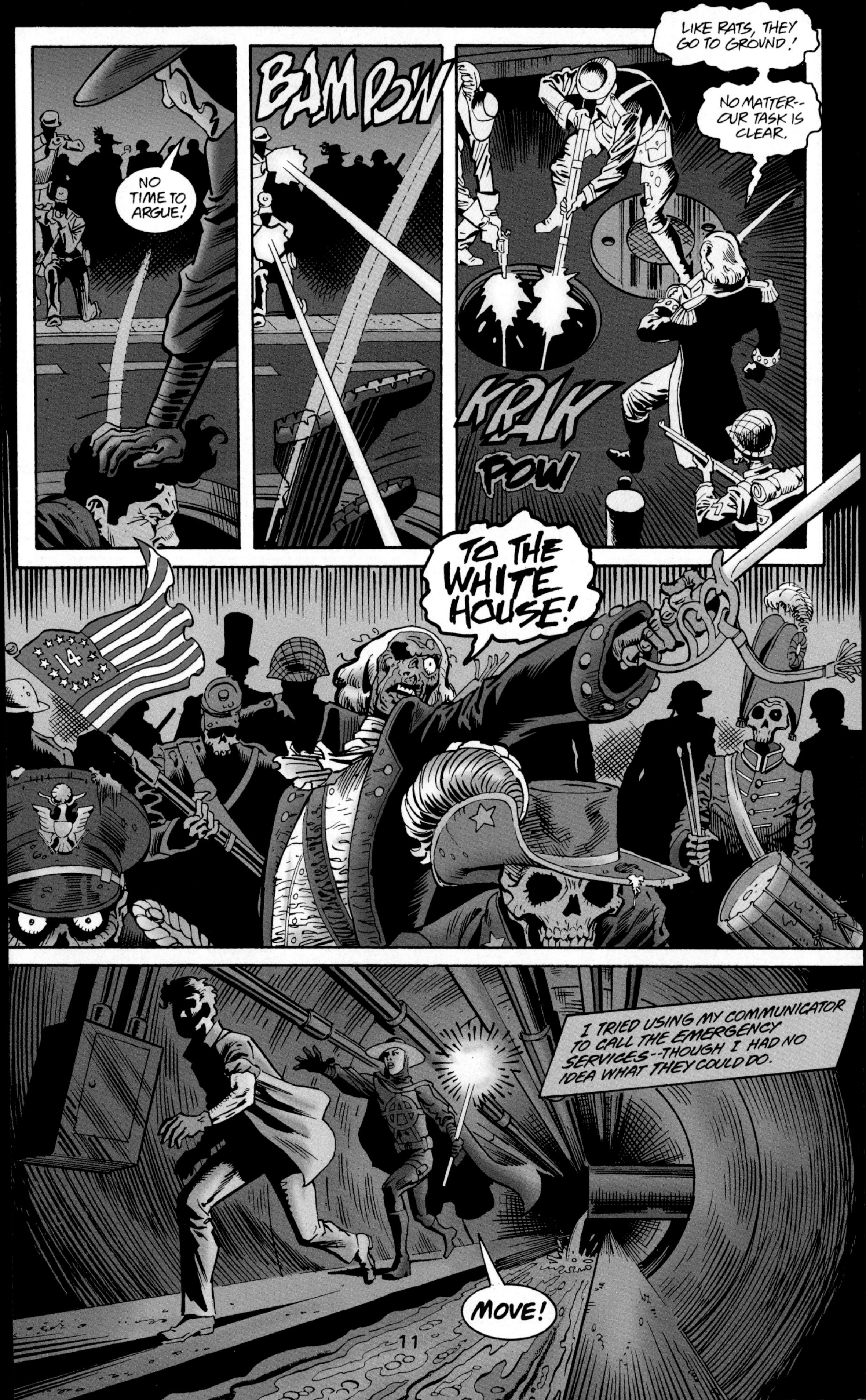
NO TIME TO ARGUE!
BAM POW
LIKE RATS, THEY GO TO GROUND!
NO MATTER-- OUR TASK IS CLEAR.
KRAK
POW
TO THE WHITE HOUSE!
I TRIED USING MY COMMUNICATOR TO CALL THE EMERGENCY SERVICES--THOUGH I HAD NO IDEA WHAT THEY COULD DO.
MOVE!

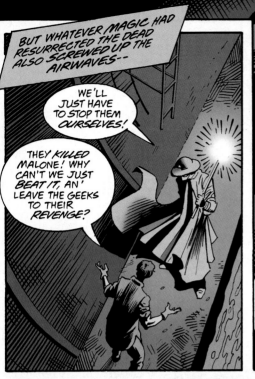

BUT WHATEVER MAGIC HAD RESURRECTED THE DEAD ALSO SCREWED UP THE AIRWAVES--

WE'LL JUST HAVE TO STOP THEM *OURSELVES!*

THEY *KILLED* MALONE! WHY CAN'T WE JUST *BEAT IT,* AN' LEAVE THE GEEKS TO THEIR *REVENGE?*

BECAUSE THEY'RE *DEAD!* AND EVEN IF THEIR *CAUSE* IS *JUST--* MURDERING THE *LIVING* WON'T EVER MAKE THINGS *RIGHT!*

I'M GOING UP!

N-NOT ME, MAN! I AIN'T NO *HERO!*

I'M A *CRIMINAL!* I'VE PULLED DOZENS OF CARJACKS!

I DEMAND MY *RIGHTS!* TURN ME OVER TO THE *COPS!*

WAIT FOR ME!

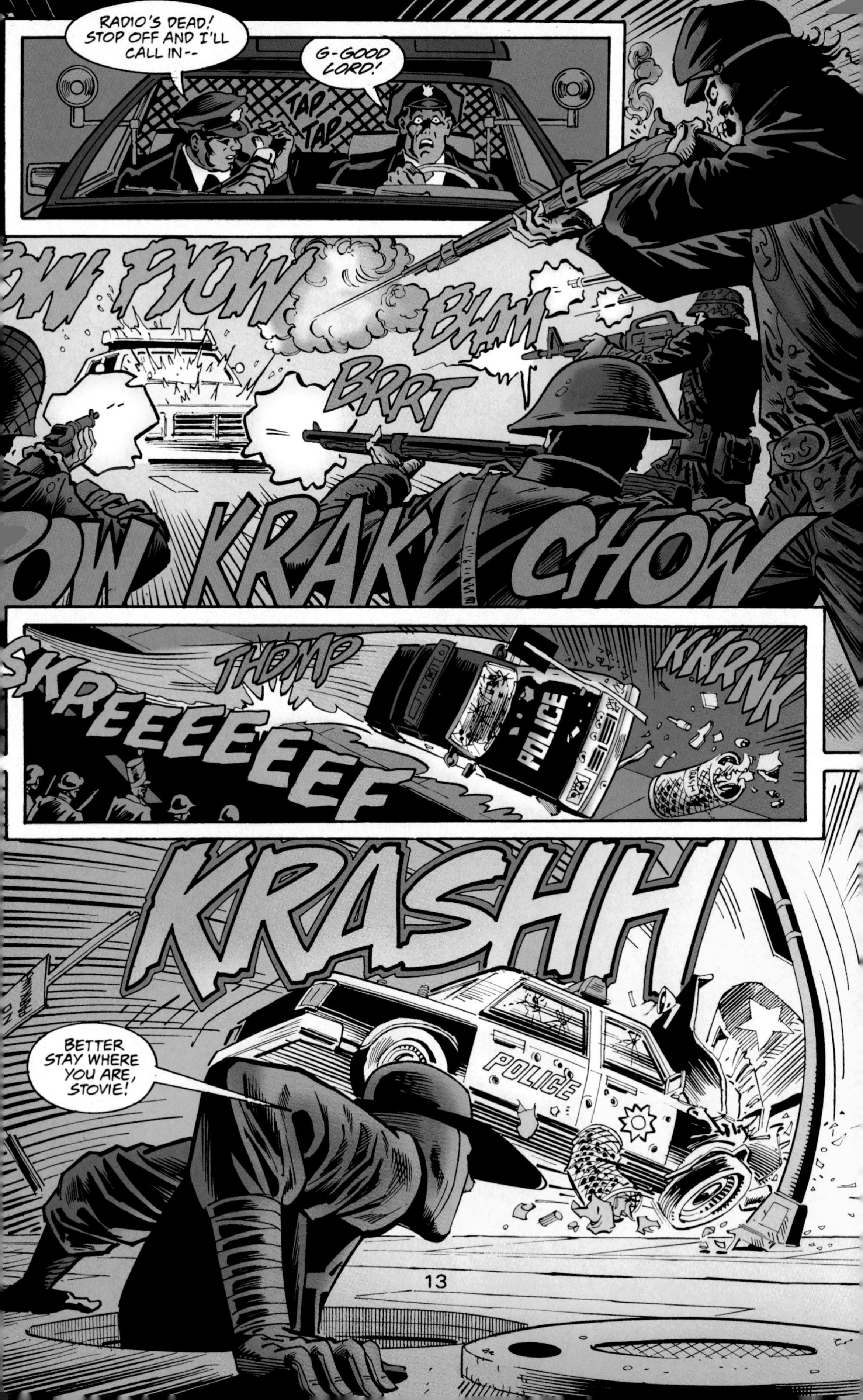
RADIO'S DEAD! STOP OFF AND I'LL CALL IN--
G-GOOD LORD!
TAP TAP
OW PYOW
BLAM
BRRT
OW KRAK! CHOW
SKREEEEEEEEF
THDMP
KKRNK
KRASHH
BETTER STAY WHERE YOU ARE, STOVIE!

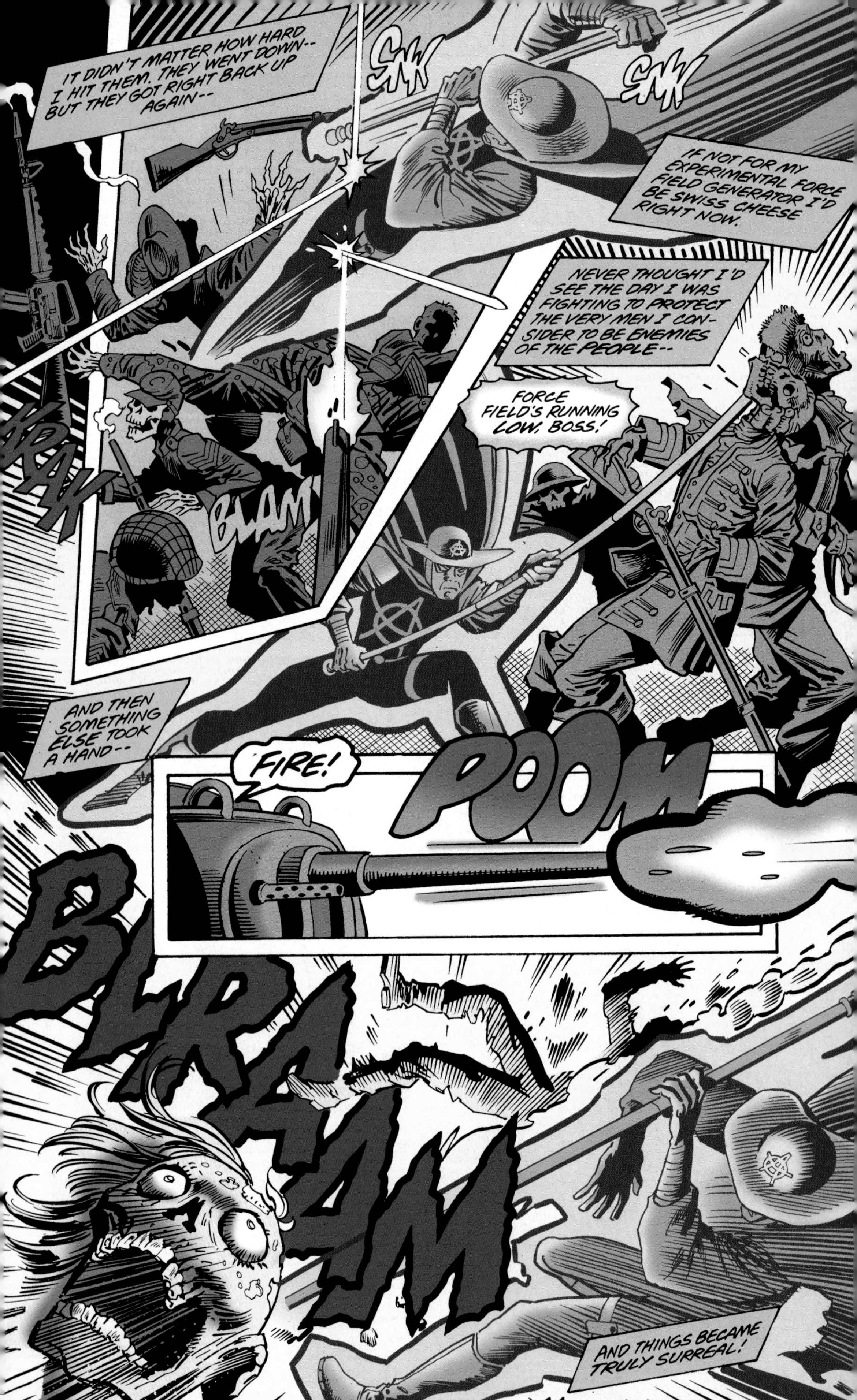

IT DIDN'T MATTER HOW HARD I HIT THEM. THEY WENT DOWN-- BUT THEY GOT RIGHT BACK UP AGAIN--
SNK
SNK
IF NOT FOR MY EXPERIMENTAL FORCE FIELD GENERATOR I'D BE SWISS CHEESE RIGHT NOW.
KRAK
BLAM
NEVER THOUGHT I'D SEE THE DAY I WAS FIGHTING TO PROTECT THE VERY MEN I CONSIDER TO BE ENEMIES OF THE PEOPLE--
FORCE FIELD'S RUNNING LOW, BOSS!
AND THEN SOMETHING ELSE TOOK A HAND--
FIRE!
POOM
BLRAAM
AND THINGS BECAME TRULY SURREAL!

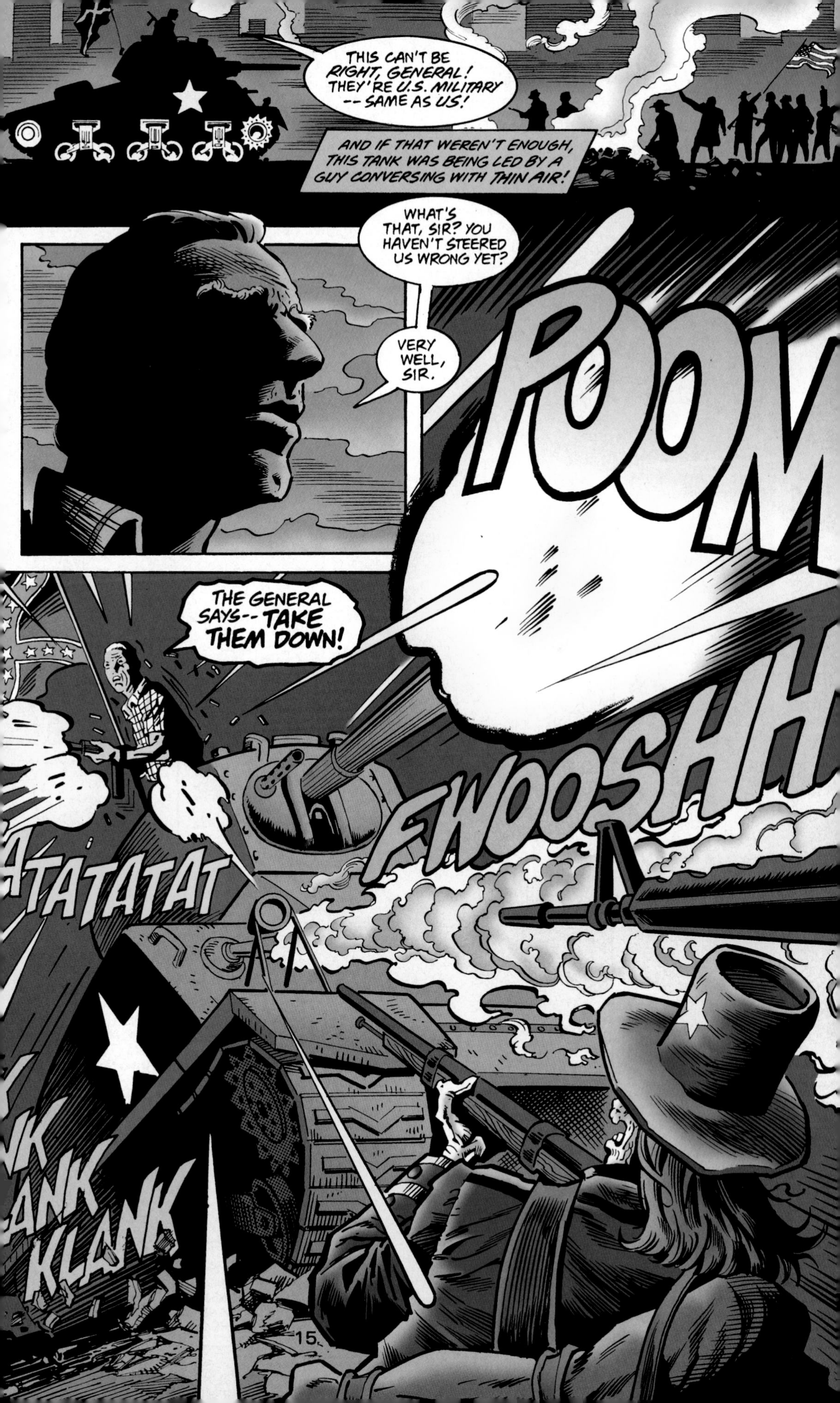
THIS CAN'T BE RIGHT, GENERAL! THEY'RE U.S. MILITARY -- SAME AS US!
AND IF THAT WEREN'T ENOUGH, THIS TANK WAS BEING LED BY A GUY CONVERSING WITH THIN AIR!
WHAT'S THAT, SIR? YOU HAVEN'T STEERED US WRONG YET?
VERY WELL, SIR.
POOM
THE GENERAL SAYS--TAKE THEM DOWN!
FWOOSHH
TATATAT
ANK
KLANK

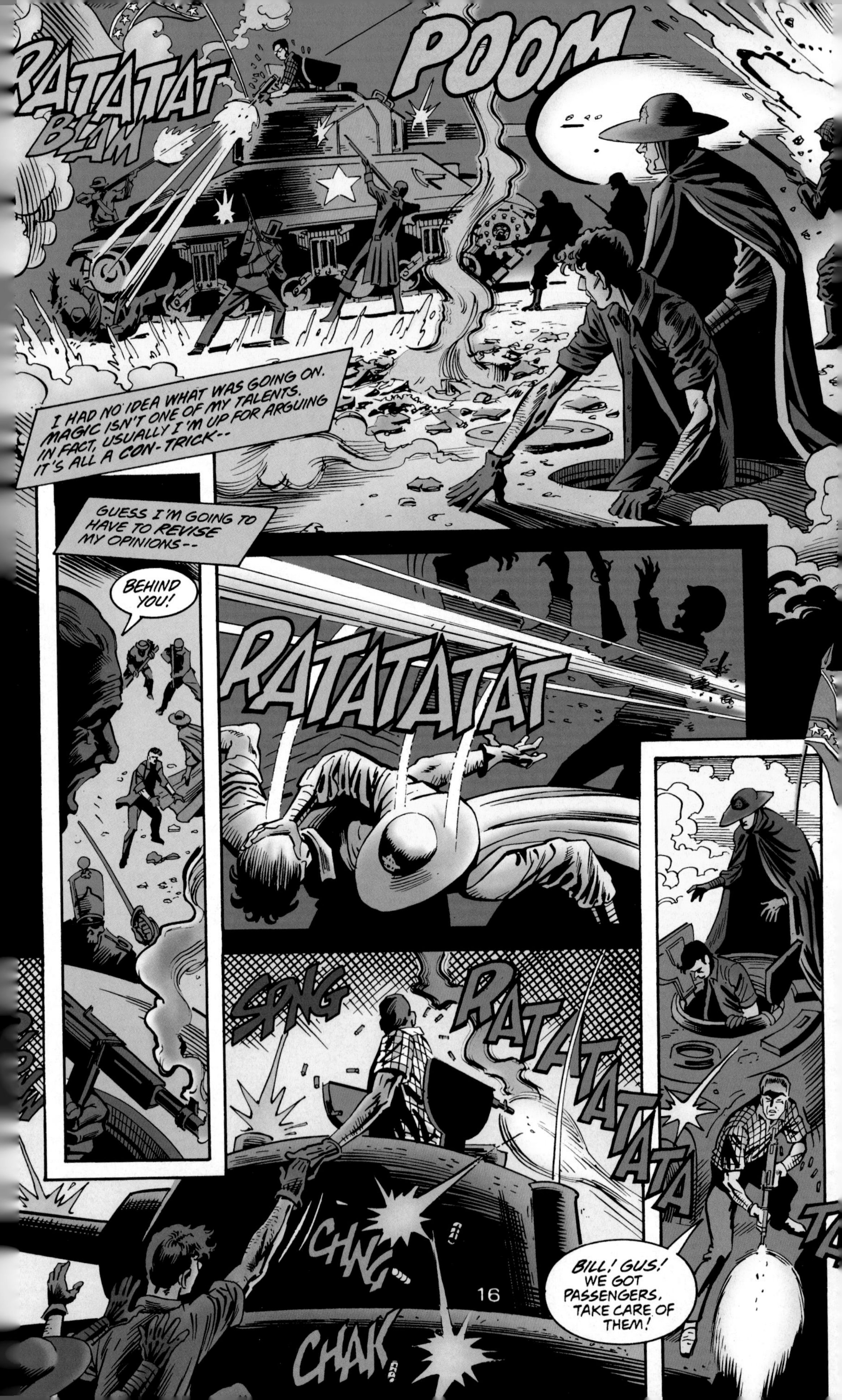
RATATAT
BLAM
POOM
I HAD NO IDEA WHAT WAS GOING ON. MAGIC ISN'T ONE OF MY TALENTS. IN FACT, USUALLY I'M UP FOR ARGUING IT'S ALL A CON-TRICK--
GUESS I'M GOING TO HAVE TO REVISE MY OPINIONS--
BEHIND YOU!
RATATATAT
SPNG
RATATATATATA
CHNG
CHAK
BILL! GUS! WE GOT PASSENGERS, TAKE CARE OF THEM!

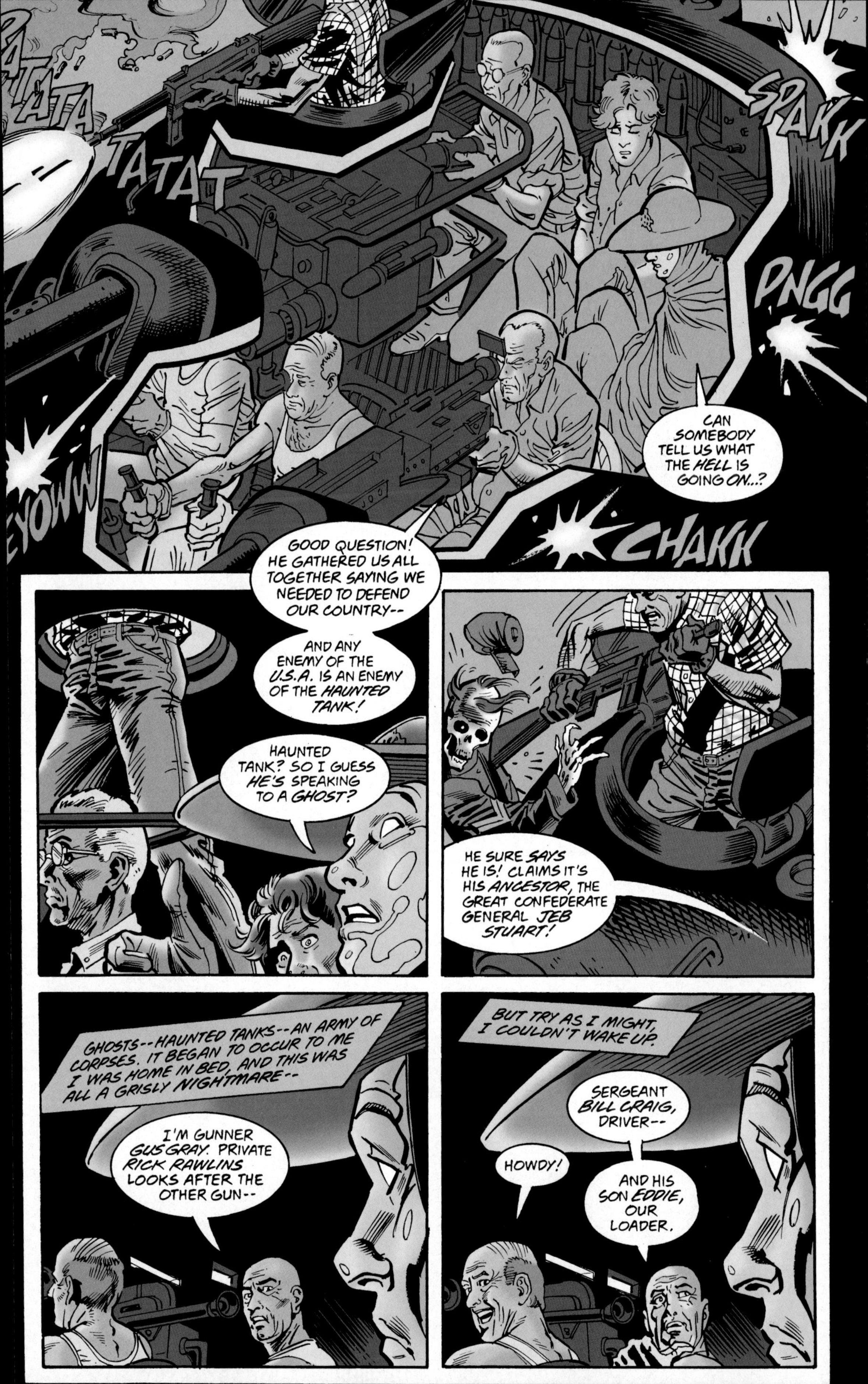
TATATAT
SPAKK
PNGG
EYOWW
CAN SOMEBODY TELL US WHAT THE HELL IS GOING ON...?
CHAKK
GOOD QUESTION! HE GATHERED US ALL TOGETHER SAYING WE NEEDED TO DEFEND OUR COUNTRY--
AND ANY ENEMY OF THE U.S.A. IS AN ENEMY OF THE HAUNTED TANK!
HAUNTED TANK? SO I GUESS HE'S SPEAKING TO A GHOST?
HE SURE SAYS HE IS! CLAIMS IT'S HIS ANCESTOR, THE GREAT CONFEDERATE GENERAL JEB STUART!
GHOSTS--HAUNTED TANKS--AN ARMY OF CORPSES. IT BEGAN TO OCCUR TO ME I WAS HOME IN BED, AND THIS WAS ALL A GRISLY NIGHTMARE--
I'M GUNNER GUS GRAY. PRIVATE RICK RAWLINS LOOKS AFTER THE OTHER GUN--
BUT TRY AS I MIGHT, I COULDN'T WAKE UP.
SERGEANT BILL CRAIG, DRIVER--
HOWDY!
AND HIS SON EDDIE, OUR LOADER.

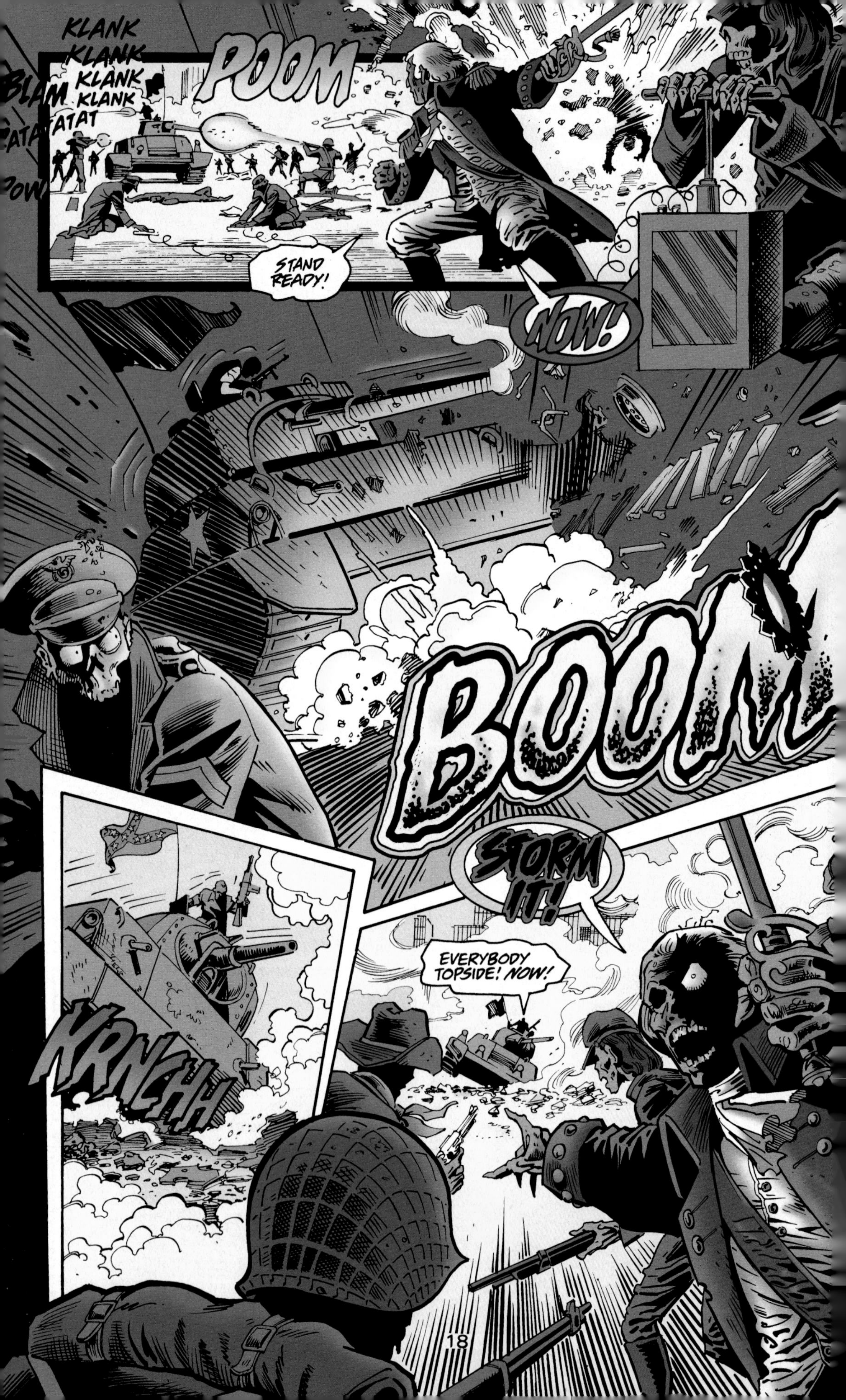
KLANK KLANK KLANK KLANK
POOM
BLAM
TATATATAT
POW
STAND READY!
NOW!
BOOM
STORM IT!
KRNCHH
EVERYBODY TOPSIDE! NOW!

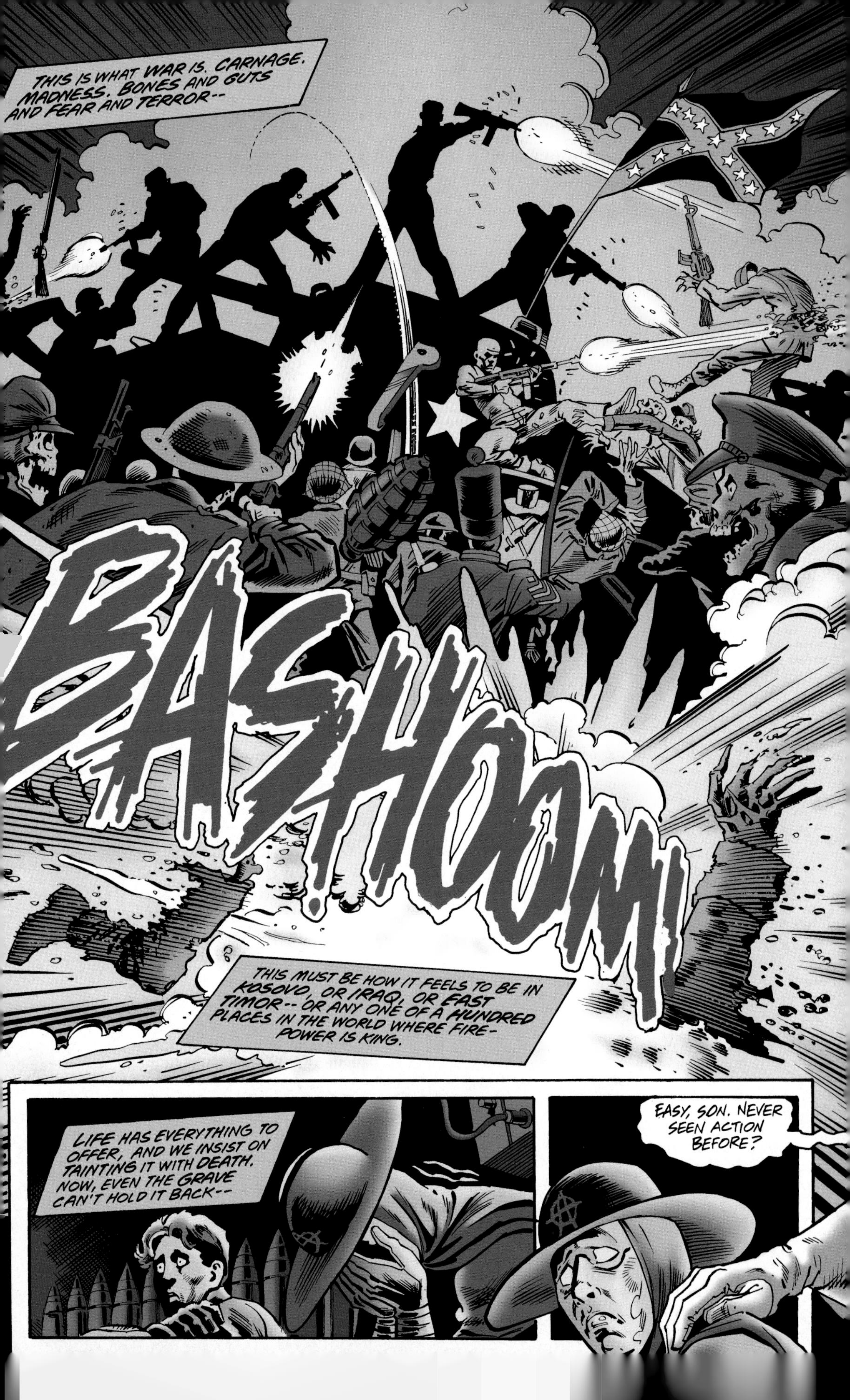
THIS IS WHAT WAR IS. CARNAGE. MADNESS. BONES AND GUTS AND FEAR AND TERROR--
BASHOOM!
THIS MUST BE HOW IT FEELS TO BE IN KOSOVO, OR IRAQ, OR EAST TIMOR-- OR ANY ONE OF A HUNDRED PLACES IN THE WORLD WHERE FIRE-POWER IS KING.
LIFE HAS EVERYTHING TO OFFER, AND WE INSIST ON TAINTING IT WITH DEATH. NOW, EVEN THE GRAVE CAN'T HOLD IT BACK--
EASY, SON. NEVER SEEN ACTION BEFORE?

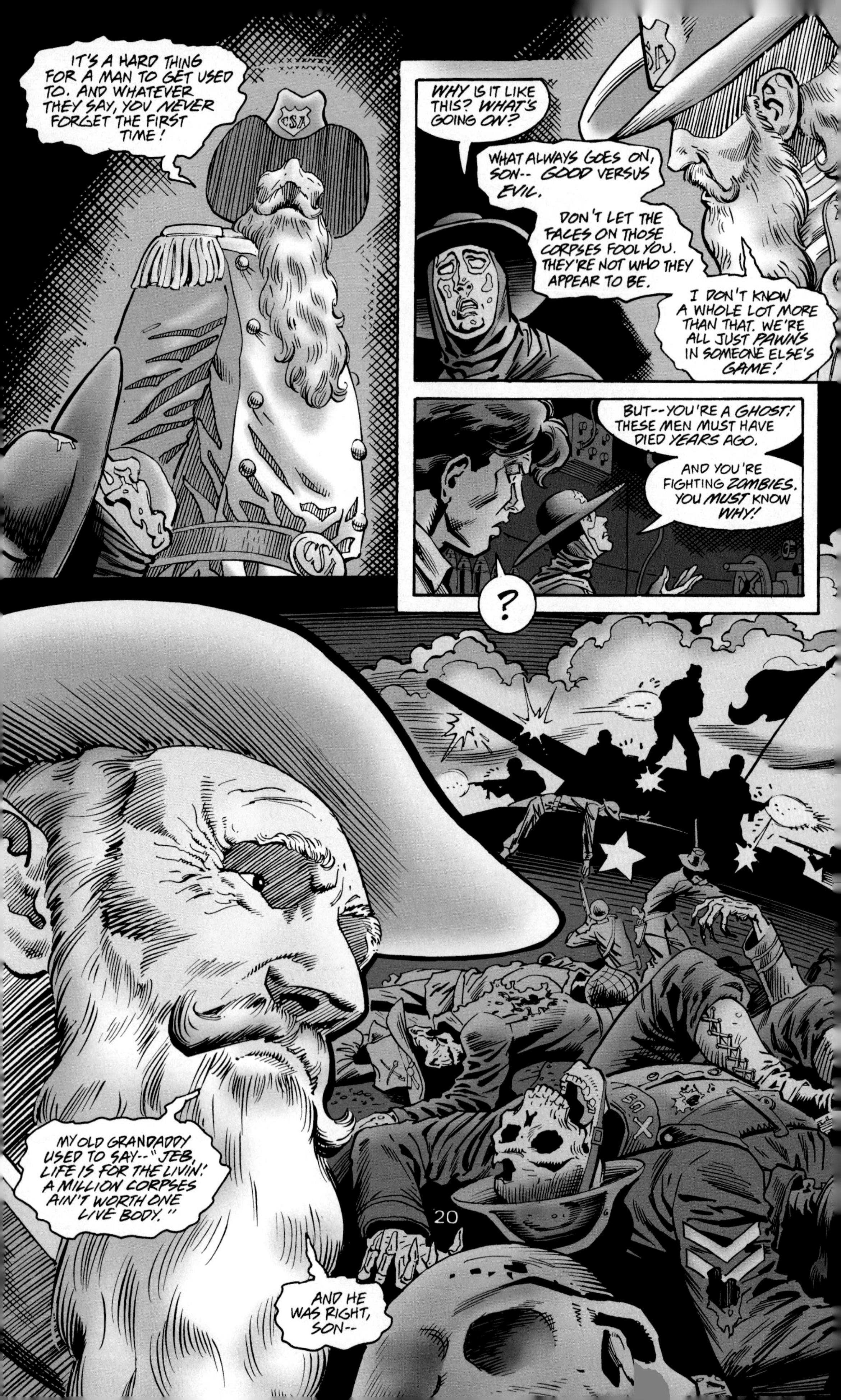
IT'S A HARD THING FOR A MAN TO GET USED TO. AND WHATEVER THEY SAY, YOU NEVER FORGET THE FIRST TIME!
WHY IS IT LIKE THIS? WHAT'S GOING ON?
WHAT ALWAYS GOES ON, SON-- GOOD VERSUS EVIL.
DON'T LET THE FACES ON THOSE CORPSES FOOL YOU. THEY'RE NOT WHO THEY APPEAR TO BE.
I DON'T KNOW A WHOLE LOT MORE THAN THAT. WE'RE ALL JUST PAWNS IN SOMEONE ELSE'S GAME!
BUT--YOU'RE A GHOST! THESE MEN MUST HAVE DIED YEARS AGO.
AND YOU'RE FIGHTING ZOMBIES. YOU MUST KNOW WHY!
?
MY OLD GRANDADDY USED TO SAY--"JEB, LIFE IS FOR THE LIVIN'. A MILLION CORPSES AIN'T WORTH ONE LIVE BODY."
AND HE WAS RIGHT, SON--

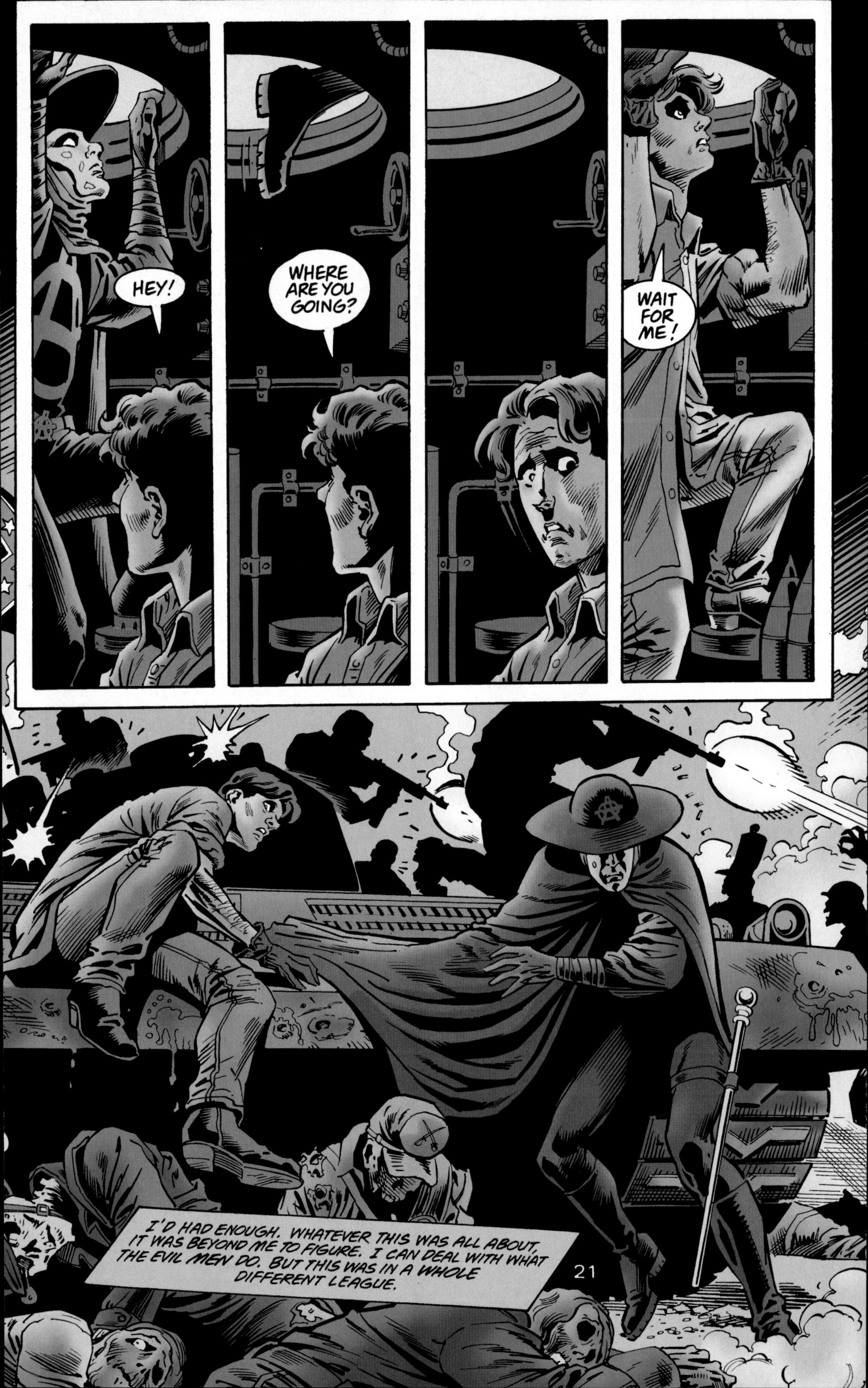
HEY!
WHERE ARE YOU GOING?
WAIT FOR ME!
I'D HAD ENOUGH. WHATEVER THIS WAS ALL ABOUT, IT WAS BEYOND ME TO FIGURE. I CAN DEAL WITH WHAT THE EVIL MEN DO. BUT THIS WAS IN A WHOLE DIFFERENT LEAGUE.

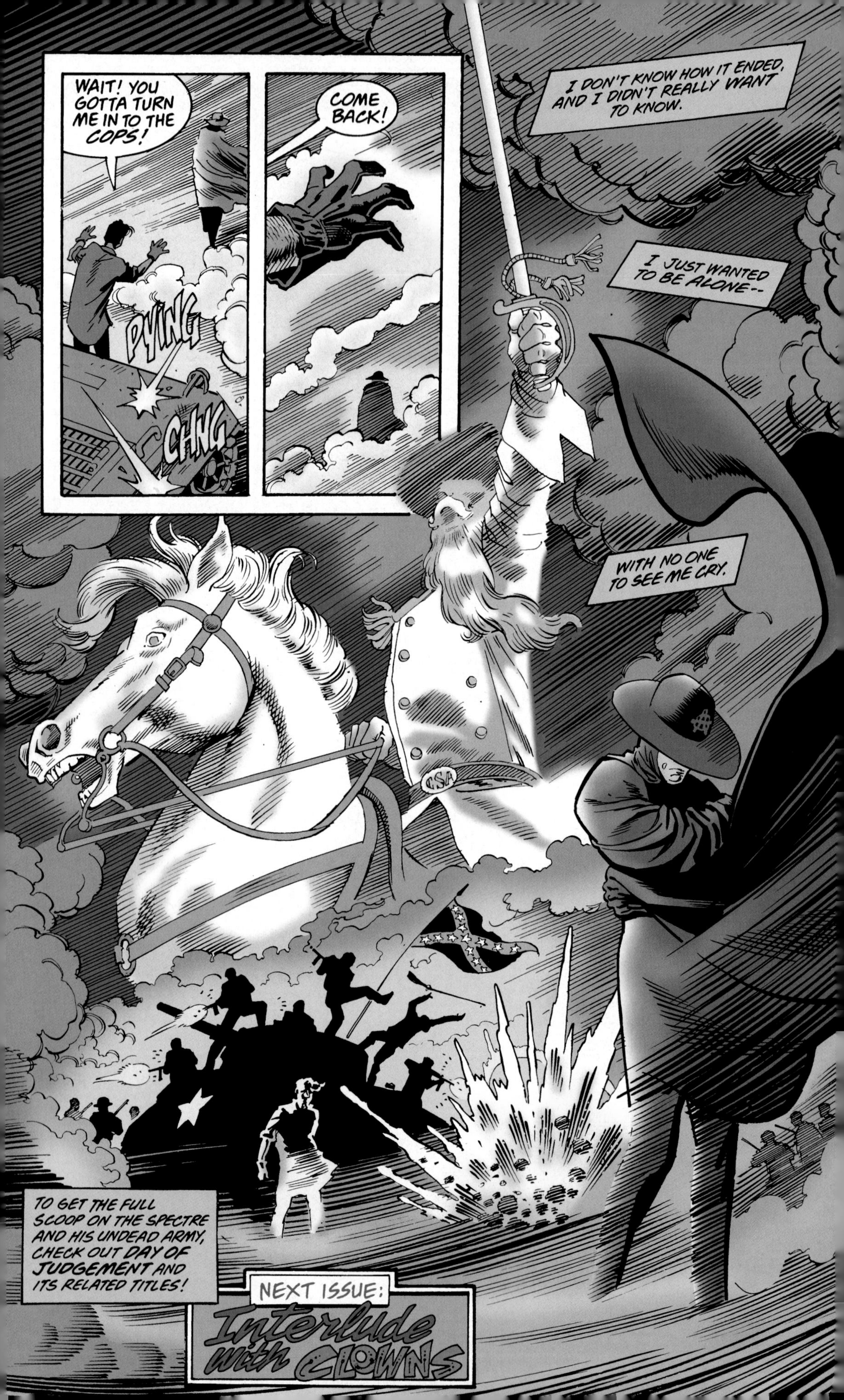
WAIT! YOU GOTTA TURN ME IN TO THE COPS!
PYING
CHNG
COME BACK!
I DON'T KNOW HOW IT ENDED, AND I DIDN'T REALLY WANT TO KNOW.
I JUST WANTED TO BE ALONE--
WITH NO ONE TO SEE ME CRY.
CSA
TO GET THE FULL SCOOP ON THE SPECTRE AND HIS UNDEAD ARMY, CHECK OUT DAY OF JUDGEMENT AND ITS RELATED TITLES!
NEXT ISSUE:
Interlude with CLOWNS

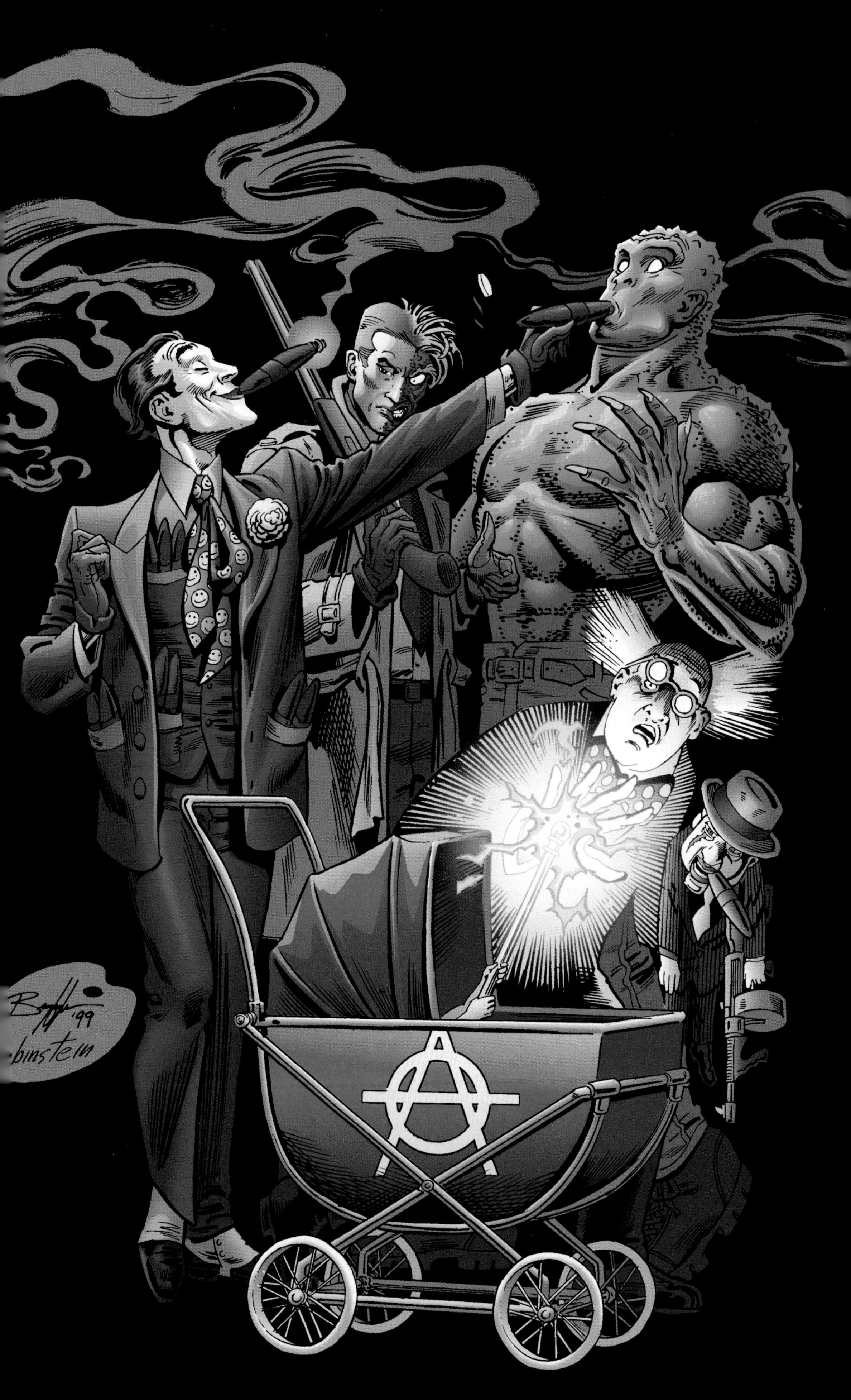

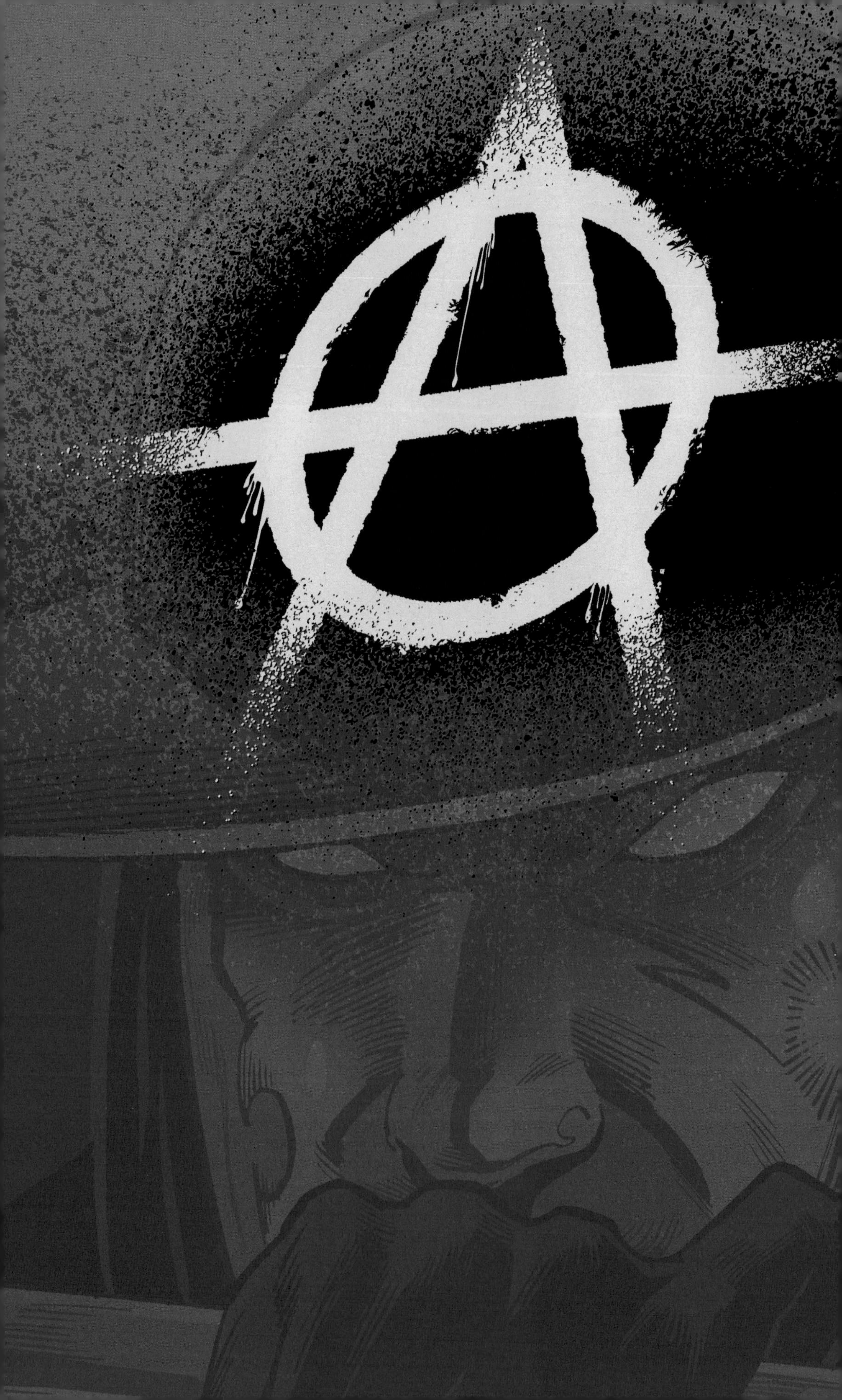

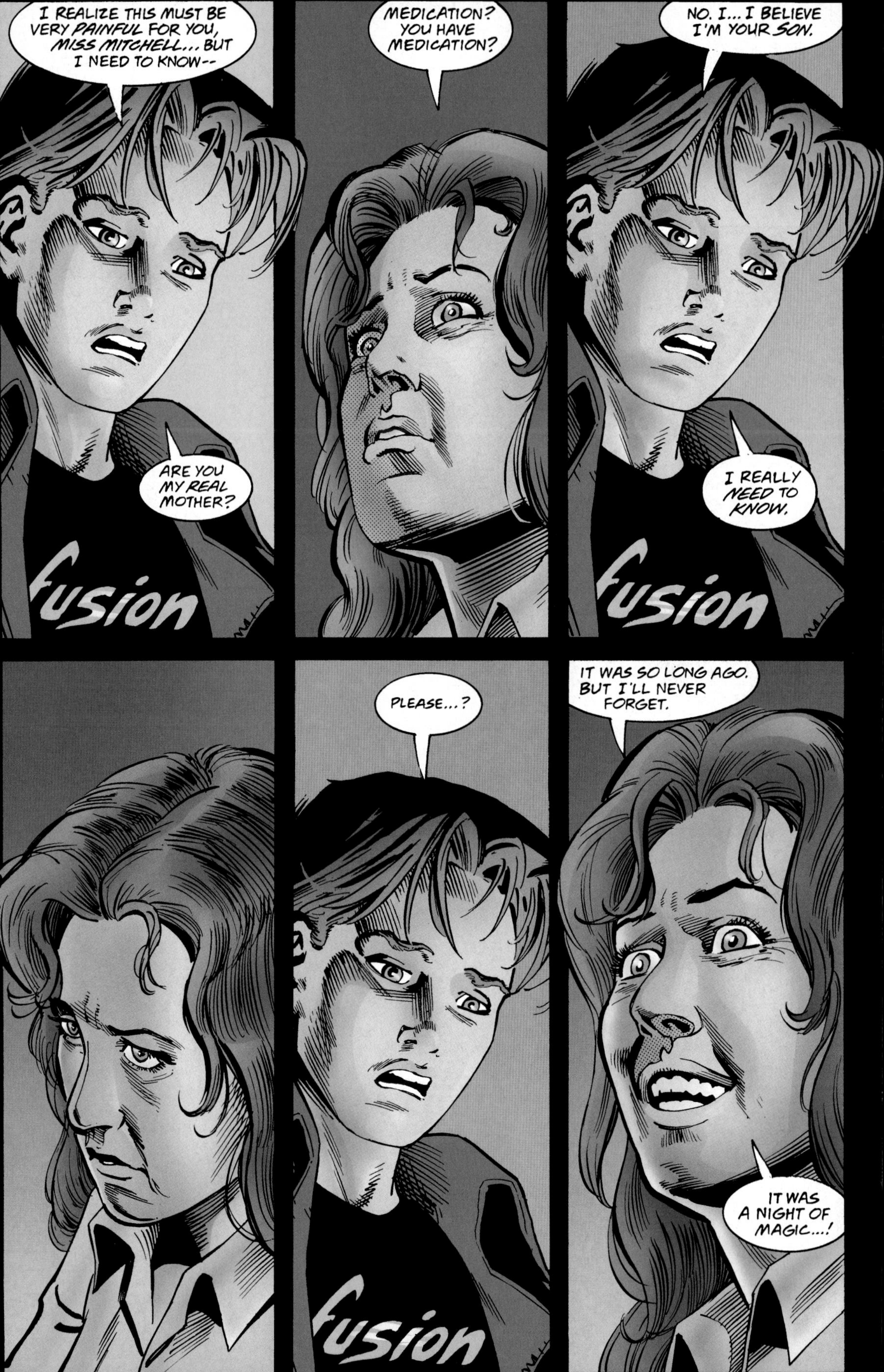
I REALIZE THIS MUST BE VERY PAINFUL FOR YOU, MISS MITCHELL... BUT I NEED TO KNOW--
ARE YOU MY REAL MOTHER?
MEDICATION? YOU HAVE MEDICATION?
NO. I... I BELIEVE I'M YOUR SON.
I REALLY NEED TO KNOW.
fusion
fusion
PLEASE...?
fusion
IT WAS SO LONG AGO. BUT I'LL NEVER FORGET.
IT WAS A NIGHT OF MAGIC...!

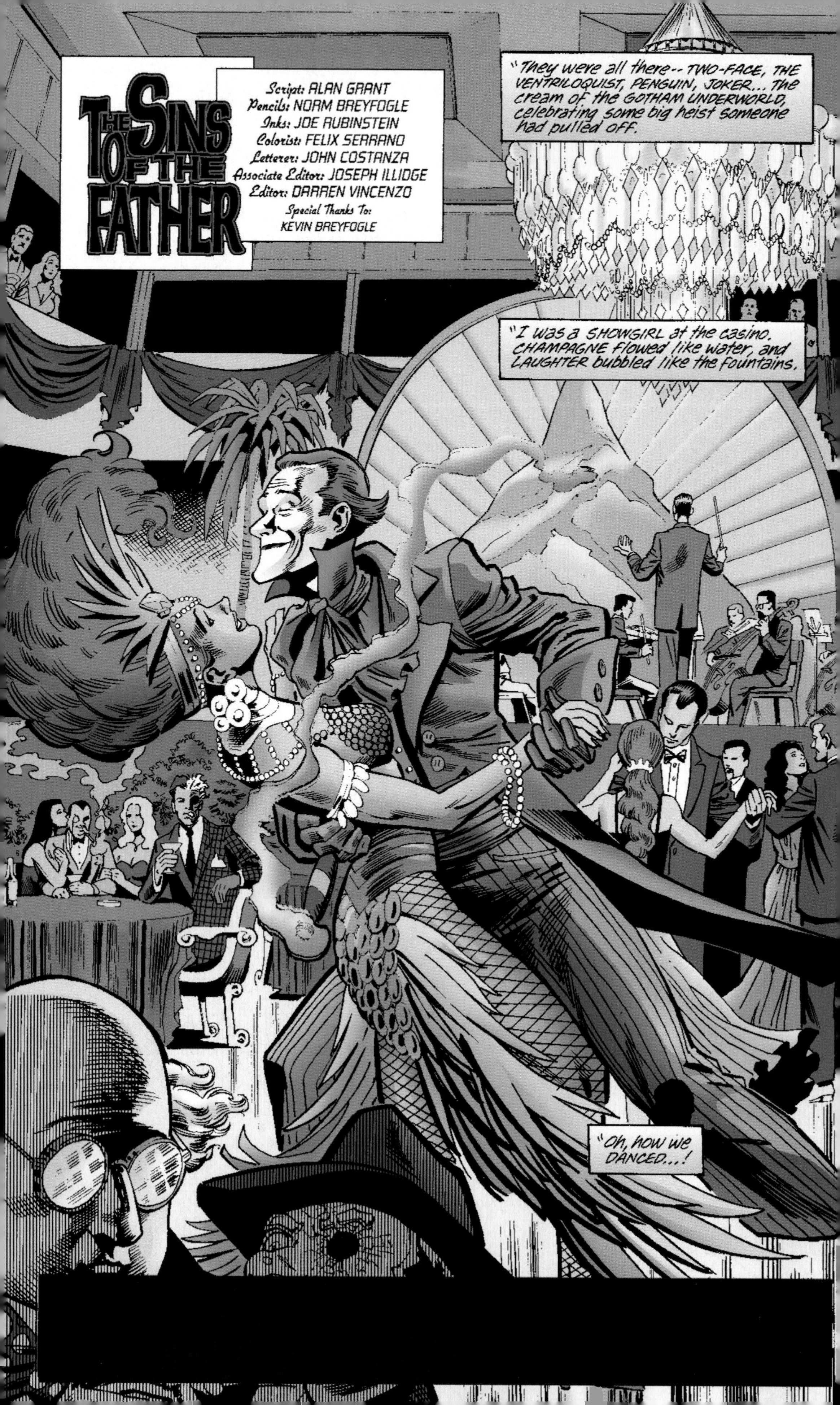
THE SINS OF THE FATHER
Script: ALAN GRANT
Pencils: NORM BREYFOGLE
Inks: JOE RUBINSTEIN
Colorist: FELIX SERRANO
Letterer: JOHN COSTANZA
Associate Editor: JOSEPH ILLIDGE
Editor: DARREN VINCENZO
Special Thanks To:
KEVIN BREYFOGLE
"They were all there-- TWO-FACE, THE VENTRILOQUIST, PENGUIN, JOKER... The cream of the GOTHAM UNDERWORLD, celebrating some big heist someone had pulled off.
"I was a SHOWGIRL at the casino. CHAMPAGNE flowed like water, and LAUGHTER bubbled like the fountains.
"Oh, how we DANCED...!
[redacted]

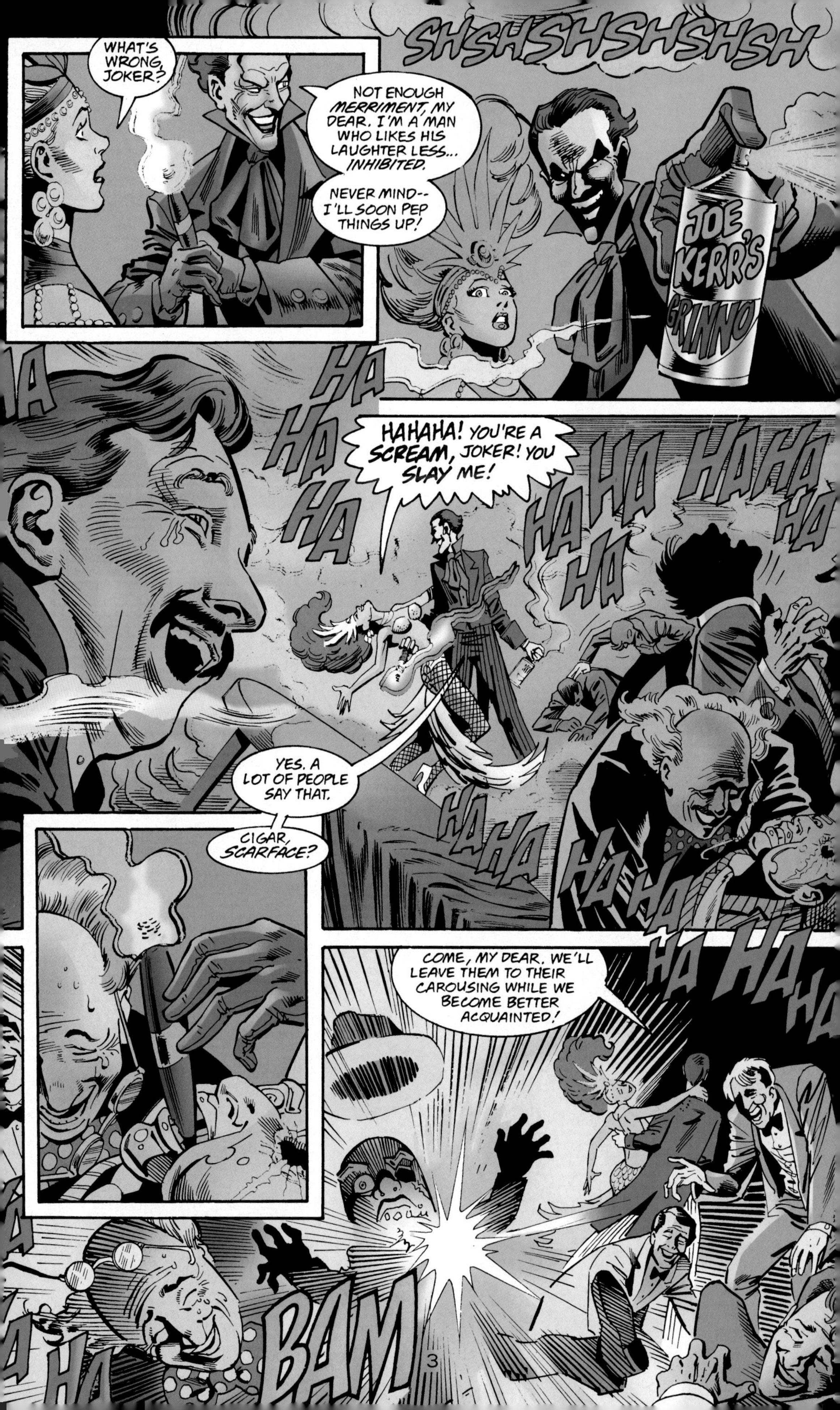
WHAT'S WRONG, JOKER?
NOT ENOUGH MERRIMENT, MY DEAR. I'M A MAN WHO LIKES HIS LAUGHTER LESS... INHIBITED.
NEVER MIND-- I'LL SOON PEP THINGS UP!
SHSHSHSHSHSHSH
JOE KERR'S GRINNO
HA HA HA HA
HAHAHA! YOU'RE A SCREAM, JOKER! YOU SLAY ME!
HAHA HAHAHA HA HA
YES. A LOT OF PEOPLE SAY THAT.
CIGAR, SCARFACE?
HAHAHA
HAHAHA
COME, MY DEAR. WE'LL LEAVE THEM TO THEIR CAROUSING WHILE WE BECOME BETTER ACQUAINTED!
HA HA HA
BAM

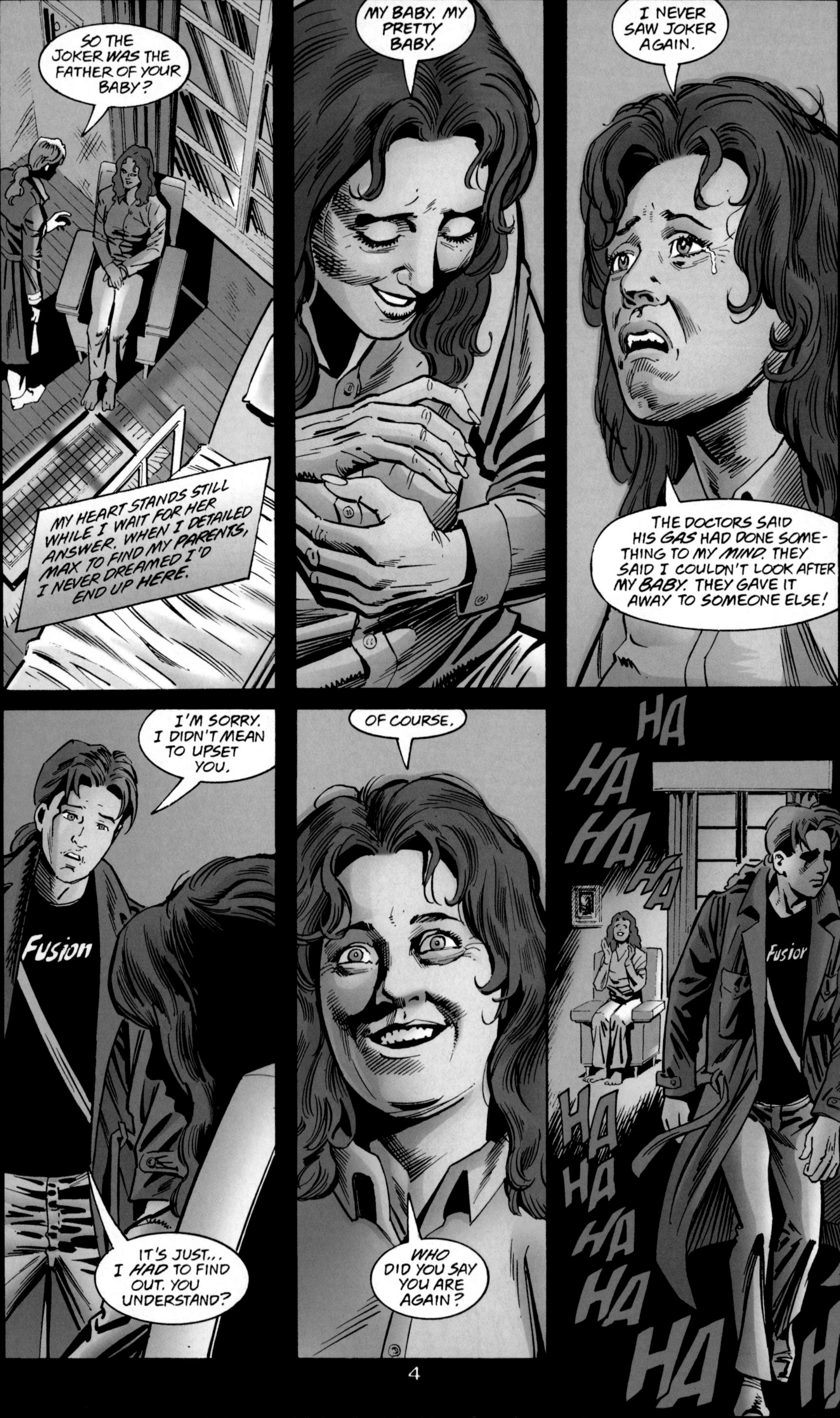
SO THE JOKER WAS THE FATHER OF YOUR BABY?
MY HEART STANDS STILL WHILE I WAIT FOR HER ANSWER. WHEN I DETAILED MAX TO FIND MY PARENTS, I NEVER DREAMED I'D END UP HERE.
MY BABY. MY PRETTY BABY.
I NEVER SAW JOKER AGAIN.
THE DOCTORS SAID HIS GAS HAD DONE SOMETHING TO MY MIND. THEY SAID I COULDN'T LOOK AFTER MY BABY. THEY GAVE IT AWAY TO SOMEONE ELSE!
I'M SORRY. I DIDN'T MEAN TO UPSET YOU.
Fusion
IT'S JUST... I HAD TO FIND OUT. YOU UNDERSTAND?
OF COURSE.
WHO DID YOU SAY YOU ARE AGAIN?
HA HA HA HA HA HA
Fusion
HA HA HA HA HA HA HA

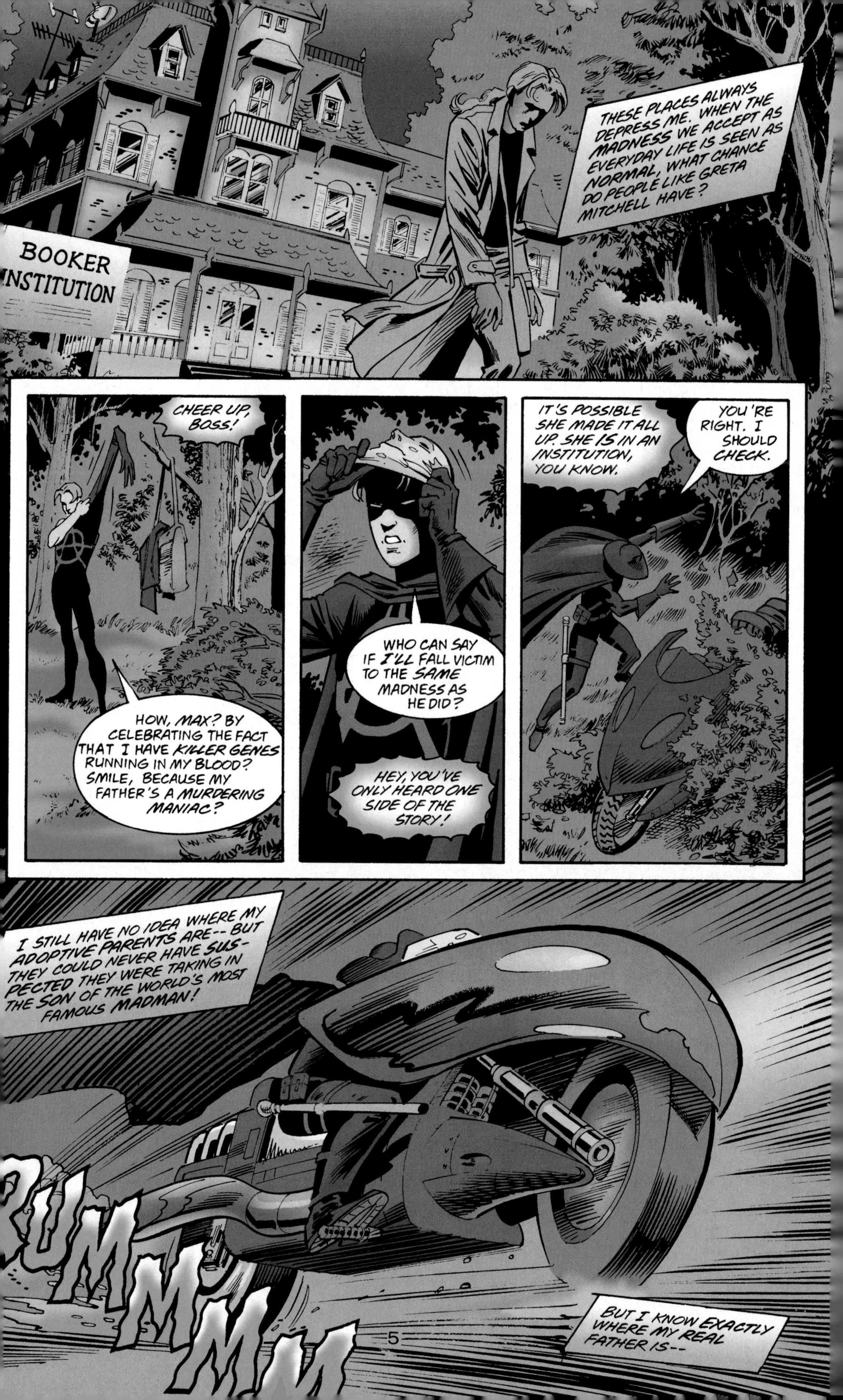

BOOKER INSTITUTION
THESE PLACES ALWAYS DEPRESS ME. WHEN THE MADNESS WE ACCEPT AS EVERYDAY LIFE IS SEEN AS NORMAL, WHAT CHANCE DO PEOPLE LIKE GRETA MITCHELL HAVE?
CHEER UP, BOSS!
HOW, MAX? BY CELEBRATING THE FACT THAT I HAVE KILLER GENES RUNNING IN MY BLOOD? SMILE, BECAUSE MY FATHER'S A MURDERING MANIAC?
WHO CAN SAY IF I'LL FALL VICTIM TO THE SAME MADNESS AS HE DID?
HEY, YOU'VE ONLY HEARD ONE SIDE OF THE STORY!
IT'S POSSIBLE SHE MADE IT ALL UP. SHE IS IN AN INSTITUTION, YOU KNOW.
YOU'RE RIGHT. I SHOULD CHECK.
I STILL HAVE NO IDEA WHERE MY ADOPTIVE PARENTS ARE-- BUT THEY COULD NEVER HAVE SUSPECTED THEY WERE TAKING IN THE SON OF THE WORLD'S MOST FAMOUS MADMAN!
RUMMMM
BUT I KNOW EXACTLY WHERE MY REAL FATHER IS--

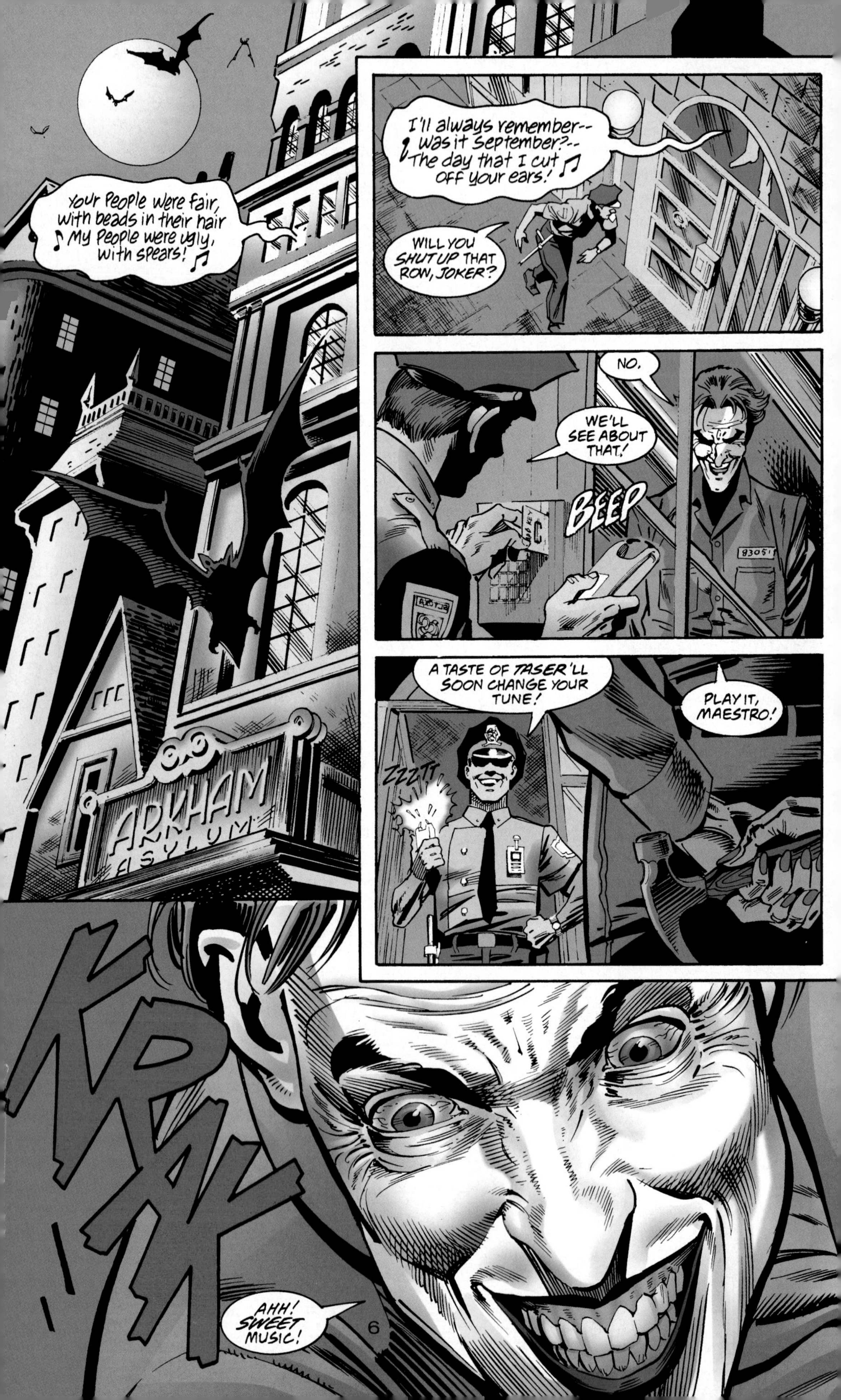

Your People were fair, with beads in their hair ♪ My People were ugly, with spears! ♫
I'll always remember-- was it September?-- The day that I cut off your ears! ♫
WILL YOU SHUT UP THAT ROW, JOKER?
NO.
WE'LL SEE ABOUT THAT!
BEEP
A TASTE OF TASER'LL SOON CHANGE YOUR TUNE!
PLAY IT, MAESTRO!
ZZZT!
KRAK
AHH! SWEET MUSIC!
ARKHAM ASYLUM

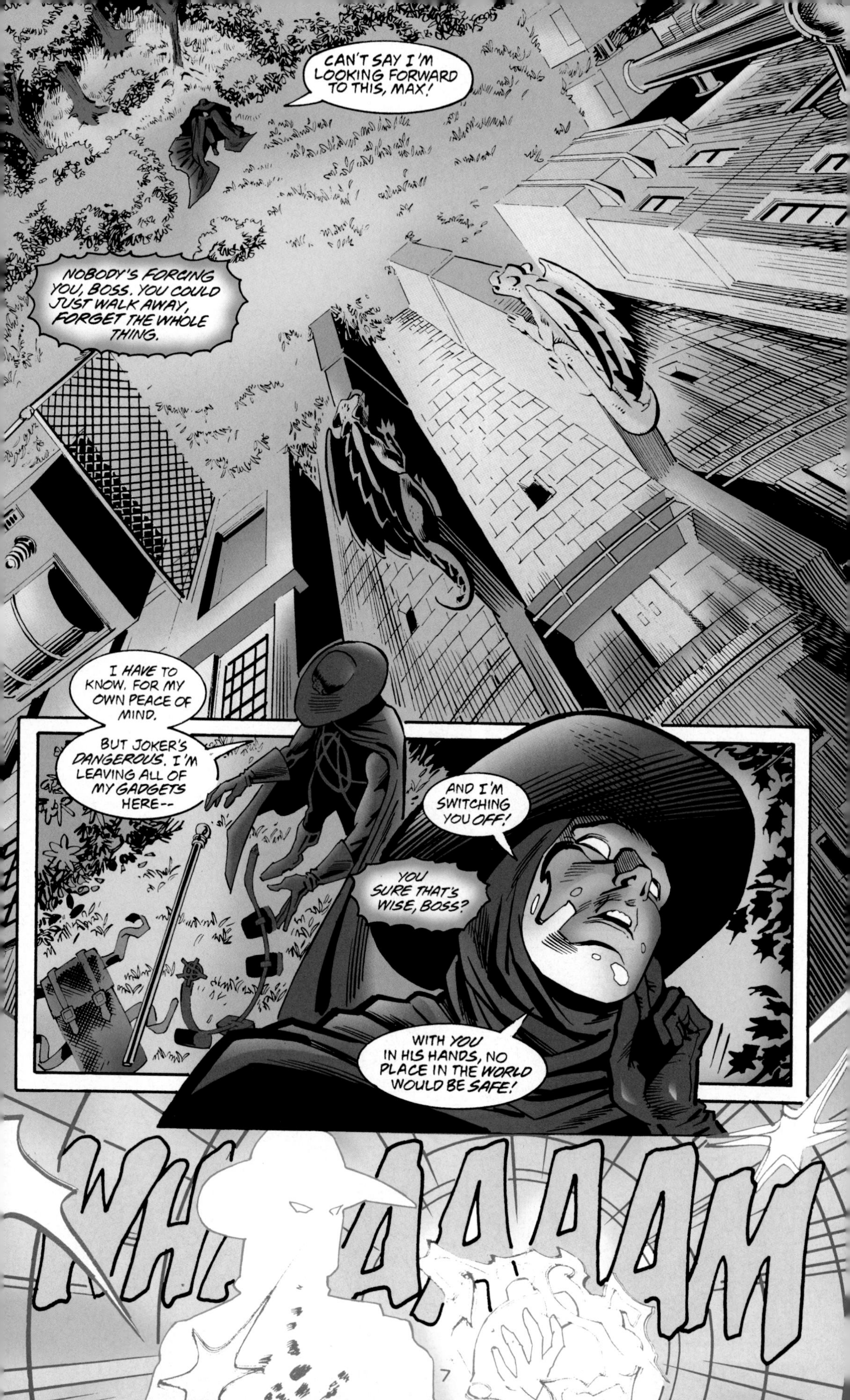
CAN'T SAY I'M LOOKING FORWARD TO THIS, MAX!
NOBODY'S FORCING YOU, BOSS. YOU COULD JUST WALK AWAY, FORGET THE WHOLE THING.
I HAVE TO KNOW. FOR MY OWN PEACE OF MIND.
BUT JOKER'S DANGEROUS. I'M LEAVING ALL OF MY GADGETS HERE--
AND I'M SWITCHING YOU OFF!
YOU SURE THAT'S WISE, BOSS?
WITH YOU IN HIS HANDS, NO PLACE IN THE WORLD WOULD BE SAFE!
WH AAAAM

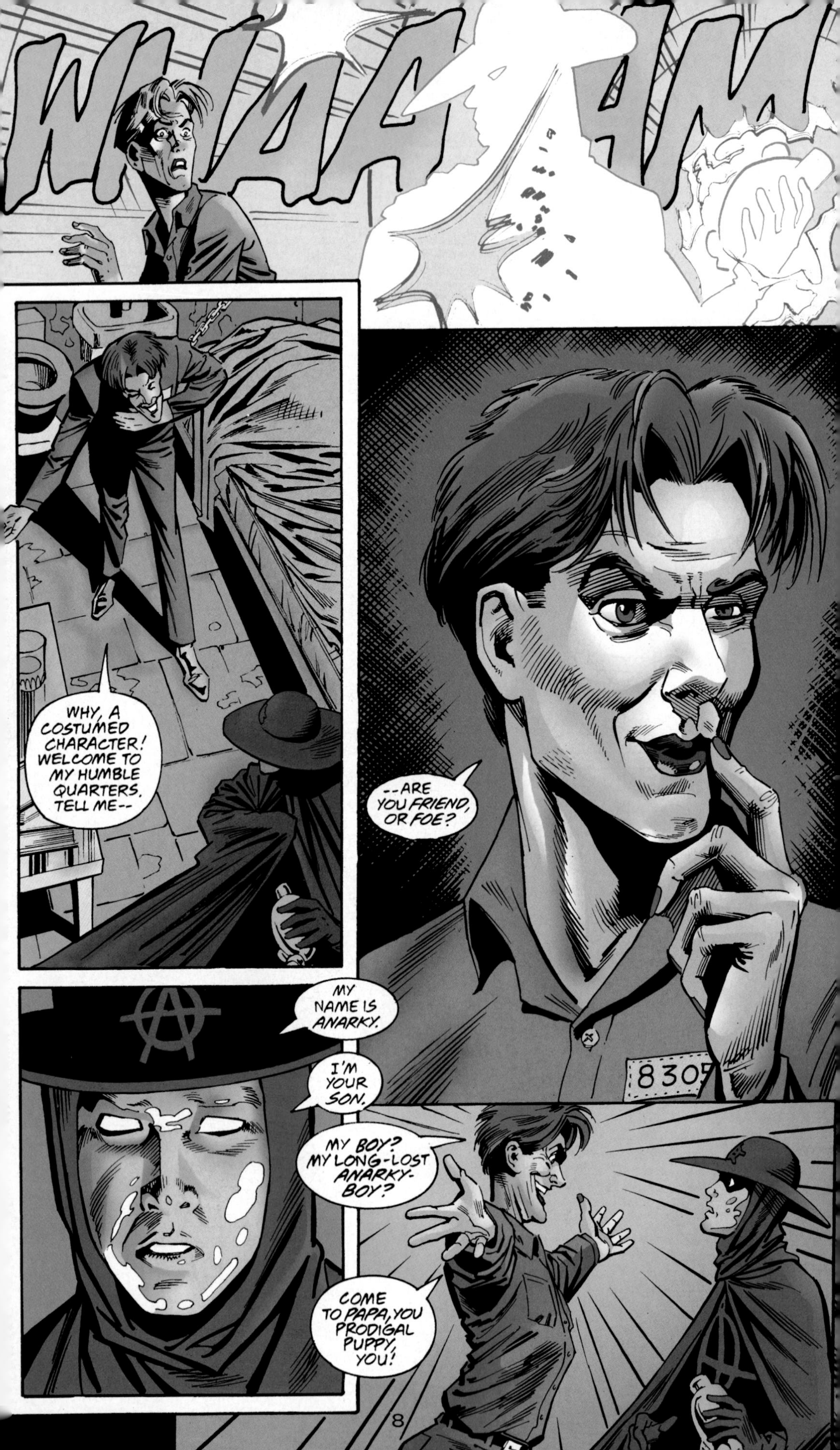
WHAAAM
WHY, A COSTUMED CHARACTER! WELCOME TO MY HUMBLE QUARTERS. TELL ME--
--ARE YOU FRIEND, OR FOE?
8305
MY NAME IS ANARKY.
I'M YOUR SON.
MY BOY? MY LONG-LOST ANARKY-BOY?
COME TO PAPA, YOU PRODIGAL PUPPY, YOU!

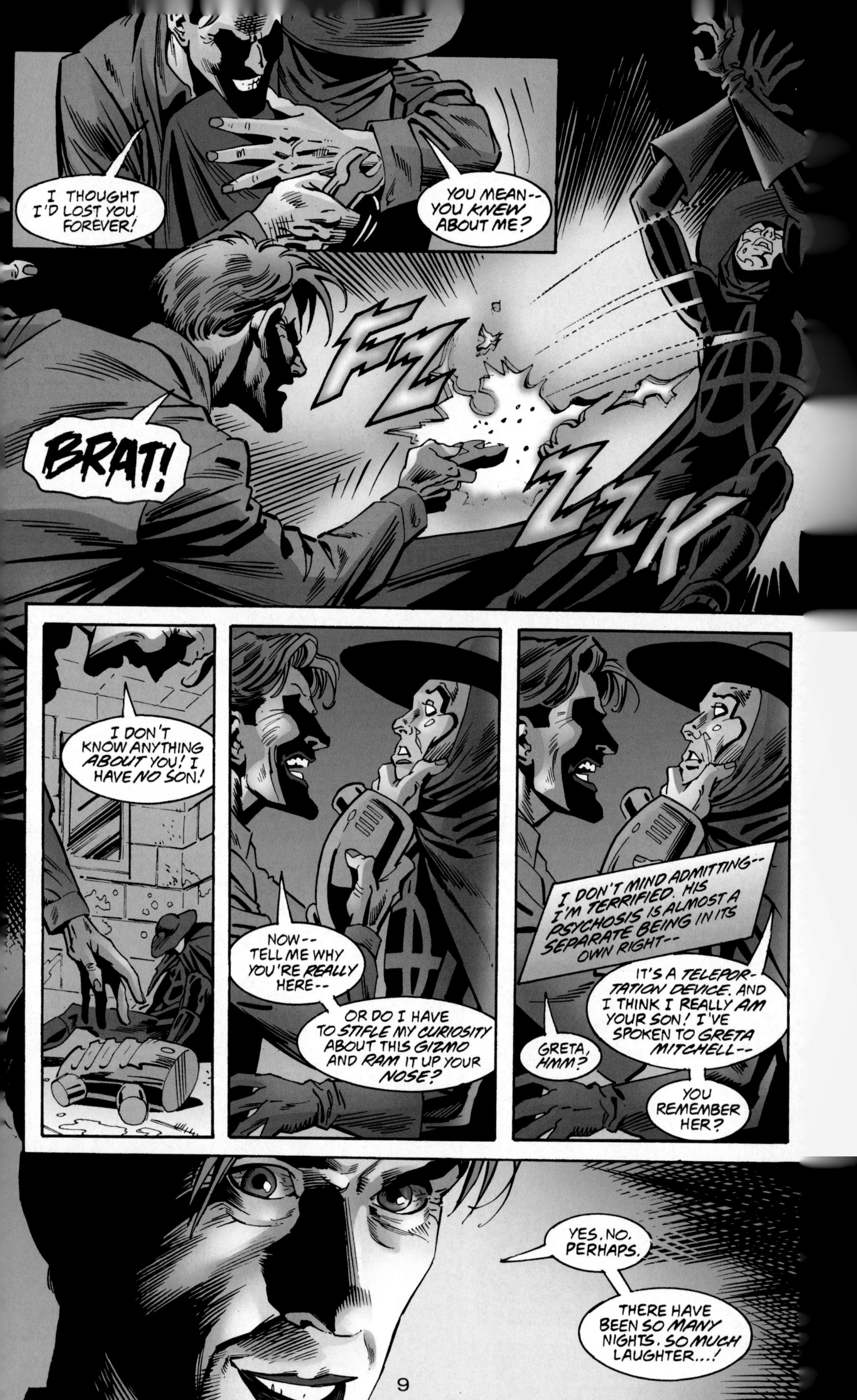
I THOUGHT I'D LOST YOU FOREVER!
YOU MEAN-- YOU KNEW ABOUT ME?
BRAT!
FZZZK
I DON'T KNOW ANYTHING ABOUT YOU! I HAVE NO SON!
NOW-- TELL ME WHY YOU'RE REALLY HERE--
OR DO I HAVE TO STIFLE MY CURIOSITY ABOUT THIS GIZMO AND RAM IT UP YOUR NOSE?
I DON'T MIND ADMITTING-- I'M TERRIFIED. HIS PSYCHOSIS IS ALMOST A SEPARATE BEING IN ITS OWN RIGHT--
IT'S A TELEPORTATION DEVICE. AND I THINK I REALLY AM YOUR SON! I'VE SPOKEN TO GRETA MITCHELL--
GRETA, HMM?
YOU REMEMBER HER?
YES. NO. PERHAPS.
THERE HAVE BEEN SO MANY NIGHTS. SO MUCH LAUGHTER...!

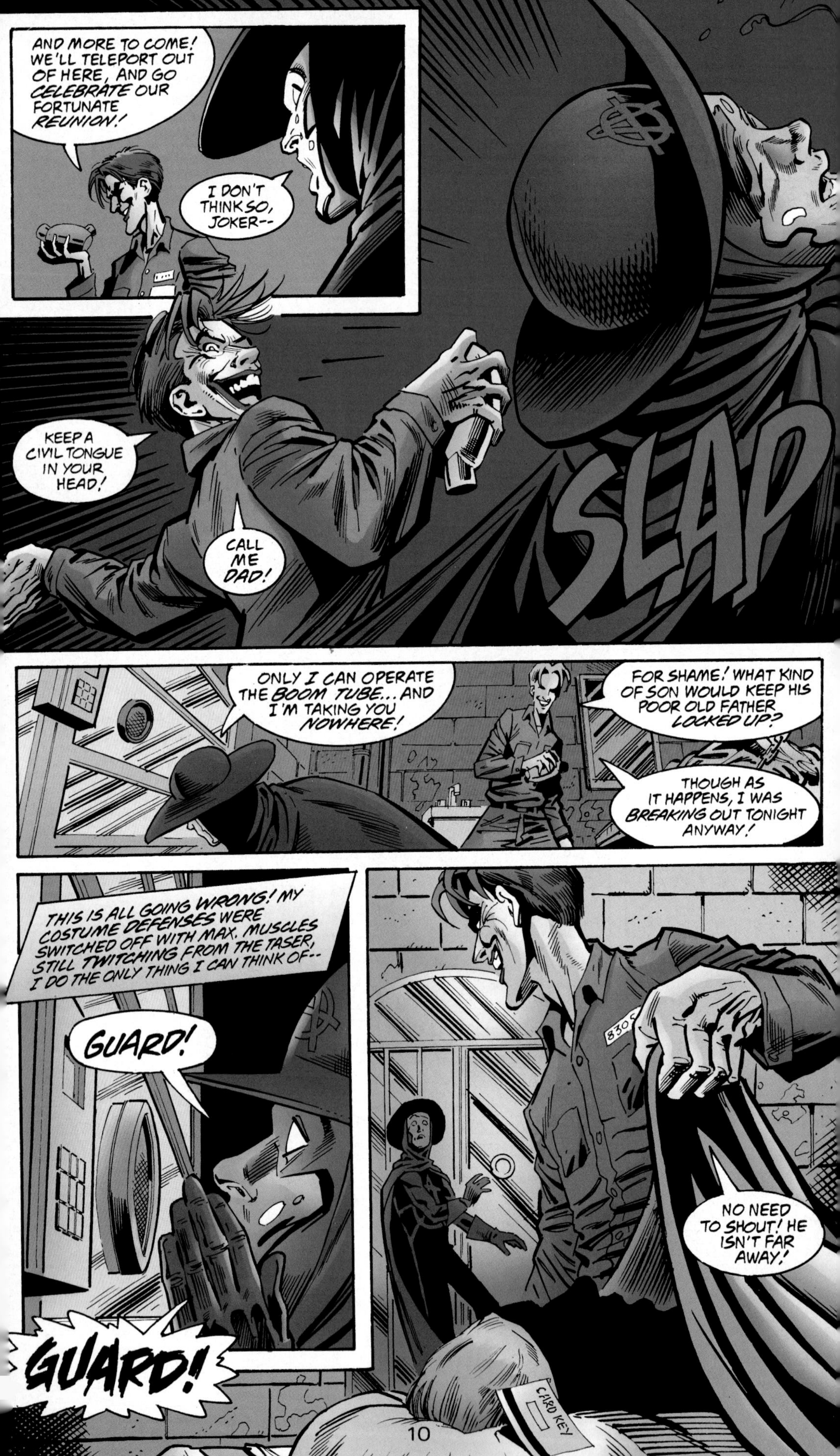
AND MORE TO COME! WE'LL TELEPORT OUT OF HERE, AND GO CELEBRATE OUR FORTUNATE REUNION!
I DON'T THINK SO, JOKER--
KEEP A CIVIL TONGUE IN YOUR HEAD!
CALL ME DAD!
SLAP
ONLY I CAN OPERATE THE BOOM TUBE... AND I'M TAKING YOU NOWHERE!
FOR SHAME! WHAT KIND OF SON WOULD KEEP HIS POOR OLD FATHER LOCKED UP?
THOUGH AS IT HAPPENS, I WAS BREAKING OUT TONIGHT ANYWAY!
THIS IS ALL GOING WRONG! MY COSTUME DEFENSES WERE SWITCHED OFF WITH MAX. MUSCLES STILL TWITCHING FROM THE TASER, I DO THE ONLY THING I CAN THINK OF--
GUARD!
GUARD!
NO NEED TO SHOUT! HE ISN'T FAR AWAY!
CARD KEY

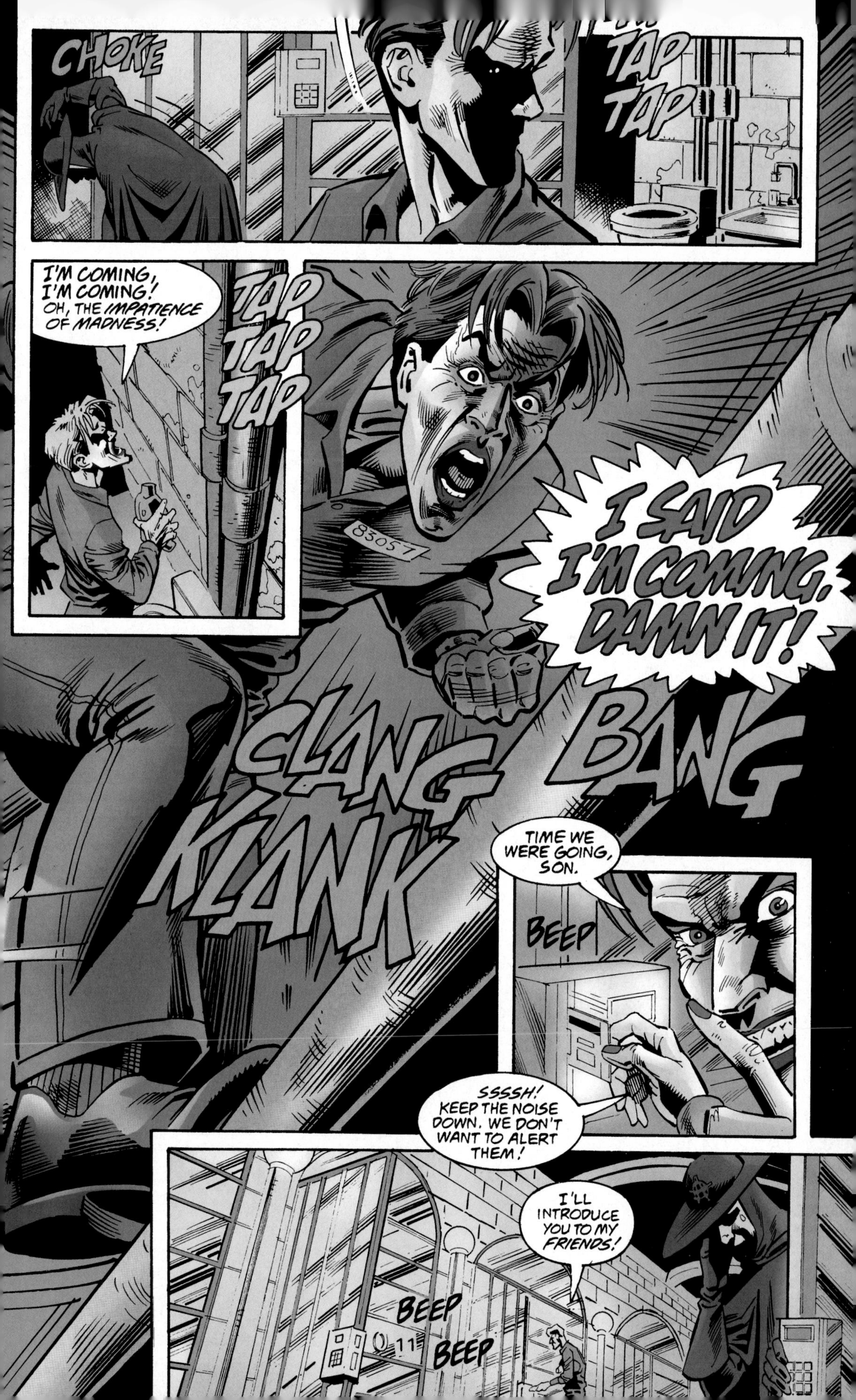
CHOKE
TAP TAP
I'M COMING, I'M COMING! OH, THE IMPATIENCE OF MADNESS!
TAP TAP TAP
83057
I SAID I'M COMING, DAMN IT!
CLANG KLANK
BANG
TIME WE WERE GOING, SON.
BEEP
SSSSH! KEEP THE NOISE DOWN. WE DON'T WANT TO ALERT THEM!
I'LL INTRODUCE YOU TO MY FRIENDS!
BEEP
BEEP
11

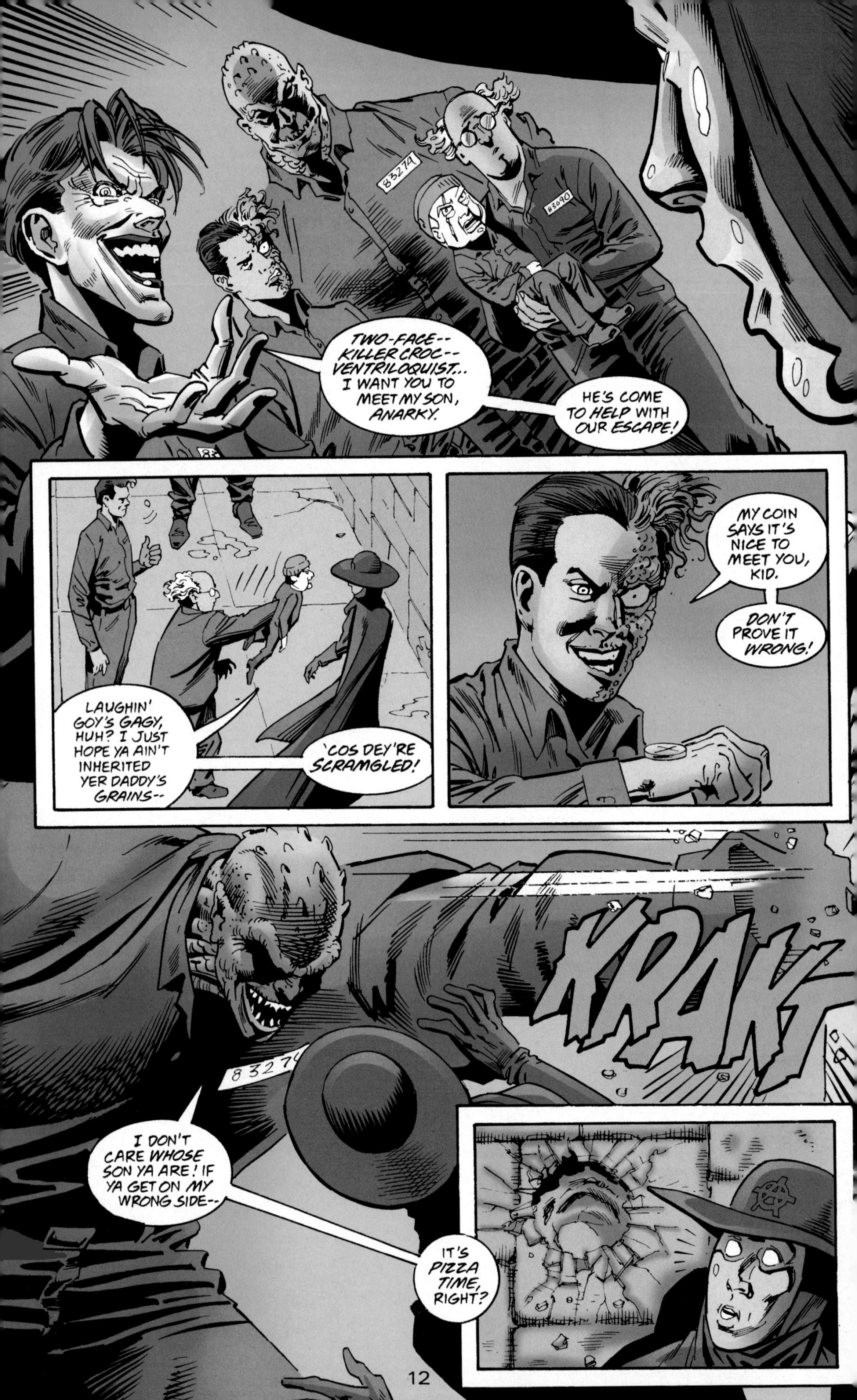
TWO-FACE-- KILLER CROC-- VENTRILOQUIST... I WANT YOU TO MEET MY SON, ANARKY.
HE'S COME TO HELP WITH OUR ESCAPE!
LAUGHIN' GOY'S GAGY, HUH? I JUST HOPE YA AIN'T INHERITED YER DADDY'S GRAINS--
'COS DEY'RE SCRAMGLED!
MY COIN SAYS IT'S NICE TO MEET YOU, KID.
DON'T PROVE IT WRONG!
KRAK
I DON'T CARE WHOSE SON YA ARE! IF YA GET ON MY WRONG SIDE--
IT'S PIZZA TIME, RIGHT?

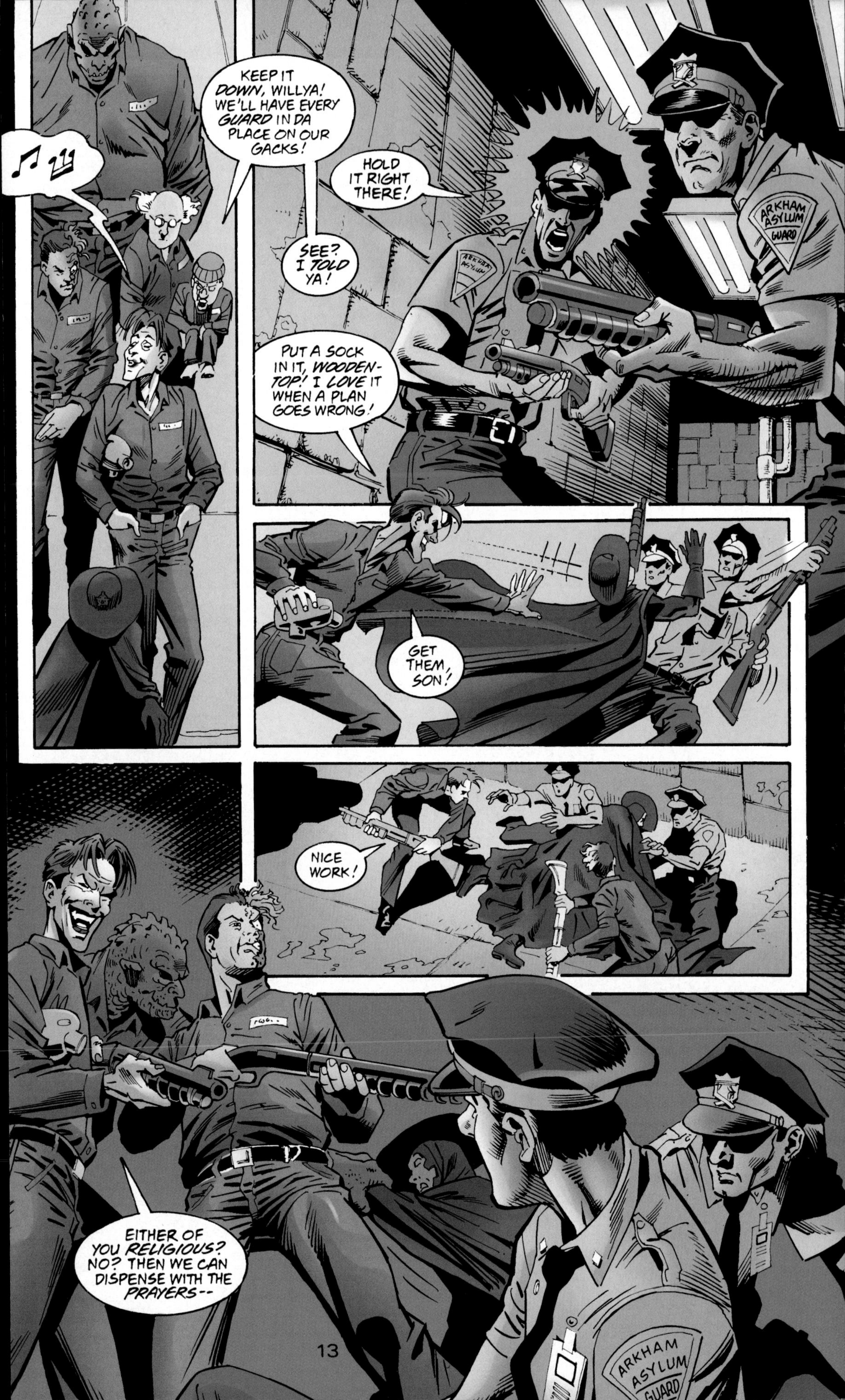
KEEP IT DOWN, WILLYA! WE'LL HAVE EVERY GUARD IN DA PLACE ON OUR GACKS!
HOLD IT RIGHT THERE!
SEE? I TOLD YA!
PUT A SOCK IN IT, WOODEN-TOP! I LOVE IT WHEN A PLAN GOES WRONG!
ARKHAM ASYLUM GUARD
GET THEM, SON!
NICE WORK!
EITHER OF YOU RELIGIOUS? NO? THEN WE CAN DISPENSE WITH THE PRAYERS--
ARKHAM ASYLUM GUARD

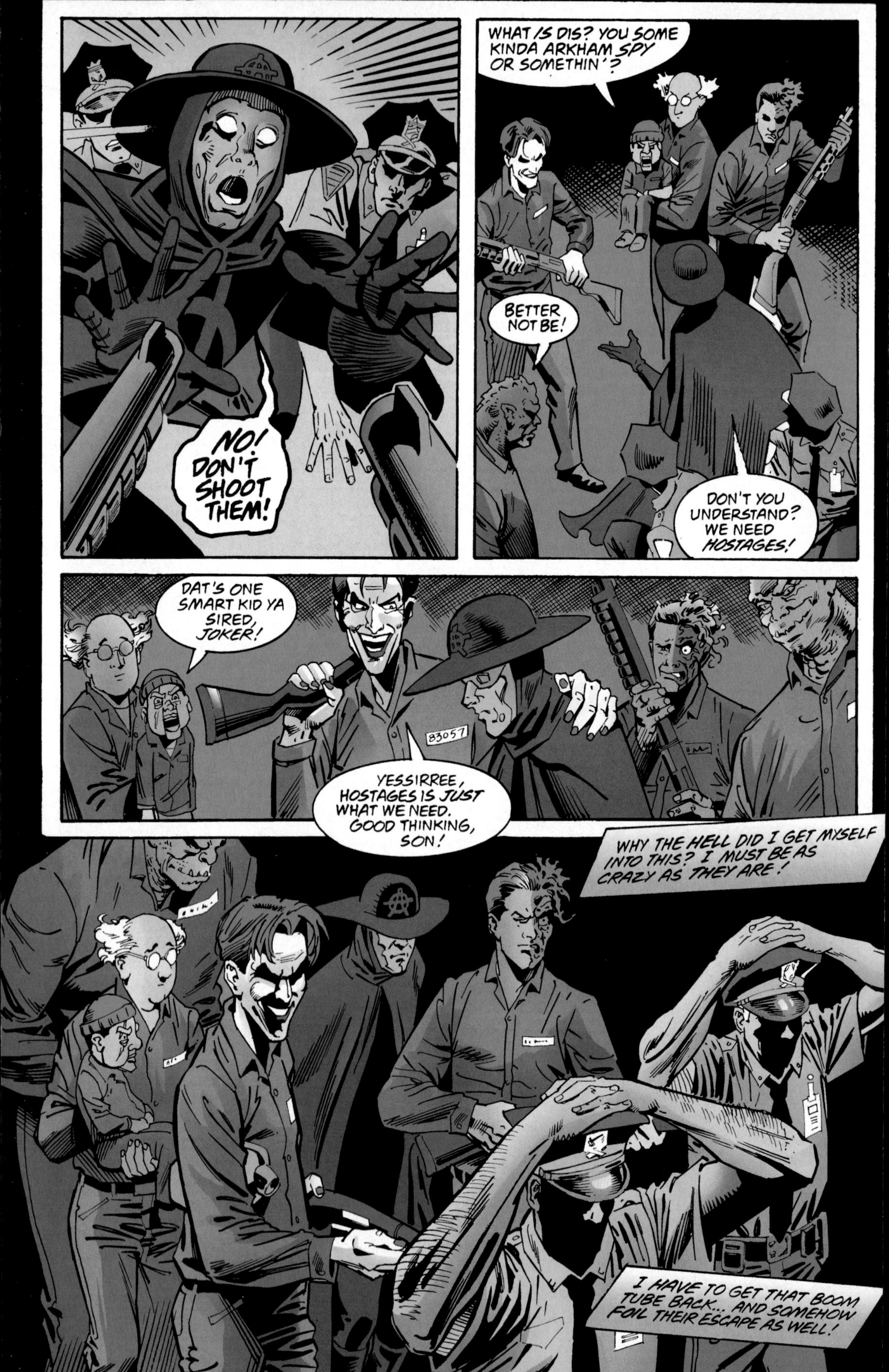
NO! DON'T SHOOT THEM!
WHAT IS DIS? YOU SOME KINDA ARKHAM SPY OR SOMETHIN'?
BETTER NOT BE!
DON'T YOU UNDERSTAND? WE NEED HOSTAGES!
DAT'S ONE SMART KID YA SIRED, JOKER!
83057
YESSIRREE, HOSTAGES IS JUST WHAT WE NEED. GOOD THINKING, SON!
WHY THE HELL DID I GET MYSELF INTO THIS? I MUST BE AS CRAZY AS THEY ARE!
I HAVE TO GET THAT BOOM TUBE BACK... AND SOMEHOW FOIL THEIR ESCAPE AS WELL!

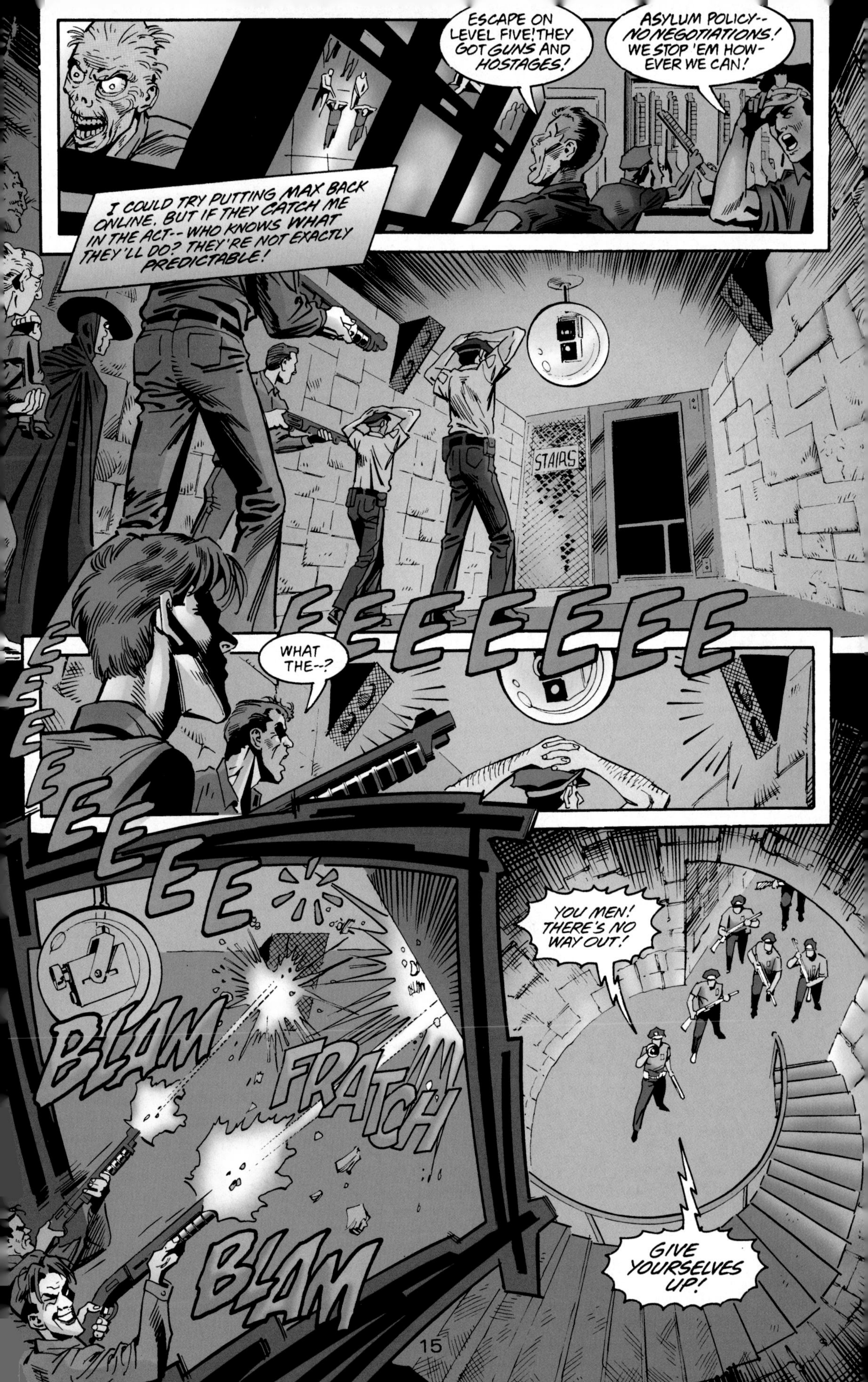
ESCAPE ON LEVEL FIVE! THEY GOT GUNS AND HOSTAGES!
ASYLUM POLICY-- NO NEGOTIATIONS! WE STOP 'EM HOWEVER WE CAN!
I COULD TRY PUTTING MAX BACK ONLINE. BUT IF THEY CATCH ME IN THE ACT-- WHO KNOWS WHAT THEY'LL DO? THEY'RE NOT EXACTLY PREDICTABLE!
STAIRS
EEEEEEEEEEEEEEEEEE
WHAT THE--?
BLAM
FRATCH
BLAM
YOU MEN! THERE'S NO WAY OUT!
GIVE YOURSELVES UP!

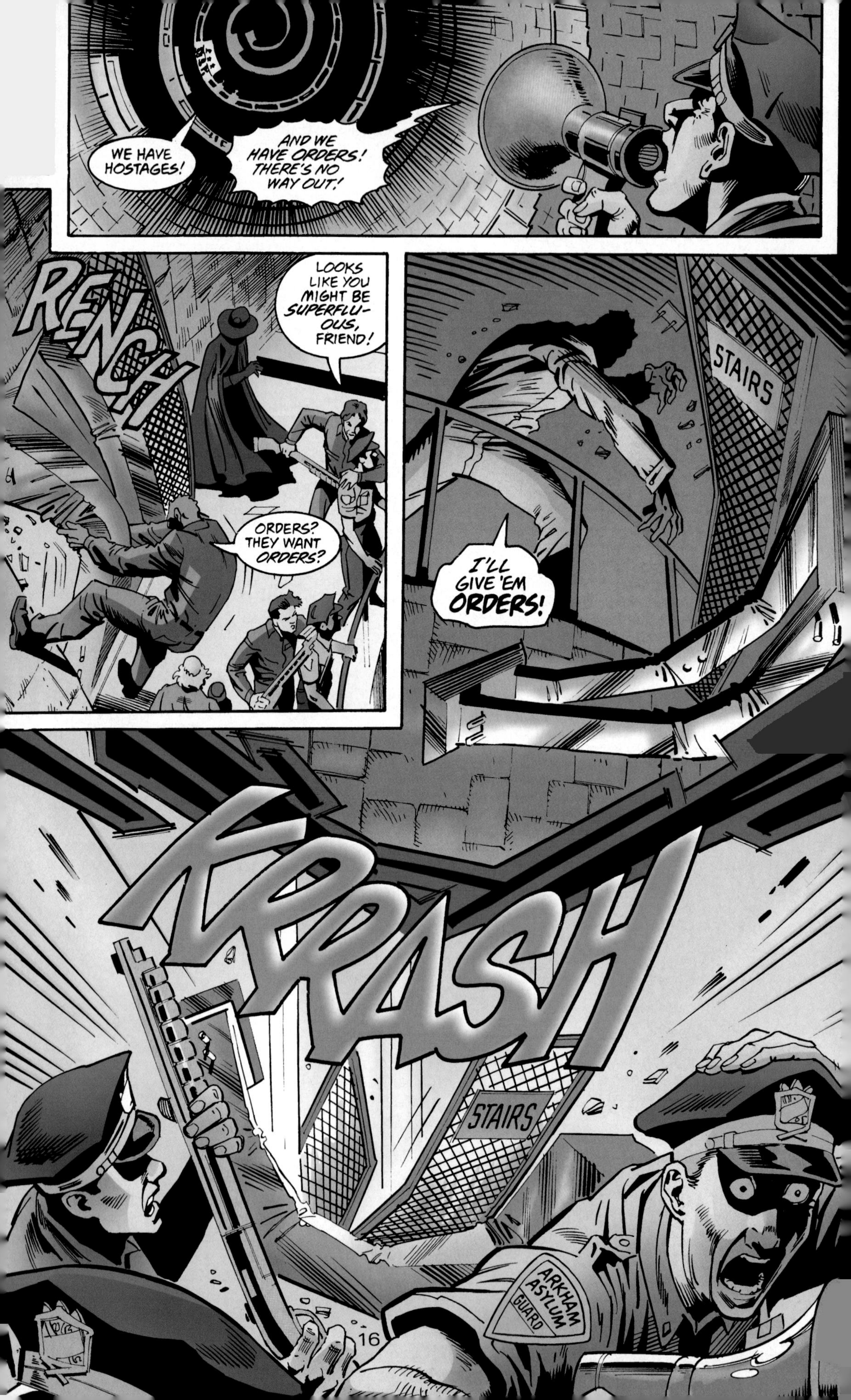
WE HAVE HOSTAGES!
AND WE HAVE ORDERS! THERE'S NO WAY OUT!
RENCH
LOOKS LIKE YOU MIGHT BE SUPERFLUOUS, FRIEND!
ORDERS? THEY WANT ORDERS?
STAIRS
I'LL GIVE 'EM ORDERS!
KRASH
STAIRS
ARKHAM ASYLUM GUARD

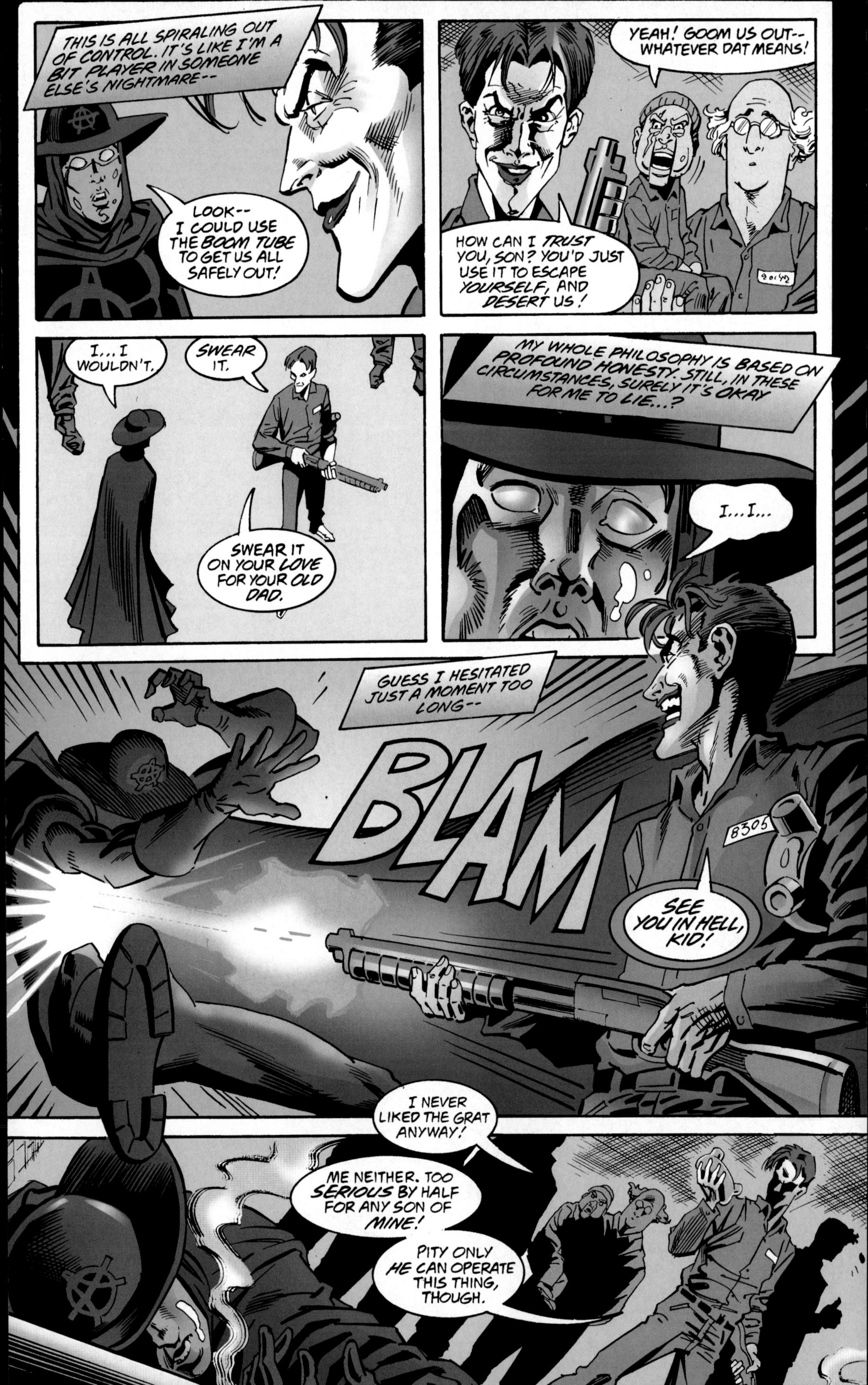
THIS IS ALL SPIRALING OUT OF CONTROL. IT'S LIKE I'M A BIT PLAYER IN SOMEONE ELSE'S NIGHTMARE--
LOOK-- I COULD USE THE BOOM TUBE TO GET US ALL SAFELY OUT!
YEAH! GOOM US OUT-- WHATEVER DAT MEANS!
HOW CAN I TRUST YOU, SON? YOU'D JUST USE IT TO ESCAPE YOURSELF, AND DESERT US!
I... I WOULDN'T.
SWEAR IT.
SWEAR IT ON YOUR LOVE FOR YOUR OLD DAD.
MY WHOLE PHILOSOPHY IS BASED ON PROFOUND HONESTY. STILL, IN THESE CIRCUMSTANCES, SURELY IT'S OKAY FOR ME TO LIE...?
I... I...
GUESS I HESITATED JUST A MOMENT TOO LONG--
BLAM
SEE YOU IN HELL, KID!
8305
I NEVER LIKED THE GRAT ANYWAY!
ME NEITHER. TOO SERIOUS BY HALF FOR ANY SON OF MINE!
PITY ONLY HE CAN OPERATE THIS THING, THOUGH.

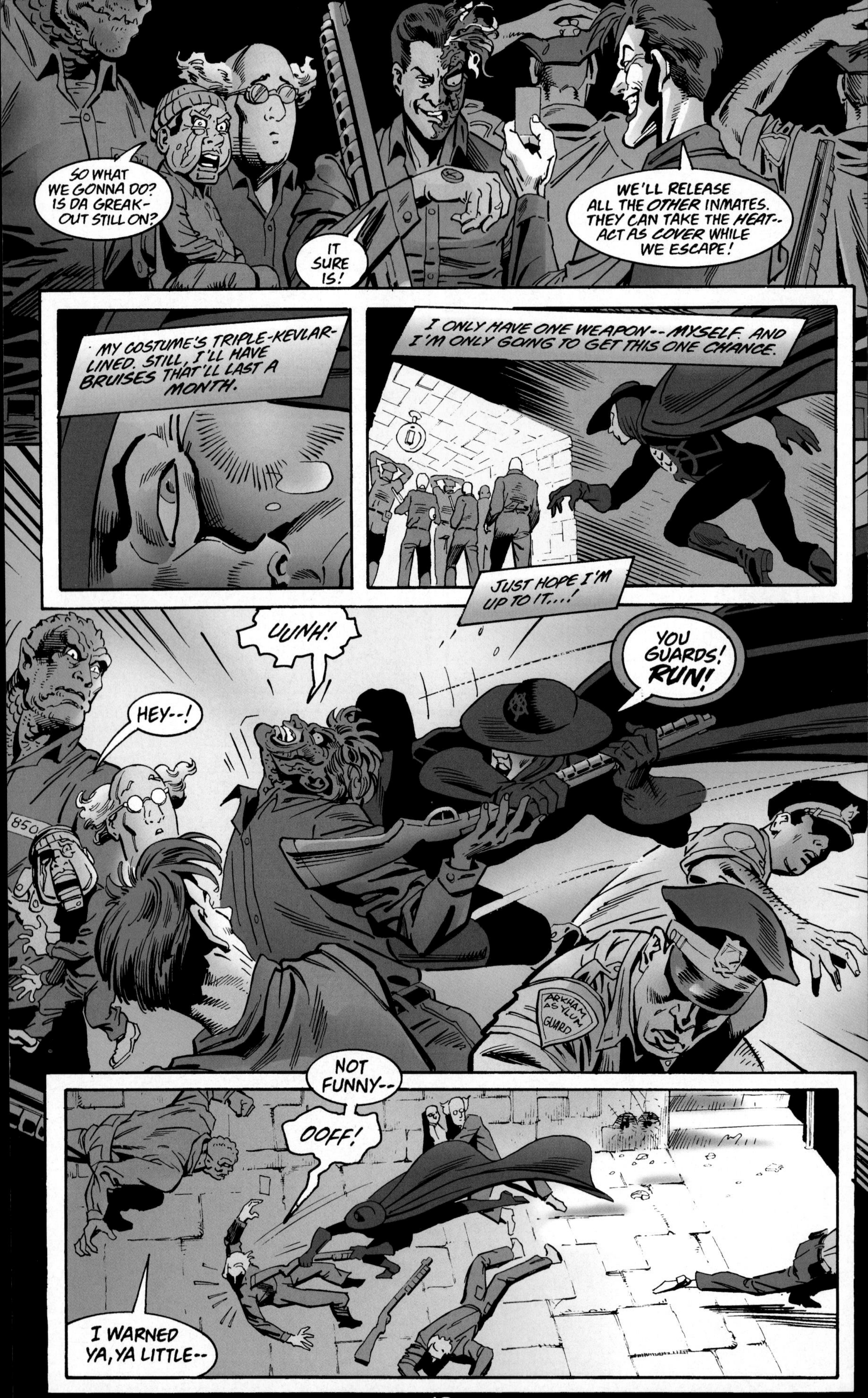

SO WHAT WE GONNA DO? IS DA GREAK-OUT STILL ON?
IT SURE IS!
WE'LL RELEASE ALL THE OTHER INMATES. THEY CAN TAKE THE HEAT-- ACT AS COVER WHILE WE ESCAPE!
MY COSTUME'S TRIPLE-KEVLAR-LINED. STILL, I'LL HAVE BRUISES THAT'LL LAST A MONTH.
I ONLY HAVE ONE WEAPON--MYSELF. AND I'M ONLY GOING TO GET THIS ONE CHANCE.
JUST HOPE I'M UP TO IT...!
UUNH!
YOU GUARDS! RUN!
HEY--!
850
ARKHAM ASYLUM GUARD
NOT FUNNY--
OOFF!
I WARNED YA, YA LITTLE--

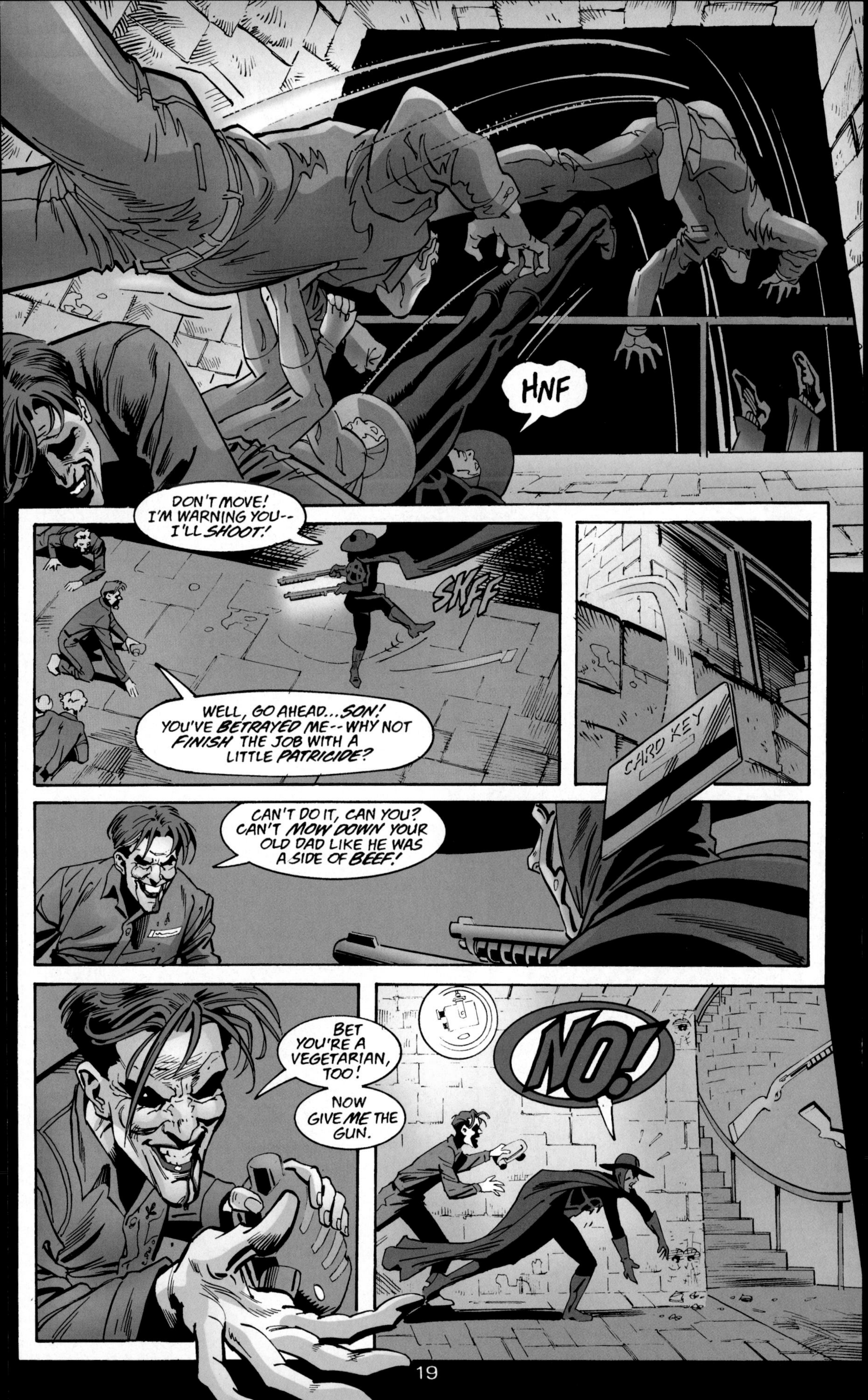
HNF
DON'T MOVE! I'M WARNING YOU-- I'LL SHOOT!
SNFF
WELL, GO AHEAD... SON! YOU'VE BETRAYED ME--WHY NOT FINISH THE JOB WITH A LITTLE PATRICIDE?
CARD KEY
CAN'T DO IT, CAN YOU? CAN'T MOW DOWN YOUR OLD DAD LIKE HE WAS A SIDE OF BEEF!
BET YOU'RE A VEGETARIAN, TOO!
NOW GIVE ME THE GUN.
NO!

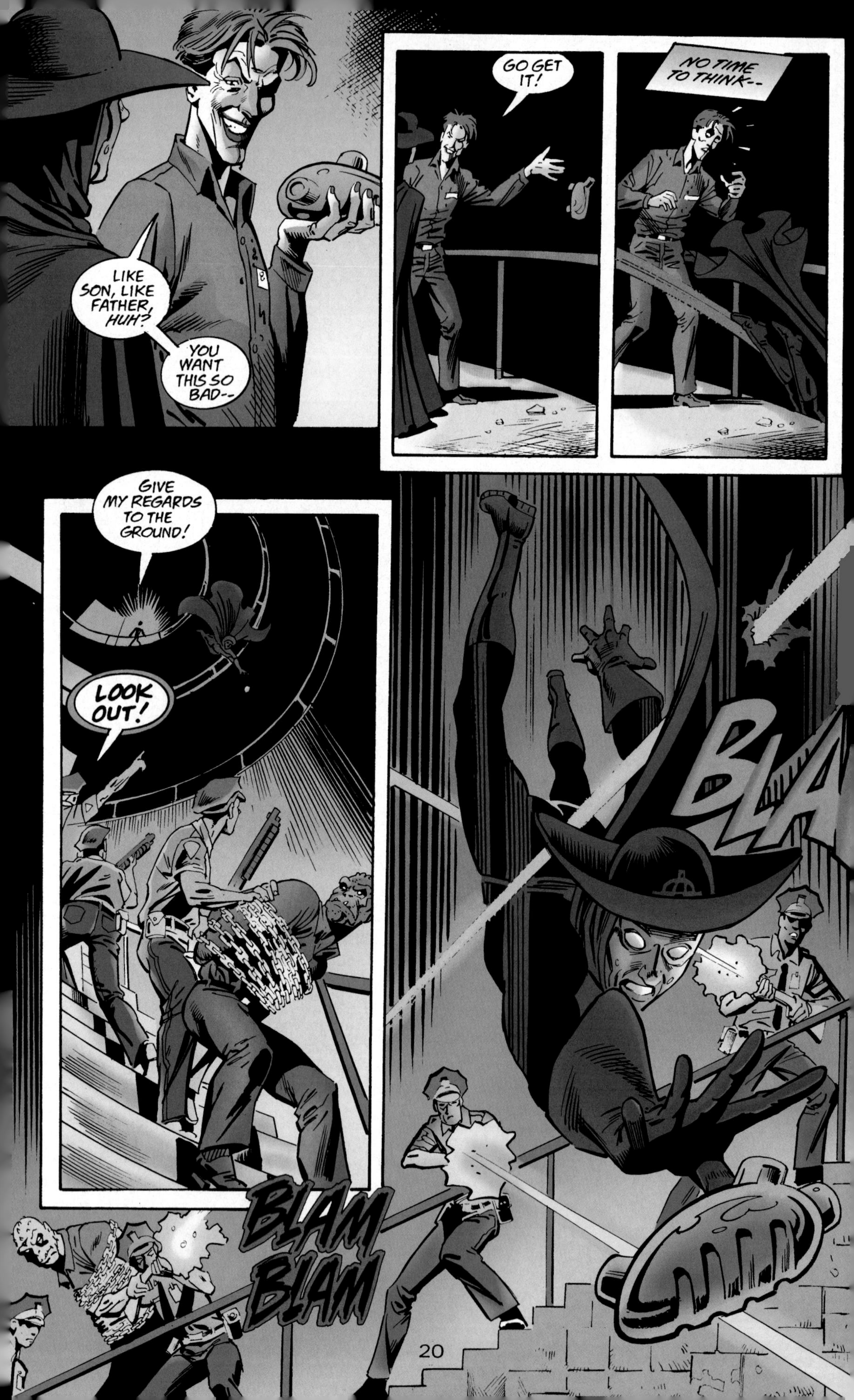
LIKE SON, LIKE FATHER, HUH?
YOU WANT THIS SO BAD--
GO GET IT!
NO TIME TO THINK--
GIVE MY REGARDS TO THE GROUND!
LOOK OUT!
BLA
BLAM
BLAM

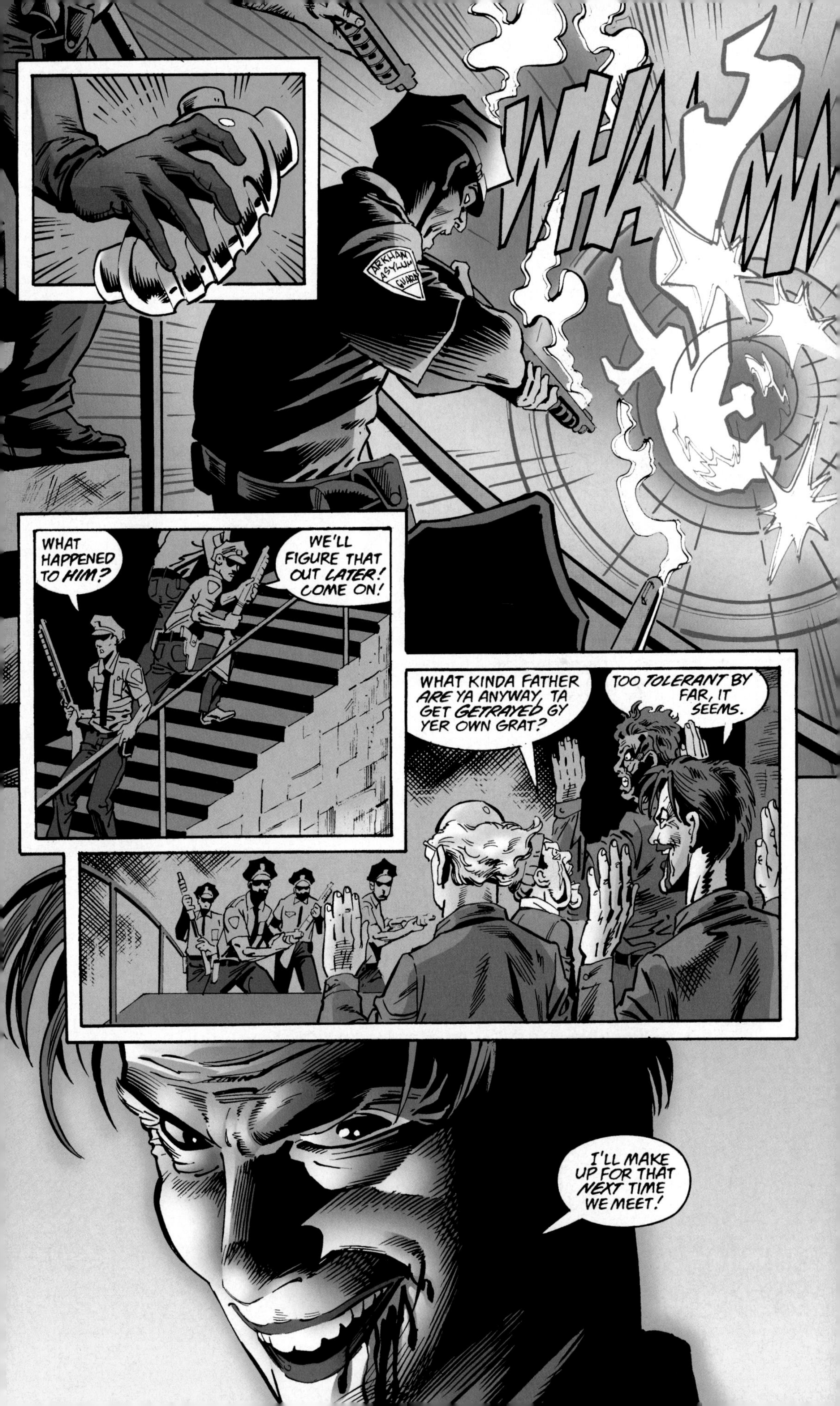
WHAM
ARKHAM ASYLUM GUARD
WHAT HAPPENED TO HIM?
WE'LL FIGURE THAT OUT LATER! COME ON!
WHAT KINDA FATHER ARE YA ANYWAY, TA GET GETRAYED GY YER OWN GRAT?
TOO TOLERANT BY FAR, IT SEEMS.
I'LL MAKE UP FOR THAT NEXT TIME WE MEET!

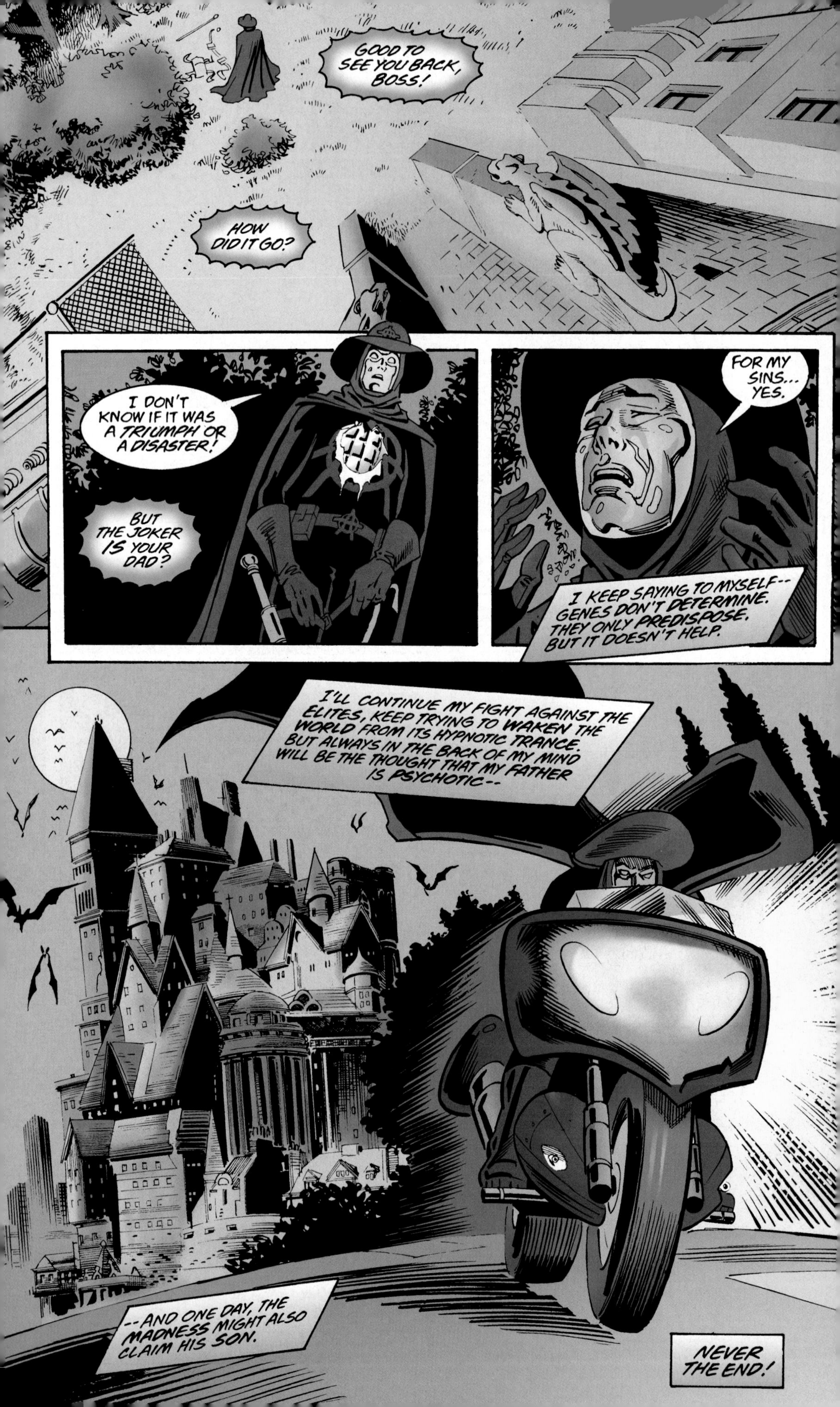
GOOD TO SEE YOU BACK, BOSS!
HOW DID IT GO?
I DON'T KNOW IF IT WAS A TRIUMPH OR A DISASTER!
BUT THE JOKER IS YOUR DAD?
FOR MY SINS... YES.
I KEEP SAYING TO MYSELF-- GENES DON'T DETERMINE. THEY ONLY PREDISPOSE. BUT IT DOESN'T HELP.
I'LL CONTINUE MY FIGHT AGAINST THE ELITES, KEEP TRYING TO WAKEN THE WORLD FROM ITS HYPNOTIC TRANCE. BUT ALWAYS IN THE BACK OF MY MIND WILL BE THE THOUGHT THAT MY FATHER IS PSYCHOTIC--
--AND ONE DAY, THE MADNESS MIGHT ALSO CLAIM HIS SON.
NEVER THE END!

ANARKY

Real Name: **Lonnie Machin**
Occupation: **Vigilante**
Base of Operations: **Washington, D.C.**
Marital Status: **Single**
Height: **5'8"** Weight: **150 lbs.**
Eyes: **Brown** Hair: **Orange**
First Appearance:
DETECTIVE COMICS #608
(November, 1989)

While still at school in Gotham City, Lonnie Machin became infuriated at all the injustice in the world. He determined to give a voice to the problems of the "common man" by adopting the secret identity of Anarky. Thwarted by Batman, Lonnie was incarcerated in a correctional center. He used his time there to hone his fighting skills and study widely before escaping to continue with his mission.

Anarky is convinced mankind is ruled by a small but evil elite, who hypnotize or force the masses to obey them. When Gotham was destroyed in an earthquake, and his parents disappeared, Anarky decided to take his fight to the heart of the vipers' nest. He relocated to Washington, D.C., establishing his secret base inside the famous Washington Monument. His genius-level I.Q. and technical mastery make him a constant threat to criminal minds everywhere.

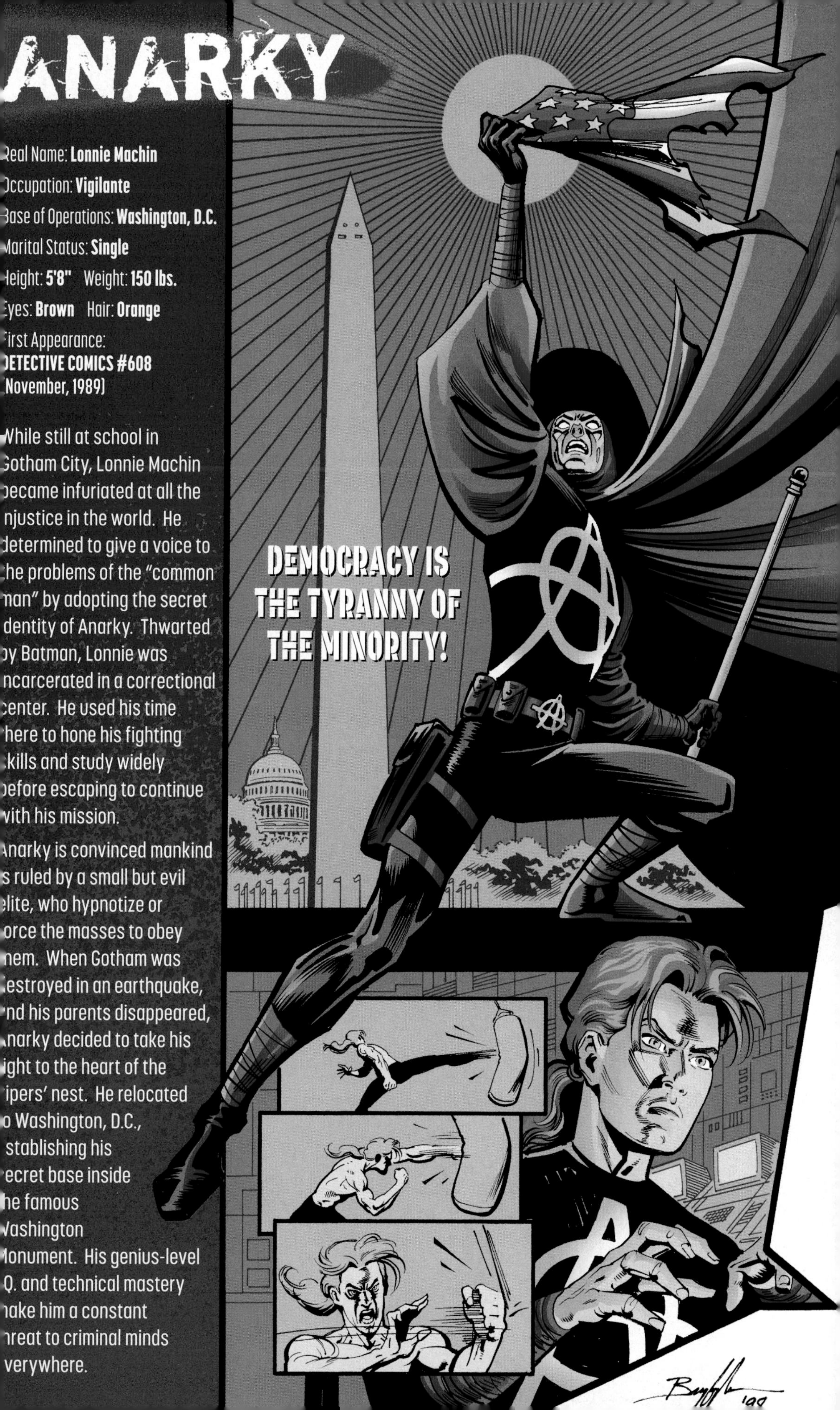
DEMOCRACY IS THE TYRANNY OF THE MINORITY!

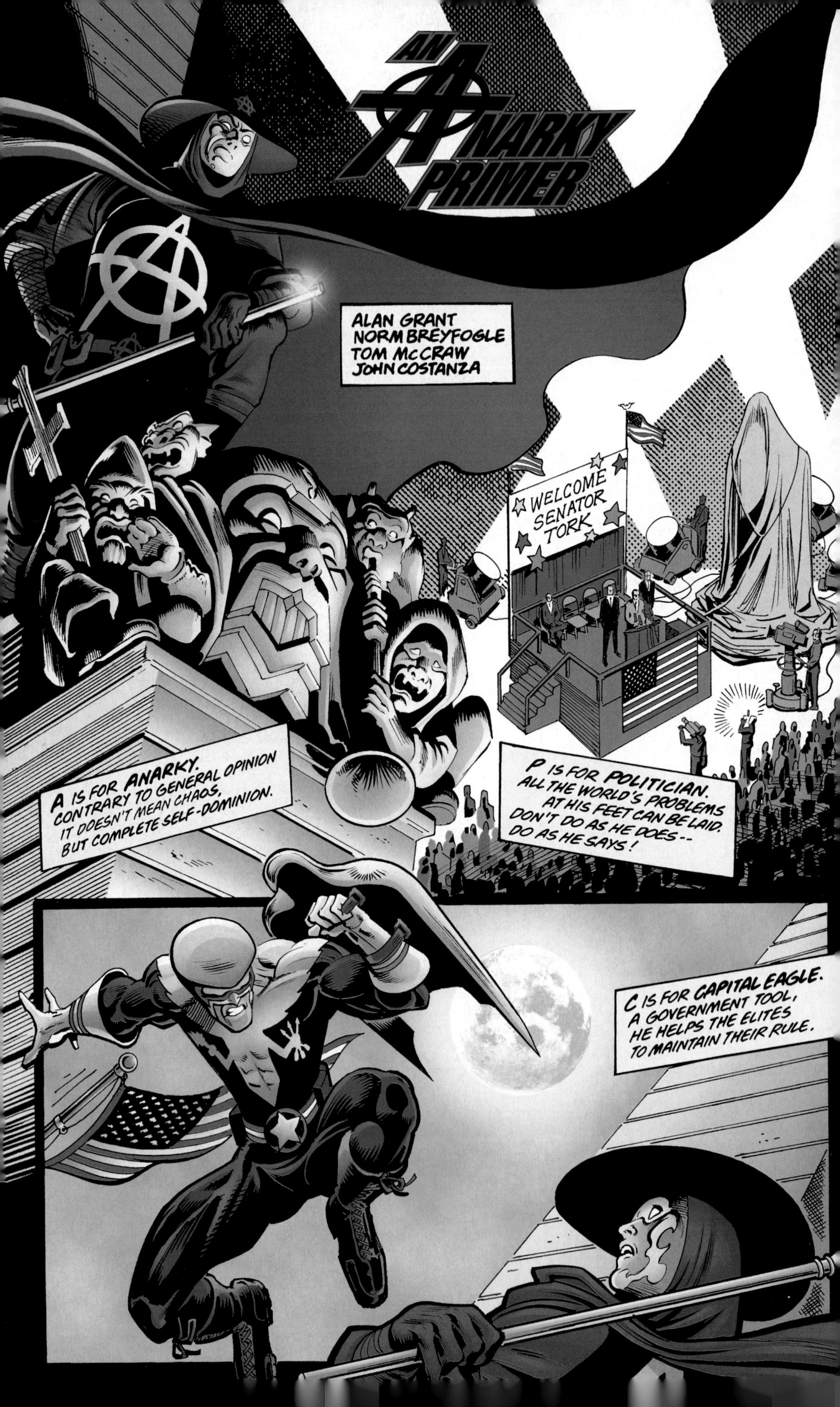
AN ANARKY PRIMER
ALAN GRANT
NORM BREYFOGLE
TOM McCRAW
JOHN COSTANZA
A IS FOR ANARKY. CONTRARY TO GENERAL OPINION IT DOESN'T MEAN CHAOS, BUT COMPLETE SELF-DOMINION.
WELCOME SENATOR TORK
P IS FOR POLITICIAN. ALL THE WORLD'S PROBLEMS AT HIS FEET CAN BE LAID. DON'T DO AS HE DOES-- DO AS HE SAYS!
C IS FOR CAPITAL EAGLE. A GOVERNMENT TOOL, HE HELPS THE ELITES TO MAINTAIN THEIR RULE.

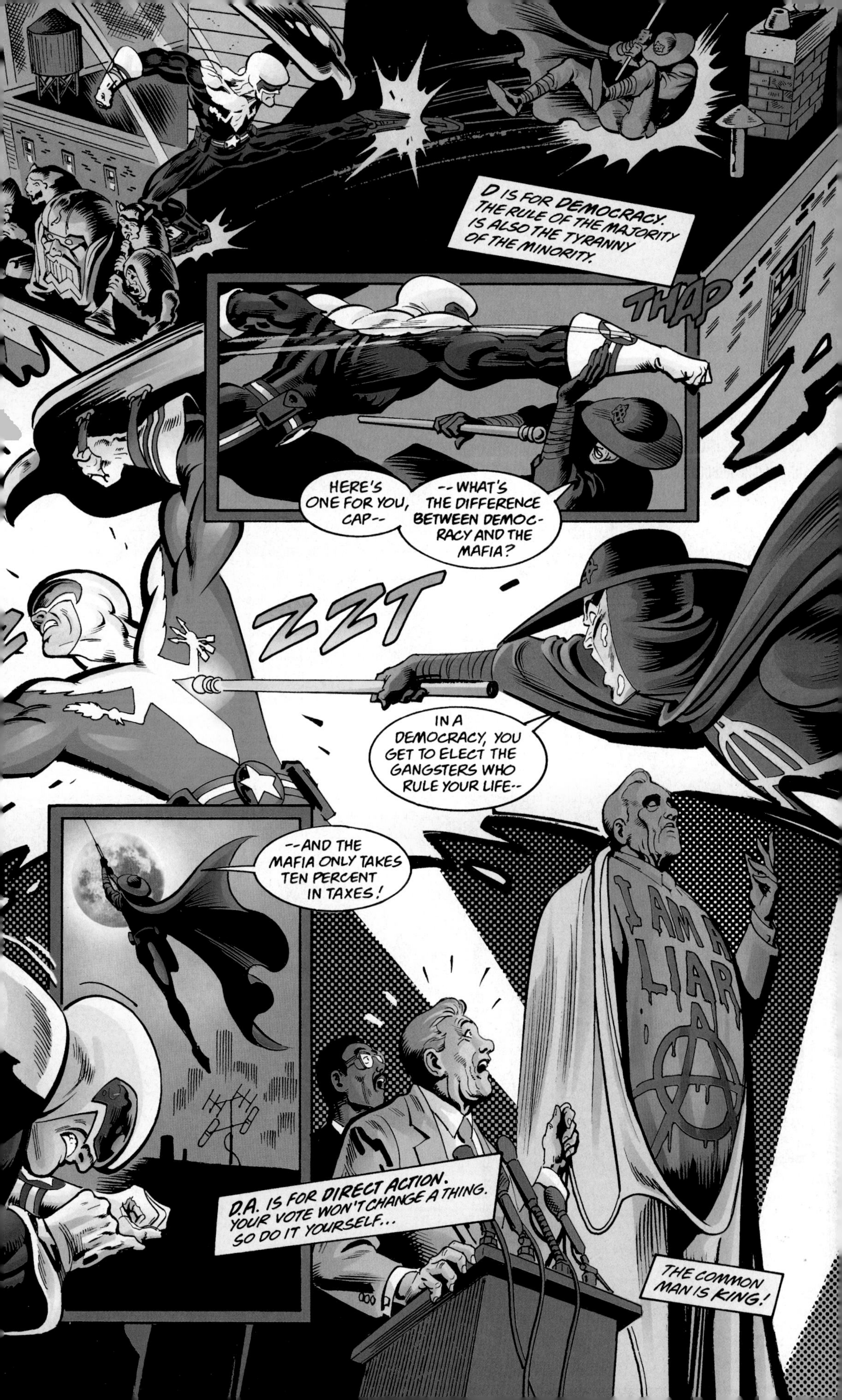

D IS FOR DEMOCRACY. THE RULE OF THE MAJORITY IS ALSO THE TYRANNY OF THE MINORITY.
THAP
HERE'S ONE FOR YOU, CAP--
--WHAT'S THE DIFFERENCE BETWEEN DEMOCRACY AND THE MAFIA?
ZZT
IN A DEMOCRACY, YOU GET TO ELECT THE GANGSTERS WHO RULE YOUR LIFE--
--AND THE MAFIA ONLY TAKES TEN PERCENT IN TAXES!
I AM A LIAR
D.A. IS FOR DIRECT ACTION. YOUR VOTE WON'T CHANGE A THING. SO DO IT YOURSELF...
THE COMMON MAN IS KING!

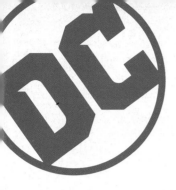

“Batman is getting a brand-new voice.”
– USA TODAY

“A great showcase for the new team as well as offering a taste of the new flavor they’ll be bringing to Gotham City.” **– IGN**

DC UNIVERSE REBIRTH

BATMAN

VOL. 1: I AM GOTHAM

TOM KING
with DAVID FINCH

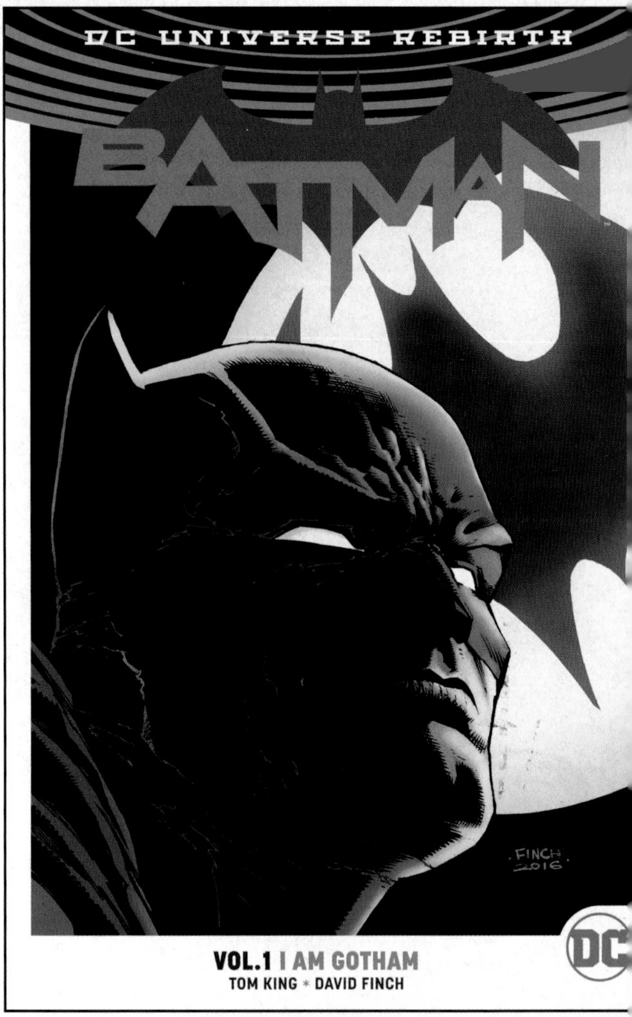

DC UNIVERSE REBIRTH
BATMAN
FINCH 2016
VOL.1 I AM GOTHAM
TOM KING * DAVID FINCH

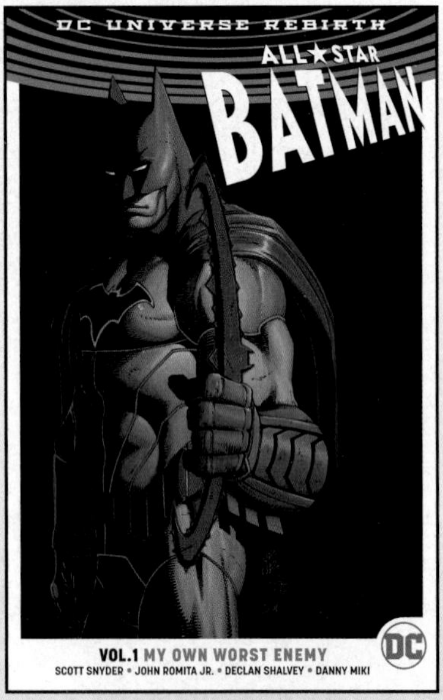

DC UNIVERSE REBIRTH
ALL★STAR
BATMAN
VOL.1 MY OWN WORST ENEMY
SCOTT SNYDER • JOHN ROMITA JR. • DECLAN SHALVEY • DANNY MIKI

ALL-STAR BATMAN VOL. 1:
MY OWN WORST ENEMY

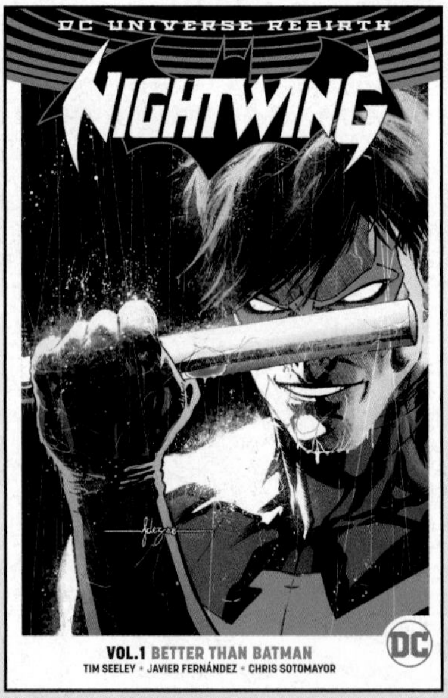

DC UNIVERSE REBIRTH
NIGHTWING
VOL.1 BETTER THAN BATMAN
TIM SEELEY • JAVIER FERNÁNDEZ • CHRIS SOTOMAYOR

NIGHTWING VOL. 1:
BETTER THAN BATMAN

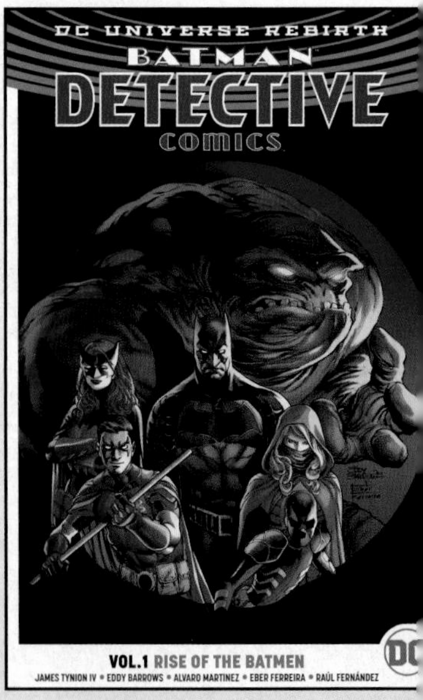

DC UNIVERSE REBIRTH
BATMAN
DETECTIVE
COMICS
VOL.1 RISE OF THE BATMEN
JAMES TYNION IV • EDDY BARROWS • ALVARO MARTINEZ • EBER FERREIRA • RAÚL FERNÁNDEZ

DETECTIVE COMICS VOL. 1:
RISE OF THE BATMEN

Get more DC graphic novels wherever comics and books are sold!